The Community
and the
Social Worker

THIRD EDITION

The Community and the Social Worker

THIRD EDITION

PHILLIP FELLIN
The University of Michigan

BROOKS/COLE
CENGAGE Learning

Australia • Brazil • Japan • Korea • Mexico • Singapore • Spain • United Kingdom • United States

BROOKS/COLE
CENGAGE Learning™

The Community and the Social Worker, Third Edition
Phillip Fellin

Editor: Janet Tilden

Production Supervisor: Kim Vander Steen

Cover Design: Lucy Lesiak Design

Composition: Point West, Inc.

For product information and technology assistance, contact us at **Cengage Learning Customer & Sales Support, 1-800-354-9706**

For permission to use material from this text or product, submit all requests online at **cengage.com/permissions** Further permissions questions can be emailed to **permissionrequest@cengage.com**

Library of Congress Control Number: 00134169

ISBN-13: 978-0-875-81438-4

ISBN-10: 0-875-81438-7

Brooks/Cole
10 Davis Drive
Belmont CA 94002-3098
USA

Cengage Learning is a leading provider of customized learning solutions with office locations around the globe, including Singapore, the United Kingdom, Australia, Mexico, Brazil, and Japan. Locate your local office at: **international.cengage.com/region**

Cengage Learning products are represented in Canada by Nelson Education, Ltd.

For your course and learning solutions, visit **academic.cengage.com**

Purchase any of our products at your local college store or at our preferred online store **www.ichapters.com**

Printed in the United States of America
4 5 6 7 8   12 11 10 09 08
ED023

Contents

1

The Societal Context of Communities

Understanding how communities function is essential for the practice of social work in the United States. Communities are one of many social systems that touch people's lives. Examples of social systems include families, small groups (e.g., friends, co-workers, peers), organizations, social institutions, society, and the world. A community exists when a group of people form a social unit based on common location, interest, identification, or some combination of these characteristics. This book provides a conceptual framework for understanding these multiple communities within which people have membership, social identities, and social interactions. Three major types of communities are emphasized: (1) those with geographic boundaries that are distinguished by locality or place, such as metropolitan, municipal, and neighborhood communities; (2) those created and maintained through identification and interest, such as communities based on ethnicity, culture, race, religion, lifestyle, sexual orientation, social class, occupation, ability/disability, age; and (3) those distinguished by an overlap of geographical location with identification and/or interest communities.

Two theoretical perspectives—social systems and ecological systems—provide avenues for understanding how communities function within American society. An ecological perspective is grounded in social science theories of human ecology, as well as conceptual models of ecosystems that focus on person-in-environment relationships (Germain and Gitterman, 1995; Germain and Bloom, 1999; Hawley, 1950, 1986; Longres, 1995; Norlin & Chess, 1997; Wakefield, 1996). From a social systems perspective, local communities function within larger systems: a national society and a worldwide global system.

Since the interactions and interdependencies of local communities occur within national and global social systems, in Chapter 1 we explore the societal context of communities. The concept of a global community is introduced. Next, American society is discussed from four viewpoints: (1) cultural perspectives on society; (2) civil society, social order, and social control; (3) social and economic justice in societies; and (4) society as social and ecological systems. The societal context of American communities is then extended in Chapter 2 through a focus on American society as a welfare state. Chapters 1 and 2 set the stage for understanding how individuals in local communities are linked to and influenced by the social institutions of American society (Schriver, 1998).

THE GLOBAL COMMUNITY

American society and its local communities belong to a global community—an international system consisting of nations and multinational agencies such as the World Trade Organization, the International Monetary Fund, and the World Bank. Membership in this world community has significant implications for people living in local American communities (Fisher & Karger, 1997; Leonard, 1997; Mishra, 2000). The concept of *globalization* refers to the political, economic, and social processes of nations within an international system or community. As Midgley (1997) has observed, globalization "is widely used to connote a process of global integration in which diverse peoples, economies, cultures, and political processes are increasingly subjected to international influences." A significant element of globalization is the existence of free-market capitalism in many nations throughout the world. The American national political system, through its social, economic, and foreign policies, takes a major responsibility for helping to sustain relationships among nations, especially in regard to the economic systems of the world. This role is assumed by the American government as a way of responding to the impact of globalization on the political, economic, educational, and health and social welfare systems of the United States, as well as on these subsystems in local communities.

A major international organization related to economic globalization is the World Trade Organization, of which the United States is a member. The deliberations of this world organization indicate that the interests of industrialized nations such as the United States are often at odds with those of developing nations. The philosophy of the WTO is that "when countries can trade freely with each other, without import tariffs or measures to protect the domestic market from competition, the world economy grows and everyone in general benefits" (Associated Press, 1999i). Opponents of the WTO claim that the organization is an undemocratic body, setting rules for global trade and settling disputes in secret, supporting only the interests of large multinational corporations, destroying the natural environment, and exploiting workers by violating human rights. Many groups in the United States, including labor unions and environmental organizations, have protested the actions of the WTO. Major demonstrations against the WTO were carried out in November 1999 at a meeting of the WTO in Seattle, Washington. The meeting ended with a lack of consensus on any of the major issues dividing the industrialized and developing nations, particularly issues involving labor and environmental standards.

The world economy generates social, economic, and political opportunities as well as problems for societies and their communities. For example, Fisher and Karger (1997) contend that at times "the global economy has led to a shrinking tax base, more joblessness, greater insecurity in the workplace, higher numbers of people in poverty, and a climate in which the disparities between the overclass and the poor are growing." As Piven and Cloward (1997) have observed, globalization may have a negative effect on the economic well-being and power of the working class. Such economic and social problems are likely to place demands on American society as a welfare state and on its local communities as they seek to respond to the needs of all their members (Leonard, 1997). In this regard, Reisch (1999) has observed that "the interdependence of the world economy blurs the distinction between national and international issues" such as "the growing global economic recession, the impact of immigration, the spread of AIDS, and the degradation of the physical environment."

Of special interest to the social worker is the impact of economic globalization on welfare state policies. As Reisch (1999) has noted, economic globalization affects the growing inequality of income and wealth in the United States, an inequity related to such factors as "gaps in educational and job skill levels, new technologies, the decline in the power of unions, the emphasis on foreign trade, changes in the wage scale and occupational structure of societies, the reorganization and transformation of work, the spread of modes of taxation, and the stagnation or contraction of welfare benefits." All of these factors affect the ways in which government and the private sector can respond to vulnerable populations, especially through welfare policies that affect well-being, such as those related to employment, unemployment, and underemployment. These policies, in turn, reflect the need for a social justice framework to guide the welfare policies and programs of the United States (Reisch, 1999).

The specific consequences of globalization for the United States as a welfare state, and for its communities, have been identified and discussed as social policy questions. For example, Mishra (2000), in *Globalization and the Welfare State*, examines the implications of globalization on social policy and social standards. Mishra argues that globalization is as much a political and ideological phenomenon as it is an economic one, and social policy must ensure that social standards rise in line with economic growth. Another example is a People's Global Action manifesto, issued in Geneva in 1999, which examines a number of issues and concerns related to globalization, including changing forms of wealth and power, exploitation of labor, gender oppression, oppressed ethnic groups, onslaughts on nature and agriculture, militarization, migration, and discrimination (Prigoff, 2000).

The importance of local communities may increase when globalization creates or magnifies the social problems of American society. Thus, Fisher and Karger (1997) contend that the community becomes an "essential component of how people deal collectively with globalization. . . [because] the more the nation moves into a global economic model, the more people need community to give structure to everyday life." In order to be effective in the practice of community organization, social planning, and community development at the local community level, social workers need a basic understanding of globalization as a framework for "knowledge of the economic profile of communities in which they work, and knowledge of the tools, methods, and limitations of economic theory and practice" (Prigoff, 2000). The reader should consult the emerging literature on globalization in order to develop a basic understanding of the interdependence of local communities, American society, and other nations of the world (Esping-Andersen, 1996; Fisher & Karger, 1997; Midgley, 1997).

DEFINING SOCIETY

Knowledge from the social sciences about American society is particularly relevant to the study of local communities. A *society* is a special kind of human group in which members "share a common culture, occupy a particular territorial area, and feel themselves to constitute a unified and distinct entity" (Marshall, 1994). Thus, societies have social, interactional, cultural, spatial, and identity dimensions that serve to distinguish one from another. The United States of America is the territorial area commonly referred to as American society, a society made up of people who have interactions and interrelationships through various groups, social organizations, social institutions, and communities. Viewing society as a social system involves identifying its major subsystems, usually referred to as its legal, political, economic, educational, social welfare, health, and religious institutional structures (Germain & Bloom, 1999).

In their classic study, *Industrial Society and Social Welfare*, Wilensky and Lebeaux (1958) identify some basic features of society, or "necessary conditions of societal survival," including population, specialization and stratification, solidarity or integration, and perpetuation of the social system. These features are described in terms of problems a society must solve in order to survive. Thus, societies must assure that their members receive food and shelter, have the opportunity to reproduce, and are able to protect themselves from extinction. Role differentiation and role assignment are necessary to assure a division of labor, the production of goods and services, the maintenance of social order, and the provision of child care. Social bonds developed in a society provide social integration of members through norms and values. Social roles, a division of labor, social bonds, socialization, social norms, and social order assure the continuation of a society as a social system.

The concept of society is often used interchangeably with the idea of American culture, suggesting that there is a core set of values based on individual worth and equal justice that exists within American society. In recent years, the subcultures of American society, especially ethnic, racial, and religious communities, have gained increased recognition. It is now generally acknowledged that people have sets of values based on one or more of these subcultures as well as values associated with American mainstream culture. Mainstream values are often represented by political and economic terms, i.e., American society is described as a nation-state, with a political system characterized as a free, democratic, civic society, with economic opportunities in a capitalistic system. As American society changes, new labels are attached to it, such as a post-industrial society, a multicultural society, an urban society, a postmodern society, or a mass society. Social changes identified with these labels provide a context for the study of the influence of American society as a social system on people, groups, and organizations in local communities. These changes are debated in terms of the positive or negative influences of social change on the society and local communities.

A relatively recent conceptualization of society depicts the United States as a *communitarian* society—that is, a national community that shares certain values related to identity, history, and culture (Etzioni, 1996a, 1996b). Communitarians speak of a national community that is equated with society-at-large, with American society identified as a community of communities. This perspective views American society as a system that is made up of individuals, groups, and social institutions within local geographic communities. Communitarians emphasize the fact that people in local communities have rights and responsibilities vis-à-vis the national society. In this regard, the national society is guided in its relationships to states and local communities by the Constitution and its Bill of Rights, additional amendments, by the Supreme Court, and by its political structures, in assuring freedoms such as speech, association, and assembly. At the same time, communitarians maintain that local communities should be able to make some decisions on their own and have primary jurisdiction over local affairs (Etzioni, 1996a).

The idea of society as a national community recognizes that there are multiple communities within American society, including geographic communities and communities based on identification and/or interest. The question arises, then, as to how the unity of American society as a national community can be maintained in the presence of diversity and pluralism in local communities. One perspective on this question is to view the United States as a multicultural society with a number of equal subcultures based on characteristics such as race, ethnicity, religion, and national origin. Another perspective recognizes the pluralistic nature of the United States but emphasizes the existence of a dominant, mainstream American culture. Communitarians take the second position, asserting that American citizens belong to multiple communities under a national community, possessing "layered loyalties" to these communities (Etzioni, 1996a).

CULTURAL PERSPECTIVES ON SOCIETY

The concept of *culture* is often used in conjunction with and as an alternative term for *society*. It has been widely acknowledged that "all societies possess an individual culture of their own," and "all human societies are cultural phenomena" (Tenbruck, 1989). Increasingly, however, the culture of American society is characterized as multicultural rather than monocultural. A common view of the culture of a society includes reference to its history, communication patterns and shared meanings, norms, values, attitudes, roles, beliefs, behaviors, language, and lifestyles (Phinney, 1996; Betancourt & Lopez, 1993). These features of a society are often regarded as its subjective culture, described as systems of meanings that are learned, shared by a people, and passed on from one generation to another. "These subjective elements include a wide range of topics, such as familial roles, communication patterns, affective styles, and values regarding personal control, individualism, collectivism, spirituality, and religiosity" (Betancourt & Lopez, 1993).

Societies are also associated with a physical, material culture. One aspect of this culture is the artistic and intellectual production in the society: "the social practices, products and consumption of literature, visual arts, music, theatre, film and television" (Leonard, 1997). We can examine the role of this type of culture in American society by looking at the number of books published in a given year, the number of American college students enrolled in the U.S. and abroad, the number of Americans who visit museums each year, and the number of Americans who listen to classical music, attend symphony orchestra concerts, or support the performing arts. Surveys indicate not only increased participation in these forms of culture in the United States in recent years, but a diffusion of these symbols of culture to small towns and rural areas.

CULTURE AS VALUES

The study of American cultures usually begins with an identification of the major sets of values associated with the national culture. Historically, American society has been viewed as monocultural—dominated by a single culture of Western European origin, predominantly based on white Anglo-Saxon Protestant values. Some of the dimensions of American society associated with this Western culture include values about work, mobility, status, independence, individualism, moralism, and ascription (Tropman, 1989, 1998). Tropman has illustrated each of these values in relation to dilemmas facing an American welfare state: work (worthy vs. unworthy); mobility (outside vs. inside society); status (lumping vs. categorizing); independence (internal vs. external control); individualism (micro vs. macro); moralism (punishment vs. compassion); ascription (white vs. other). According to Tropman, Americans are likely to be conflicted over these dilemmas, sometimes following dominant values such as individualism, and at other times following subdominant (moderating) values such as cooperation.

These "value pairs" are likely to be influenced by factors such as one's gender, ethnicity/race, social class level, and age.

American society has embodied social, cultural, and legal structures that call for a commitment of its citizens to protecting a democratic way of life. Thus, American culture has historically been based on an American creed, with the expectation that newcomers would assimilate into the society and become part of a cultural "melting pot," sharing a common culture and achieving an "American Dream." This "Dream" has involved attainment of goals associated with lifestyles, home ownership, wages, social security, and medical care. In this monocultural vision of American society, only one culture was expected to inform "the civic, economic, and social structure of the United States"—the dominant, white, mainstream culture (Lugones & Price, 1995). In Schlesinger's (1992) terms, "The point of America was not to preserve old cultures, but to forge a new American culture." This vision has been challenged in recent years by a multicultural perspective of American society.

SOCIAL PROCESSES AND AMERICAN IDENTITY

The social processes of acculturation and assimilation describe the relationships of many Americans to their individual subcultures and to American society. *Acculturation* involves adherence to the cultural patterns of mainstream America in areas related to secondary group and institutional interactions that take place in workplaces, schools, churches, health organizations, social welfare agencies, governmental agencies, courts, and community organizations. Acculturation allows people to belong to an American culture while at the same time retaining their identity and social participation in subcultures such as racial, ethnic, religious, and/or social class groups. This form of attachment is sometimes called bicultural, with one's primary identification seen as being American and secondary identities based on belonging to one or more subcultural groups. A prevailing trend among new immigrants to the United States has been to become acculturated to mainstream American culture while at the same time retaining some cultural features of their nation of origin.

Assimilation, on the other hand, represents full integration into American society and its social institutions. In contemporary American society, most white ethnics have become acculturated or assimilated into the mainstream culture, while the dominant society has prevented the full integration and assimilation of many members of ethnic minority groups of color, especially African Americans (Glazer, 1993, 1997). Evidence of this social condition within society is found in local communities. For example, residential housing and public school systems in large urban metropolitan areas are likely to be segregated by race and social class. In such areas many people of color are not fully assimilated into American society but are involved in a bicultural form of identity and social interaction, limited in their participation in the majority culture and more strongly identified with their minority culture.

Historically, many white ethnic immigrants have gradually acquired a new American identity and full participation in the full benefits and rights of citizenship in the American society. For some immigrant groups, religious affiliation (especially for Catholics and Jews) and nationality (e.g., Irish or Italian) has provided a basis of cultural values which in the past limited full integration into mainstream American society. Perhaps even more significant were features of a WASP society that constituted barriers to assimilation of these groups into American society. These features, especially involving discrimination and privilege, have been examined in "whiteness" studies that show the meaning of being white in America and demonstrate how, historically, many different white ethnic and religious groups have gradually become accepted into a majority White Anglo-Saxon Protestant society (Ignatiev, 1995; Sacks, 1997).

When members of some ethnic/religious groups have been left out of significant participation in the White Anglo-Saxon Protestant society, they have often remained attached to the values of their religious cultures (Morris, 1997; Tropman, 1995). For example, in the case of American Catholics, there have been strong community supports provided by local parishes for white immigrant groups, such as Irish, Italian, Polish, and German Catholics, and resistance from the church hierarchy to full assimilation by Catholics into a White Anglo-Saxon Protestant culture. As a result, the Catholic church established its own schools, health care institutions, social services, and youth organizations (Morris, 1997). In recent decades, negative attitudes and discrimination against Catholics have declined. This has been accompanied by a breakup of the traditional nationality/religious culture through suburbanization and social and economic advancement of Catholics into the middle and upper classes of society.

In the case of the American Jewish community, religion has served as a basis for cultural identity and behavior, while at the same time being a target for anti-Semitism in the form of discrimination and oppression. A number of social indicators provide evidence that many Jewish people have become assimilated into current American society, e.g., through participation in educational institutions, professions, social affiliations, political structures (Elazar, 1995). This assimilation has led to concerns on the part of some American Jews as to how their religious/cultural group can maintain and foster its distinctive identity in the future, especially in the light of high rates of intermarriage with non-Jews (Abrams, 1997; Dershowitz, 1997). Recent books are instructive with regard to issues involving assimilation of Jews as a cultural/religious group. Tifft and Jones (1999), in *The Trust: The Private and Powerful Family Behind The New York Times*, provide insights on what it was like for Ochs-Sulzberger families to be Jewish in America, to face anti-Semitism, and to assimilate into American society during the years from the 1850s to the present. Abrams (1997), in *Faith or Fear: How Jews Can Survive in a Christian America*, asks how Jews can maintain their cultural identity amid the forces of assimilation. In *The Vanishing American Jew*, Dershowitz (1997) suggests ways in which Jewish life can survive in the next century in a country in which "Jews will become more assimilated into the American mainstream in every way: in neighborhoods, in lifestyles, and in marriages." Whitfield (1999) in his book *In Search of American Jewish Culture*, demonstrates how "the culture of Jewish Americans has shaped the culture of gentile Americans, and vice versa," citing examples such as the work of Jewish immigrants in art, music, and theater (Klinghoffer, 1999). Whitfield suggests that an important way in which Jewish culture can avoid extinction is by returning to the religion of Judaism and making a commitment to keep identifying themselves as Jews.

Elazar (1995), in *Community and Polity: The Organizational Dynamics of American Jewry*, presents an insightful examination of the assimilation of American Jews into American society. He contends that by 1976, the "first postwar generation was a decisive one, witnessing as it did the almost total integration of American Jews into American society, the establishment of the State of Israel and its emergence as a prime focus for Jewish identity and concern, the transformation of Jewish religious life so as to conform to American modes, and the revival of the sense of Jewish ethnic identity." At the same time, during this postwar period the American Jewish community more fully developed its communal structure, modes of Jewish affiliation, and basic patterns for collective action. Thus, the American Jewish community now serves its members through a polity that has five major functions: (1) religious-congregational; (2) educational-cultural; (3) community relations; (4) communal-welfare; and (5) Israel-overseas (Elazar, 1995). Strong as this "body politic" of American Jewry has been, Elazar points out that "the danger of losing millions of Jews through assimilation grows apace." In response to this problem of "assimilation versus authenticity," Elazar believes that "American Jewry has been called to a great, even a noble, purpose: that of building a viable and creative Jewish life within an open society, one that involves the preservation of Jewish individual and corporate existence while enabling Jews to participate fully in the fulfillment of the American idea. This is easier said than done, but that in no way diminishes the greatness of the task."

For many people of color, especially Americans of African heritage, racism and oppression have kept them out of the "melting pot." As a part of their quest for rights of citizenship, people of color within American society have advocated for civil rights through social movements. At the same time, ethnic minority groups of color—African American, Asian American, Native American, and Hispanic/Latino American—have reasserted their cultural foundations in order to gain recognition and maintain their own distinct cultures within a multicultural society. Social movement advocacy groups have worked for acceptance and equal opportunity for people of color to participate in the political and economic institutions of the majority culture. The advent of multiculturalism is particularly apparent in public school systems at elementary, secondary, and higher educational levels, where "cultural wars" have been waged with a demand for recognition of the history and significance of non-white, non-Western cultures. In the larger society, race as a classification system has continued but has been joined by cultural terms to identify different ethnic groups. To highlight the cultural dimensions of these groups, there is a convention of using a label as a prefix to "American," e.g., Asian American, Jewish American, or Irish American.

The multicultural movement in education has clearly established the social fact of a multiethnic, multicultural, culturally pluralistic population in the United States. In response, proponents of a common American culture have raised concerns that along with an emphasis on ethnic cultures comes a "disuniting of America" that threatens the continued existence of "America as 'one people,' a common culture, a single nation" (Schlesinger, 1992). The dilemma raised by this concern is no longer a question of whether or not America is a multicultural society, but rather, whether the existence of many subcultures permits adherence to a common national culture. This question continues to merit attention at societal and community levels of the United States, especially in the light of racial and ethnic tensions and conflicts, discrimination and oppression of people of color, and the problems of special population groups in attaining social justice.

THE FUTURE OF AMERICAN CULTURE

What will the culture of American society be like in the future in terms of race, ethnicity, and social class? While the "melting pot" of assimilation has been declared dead by multiculturalists, there are predictions that

America is becoming a post-ethnic/post-cultural society, through the increased importance of ties to a national culture and a decline in the influence of subcultures. Under this view, names with a prefix associated with a racial/ethnic group will give way to the single term "American" as a sign of group identification. In this vein, subcultures become "symbolic," and voluntary identifications become more ornamental than instrumental, with the prominent ornaments based on customs, traditions, holiday and religious rituals, music, foods, communication patterns, and language (Gans, 1996). Thus, a post-ethnic perspective emphasizes "the civic character of the American nation-state, in contrast to the ethnic character of most of the nationalism we read about today" (Hollinger, 1995).

In contrast to the prediction of a post-ethnic society, some observers of American society believe that ethnic minority groups will continue to be classified by race, ethnicity, and social class. Demographic trends indicate that the birth rates of ethnic minority groups in American society are moving the nation toward a "minority majority" society by the year 2050. There is an assumption that groups of color, through "identity politics," will gain power through numbers and move into a more influential position with regard to American social institutions. Another reading of demographic trends suggests that an increase in intermarriage of all groups, white and nonwhite, can be expected to result in a "beige society" in the future, with increased numbers of people of mixed ethnicity and mixed race making the society truly multicultural. Proponents of this view recognize that African Americans may not participate fully in this societal change, especially if there is a continuation of the low level of intermarriage of African Americans with other nonwhite and white groups. Thus, there is a concern that African Americans may be "left out of the melting pot once again" despite assimilation of all other groups into American society (Lind, 1998). Still, social integration of all ethnic minority groups may increase through social and economic upward mobility on the part of groups now disproportionately in the underclass and lower working classes. Consequently, increased numbers of African Americans and Hispanic Americans may become assimilated through upward mobility if barriers of racism and classism are reduced or eliminated in the social and political institutions of the society.

MASS CULTURE AND MASS SOCIETY

There is a continuing debate over the extent to which people possess strong cultural bonds with groups at the local community level and with American society as a whole. Theories of mass culture and mass society claim that there is a social trend for individuals to have strong ties and affiliations with a national, mass society, leaving them with weak attachments to local communities of place and interest (Strinati, 1995). The idea of a mass society or "mass culture" is based on the premise that the mass media—television, movies, newspapers, magazines, and advertising—promote a national culture centered around values, norms, lifestyles, consumption of goods and services (such as clothes, music, foods, cinema, books, and automobiles), leisure-time activities, and political affiliations. Public opinion polls are employed to discover the views, opinions, and tastes of Americans as a representation of American culture. The national culture has become associated with the nature of social problems, such as crime, homelessness, mental illness, children living in poverty, and health problems of cancer, AIDS, and substance abuse. Problems such as these are often attributed to American culture, identified as a culture of violence, the media culture, kid culture, gun culture, or secular culture (Gopnik, 1999).

From a mass society perspective, local communities of place and identification are thought to have minimal influence over people's lives vis-à-vis the national society. This perspective suggests that people use the mass culture as a point of reference for consumption of goods and adherence to societal values. National magazines and newspapers, including those identified with special populations, such as women, youth, ethnic groups, and social classes, are said to promote popular cultures of a mass society. A modification of the mass culture perspective argues that while there is a national popular culture, there remain local community ties with one's subcultural groups based on social class, race, ethnicity, and religion. Such ties are believed to be supported by local media, schools, churches, neighborhood and community organizations, and workplaces.

Fashions in clothes may be regarded as indicators of identification with a mass society. Designer fashions have traditionally been associated with social classes, with upper-class clothes viewed as "high fashion" or signifiers of "highbrow" culture, and clothes identified with working class occupations and leisure-time activities attributed to "lowbrow" culture. The expectation has been that highbrow fashions will "trickle down" to the masses. However, currently these two levels of clothes fashions move from high to low and back to high culture rather quickly, as evidenced by the clothes worn by teenagers and young adults, and the availability of "high-fashion" clothes in the mass market, appealing to middle- and working-class people. Ethnic minority cultures also generate fashions that move into the "mainstream" culture, as well as popularizing the brands of clothes and shoes worn by people in middle- and upper-middle-class culture. In the case of young adults, merchandisers attempt to discover what clothes are "cool" and to use movie stars, athletes, and entertainers for advertisements and marketing (Gladwell, 1997). In the case of women who work away from the home, the shoe is an example of a "social signifier" that allows women to establish cultural identities, from women who wear high heels (people do their walking for them), to women who wear expensive sneakers to match their designer or dress work suits, to women who wear flat shoes for comfort as well as style, to women who wear Chinese-inspired slippers that connote a spiritual image, to women who wear "ugly" shoes, such as Doc Martens, to make an anti-fashion statement (Steinhauer, 1998).

CIVIL SOCIETY

One of the distinguishing marks of a democratic society is its conception of the role of citizenship and voluntarism in creating a civil society. "As a first approximation, civil society may be defined as all social interests not encompassed by the state or the economy" (Dryze, 1996). Civil societies are those "free societies where government, commerce and civic institutions are balanced, citizens participate in their communities, and the culture promotes civility" (Merida & Vobejda, 1996). Civil engagement occurs at several levels: in relation to local community groups, state associations, and national organizations. This engagement depends on people accepting the responsibilities of democratic citizenship through participation in voluntary associations and social institutions. Alexis de Tocqueville (1988) recognized this feature of democracy during his visit to the United States in 1831. In a civil society, citizens are involved in private and voluntary institutions and associations that mediate between government and the market (Elshtain, 1996). For example, citizens have an opportunity to influence the national political system by way of a variety of activities engaged in at the local community level, including voting, political party activities, elected offices, social movements, interest groups, financial contributions, and other forms of philanthropy. The non-governmental, nonprofit associations of a civil society provide a location for power and leadership by women (Fisher, 1999). Many civil organizations have been created or led by women, such as MADD, Planned Parenthood, Girl Scouts of the USA, the League of Women Voters, and EMILY, the national women's political fund raising group based on the principle that Early Money Is Like Yeast.

Measures of the strength of civil society in the United States include the extent to which citizens participate in the civic life of their communities through voluntary associations and the extent to which citizens place trust in their representatives in the several levels of government. The civic condition of local communities throughout the nation is viewed as a measure of the health of a civil society. Two major views have emerged regarding whether or not voluntarism and participation in civil society are on the decline. Putnam (1995) and others have argued that "the republic is in danger as the number of couch potatoes grows, as watching television replaces civil participation" (Rich, 1999). Putnam's (1995) concept of "bowling alone" suggests that a decline in bowling leagues as well as other similar groups, plus lower participation in civic organizations, signifies a decline in social ties and a threat to democracy. Concerns based on this perception of a serious decline in active citizenship related to civic life at local, state, and national levels led to the creation of a National Commission on Civic Renewal (1998). Such a decline was said to involve a weakening of "individual responsibility and a felt sense of obligation to the common good." The Commission's report suggested that "America is becoming a 'nation of spectators,' with too many people disengaged from government and community work." The report also criticized the nation's colleges and universities for moving away from liberal education, which traditionally has reinforced the values of a civil society (Schneider, 1998).

The report of the National Commission on Civic Renewal (1998) emphasized the responsibilities of citizenship in overcoming the civic ills of American society—ills demonstrated by the "weakness of our families, the poor performance of our public schools, the negative influences of popular culture on our young people, the election of public officials we mistrust, leading to a degradation of our civic environment." Starting with the premise of democratic self-government, this National Commission expressed the belief that "democratic citizenship must be nurtured in institutions such as families, neighborhoods, schools, faith communities, local governments, and political movements." At the same time, efforts for the creation of effective national public institutions were recommended, particularly through leadership in generating public trust in the national political system.

A second and contrasting view of civil society suggests that "voluntarism is alive and well" (Rich, 1999). This argument holds that societal changes have meant that people participate in the voluntary sector of society in new and different ways. Increased participation has occurred in social service and non-professional organizations, ethnic organizations, and other types of civic activities (Rich, 1999). An example is the growth of religious groups, as "churches and synagogues have been 'reinventing' themselves in order to attract members" and to offer them opportunities for civic involvement (Rich, 1999). Smidt's (1999) study of religious involvement and civic engagement found that "Religious life, in particular, serves as an important contributor to civil society. . . . Congregations are often regarded as important components of civil society in local communities, as they frequently provide physical care, spiritual guidance, and social networks to their members and others in the community" (Smidt, 1999). Religious participation is said to contribute to civil society in several ways, including the fostering of social connectedness, social and political participation, and the promotion of civic behavior outside the institutional life of the church (Smidt, 1999).

Participation in religious associations helps generate *social capital*—that is, the kinds of social relations and resources that support a civil society and local communities through norms and sanctions, mutual reciprocity, and mutual trust (Fellin, 1998; Edwards & Foley, 1997). As noted by Cnaan (1998), local religious congregations are regarded as a major source of social and human capital, as they promote social activism and civic engagement and "operate as sources of skill acquisition, social interactions, mutual exchanges, mutual obligations, and trust." As voluntary associations, religious congregations are believed to support a civil society by their emphasis on social responsibility, the group processes of congregational life, and the "cultural norm which dictates that congregations will be involved in enhancing the quality of life of others in their community" (Cnaan, 1998).

SOCIAL ORDER AND SOCIAL CONTROL IN AMERICAN SOCIETY

One of the major functions of a society is the creation and maintenance of social order and social control. Mechanisms of social order and social control established at a societal level have a significant influence over the behaviors of people in local communities. As Wrong (1994) has observed, "Order consists of the predictability of human conduct on the basis of common and stable expectations." American society, as a social system made up of social institutions, seeks to maintain order, stability, and equilibrium and to avoid conflict, deviance, and social disorganization in the nation as a whole and within its local communities. Sources of social order within society include formal social institutions such as government, schools, and religious organizations, as well as individuals, families, small groups, and voluntary associations.

Social control is a term given to "the processes through which individual participation in a system is limited or constrained" (Longres, 1995). It involves expectations of a social group, such as a family, organization, community, or society, to regulate itself. Control is implemented in various ways, including rules, rewards, and punishments. One source of social order comes from external forms of social control that provide legitimate coercion—e.g., the legal system and the criminal justice system. Internal control comes about when people voluntarily adhere to social norms, usually as a result of socialization within families, religious organizations, or schools (Liska, 1992). Socialization is often considered a major source of social control, as it is "the process of teaching new members the rules by which the larger group or society operates. Socialization involves imparting to new members the knowledge, values, and skills according to which they are expected to operate" (Schriver, 1998). Socialization is also a major way in which culture is passed on from one generation to another within a society.

Social order and social control are a matter of degree, and their levels are not always viewed in a positive way within American society. Sometimes these processes are viewed as "conservative opposition to social change and to group conflict as a source of change" (Wrong, 1994). Thus, some social workers and social scientists argue "that social control is directed against those who are least able to resist (the disadvantaged and the unfortunate) and that social control agencies are used by the powerful to control the behavior of others" (Liska, 1992). This charge is directed especially toward mental health, criminal justice, and welfare systems as agencies of social control (Borgatta & Borgatta, 1992; Dodenhoff, 1998; Piven & Cloward, 1971). As Liska (1992) notes, "Welfare is frequently conceptualized as a form of social control." An example of this position is found in the writings of Piven and Cloward (1971), who argued in *Regulating the Poor* that expansion of welfare benefits in the late 1960s was not done to help the poor but to maintain civil order and regulate labor markets. Under this formulation, welfare becomes a social control response to civil unrest, urban riots, and community disorder (Dodenhoff, 1998; Dobelstein, 1999).

The Piven and Cloward (1971) argument has been challenged by authors such as Dodenhoff (1998) and Schram and Turbett (1983) on methodological grounds and by Gronbjerg (1977) on conceptual grounds. For example, in explaining periods of expansion of social welfare indicated by increased numbers of people on public assistance, Gronbjerg (1977) proposed that this expansion is related to the emergence of a mass society in the United States. In this mass society, "all persons are seen by the state as having legitimate entitlements as citizens," with citizenship including not only political rights but social and economic rights as well. As a result, Gronbjerg explains the growth of AFDC rolls in the 1960s and 1970s as a function of "mass society" rather than "social control." Given these different perspectives on social control, there seems to be no universally accepted explanation for expansion of the programs of the American welfare state.

MAINTENANCE OF SOCIAL ORDER

In trying to maintain social order, American society faces a dilemma: balancing personal rights and individual autonomy with forms of social control based on institutional authority. One way to resolve the dilemma is to promote "an order that is aligned with the moral commitments of the members" (Etzioni, 1996a). The Constitution and its Bill of Rights, which are based on institutional authority, provide for the autonomy and rights of individuals. An important task of American society is to establish and maintain some equilibrium between social order and individual autonomy. This principle of equilibrium applies to the relationship between individuals and the society at large, as well as between individuals and the various communities that exist within American society. Good communities require social order to avoid anarchy, and individual autonomy to avoid being authoritarian villages. From this perspective, residential, racial, ethnic, and religious communities serve as "intermediary bodies" between the individual and the society. Communities maintain an equilibrium between personal autonomy and social control (Etzioni, 1996a).

American society relies heavily on law for social order, through legislation and regulation of all levels of government and the criminal justice system. For example, the criminal justice system uses punishment as an external means of social control (Liska, 1992). At the same time, society depends upon laws to promote and protect individual liberties. Given the dominant position of the federal government in relation to local communities, a good society ensures that public policies of the national government do "not take over activities that provide opportunities for communities to act" on behalf of their residents (Etzioni, 1996a). One application of this principle is the process of devolution as a public policy, with resources and authority of the federal government assigned to the governments and voluntary agencies of states and local communities, e.g., block grants from the federal government to the states for social welfare programs.

At the same time, the federal government represents the society at large when it "upholds core values in the form of limits on local policies" (Etzioni, 1996a). Society and communities must address the question, "What are the issues that a community is entitled to decide on its own, and when must it yield to society at large, the community of communities?" How can American society support social justice and equality within its local communities? Etzioni (1996a) suggests that "a measure of social justice is required both to sustain moral order and to advance autonomy for all the members of the community." He suggests that a new "golden rule" needs to be established at societal and community levels, one that involves a "commitment to moral order that is basically voluntary, and to a social order that is well balanced with socially secured autonomy."

SOCIAL AND ECONOMIC JUSTICE IN SOCIETY

A significant feature of a society is the way in which social and economic justice are promoted or denied. Several meanings can be given to justice and injustice, as well as to related concepts of oppression and discrimination. Barker (1995a) defines social justice as an "ideal condition in which all members of a society have the same basic rights, protection, opportunities, obligations, and social benefits." From Flynn's (1994) perspective, "Social justice refers to equity, equality, and fairness in the distribution of social resources." Another definition says that "justice is about people getting what is coming to them"—equal opportunities, equal rewards, and equal punishments (Schmidtz & Goodin, 1998). What are the forms of social, economic, gender, and environmental justice and injustice, and how does one determine that a society is just? Injustice is said to prevail "when a society infringes on human rights, holds prejudicial attitudes toward some of its members, and promotes inequality by discriminating against segments of its citizenry" (Miley, O'Melia, & DuBois, 1998). Injustice occurs through encroachments on human and civil rights that deny equal access to opportunities and resources, limiting full participation in society. Discrimination and oppression in the institutional order and culture of American society perpetuates injustice for many Americans through processes of domination and exploitation.

Promotion of social and economic justice is required of social workers by the profession's Code of Ethics and has been the goal of many social movements in the United States. Thus, our study of communities needs to address the questions of what constitutes a just society, and how injustice and oppression can be eliminated (Gil, 1994, 1998; Gil &

Gil, 1995; Rawls, 1971). Gil (1998) uses a model of work, exchange, and distribution to contrast non-oppressive and oppressive societies. According to Gil, "Societies and work systems are non-oppressive when all people are considered and treated as equals, and therefore, have equal rights and responsibilities. . . Systems of exchange and distribution are just when terms of exchange. . . are consistently fair and balanced." In a welfare state, social and economic justice involves access to goods and services, and the distribution and redistribution of resources (Shatz, 1995). This view of justice is referred to as distributive justice, based on egalitarian principles developed by Rawls (1971).

Without dismissing the importance of distributive justice, Young (1995) calls our attention to institutional conditions that promote injustice in society through "two forms of disabling constraints, oppression and domination." In responding to such injustice, for contemporary social movements such as "socialists, radical feminists, American Indian activists, Black activists, gay and lesbian activists... oppression is a central category of political discourse." Injustice toward these groups is "systematically reproduced in major economic, political, and cultural institutions." The five faces of oppression described by Young (1995) provide a useful framework for recognizing groups within society as oppressed. This framework recognizes that there are similarities and differences in the injustices imposed on different groups, including injustice from exploitation, marginalization, powerlessness, cultural imperialism, and violence.

SOCIAL MOVEMENTS AND SOCIAL JUSTICE

A major proposition of the American Constitution is that of equal political and civil rights based on the principles of liberty and equality (Kerchis & Young, 1995). Throughout American history, however, some residents of the United States have been denied these rights. Social movements have confronted American society with demands for equal rights through legislation and the legal system with laws that seek to assure these rights for all citizens. Nevertheless, injustices based on discrimination and oppression of people of color, women, persons with disabilities, older adults, members of religious groups, gay and lesbian persons, continue within American society. When we explore social movements in relation to social justice, we should keep in mind that "Movements for social justice in America are at once products of the culture and shapers of the culture. American beliefs and values have provided both opportunities and limitations for organizations pressing for justice" (Horton, 1985). Among the dimensions of American culture that influence social movements for social justice are "attitudes toward change; religious beliefs and principles, and the commitment to equality."

Social movements may be defined as "a wide variety of collective attempts to bring about change in certain social institutions or to create an entirely new order," on the basis of "socially shared demands for change in some aspect of the social order" (Brandwein, 1985). Such movements may operate at all levels of society, from the nation to states to local communities, as people associated with a movement seek to effect social changes that will bring about justice in social institutions and organizations. Fisher and Karger (1997) argue that effective social movements require the involvement of community organizations, neighborhoods, agencies, and social activists in order to achieve a just public society. Thus, social movement organizations link local communities to the society. For example, during the civil rights movement local communities provided a place for African Americans to organize against discrimination and unequal access to public accommodations and other community facilities, thus influencing state and federal systems and leading to the passage of the Civil Rights Act of 1964 (Schriver, 1998).

Social movements are vehicles "through which people mobilize and engage in collective action," especially through grassroots settings and networks related to churches and neighborhood (McAdam, McCarthy, & Zald, 1996). Social movements often seek social change through mobilization of protest actions and use of resources to influence change (Rucht, 1996). Examples of social movements within American society include the ecology (environmental) movement, peace movements, gay and lesbian movement, the women's movement, civil rights movement, labor movement, African American movement, and American Indian movement. In some of these movements, such as those related to people of color, there has been an emphasis on organizing around difference and cultural identity "as a strategy for achieving power and participation in the institutions of social and political life" (Kerchis & Young, 1995). This approach is labeled "identity politics" or the "politics of difference," a politics that rejects the idea of assimilation into American society by these groups.

Kerchis and Young (1995) argue that the key difference between these "liberation movement" approaches and assimilation is the way in which group difference is defined. "The politics of assimilation defines group difference in a negative way, as a liability or disadvantage to be overcome in the process of assimilating into mainstream society. In contrast, the politics of difference defines group difference in a positive way, as a social and cultural condition that can be liberating and empowering for oppressed groups."

A major goal of liberation movements has been to open up and assure equal opportunities for participation in social and political institutions. Social movements have the capacity to influence the political system at all levels of government, as is evidenced by rights legislation, by executive orders, and by decisions of the courts. Political actions taken at these levels help to create a just society for oppressed groups. Social movements also influence opportunities for participation and social equality in a range of non-governmental social groups, such as workplaces, schools, social service organizations, community groups, and other social institutions (Kerchis & Young, 1995).

Social movement activities at the local community level are described by Fisher and Karger (1997) as new strategies that have emerged "into the 'live space' of neighborhoods and communities of interest." Thus, social change through social movements has moved to groups emphasizing their cultural identities in terms of race, ethnicity, gender, and sexual orientation. All of these groups challenge the power exerted within society in relation to discrimination and oppression. At the same time these groups vie with each other as they seek to empower themselves within communities and society vis-à-vis the dominant culture. Fisher and Karger (1997) suggest that social change efforts must go beyond "identity and democratization to include an emphasis on economic equality and social justice." As a consequence, social change must go beyond the local communities to the societal level in order to obtain public-sector resources and power. Thus, Fisher and Karger (1997) advocate moving beyond community and cultural identity: "Communities need help from outside, and cultural issues, such as gender and race, need to be connected with those of class," thus grounding change efforts and social movements in both political economy and cultural identity.

AMERICAN SOCIETY AS A SOCIAL SYSTEM

Since systems perspectives guide our understanding of local communities, it is useful to identify ways in which American society can be viewed as a social system and an ecological system. Systems theory "portrays society as a set of functionally interrelated units" (Fay, 1996). These social units are often referred to as social institutions, institutional structures, or subsystems that perform certain functions for the members of a society. In Parsonian terms, society as a social system carries out patterned functions. Patterns involving a system's external activities serve adaptive and goal attainment functions and are carried out in large part by the economy and the polity. Internal patterns involve integrative functions found within the juridical system and pattern-maintenance functions that are exercised within groups such as families, schools, and cultural institutions (Parsons, 1951). Major subsystems of American society that respond to the needs of citizens include political, economic, religious, education, health and social welfare systems and social structures. These subsystems are influenced in significant ways by the national society as a social system. As Longres (1995) has noted, social institutions within society serve a variety of functions that can be grouped under institutional social orders, such as the political, economic, military, kinship, religious, and social welfare orders. These social orders relate directly to the operation of the local community as a system made up of corresponding subsystems.

The influence of the social structures of society on local communities is most apparent in the functioning of the federal government. While local community subsystems or social orders operate independently at times, they are influenced to a high degree by the political system of the federal government—that is, the legislative, executive, and judicial branches (Ginsberg, 1994; Segal & Brzuzy, 1998). The executive branch of government includes *cabinets*—departments that carry out the policies of all three branches of government. These departments include the Departments of State, Treasury, Defense, Justice, Interior, Agriculture, Commerce, Labor, Health and Human Services, Housing and Urban Development, Transportation, Energy, Education, and Veterans Affairs.

The Department of Health and Human Services is a good example of how a unit of the executive branch of government implements the actions of the legislative branch. "Health and Human Services is the government's principal agency for protecting the health of all Americans and providing essential human services, especially for those who are least able to help themselves" (HHS, 1999). HHS oversees programs such as Medicare (health insurance for elderly and disabled Americans) and Medicaid (health insurance for low-income people), financial assistance for low-income families, child support enforcement, programs for improving maternal and infant health, Head Start (preschool education and services), programs for preventing child abuse and domestic violence, substance abuse treatment and prevention, services for older Americans, and services for American Indians and Alaska Natives. The department works closely with state and local governments, with many HHS-funded services provided at the local level by state or county agencies, or through private sector grantees.

The political branches of state governments—executive, legislative, and judicial—have a significant impact on local communities. They are linked to individual citizens through the political process that includes political parties, interest and advocacy groups, elections, state representatives, and government personnel (civil service) (Karger & Stoesz, 1998). These are some of the mechanisms through which individuals and community organizations seek to influence public policy at state and federal levels of government. The reader can obtain an overview of the way in which governments make decisions about social policy by reading Ginsberg's (1994) *Understanding Social Problems, Policies, and Programs*, Karger and Stoesz's (1998) *American Social Welfare Policy*, and Segal and Brzuzy's (1998) *Social Welfare Policy, Programs, and Practice*. An important feature of government in the United States is the existence of a federal system of government, a state system, and a local governmental system. The powers of each level are defined in the Constitution and through the actions of the Courts, as are the powers of the executive, legislative, and judicial branches of government. It is common for social programs to be financed by the federal government, partly financed by states, and delivered (and sometimes funded) at local community levels (Ginsberg, 1994).

AMERICAN SOCIETY AS AN ECOLOGICAL SYSTEM

American society can be viewed as an ecological system, based on a definition of ecology as "the study of the relation of populations to their environment" (Hawley, 1950). Ideas from human ecology and systems theory have been used in social work to formulate an ecosystems perspective for practice, a perspective that is often labeled person-in-environment, with an emphasis on "the interdependence of people and their environments at multiple and interlocking levels of systems" (Kemp, 1995). This ecological perspective in social work has emphasized the ways in which people adapt to their social and physical environments, especially through the "continuous reciprocal exchanges, or transactions, in which people and environments influence, shape, and sometimes change each other" (Germain & Bloom, 1999). An important context for these relationships from an ecological system perspective is the spatial organization of society and its communities—that is, "the distribution of people and services operating in a system of interdependence" (Hawley, 1950, 1986). An ecological perspective includes attention to population characteristics of geographic areas such as size, density, and heterogeneity, as well as the physical characteristics of the environment, such as the distribution of populations in spatial areas.

The U.S. Bureau of the Census provides data that illustrate the demographics of American society and its communities, including information on features of population groups such as social class, racial and ethnic composition, age and gender structures, aspects of family composition, and economic division of labor (Frey & First, 1997; Andrews & Fonseca, 1995). An ecological perspective leads to an understanding of societal changes, such as movements of population groups, patterns of migration, immigration, and population growth dynamics, patterns of residential segregation and integration, patterns of social stratification, land use, and the impact of technological forces on society and communities. Information on these topics comes from a "long" census form (38 pages) distributed to about 1 in 6 residents. Most people complete a short form that lists only a few questions for each person in a household.

Data about the American population are available from sources such as The National Center for Education Statistics, Centers for Disease Control and Prevention, and the National Center for Health Statistics. A picture of American society in which "the primary focus is on people" can be presented through maps, graphics, and tables on topics such as urban vs. rural, vital statistics, population migration, mobility and change, poverty vs. affluence, racial/ethnic diversity, health and disease, medical care and costs, lifestyle risks, education K-12, higher education, crime, status of women, children, senior citizens, and politics and religion (Andrews & Fonseca, 1995). Data from the U.S. Census on these features of American society provide a context for understanding the demographic development of local geographic communities, such as metropolitan areas, cities, towns, and neighborhoods.

A census of the American population is conducted at ten-year intervals, with annual estimates of selected population characteristics published in Statistical Abstracts. The requirement for a decennial count of the population comes from the U.S. Constitution, with the central purpose being to provide a basis for apportioning congressional representatives and for gathering economic, social, and demographic data about the United States. A major issue for the year 2000 census has involved the methods used to determine the population totals. The Census Bureau recognized a need for new procedures after an estimated 1990 census undercount of some 8.4 million people and 4.4 million counted either twice or in the wrong place. Of special concern were indications that there was a "differential undercount," that is, of children, renters, and racial and ethnic minorities. New immigrants, in particular, have posed challenges for census takers, in part due to language difficulties, group housing arrangements, a mistrust in government, and fear of being deported by Immigration and Naturalization officials (Sachs, 1999a). Recognizing the continuing problem of under-enumeration, with more than 8.4 million people overlooked in 1990, the Census Bureau introduced an advertising campaign prior to the 2000 census. The campaign included advertisements in 17 languages, through television networks, radio stations, and billboards. A special feature of the campaign was to appeal to racial or ethnic solidarity and self-interest by emphasizing the fact that federal financial aid designed to help a person's community is distributed on the basis of census data. Also, all census forms stated that a response was required by law. An introductory letter explained that "your answers are important," because "the number of representatives each state has in Congress depends on the number of people living in the state" and "the amount of government money your neighborhood receives depends on your answers." Further, "money gets used for schools, employment services, housing assistance, roads, services for children and the elderly, and many other local needs." Citizens were assured that "your privacy is protected by law."

The traditional method for counting the population has been to make an "actual enumeration" by door-to-door and mail collection of information from people in households. In order to overcome the problem of undercount, a procedure of statistical sampling was proposed by the Census Bureau as a method of adjusting the numbers generated by the traditional headcount enumeration. This proposal was supported by the Clinton Administration and by Democrats in Congress, and opposed by Republican Congressional members. The House of Representatives filed a lawsuit against the Commerce Department over the proposed use of statistical sampling in the 2000 census. The U.S. Supreme Court ruled that the Census Bureau was to use the traditional enumeration procedures for purposes of apportionment of House of Representatives seats among the states. At the same time, the Court left open the option by the Bureau of using statistical sampling to adjust the traditional counts for purposes of distribution by federal agencies of federal funds and redrawing of political boundaries (Biskupic, 1998; Holmes, 1998).

A major approach to understanding the societal context of American communities is through the use of social indicators. Social indicators are statistics in a time series that identify social changes, such as unemployment rates, crime rates, estimates of life expectancy, health status indices, school enrollment ranges, and voting rates (Land, 1992). Reports on social changes include data on issues regarding health and illness, social mobility, the physical environment, income and poverty, public order and safety, learning, science and art, participation and alienation (Land, 1992). Thus, there is a collection of data on social, economic, and demographic characteristics of the society that provides a context for studying communities. Data from the U.S. Bureau of the Census can by analyzed in order to better understand "a whole range of social and economic issues that are facing society today" such as "racial inequality, immigrant assimilation, gender inequality and the glass ceiling, as well as differences in poverty levels among children and the elderly" (Frey & First, 1997).

Of central importance to understanding the nature of local communities is being able to recognize social stratification within American society. Data from the U.S. Bureau of the Census provides a descriptive picture of various strata of society, particularly in relation to social class, race, ethnicity, religious affiliation, age, and gender. The social composition of the society is part of the societal context for understanding local communities. It is based on classification of groups of people and the interactions of these groups with each other and their environment. An important feature of an ecological systems perspective is stratification by social class.

The combined measures of occupation, income, and education make up what is called *socioeconomic status*, or SES. Social class groups are identified within the society on the basis of SES. Lifestyles become associated with these groups, based on the ways in which class groups spend their money, the location and nature of their housing, and other consumption patterns. Still, there is little agreement about where to draw the lines to distinguish one class from another and what to call the various class levels. The boundaries of the various social classes are fluid, but the census data do provide a basis for describing the social class structure of the society.

Data from the U.S. Bureau of the Census are used to describe the social stratification of Americans by race and ethnicity. For Census 2000, designations regarding race and ethnicity have been expanded so that a person can identify as a member of more than one group. Respondents are asked to answer questions 7 and 8 for each person in a household.

Q. 7. Is Person 1 Spanish/Hispanic/Latino?
____ No.
____ Yes, Mexican, Mexican-American, Chicano.
____ Yes, Puerto-Rican.
____ Yes, Cuban.
____ Yes, other Spanish/Hispanic/Latino.
Print Group:

Q. 8. What is Person 1's race? Mark (X) one or more races to indicate what this person considers himself/herself to be:
____ White
____ Black, African American, or Negro
____ American Indian or Alaska Native: Print name of enrolled or principal tribe:

_____ 4. ___ Asian Indian   ___ Japanese   ___ Native Hawaiian
          ___ Chinese   ___ Korean   ___ Guamanian or
                                                 Chamorro
          ___ Filipino   ___ Vietnamese
          ___ Other Asian: Print Race:
          ___ Samoan   ___Other Pacific Islander: Print Race:
          ___ Some other race: Print Race:

Chapter 1 Review

In this chapter we examined the growing interdependence between the global community, American society, and local communities. Characteristics of American society were selected to illustrate how the societal context impacts on local communities. In exploring society as a national culture, we highlighted how conceptions of American culture have changed from a monocultural society to a multicultural society. We discussed ongoing debate concerning relationships between various subcultures and the national culture. Because a multicultural society incorporates various ethnic and social groups into a national social system, the question arises as to whether assimilation will produce a post-ethnic society. A second issue regarding culture concerns the extent to which a national, "mass society" culture dominates the society, and the nature of the influence subcultural groups have on individuals, groups, and organizations.

Connections between a national society and local communities were explored in relation to the United States as a civil society. The report of the National Commission on Civic Renewal (1998) served as a context for examining the engagement of individuals and groups in the civic life of American society. An emerging issue involves ways in which the civil society can be strengthened by building communities and linking local groups to the national enterprise. Closely related to our discussion of civil society is the question of how social order and social control are maintained within American society. A special issue in this regard involves the extent to which the nation and local communities can balance individual rights and autonomy so that anarchy is avoided and social order is maintained. Social and economic justice were identified as important goals of American society. Attention was given to how social movements strive to promote justice by fighting discrimination and oppression that has been directed at specific groups.

Finally, American society was viewed as a social system and an ecological system, the conceptual frameworks we will use to examine local communities. A social systems perspective was illustrated by reference to the functioning of the federal government. An ecological perspective in relation to the national society was illustrated through reference to the U.S. Bureau of the Census as the provider of demographic and social information on the U.S. population.

2

American Society as a Welfare State

The term *welfare state* is used throughout the world to refer to a country that provides substantial health and human services to its citizens. The term is used by academicians and professionals in the United States to refer to the health and social welfare policies, programs, and services of the nation, following the British use of the term "welfare state" for nation (Titmuss, 1974). American citizens, on the other hand, rarely use the term "welfare state" and reserve the term "state" for one of the fifty states of the United States. They more commonly refer to government programs as "welfare" and assistance provided within the voluntary, private sector as "charity."

The concept of a welfare state is sometimes restricted to the public sector, but in this text the term applies to the combination of public and private health and social welfare systems of the nation. These systems are characterized by extensive policies, programs, and expenditures for all citizens, but especially those who are disadvantaged by social and economic problems and/or by physical and mental disabilities. General categories of assistance provided usually include education, employment, social services, health care, income security, housing, and nutrition.

Another way of characterizing the American welfare state is to think of social welfare as a goal and social condition. Midgley (1995) follows this approach, arguing that "a condition of social welfare exists when families, communities, and societies experience a high degree of social well-being." Segal and Brzuzy (1998) define social well-being in terms of "people's health, economic condition, happiness, and quality of life." Well-being at these social levels can be evaluated in terms of three elements of social welfare: (1) "the degree to which social problems are managed; (2) the extent to which needs are met; (3) the degree to which opportunities for advancement are provided." According to Midgley (1995), achievement of these goals results in a community or society with a satisfactory level of welfare and well-being. Achievement of these goals is gained through a *social welfare system*—that is, "the organized efforts and structures used to provide for our societal well-being" (Segal & Brzuzy, 1998). This system, as characterized by Segal and Brzuzy (1998), includes four interrelated parts: social issues, policy goals, legislative regulation, and social welfare programs. Social workers play important roles within the American social welfare system. The social work profession's Code of Ethics identifies the social worker's ethical responsibilities to the broader society and social welfare as follows: "Social workers should promote the general welfare of society, from local to global levels, and the development of people, their communities, and their environments. Social workers should advocate for living conditions conducive to the fulfillment of basic human needs and should promote social, economic, political, and cultural values and institutions that are compatible with the realization of social justice" (NASW, 1997).

SECTORS OF THE WELFARE STATE

Three major sectors make up the U.S. welfare state: the government, the private/voluntary sector, and the business/corporate sector. This "pluralistic mix of private and public services is an essential feature of American social welfare" (Karger & Stoesz, 1998). The interrelationships between government, private, and corporate welfare structures constitutes a complex web of social policies and programs devoted to the well-being of all Americans. An understanding of the historical development of these welfare systems can be gained by reading works such as *Controversial Issues in Social Welfare Policy* by Chelf (1992); *Moral Authority, Ideology, and the Future of American Social Welfare* by Dobelstein (1999); *American Social Welfare Policy* by Karger and Stoesz (1998); *Social Work in Contemporary Society* by Garvin and Tropman (1998); *Industrial Society and Social Welfare* by Wilensky and Lebeaux (1958); *The Welfare State and Equality* by Wilensky (1975); *Race, Money, and the American Welfare State* by M. K. Brown (1999); and *The National Government and Social Welfare* by Hansan and Morris (1997). These books cover the various historical periods of the American welfare state, emphasizing the development of public welfare after the enactment of the Social Security Act of 1935. Many policy makers agree with Chelf's (1992) observation that two basic components of the Social Security Act—a system of social insurance based on employer/employee contributions, and a non-contributory program of social assistance—made Social Security the "cornerstone for the federal welfare state." The future of the Social Security system has become an important agenda for the public and for politicians, and health and social welfare professionals need to have a basic understanding of "how social security works." A reading of Peterson's (1999) *The Social Security Primer* will contribute to this understanding of the present system and issues related to its future.

The development of the welfare state in the United States continues to be influenced by the political and economic systems of the nation. The laws and policies of an economic system and their interactions are referred to as the *political economy* of the society. The American political economy is labeled "democratic-capitalist," "reflecting an open, representative form of government coexisting with a market economy" (Karger & Stoesz, 1998). What makes the United States a welfare state is the fact that the social welfare system is expected to "modify the play of market forces and to ameliorate the social and economic inequities that the market generates" (Karger & Stoesz, 1998). The federal systems of health and social welfare operate within a context of the political economy of the nation as they represent the major source of policies and programs carried out in the states and local communities.

An important aspect of political economy is the impact of race and social class on the development of the federal social policies of the American welfare state. According to M. K. Brown (1999), racial stratification has led to "the relative exclusion of minority and female-headed families from the salient, non-means-tested, and private forms of social protection, and the regulating of "African Americans and other subordinate racial groups to charity or the public system of social provision, normally relief." In this regard, Quadagno (1994) claims that the "American Creed" of liberty, justice, and equality has clashed with a history of active racial discrimination, resulting in social welfare programs such as the War on Poverty in the 1960s and present-day welfare reform developments. This perspective is expressed by Esping-

Anderson (1996), who argues that "the welfare state is not just a mechanism that intervenes in, and possibly corrects, the structure of inequality; it is, in its own right, a system of stratification." Thus, social programs "help determine the articulation of social solidarity, divisions of class and status differentiation."

The role of political and economic forces in promoting the "public good" through a national social welfare system is influenced by the ideologies of the American people. The major ideologies are usually viewed along a continuum from conservatism to liberalism (Chelf, 1992; Dobelstein, 1999; Karger & Stoesz, 1998). Thus, as Mullaly (1997) contends, "The welfare state is a social construction based on subjective and ideological grounds, existing to deal with social and economic problems." Hence, "Every Western industrial country has a social welfare state, but no two countries have identical welfare systems." Ideologies expressed in terms of liberal and conservative beliefs have a significant impact on the way people answer two questions posed by Gilbert (1983): "How much social welfare can society afford?" and "How large an allocation of resources through the social market will a capitalist economy tolerate?" These questions are a central part of all attempts of the federal government to engage in "welfare reform." The ways in which these questions are answered impose significant opportunities and constraints on local communities, especially in regard to their ability to fund social programs and to respond to local community problems.

GOVERNMENTAL WELFARE SECTOR

Federal, state, and local governments play key roles in the functioning of American society as a welfare state. At the national level, three branches of government—executive, legislative, and judicial—are involved in making social policies that affect the welfare of all citizens. The basic powers of these branches of government have been established by the U.S. Constitution and its amendments. The Constitution specifies areas of federal authority, leaving sovereignty to the states in all other areas. The U.S. Supreme Court often rules on cases involving challenges to the authority of the federal government or of the states. Major social policies and social programs established by federal and state governments are carried out in local communities. At the same time, local community governments have jurisdiction over some activities delegated to them by higher levels of government, as well as authority to create policies and programs of their own.

A key question regarding the welfare state is "What is an appropriate role for the national government in social welfare?" Hansan and

Morris (1997) respond to this question by asserting that "the national government is a necessary partner in dealing with the difficult problems of poverty, dependency, illiteracy, unemployment, delinquency, alienation, environmentally dangerous waste, and so forth." These authors propose that the role for the federal government include active involvement in policies and programs that promote both economic and social goals, such as employment and wages, Social Security, health care, housing, education, social services, and public assistance. The nature of this involvement by the federal government is often characterized by the terms "liberal" and "conservative," with a tendency during the past decade of drifting toward conservatism, as illustrated by welfare reform legislation passed in 1996.

Department of Health and Human Services

At the federal level of government, most health and human service policies and programs are administered by the Department of Health and Human Services. This department is the "principal agency for protecting the health of all Americans and providing essential human services, especially for those who are least able to help themselves" (HHS, 1999). Operating divisions include the Health Care Financing Administration (for Medicare and Medicaid Programs), Administration for Children and Families (for Temporary Assistance to Needy Families), Head Start (early childhood education), and Administration on Aging (services to the elderly). Since 1995 the Social Security Administration, formerly part of Health and Human Services, has operated as an independent agency.

Public health and social welfare services are for the most part financed by federal and state governments and delivered at the local community level. Yearly, the U.S. Bureau of the Census publishes information in its Statistical Abstracts on the expenditures of the federal government for health and social welfare programs. State and local municipalities contribute to the financing of health and welfare services through state and local taxes. Thus, given the nature of the political systems in the United States, financing of welfare state programs requires an interdependence between the three levels of government and the corporate/business and voluntary sectors of the nation.

As already noted, the American welfare state is influenced both by the political system and the economic system of the society. Capitalism is the hallmark of the U.S. economic system and provides the foundation for the health and social welfare of Americans (Myles, 1996). Thus, the key to economic well-being for most people is employment, with many health and welfare benefits coming through workplace programs. However, the workplace does not provide access to these benefits for many people who work part-time, earn low wages, or are employed in small businesses that do not offer benefits. A number of people rely heavily on public and voluntary health and social welfare services, especially many older adults, ill persons, children, low-income individuals and families, and persons unable to work due to disabilities.

Ever since the New Deal initiated during President Franklin Roosevelt's administration (especially the Social Security Act of 1935), American society has had major provisions for income maintenance and services for people unable to participate in the market economy or to provide for themselves. The public sector's response to this social problem has been the provision of government-financed social and economic programs, but in many instances "assistance tends to be minimal, is intended to be short term, and is often punitive and stigmatizing in nature" (Myles, 1996). For people eligible for governmental programs, "Welfare transfers in the form of housing, education, health care, and personal social services subsidize the consumption of resources that, for the most part, would otherwise require expenditures of personal income" (Gilbert & Gilbert, 1989).

The American welfare state makes a significant contribution to the welfare of all citizens, especially those who are unable to participate in the labor force. Health and social welfare services are provided through government programs such as social insurance—e.g., Old Age, Survivors, and Disability Insurance (OASDI), unemployment insurance, workers' compensation, earned income tax credit, Supplemental Security Income (cash payments to adults who are older, blind, or disabled, with an income below the poverty line), Medicare, and Medicaid. Some of these programs are a mixture of insurance and public assistance. Public assistance programs are means-tested (based on income levels) and include Temporary Assistance to Needy Families (TANF), the 1996 replacement for AFDC, and General Assistance (GA). State and local general assistance programs provide benefits to families and individuals who are not eligible for federal programs.

Welfare Reform Act of 1996

The most recent major change in the American welfare system occurred with the passage of the Personal Responsibility and Work Opportunity Reconciliation Act of 1996. This act was initiated by a Republican Congress as part of a political agenda referred to as a "Contract with America." The 1996 act, signed by President Clinton, represented a strong shift of responsibility of administration of federal funds and policy making to the states and localities. Several changes in the public welfare system were implemented under the 1996 act. Aid to Families with Dependent Children (AFDC), Emergency Assistance, and Job Opportunities and Basic Skills Training programs were replaced by the Temporary Assistance for Needy Families (TANF) block grant (Title I). Other parts of the act included Title II: Supplemental Security Income; Title III: Child Support; Title IV: Restructure of Welfare and Public Benefits for Non-citizens; Title V: Reductions in Federal Government Positions; Title VI: Public Housing Benefits; Title VIII: Child Care Block Grant; Title IX: Child Nutrition; and Title X: Food Stamps and Commodity Distribution. The welfare reform act also included a Child Protection Program, Foster Care Adoption Assistance, and Foster Care and Adoption Maintenance Program (Dobelstein, 1999).

The welfare reform act of 1996 funded state programs under a federal block grant approach, *devolution*, that gave states new control and primary responsibility over welfare programs that deliver services in local communities. The new act eliminated a federal guarantee of cash assistance for poor families and children and gave the states new authority to run their own programs within federal guidelines. The act resulted in states providing public welfare through an assortment of plans, and it allowed states to cut their welfare spending up to 25 percent without penalty from the federal government.

The federal goal established in the 1996 act is to have at least one half of adult welfare recipients working by the year 2002 (Pear, 1998a). The act introduced a new set of requirements for welfare recipients, in terms of job training and expectations regarding work and retention of welfare payments. Welfare recipients were given two years to begin work or have their benefits reduced, and a limit of five years was placed on receipt of federal cash assistance. States were allowed some exceptions, such as waivers of the work requirement for mothers with young children and waivers of the lifetime rule for up to 20 percent of recipients. New restrictions were introduced regarding benefits for special groups, including legal immigrants and teenage unmarried mothers. Teenage mothers were required to attend school and live with an adult in order to receive assistance.

The 1996 welfare reform act made it more difficult for immigrants to become eligible for public assistance. Restrictions were placed on legal immigrants for benefits of SSI, food stamps, and Medicaid. Strict regulations regarding income and assets of the immigrant's sponsor were introduced for immigrants entering the U.S. after the passage of the act. In reaction to these restrictions in eligibility for welfare benefits by immigrants, state and local governments, as well as rights organizations, pressed for changes in the act. As a result, some of the provisions of the act with regard to immigrants were repealed, such as SSI and food stamp regulations (Borjas, 1999). Still, in March 2000 the Supreme Court refused to hear a challenge by the City of Chicago to the provisions in the 1996 act that prevented legal immigrants from receiving some types of federal welfare benefits. Concerns have been raised about declining use of welfare benefits by immigrants and refugees, with a survey by the U.S. Bureau of the Census showing that the 1996 act had restricted benefits and discouraged use of services and health benefits, especially by immigrant families with children (Branigin, 1999).

As of the year 2000, studies of the effects of the welfare reform act indicated that welfare rolls had been reduced and employment of aid recipients had increased. A number of states received "bonus" money from the government for moving welfare recipients into jobs. New categories for bonuses were established for the states: "Improvement in the percentage of families moving from welfare to work who have health insurance through Medicaid or the new Children's Health Insurance program; improvement in the percentage of low-income working families who are eligible for food stamps and get them; improvement in the percentage of children living below 200 percent of poverty who reside in a family with married parents" (Associated Press, 1999j). At the same time, concerns remain about the limitations of the Temporary Assistance for Needy Families program, since "(1) Many of the jobs available in the private sector do not pay wages sufficient to support a family, particularly single-parent families; and (2) There are some parents in our society whose physical, mental, emotional, or family circumstances prevent them from working successfully in the private sector; and (3) State and local governments do not have the finances or taxing authority to cope with serious unemployment and poverty during times of economic recessions" (Hansan & Morris, 1999). A positive response to these concerns by states and local communities will require investment in work-related programs, such as the creation of community jobs, job initiatives for the hard-to-employ, increases in vocational training, and enhancing of earned income disregards (raising of asset limits, and investments in child care assistance) (Hansan & Morris, 1999).

HEALTH CARE SYSTEM

The American health care system may be viewed as a significant part of the welfare state. The system relies on the public, private, and corporate sectors for the funding and provision of health benefits and health care. Most health care costs are covered through employment-based insurance programs in the corporate sector, with services delivered by private-sector health care providers. The role of the public sector is still extensive; various public health services are provided via federal, state, and local funding, such as family planning, prenatal and postnatal care, school health services, disease prevention and control, immunization, sexually transmitted disease services, environmental sanitation, and health education.

The federal government sponsors health care in Veterans Administration hospitals and clinics, Community and Migrant Health Centers, maternal and child health care services, and through programs within the Social Security system (Medicare and Medicaid) (Dobelstein, 1999; Karger & Stoesz, 1998). Medicare was added to the Social Security Act in 1965 as a health insurance program for people entitled to receive Social Security, including all older adults as well as spouses and some children. Medicare has two parts: Part A: hospital insurance (inpatient hospital care, skilled nursing facility care); and Part B: voluntary medical insurance, with premium payment (physician services, outpatient services). Since its establishment Medicare has expanded to include coverage for home health care, medical care for disabled persons, hospice care, payments for health equipment, and hospital clinic care (Dobelstein, 1999). Medicaid is a medical care program for low-income persons, covering aged, blind, and disabled persons, families with dependent children, and eligible pregnant women and children (Dobelstein, 1999). Funding is provided for this program through federal funds and state matching funds, with considerable variation among the states. Customarily, people receiving benefits for SSI and TANF receive medical care assistance through Medicaid.

The nature, extent, and costs of health care services in local communities continue to be problematic. Of special concern is the organization of health care in the private sector that includes solo physicians, group physician practices, hospitals, and outpatient services. Due mainly to the increasing costs of medical care, managed care through various forms of Health Maintenance Organizations has become the major vehicle for health care delivery. Efforts to establish a national health care system have not succeeded; the most recent failed attempt was the Health Security Act proposed in 1993 by the Clinton administration. Thus, in the year 2000 some 43 million citizens lacked health insurance coverage. The private health-care sector provided care for some members of this group, particularly with regard to serious health care needs of people living in poverty.

PRIVATE AND CORPORATE WELFARE SECTORS

The private sector not only provides a major proportion of medical care for Americans, but is also a major player in the provision of social welfare services. These programs are funded by voluntary contributions and governmental contracts, and delivered through not-for-profit and for-profit social agencies and volunteer programs. A significant part of the voluntary sector is composed of faith-based groups that provide social welfare services through organizations such as hospitals, clinics, and social welfare agencies. These organizations employ professionals, while also making extensive use of volunteers for a wide variety of non-professional services and activities. They provide services funded by the private sector through voluntary giving and fees, as well as through contracts from state and federal governments as part of a process called privatization. Yet another source of private voluntary sector services is an array of self-help groups that are independent of formal health and human service organizations. Self-help groups are often related to recovery from illnesses, social support, education, and advocacy for groups stigmatized within American society (Kurtz, 1997). Many self-help groups are linked with the local community through social agencies and with the society by national organizations that have local chapters.

A sizable component of the welfare state is composed of business organizations that contribute to employee benefits through various types of insurance for health and social welfare services, pensions, in-house employee assistance programs, child day care, recreational programs, and other fringe benefits (Garvin and Tropman, 1998). Philanthropic foundations established by large for-profit organizations, such as General Motors, General Electric, Ford Motor Company, Wal-Mart, and the Kellogg Company, make sizable contributions to health and social welfare programs. The corporate sector also includes health and social welfare for-profit organizations, including nursing homes, child care and child welfare services, correctional facilities, mental health and health care clinics, social services, and educational services. Included under the corporate sector are professionals in private practice, such as physicians, psychiatrists, psychologists, social workers, and nurses. Increasingly, governmental health and social welfare programs look to the corporate sector for providing the delivery of services through public funding arrangements.

SOCIAL DEVELOPMENT AND THE WELFARE STATE

Up to this point, our discussion of the welfare state has emphasized the nation's political and economic systems, their interrelationships, and their impact on health and social welfare policies and programs. An important issue concerns the extent to which the various levels of government can support economic development and at the same time meet the social needs of people. Meeting these needs involves expenditures of public monies for health and social welfare programs. Midgley (1999) explores this issue from a social development perspective, suggesting that interventions be directed toward bringing people "currently dependent on social benefits. . . into the productive economy." Thus, Midgley's (1999) social development approach within a welfare state is "concerned not only with increasing labor market participation but with promoting human capital formation, accumulating assets, mobilizing social capital in poor communities, and developing microenterprises. . . At a broader level, social development seeks to remove impediments to economic participation, such as racial and gender discrimination, and to create a climate conducive to economic development."

Examples of human capital investments come from the field of child welfare services, which emphasizes the use of day care centers and other community programs to nurture human potential and prevent child neglect. Capital investments in regard to persons with disabilities include skills training and promotion of workforce participation through education and health care programs. Examples of development of social capital are found in community practice in low-income communities, where there is a focus on local community economic growth projects (Midgley & Livermore, 1998; Midgley, 1999). These social development programs within a welfare state concentrate on local community programs that involve development of social and human capital, and of individual and community assets (Sherraden, 1991; Page-Adams & Sherraden, 1997). Some programs focus on removing barriers to economic participation, such as discrimination based on race and ethnicity, gender, nationality, disability, age, and other factors. Finally, efforts are directed toward creating a social climate conducive to development, through efforts such as responding to problems of crime and violence in low-income areas that arise from poverty and social disorganization.

THEORIES OF THE WELFARE STATE

Our discussion of American society as a welfare state highlights the role of the federal government in providing social benefits and responses to social problems through health and social service programs that are delivered at the local community level. Views of the nature of a welfare state, sometimes referred to as theories of the welfare state, provide a framework for thinking about the future of the American welfare state. These theories may be characterized in ideological terms, such as conservative, moderate, or radical (Blau, 1989). These ideological positions represent ways in which health and social welfare programs are believed to contribute to the creation and maintenance of a responsive society. From the conservative point of view, social benefits provided by the government have a negative effect on the capitalistic economic system and foster dependency on government aid. In terms of the rights of individuals, a conservative perspective suggests that "social welfare policies represent a form of charity organized by the state," and recipients of aid have no inherent entitlement to such help (Blau, 1989). A moderate philosophical perspective asserts that there should be social spending, with neither charity nor absolute entitlements, but with fiscal constraints imposed on the welfare state. Such fiscal limits should be imposed on social welfare programs in keeping with political and economic interests. Finally, a radical perspective challenges the welfare state to provide more benefits to the disadvantaged, to view such needs as medical care, housing, and social wages as rights, and to back away from some of the political and economic functions of the welfare state, such as regulating the poor.

These views of the welfare state suggest different approaches to American welfare politics, from the right, to the center, to the left in ideological positions. As such, they deal with public versus individual responsibilities, individual rights, and how the welfare state configures the provision of health and welfare services through the public, private, and corporate sectors of the society. In particular, they focus on "what groups of people the government programs should target for help," i.e., all people (e.g., all children), some people (e.g., people with disabilities), or poor people (e.g., unemployed) (Garvin & Tropman, 1998). The future of the American welfare state depends, at least in part, on how the public and their political representatives answer this question, as well as the question of how to distribute responsibility for social welfare benefits among the public, private, and corporate sectors of the welfare state.

THE FUTURE WELFARE STATE

The American welfare state of the future will influence the ways in which the needs of people are met in their residential communities, that is, how well the subsystems of the community are able to meet "common human needs." Major perspectives toward the future American welfare state can serve as a framework for thinking about how governments and economic systems might affect local communities. One perspective is to focus on the values Americans hold and how they influence the future development of the welfare state. Dobelstein (1999) identifies values such as freedom, independence, responsibility, personal well-being, family values, and religious values. He suggests that these values influence how people respond to three basic value questions: Who should get welfare? What should it be? How should it be given?

One of the major characteristics of the present social welfare state is the fact that changes in it are incremental, reflecting the ideologies of political parties and the American people as well as changes in the economic systems of the nation and the world (Dobelstein, 1999). As a consequence, it is difficult to predict the future of the federal welfare state and to determine its effects on states, counties, districts, and municipalities. It is clear that the future of the American welfare state is intertwined with that of government and economic systems. These systems rely heavily on the values of the American people that support health and social welfare policies and programs, as well as the rights and responsibilities of citizens. The values associated with social policies of the American welfare state are highly influenced by the political system, the functioning of the economic system, and the roles played by private/voluntary and corporate sectors in relation to the well-being of members of the society.

The Enabling Welfare State

An interesting perspective on the future of the American welfare state has been advanced by Gilbert (1998). Gilbert proposes the idea of an "enabling welfare state" as a basis for responding to demographic and economic changes in American society. He suggests that a new form of welfare state is necessary to respond to special groups, such as single parents and children, and older adults with income, health, and social service needs. Gilbert (1998) argues that changes in family composition have reduced "the modern family's capacity to discharge traditional responsibilities for the care of children, elderly, and other infirm relatives," leading to "demands for the state to provide child care, financial assistance, and other supportive services." At the same time, with the globalization of the economy, "capital mobility has intensified the pressures of the global market on local and national markets," posing problems for any increases in social spending. In the light of changes in the economic systems of the world and the pressures of the welfare state for increased spending for social programs, there has been a privatization of governmental programs. This privatization has involved changes in delivery of services from the public to the private sector, and a move from "social rights to welfare and toward social responsibilities to work, cost containment, and privatization." This means that there is a "new institutional framework that subordinates social welfare policies to economic considerations. . . . social welfare policies are increasingly designed to enable more people to work and to enable the private sector to expand its sphere of activity" (Gilbert, 1998).

Gilbert (1998) suggests that these changes are leading American society to replace the current welfare state by an "enabling state," with social benefits based on private responsibility and work. The Personal Responsibility and Work Opportunity Reconciliation Act of 1996, in establishing the Temporary Assistance to Needy Families program, illustrates this principle. Gilbert suggests that this shift in the welfare state "is likely to dilute social protection for the weakest and most disadvantaged members of the community. . .those most in need of help and care," as well as the working poor. The idea of an enabling state offers "public support for private responsibility" by supporting a market-oriented approach to social welfare by expecting individual and family responsibility, and by providing aid and social protection for those unable to participate in the labor force (Gilbert & Gilbert, 1989; Gilbert, 1998). Thus, the fact that some people are still "left behind," left out of the mainstream, and make up a "hardcore" population dependent on the welfare state challenges policy makers to create policies and programs that will be in keeping with the idea of an "enabling welfare state."

The Reluctant Welfare State

Another approach to the future American welfare state has been developed by Jansson (1997) in his discussion of a "reluctant welfare state." The term "reluctant welfare state" was coined by Wilensky and Lebeaux (1958) in their classic book entitled *Industrial Society and Social Welfare*. Jansson's history of welfare policies at the societal level, from colonial times to the present, provides a context for understanding social welfare systems in local communities. Jansson notes the mixed response of public policies and private philanthropy to social problems and people in special need. This combination of both punitiveness and generosity in social reforms, particularly in comparison to European nations, is the basis for calling American society a reluctant welfare state (Jansson, 1997; Esping-Andersen, 1996). The American welfare system, in contrast to European welfare states, is more likely to spend a lower percentage of GNP on social programs; to use means-tested rather than universal programs; to have policies that fluctuate over time; to have citizens pay for social needs; to impose restrictions on welfare; to have a concentration of minority, elderly, and children with special needs who require government support; and to rely heavily on non-governmental social programs from the private and corporate sectors of society (Jansson, 1997; Brilliant, 1997).

Despite these indicators of reluctance, the American welfare state provides substantial resources to all social class groups, including the middle and upper classes. Jansson (1997) identifies a number of government social policies that affect states and localities in a positive way, such as "regulations that protect people from hazards; needs-meeting policies, such as health and economic benefits; opportunity-enhancing policies, such as education, affirmative action; social services, such as mental health, child welfare; referral and linkage programs, such as case management; equality-enhancing policies, such as Medicaid, AFDC, food stamps, progressive taxation; rights-conferring policies, such as civil rights legislation; public-improvement policies, such as parks, transportation, roads; asset-accumulation policies, such as income tax benefits."

Tropman (1998) explains the reluctance of the welfare state in terms of both the social culture or value system of Americans, and the social structure—that is, social policies and programs of American society. Under this formulation, public and private expenditures on social welfare programs are viewed by Americans as being too high but do not seem as high when compared to European welfare states. However, public support for social programs is mixed, due to conflicting values regarding obligations of society to the poor. Tropman (1998) maintains that these values are "generally negative and hostile with respect to the public welfare system." These values are embedded in a "poorfare culture" that emphasizes work over welfare, and is not "sympathetic to the disadvantaged or to the poor." Yet, there are contradictions in the value systems of Americans, especially tied to religious beliefs that regarding helping the poor, that permit support of some minimal level of welfare state programs.

WELFARE REFORM AND SOCIAL JUSTICE

Proposals for changes in the American welfare state may be viewed in terms of their relationship to social justice. For example, Karger and Stoesz (1998) have proposed five principles related to welfare reform as a foundation for thinking about the future of the American welfare state in relation to social justice. These principles include greater economic productivity, strengthening the family, increased social cohesion, the strengthening of community, and greater social choice. In regard to the principle of greater economic productivity, Karger and Stoesz propose that integration of welfare clients into the work force be accompanied by the assurance of basic health and child care benefits for the working poor. This principle is illustrated in the Personal Responsibility and Work Opportunity Reconciliation Act of 1996. To strengthen families, there is a need for a national family policy that helps keep families out of welfare by providing benefits such as maternity and sick leave, day care, medical insurance, after-school programs, adequate unemployment insurance compensation, and affordable housing. The call for social policies that support neighborhood and community cohesion and civic involvement is a response to the negative effects of racism and of the separation of classes and races in residential settings. An example of policies that support community development is the Empowerment Zone initiative under the Clinton administration. These zones were established in a few large American cities in order to encourage and support the development of businesses, jobs, social services, and housing in poor neighborhoods. Finally, the idea of greater social choice involves programs such as vouchers for housing and education, and an increase in choices related to medical and social services, especially through privatization via public/private-sector funding and service delivery arrangements.

Karger and Stoesz (1998) link these values to the achievement of social justice through social welfare programs. They propose three main programs: (1) a family conservation program, (2) a community revitalization initiative, and (3) a national service program. Family conservation would be the target of preventive as well as remedial programs such as improvements in the unemployment insurance program, in the minimum wage program, in a minimal benefits package, in day care, in Individual Development Accounts (IDAs), in Individual Retirement Accounts (IRAs), in health care, in a Stable Incomes Program, and in social service vouchers. Community revitalization programs would involve further development of Community Enterprise Zones, rebuilding of community physical and social infrastructure in low-income areas of inner cities, and improvements in public safety programs. Closely related to the community revitalization programs is a proposal for national service programs such as Americorps.

WELFARE CAPITALISM

Many of the principles and programs advanced under our discussion of the "enabling welfare state" and "welfare reform and social justice" are included in the proposal by Stoesz and Saunders (1999) for poverty policies based on the idea of "welfare capitalism." These authors define welfare capitalism as "the application of market principles to enhance social welfare," and propose this type of policy "as an agenda for alleviating poverty." They contend that a welfare state based on welfare capitalism can strengthen "the social and economic infrastructures that are the preconditions to prosperity" through three strategies: (1) wage supplements, (2) asset development, and (3) community capitalism. Wage supplements include tax credits for low-wage workers and their employers, such as the federal Earned Income Tax Credit program of the Internal Revenue Service, and state programs of supplemental Earned Income Credits.

An assets strategy is well developed in Sherraden's (1991) *Assets and the Poor*. This strategy seeks to implement IDAs (Individual Development Accounts) to encourage saving and asset accumulation by low-income individuals and families. "IDAs are special savings accounts that are designed to help people build assets for increased self-sufficiency and long-term economic security" (Sherraden et al., 2000). A national demonstration of 200 IDAs has been funded by eleven foundations and implemented in fourteen programs run by private, not-for-profit organizations throughout the United States from 1997 through 2001. Participants' savings are matched by the IDA programs. An evaluation of the IDA programs is measuring the relationship between program and participant characteristics and savings outcomes. Sherraden's history of IDAs shows that they were first initiated in the early 1990s by community-based organizations. More than 200 community IDA programs are now operating, sponsored and funded by organizations such as United Way, and by state and federal welfare programs under the Assets for Independence Act of 1998.

An "asset-based community development" plan is presented by McKnight and Kretzmann (1993) as an approach to rebuilding "troubled" communities and neighborhoods. These authors provide a guide for mapping the assets of individuals, associations, and institutions in locality-based communities. This strategy emphasizes the assets in neighborhood communities, but recognizes the need in low-income urban areas for outside resources. This approach is "internally focused" on the problem-solving capacities of local residents and groups. It is also "relationship driven," meaning that community developers constantly build and rebuild relationships between and among local residents and organizations, in order to utilize the strengths and capacities of these social groups.

Another strategy associated with welfare capitalism is community capitalism, as exemplified by the development of programs under

Community Development Corporations, community development banks and credit unions, and empowerment zones. These programs have the potential for revitalizing poor neighborhoods through the use of monetary capital in local neighborhoods. Examples of this strategy are the creation of 100 community development banks authorized under the Bank Enterprise Act of 1994, and the programs of private financial institutions in inner-city areas. Given the potential of these strategies for alleviating poverty, Stoesz and Saunders (1999) suggest that welfare capitalism "will not be [used] as a replacement for public welfare, but rather as its sequel." By this they mean that income maintenance and other public welfare assistance would still be necessary for destitute families, but that "welfare capitalism builds on welfare-to-work by offering individuals additional income, families upward mobility, and communities stronger economies."

Chapter 2 Review

The U.S. welfare state is often viewed by the American public as consisting of public-sector political and economic social policies and programs. However, our more comprehensive view of the welfare state includes the voluntary/private sector and the corporate sector, so that the welfare state consists of a mix of public and private services directed toward the "general welfare" and "public good" of the American population.

Ideologies of the American people regarding the nature and role of the federal government and the national economy, particularly as represented by political parties, affect the ways in which welfare reform has occurred in the United States. The major features of the Personal Responsibility and Work Opportunity Act of 1996 are described as an example of how federal legislation affects social welfare programs at state and local levels. The present trends of the welfare state include a new federalism and a devolution of responsibility for welfare from the federal government to the states, e.g., through block grant funding arrangements. The American health care system, at federal, state, and local community levels, is viewed as a significant part of the welfare state. Private and corporate sectors of the nation are described, followed by an examination of social development programs in local communities. These programs are introduced as examples of ways in which forms of capital can be developed to enhance the achievement of welfare state goals. Trends and proposals regarding the future of the welfare state are explored in terms of an "enabling welfare state," as illustrated by the welfare reform act of 1996; a "reluctant welfare state," with ongoing constraints imposed on expenditures devoted to social welfare programs; "welfare reform," with policies and programs to promote social justice; and "welfare capitalism," with a focus on encouraging the development of personal assets and strengthening the economic base of local communities.

3

Defining Communities

Historically, the concept of *community* has been defined in many different and overlapping ways. In Chapter 1 we defined a community as a group of people who form a social unit based on common location, interest, and/or identification. A traditional meaning for a *locational* community is a collective group of people living in a common place, such as a neighborhood, town, city, or metropolitan area. We refer to these communities with several similar terms: locality-based, geographic, spatial, or place communities. The boundaries of these communities are usually established by the local political system, e.g., city limits, neighborhood areas, or school districts. Under this definition, all the persons and families living in a specified spatial area are considered to be members of a community. In addition, there are many groups and organizations within locality-based communities that provide varying degrees of social interaction, social resources, and social arrangements "through which and by which people can meet their common needs, deal with their common problems, and advance their sense of well-being" (Norlin & Chess, 1997). Thus, a locality-based community is a form of social organization or social system that includes individuals, families, kin and friendship groups, work groups, associations, and formal organizations in a defined spatial area (Longres, 1995; Schriver, 1998).

Membership in some communities does not depend on presence in a locality; instead, members share certain characteristics or interests. *Identificational* communities are usually based on common individual and group features such as ethnicity and culture, race, religion, lifestyle, ideology, sexual orientation, ability, or social class. Communities of interest are a form of identificational communities, but may have a more narrow focus based on shared interests, goals, and objectives (Longres, 1995). Communities of interest include advocacy and social movement groups such as a gay, lesbian, and bisexual community, a faith-based community, an ethnic minority community, a community of persons with disabilities, or a professional/occupational community. These communities of identification and interest often overlap with a community of place, especially in instances where residential areas have a high proportion of people who identify with a specific group.

People belong to multiple communities with varying degrees of involvement, identification, and interest, and hence have "multiple community identities." One way of recognizing this fact is to use the term "personal community" to designate a person's membership in a range of place and non-place communities (Davidson, 1986). The concept of personal community allows for a focus on all the communities in which a person engages in social interaction, in use of services and resources, in employment activities, in leisure-time pursuits, and in attachment and involvement through identification and/or interest. This view of community broadens the scope of potential social interactions and social resources, including both formal and informal helping networks and other sources of social support. A personal community perspective can provide a context for the social worker's development of interpersonal change and social service intervention goals.

Our approach to understanding communities of place is to use perspectives from theories of ecological and social systems. Whenever appropriate, we consider communities of identification and interest as they interact and overlap with communities of place. From an ecological perspective, a spatial community may be defined as "a structure of relationships through which a localized population provides its daily requirements" (Hawley, 1950). In social work education and practice, this perspective focuses on ecosystems—that is, "the interdependence of people and their environments in multiple and interlocking systems" (Kemp, 1995). Under this formulation, attention is given to the spatial organization of a community, the physical environment, demographic characteristics of the population, the social stratification of communities, and the processes of community stability and social change.

From a social systems perspective, a community may be defined as "that combination of social units and systems which perform the major social functions having locality relevance" (Warren, 1963). These functions include production/distribution/consumption of goods and services, socialization, social control, social participation, and mutual support. Each of these functions is the primary topic of chapters in this book on the subsystems of a municipality as community, including health and social welfare, education, economic, and political subsystems. The concept of community competence guides the assessment of how well a community's subsystems operate in carrying out social functions, thereby contributing to the level of competence of the total community as a social system.

LOCALITY-BASED COMMUNITIES

Individuals and the social groups with which they are affiliated usually belong to multiple and overlapping locality-based communities, i.e., a neighborhood community, a municipal community (village, town, city), a metropolitan community, a national community, and a global community. Since these communities overlap in terms of geography and membership, individuals and social groups may be regarded as being members of communities within communities. At the same time individuals may have closer attachments and higher social participation in one or more of these communities than in others. People in urban areas are more likely to live in "layered" communities than residents of rural areas, where individuals may not live in neighborhoods or municipalities but still reside in a rural community.

The population of locality-based communities varies by size, density, and diversity. Communities with populations less than 2,500 are usually referred to as villages or small towns. Those with populations from 2,500 to 50,000 people are usually called small cities, and those over 100,000 considered to be large cities. Density refers to the number of people within a physical space. The density of population in large cities is much higher than in suburban communities or non-metropolitan areas. The diversity of populations varies in locality-based communities, especially with regard to demographic factors such as ethnicity and race, religion, social class, and age/gender/family composition. In this regard, large central cities in the United States tend to have segregated neighborhood communities with high proportions of people of color, while suburban communities tend to have a majority of white residents.

The following dimensions are useful in studying locality-based communities: (1) the extent to which the community is a form of social organization with resources that meet sustenance needs, especially housing, employment, social participation, education, health and social welfare, and safety; (2) the level of social interaction in the community; (3) the extent to which the community is a source of collective identity, providing a "sense of community." These dimensions guide our discussion of communities of place, from an ecological systems perspective, i.e., neighborhoods, villages, towns, central cities, suburban cities. By way of illustration of these dimensions, a number of planned communities are described. We give special attention to neighborhoods, especially in relation to diversity of populations in these localities by social class, ethnicity, people of color, religious affiliation, and sexual orientation. This examination of communities is based on an ecological systems perspective. In the second section of the book we examine communities from a social systems perspective, with chapters on the subsystems that make up locality-based communities, including the health and welfare, economic, political, and educational systems.

PLANNED COMMUNITIES

In addition to traditional communities of place, there are a number of types of non-conventional communities and planned communities that continue to emerge in American society. Such communities are examples of efforts to create competent, good, healthy communities of place. Goals for these communities include increasing the residents' opportunities for development of primary group relationships; promoting residents' sense of attachment to their community; providing solid, functional, safe business areas and neighborhoods; offering opportunities for education, employment, and recreation; and creating a positive physical and cultural environment. These communities are sometimes described by residents in terms of being a "good place to live," a "good place to work," a "good place to raise kids," or a "good place to retire," with each person and family having a somewhat different definition or image of what is "good" about their community.

There are many historical examples of planned communities that emphasized the proximity of living together and the development of a sense of community through shared values, such as utopian communities, communes, garden cities, and faith-based communities. Some suburban communities and neighborhoods that were created following World War II represent a type of planned community, with developers mixing houses, park areas, swimming pools, golf clubs, and schools into residential subdivisions. Classic examples of such communities are Reston, Virginia; Columbia, Maryland; Radburn, New Jersey; Levittown, New York; and, most recently, the Disney community of Celebration, Florida. Such community development occurs today in areas beyond suburban communities through a process of "urban sprawl." Recently urban planners, architects, and home builders have developed new community types while also "rebuilding" older communities through gentrification and community development rehabilitation projects. Some examples of older and newer forms of "community building" are described now to illustrate attempts to create competent, good communities.

Roosevelt, New Jersey, as a Utopia

Roosevelt, New Jersey, was created in 1936 as a new, utopian community called Jersey Homesteads for garment workers fleeing Manhattan tenements. The workers would live there and own and run a clothing factory and farm (Hanley, 1999). The new community was established with the support of Albert Einstein, but the co-op failed before World War II. After the war the community was renamed Roosevelt after President Franklin Roosevelt. "From its original settlers to a postwar influx of artists and musicians, and now, to refugees from the suburbs, Roosevelt has been a place of solace and slow pace on a two-lane country road, of communal spirit, of woods, cornfields, and little commerce," a town of about 320 homes, 607 registered voters, an elementary school, a post office, a town hall with firehouse, and a pizzeria (Hanley, 1999). It has a theater group, a string band, a monthly newspaper, but no stores (other than the pizzeria), banks, gasoline stations, pharmacies, or ball fields. Residents view Roosevelt as a town with a "unity and communal quality which we all appreciate."

Threatening to disturb this "Utopian" town is a 1999 proposal for new housing developments that would include about 65 single-family houses in a 100-acre area and 350 townhouses for people age 55 and over on what is now a 150-acre cornfield. Proponents of the new developments believe new housing is needed in order to have more taxable property and to keep current tax rates from increasing. Opponents of the proposed housing take the view that "this is a precious community, an American dream community, a real place, not a development." As one resident put it, "We moved here because of the way it looks. It's been beautifully planned, with a sense of space. I would hate to see the town turned into another sprawling development" (Hanley, 1999).

A Disney Community

Some thirty years ago Walt Disney had an idea of building a new town, an Experimental Prototype Community of Tomorrow (EPCOT) that would represent his vision of a city of the future (Rybczynski, 1996). In 1994, Disney's vision was implemented in the development of an actual town called Celebration on 4,900 acres near Disney World in central Florida. This new town has a school, a health campus, an office park, a downtown, and a mix of townhouses and homes of traditional styles that range in price from about $160,000 for "tract" houses to more than one million dollars for "estate" houses. The town is built on "a very old utopian idea, with deep roots in the American landscape: that the proper arrangement of streets and houses can help usher in a specific sort of community. . . helping to realize a vision of the good society" (Pollan, 1997). The downtown includes business buildings, a town hall, a post office, apartments above shops, and a school in the center of town. Municipal services, such as garbage pickup, maintenance of recreational facilities, and public safety, are privatized. There is a homeowners' association that serves as a private government, organized to "strike a balance between individual freedom and communal responsibility" through "rules and more rules," based on a philosophy that "you need controls—you can't have community without them" (Pollan, 1997).

The planners and many residents now recognize that Celebration is not a perfect town and that it has some of the usual disputes and problems of most American towns. For example, children can walk or bike to the public school in the center of the town. However, this K–12 experimental school has not been without controversy, as it follows a "values-based" curriculum, with kids divided into multi-age "neighborhoods" rather than grades. School-community controversies in Celebration are described in two books published in 1999: *The Celebration Chronicles* by Berendt (1999) and *Celebration, U.S.A.* by Frantz and Collins (1999). The authors of these books discuss how some parents objected to what they regarded as a lack of structure and discipline in the school, with parents' attitudes toward the school causing a major rift in the community (Andersen, 1999; Pollan, 1997; Weeks, 1999). Another area of controversy emerged as some early residents had problems with the home builders, such as leaky roofs, walls, and windows, especially since the Disney Company was not involved in the building of the houses or assuring their quality (Salant, 1999). These problems seemed similar to those encountered in the building of "tract" houses in new suburban communities after World War II, such as Park Forest, Illinois, Levitttown, New York, and St. Anne, Missouri.

Still, despite Celebration's "growing pains," some observers and residents view the town, planned for about 20,000 people, as an example of a small planned community at the edge of an urban area that offers residents a "sense of belonging." It appears to provide what many residents seem to want—that is, a "civil society—the informal network of clubs, volunteer groups and civic and religious organizations that traditionally knit a community together" (Pollan, 1997).

Old-Style Towns

Rancho Santa Margarita, a community in Orange County, California, is an example of the planned development of an old-style town. This community was designed to include "medium-priced homes, shops, industry, and plenty of open space within a well-defined area, so people can get out of their cars and actually meet each other" (Hirsch, 1991). The goal was to "create a self-contained community where all activities—working, shopping, playing—are woven together like the strands of a spider web." The developers of this community used ideas from urban planners and psychologists, such as Maslow's hierarchy of needs, to create a community that "looks at wellness as a lifestyle need." Priority was placed on affordable housing, shared open spaces, jobs, small yards, porches and patios, general stores, and walking paths.

Seaside, Florida, developed by an architecture firm headed by Andres Duany and Elizabeth Plater-Zyberk, is another example of an old-style town. Seaside, established in 1981, represents the architects' idea of "the quintessential neotraditional town" (Goldberger, 2000). Their image of a "good community" is one in which people are less dependent on cars, and where there are strict building codes, streets that diffuse traffic (not cul-de-sacs), a mix of commercial and residential areas, mixed housing and apartments, and residents of mixed ages and incomes. Following ideas from New Urbanism, these architects have designed a number of towns in the United States, with features thought to promote the friendly ambience of old-fashioned villages. In *Suburban Nation: The Rise of Sprawl and the Decline of the American Dream*, Duany, Plater-Zyberk, with their colleague, Speck (2000) point out the need to build communities by creating villages rather than the conventional suburban neighborhoods.

A quite different model of a new community has been developed in Winslow, Washington, on Bainbridge Island. This is a village created for about 70 people with co-housing rather than single units, designed by its future residents, pedestrian-oriented, with privacy and substantial facilities shared by all the residents (Giese, 1990). The houses in Winslow are in the style of traditional Bainbridge farmhouses. All are attached and clustered in three neighborhoods, one with large units and two with one-bedroom apartments. There is a common house with dining options and meeting room, library, day-care center, and laundry, as well as a guest house. Each unit has a kitchen, but communal dining is an option. All decisions about the community are made by a consensus of the residents. Examples of this type of co-housing can be found in Denmark, Sweden, Norway, France, and West Germany.

Retirement Communities

When housing areas are age segregated—i.e., when they seek residents who are at least 55 years old—they are labeled retirement communities. These communities, such as Sun Cities in Arizona and Florida, are built outside central cities and usually include a golf course, recreational clubhouse, and small house and condo housing units. Upkeep of grounds and buildings is provided by a community association, with the services funded with monthly fees from residents. In contrast, some housing for older adults is now being built in the center of downtown areas of central cities, resulting in a form of "new urbanism" that involves age integration. An example is a retirement center in Hinsdale, Illinois, an affluent suburb west of Chicago (Collins, 1999). The location of the center fosters walking, neighborliness, and volunteer work in nearby schools, hospitals, libraries, churches, and synagogues. Another example is the building of public housing for older adults in downtown areas of both central cities and suburban communities throughout the United States.

COMMUNITIES OF IDENTIFICATION AND INTEREST

Some communities are defined in terms of a common characteristic that is not necessarily locality based, such as identity, interest, or culture. These communities are formed by people who identify themselves on the basis of ethnicity, race, religion, national ancestry, language, lifestyle, ideology, sexual orientation, social class, age, disability, political affiliation, profession, type of employment, college/university background, and so forth. Many communities of identification rely heavily on cultural characteristics as a foundation for distinguishing their group from other groups, e.g., communities of people of color. While we view communities of identity and interest as one type of community, some authors, such as Longres (1995) and Schriver (1998), distinguish between these communities. Accordingly, identificational communities include members who have "ties based on affection and common identity," and often think of themselves as members of a specific social group, such as the African American community, the Asian American community, the Jewish community, the Catholic community, the Irish American community, the Italian American community, or the gay community. Communities of interest are regarded as more narrow that those of identification, with membership based on common interest and objectives, such as professional associations, occupational groups, and advocacy or social movement organizations. A newly emerging form of a community of interest is the virtual community, a group established by people engaged in discussions on a common topic through interaction in the World Wide Web of the Internet.

Identificational and interest communities often engage in some level of organizational activity, e.g., meetings of professional groups, religious organizations, ethnic organizations, or advocacy groups. Just as communities of place are "layered"—that is, communities within communities—so are communities of interest/identity/culture. Thus, a person may belong to and participate in the activities of a community of identification through neighborhood, city, metropolitan, state, and national organizations, e.g., a local chapter of NAACP as well as affiliation with state and national NAACP branches.

MULTIPLE IDENTITIES AND COMMUNITY AFFILIATIONS

People often belong to more than one identificational/interest community. Multiple identities may be a mix of characteristics such as national origin, gender, social class, sexual orientation, disability, or age. Identification with these multiple communities will vary by intensity, attachment, and social involvement. In many instances, membership of individuals in communities of identification and/or interest coincides with identification with a locality-based residential community. For example, individuals with a primary identification with a cultural/ethnic group may live in residential areas that have a high proportion of people with one or more of these characteristics, such as a middle-class Italian neighborhood, a middle-class African American neighborhood, or a gay retirement community. In many large American cities, such as Chicago, Los Angeles, New York City, Boston, Philadelphia, and Miami, the names given to community areas or neighborhoods are associated with specific ethnic, racial, or religious groups. We take into account the overlap of communities of place and non-place in our examination of social stratification of municipal communities and neighborhoods, especially in regard to the demographic development of communities and emergence of social class and ethnic minority neighborhoods.

EXAMPLES OF IDENTIFICATIONAL COMMUNITIES

Individuals often reside in communities of place that have a high proportion of people who identify with a specific group. Other persons who identify with such groups may live in more heterogeneous communities and neighborhoods. Some examples of identificational communities are now presented, such as those linked to social class, race/ethnicity, religion, sexual orientation, gender, or abilities. These examples have been selected to show the wide diversity of community groups within American society and to demonstrate majority/minority relationships within society in terms of power and status. In Chapter 4 we identify some of the forms of discrimination and oppression that these groups encounter in American communities of place, such as municipalities and neighborhoods. We also highlight some of the strengths that individuals associated with these communities derive from other members, their culture, and organizations related to their communities.

Social Class Communities

At first glance, social classes do not appear to be social communities. Yet the characteristics of socioeconomic status, such as occupational position, income, education, and lifestyle, tend to produce a stratification of discrete social class communities. These groups do not have rigid boundaries, and there is some overlap in membership and identification between social class groups. Still, Americans use social class factors as the basis for identifying themselves as belonging to a social group defined in terms of community. As Longres (1995) has noted, social classes can "give rise to communal action, that is, the development of common neighborhoods, a common identity, and common interests."

As we discussed in Chapter 1, American society can be stratified through measures of social class into a hierarchy of social communities, such as upper class, middle class, lower/working class, and underclass. As people consider their socioeconomic status within American society, they may locate themselves into a class category within a national context that is independent of a local community of place. However, for most Americans, there is an overlap between their identification with a social class and their residence in a neighborhood or municipality that can be characterized by a social class label. Thus, the municipal community of residence is often associated with a class label; for example, a city may be called an affluent community, a middle-class community, or a working-class community. Sometimes this label is given to the municipality, and at other times to a neighborhood community. With few exceptions, such as planned communities with mixed social classes, neighborhoods in the United States can be identified through the membership of their residents in a particular social class.

While they may use different bases for classification, many Americans appear to identify themselves with a social class and believe they belong to a social class community. There is little evidence that the United States is a "classless" society. Instead, "Social class is a major source of group identity for most Americans" (Jackman & Jackman, 1983). There is also reason to believe that Americans sometimes identify in a subjective way with a social class that is not consistent with their status in the class structure—e.g., there is a tendency for many upper-class people to claim membership in the middle class, while some people in a middle class see themselves as members of the working class. This is especially true when social class communities are viewed in terms of economic groups and their lifestyles (Jackman & Jackman, 1983). In fact, the traditional classifications and labels for social class do not seem to fit current American society. For example, some sociologists observe that the middle class has disappeared, with some members moving up to an upper-class group and others moving downward to the lower or "working poor" class. They suggest that two extreme class groups have emerged, a wealthy elite and a poor underclass. In between these two groups are a highly educated professional group and a group of less-educated and less-skilled workers, leaving no middle class (Cassidy, 1995).

In many discussions of social classes as communities, there is a recognition that members of ethnic minority groups are disproportionately located within the lower part of the class structure and reside in lower-class and underclass communities of color. In their classic study of *Class Awareness in the United States*, Jackman and Jackman (1983) discovered that "class is more keenly felt by those who experience its deprivations than by those who enjoy its privileges." The higher one's position on the class hierarchy, the more likely one is to have access to opportunities, to resources, and to personal, interpersonal, and political power. People in lower-class positions, especially the poor and underclass, usually have little access to or control over "a wide range of opportunities, including employment, education, housing, health care services, and public amenities" (Kemp, 1995). When people of color are in these class positions, the negative effects of race and residential segregation and concentration of underclass residents in inner-city neighborhoods compound the disadvantages imposed by social class (Wilson, 1987).

Communities of Color/Ethnicity

Many Americans use race, color, ethnicity, and culture, or some combination of these factors, as the basis for an identificational community. Our references to communities of color do not include non-Hispanic white groups, although people who identify themselves as white can be regarded as communities. A person's identification with such communities may be at any one of several levels: national, local municipal community, and/or neighborhood community. For example, a person may identify with membership in the African American community, meaning all African Americans in society, and/or with African Americans living in a specific city or neighborhood. When these identificational communities coincide with a geographic community, such a community may be regarded as a community of color whose residents consider themselves African American, Asian American or Pacific Islander, Hispanic/Latino American, or Native American. Members of these communities may identify with one of these groups, belong to a group of mixed race or culture, or identify with a specific sub-group based on national origin, e.g., Japanese, Chinese, Korean, Puerto Rican, or Mexican. Identification by color and culture is a complex process, given the differences and similarities of the subgroups of the major communities of color, involving aspects such as "culture, language, economic, political, and social histories" (Rivera & Erlich, 1998). Rivera and Erlich (1995) have argued that ethnic minority communities are *gemeinschaft* in nature, that is, they form social systems "in which relationships are personal, informal, traditional, general, and sentiment-based." In contrast, American society is regarded as *gesellschaft* in nature, that is, "a system in which relationships are impersonal, contractual, utilitarian, specialized, and realistically based on market conditions." Communities of color are said to differ from mainstream society in terms of culture, identity, minority status, social structure, power structure, leadership patterns, economics, physical appearance, and social networks (Phinney, 1996; Rivera &

Erlich, 1995). High proportions of people who identify with a community of color reside in residential areas with members of their own racial/ethnic group.

As Lewis (1995) has noted, while "the view of most Americans and the federal government is that American Indians are just another minority group. . . .The American Indian is not just another minority. Indian people possess a unique constitutional right to special recognition that allows them to be separate and apart from the rest of U.S. citizens." Most of the American Indian population resides in the states of Oklahoma, Arizona, and California, reflecting "themes of forced migration, isolation of Indian people, and a migration from rural reservations to the cities." Under relocation programs of the U.S. government, many American Indians have been moved to urban areas, with these groups forming "an American Indian community that interacts socially while forming social and political ties that have evolved into traditions and customs." Approximately two thirds of the 1.4 million people who identify themselves as American Indian do not live on reservations, with many living in urban areas where "they have developed creative and adaptive responses to the urban environment, which makes them distinctly American Indian."

According to Lewis (1995), American Indian communities exist in urban, rural, and reservation areas, with "a clustering of individuals into a unit" that "constitutes a way of life that allows the people to be involved in an intimate association with each other; offers them the ability to form a social cohesion that bonds the community into units." Having been "forced upon reservations and forcefully separated from mainstream Americans" by the U.S. government, many American Indians prefer to reside on reservations. For them, "America itself has a lot to do with why the Indian people are reluctant to give up their language, culture and spirituality and disappear into the melting pot" (Giago, 2000). American Indians in urban areas are a part of American society, facing many of the problems of this society, and having to adapt to their surrounding social and natural environments. This adaptation is problematic for many due to the fact that "American Indian people represent a departure from mainstream values and worldviews," especially in relation to the importance of tribal and family networks, child rearing practices, religious practices, cultural values and attitudes, and relationship to nature (Lewis, 1995; Locke, 1992). The diversity among American Indians is demonstrated by their affiliation with some 542 unique tribes (Edwards & Egbert-Edwards, 1998).

Communities of color have dimensions of social interaction, social exchanges and mutual aid, and identity related to extended family relationships and local community institutions. Members of these communities benefit from the considerable strengths of their minority group, but many are negatively affected by their social class position. At the same time, racism and discrimination against such groups by the mainstream white society hinder their full participation in the broader community. Thus, members of ethnic minority groups may be subjected to discriminatory policies and practices found in economic institutions and in the political, health, education, and social welfare subsystems of their locality-based communities.

White Ethnic Communities

Historically, many white Americans have identified with ethnic groups based on national origin. People who immigrated to the United States from countries other than England, mainly southern and eastern European countries, have been labeled "white ethnic" groups. Often these non-WASP immigrants were identified as ethnics in terms of their religion and nationality, such as Irish Catholics and Italian Catholics, or German Jews and Russian Jews. These groups have tended to identify with their nationality of origin and to reside in ethnic neighborhoods within large urban areas, especially on arrival to the United States. Longres's (1995) brief social histories of some of these immigrant ethnic communities show how they were distinguished from "Americans"—that is, the surrounding White Anglo-Saxon Protestant society. This distinction was captured in the year 2000 exhibition of pictures of immigrants and their communities at the New York Historical Society, "The Italians of New York: Five Centuries of Struggle and Achievement." In her review of this exhibition, Barbara Grizzuti Harrison (1999) reflects on her childhood in Bensonhurst, Brooklyn, an Italian village with "three distinctive and different groups, entities, peopling Our Town: Italians, Jews, and Americans. Americans were blond and fair and lived in one-family houses, and there weren't a lot of them" in "Our Town." Furthermore, Harrison observes that Our Town was further distinguished from another place: New York, "the city," Manhattan.

Many of the white ethnic group immigrants, especially the Irish and Italians, were faced with discrimination and second-class status within mainstream society. What is distinctive about these "new immigrants," in contrast to ethnic minority groups of color, has been their eventual acculturation and assimilation into mainstream American society. While some groups became assimilated more quickly than others, eventually most white ethnics have participated in upward educational, occupational, and residential mobility to a greater extent than African Americans and Hispanic/Latino Americans. While white ethnic neighborhoods continue to exist in some large American cities, for the most part people who identify with a white ethnic group no longer reside in these neighborhoods. They are located mainly in non-ethnic middle-class neighborhoods or in residential suburban communities. While some white ethnics continue to identify with their ancestry and claim membership in an ethnic community, many have become Americanized and are completely assimilated into American society (Guzzetta, 1995).

To a large extent, intermarriage and other means of assimilation of white ethnics have diminished the salience of ethnic communities in today's society. Still, as Guzzetta (1995) has argued, some white ethnics have participated in an "ethnic renewal" in reaction to the civil rights movement of the 1960s, the emergence of identity politics, and the cultural wars of multiculturalism. This renewal has included a development of ethnic consciousness and an effort to achieve recognition as distinct ethnic groups within a culturally pluralistic, multicultural society. To some extent, then, for some white ethnics, there has been a rebuilding of identificational, if not geographic, community that is based on ancestry and culture.

The disadvantages of being associated with a "white ethnic" group within American society have declined to a point where most overt forms of discrimination have disappeared. Some exclusion still exists in the associations of upper-class American "society" as well as in the upper middle classes. However, for the most part barriers to education, housing, club membership, and economic status have been reduced, at least under the law, if not in practice, for almost all white Americans. At least one white ethnic group continues to identify itself as an ethnic/class community that is stigmatized and discriminated against—that is, white trash. "White trash" is a complex category consisting of people with mixed national heritages "living in (often rural) poverty, while at the same time it designates a set of stereotypes and myths related to the social behaviors, intelligence, prejudices, and gender roles of poor whites" (Wray & Newitz, 1997). Such groups are usually located in economically distressed communities of Appalachia, the Ozarks, southern rural areas, as well as in white poverty neighborhood areas of large urban cities (Harper & Lantz, 1996).

Religious Groups as Communities

Religious denominations in the United States constitute identificational communities for many people. It is common for Catholics, Protestants, Jews, Muslims, or members of other faiths to claim membership in a community based on religious affiliation. The primary focus of identification is with a religious denomination at the local community level, i.e., the parish, congregation, church, or synagogue. American religious communities at the local level are usually associated with the major faiths of Catholicism, Protestantism, Judaism, and Islam. For example, "the basic institutions of the American Jewish community are essentially local, and with few exceptions, all Jewish religious, social, welfare, and educational institutions are local both in name and in fact" (Elazar, 1995). The major institutions of the American Jewish community are the federations and synagogues (congregations) at the local community level. As Elazar (1995) notes, "Organizationally, the American Jewish community is best understood as a mosaic, a multidimensional matrix of institutions and organizations that interact with each other in their attempts to cover the range of communal concerns while preserving their respective integrities." This matrix varies from one community to another, often serving local, countrywide, and overseas constituencies.

Often, members of a religious community identify with a segment of the major group, such as Episcopal, Presbyterian, Baptist, Methodist, African Methodist Episcopal, and other branches of Protestantism, or Reform, Orthodox, or Conservative forms of Judaism. Membership in religious congregations varies in terms of degree of commitment, involvement, amount and type of individual participation in religious and related activities. For many Americans at the local community level, religious congregations provide a source of social interaction, mutual aid, in addition to spiritual activities. Faith-based organizations provide a range of health and human services at the congregational level, the community level, and the national level, constituting a significant part of the services of the welfare state (Cnaan, 1997). In many instances, the local synagogue, temple, church, or mosque is the center of a religious community, sometimes located within a residential area that contains many members of a particular religious denomination.

Many religious communities are basically local institutions, either not affiliated with or minimally attached to an organization in some hierarchy. In other instances, especially in the Catholic religion and some Protestant groups, individuals belong to a local religious congregation that is affiliated vertically with a parent organization; for example, members of a Catholic parish are part of a diocese as well as an international church. Religious congregations may be viewed as ethnic group communities when there are cultural components related to membership, such as norms, values, patterns of conduct, rituals, holidays, and a "sense of community." All of the various congregations of worship in a community make up a subsystem of the community, contributing in many ways to the fulfillment of functions of social control, mutual aid, social participation, and education. Some religious groups are active at one or more levels of the political system, especially in regard to legislation regarding controversial issues such as abortion, sex education, prayer in schools, school vouchers, assisted suicide, and separation of church and state.

Gay and Lesbian Communities

Communities are a significant part of the social environment of gay men, lesbians, bisexual, and transgendered persons. Sexual orientation creates a foundation for these individuals in forming communities of identification, interest, and place (Icard et al., 1999). Historically, gay men and lesbian women have formed their own separate communities of identification and interest, with white gay groups most often not including people of color or bisexual persons. In recent years, bisexual or transgendered persons have joined some "umbrella" gay organizations. Gay organizations may include members who identify with a specific community, such as lesbian, gay male, or bisexual, as well as members who identify with a more inclusive "gay community."

Issues related to communities of lesbian and bisexual women of color have been examined by Icard, Jones, and Wahab (1999). These authors demonstrate how various communities have "a significant effect on the personal and collective power of lesbian and bisexual minority women: the ethnic community, the gay community, the lesbian community, the ethnic gay and lesbian community, and the community of lesbian and bisexual women of color." For example, "ethnic communities are often less than nurturing," often exhibiting homophobia and sexism. Of major concern are the racism and sexism that exist within the gay community; e.g., "lesbian groups, social networks, and organizations have been largely of white women." New communities of minority men and women are being formed for "political, economic, health, social, and emotional needs" separate from white groups. There is a new development of lesbian and bisexual groups and organizations by women of color, to support ethnic identity, counteract racism, and provide resources for community members.

The various communities of identification and interest related to sexual orientation often coincide with a common locality of residence, commercial, and social activity. These geographic neighborhood and enclave areas are known to members of the gay community and often to the community at large (Fellin, 1998). The overlap of locational and identificational communities contributes to the development of a gay community cultural system, located in gay neighborhoods/enclaves.

Abrahamson (1996) provides a description of gay community enclaves in San Francisco: for gay males, the South of the Market area and the Castro district; for lesbians, Valencia Street in the Mission district. These areas are not only places of residence but usually include social and business establishments such as gay restaurants, bars, clubs, bookstores, and parks, as well as community service organizations.

Urban neighborhoods or enclaves that include large numbers of gay people can be contrasted to a more recent suburbanization of gay life, with individuals sometimes residing in suburban enclaves and at other times in neighborhoods populated mainly by straight people. Attitudes and behaviors toward gay persons vary in different cities, towns, and suburban areas. Some cities and neighborhoods have gained reputations for being hospitable, accepting, and sensitive to the needs of gay people. In other communities, gay people are not welcome and they find themselves in unsafe, inhospitable, social environments. Local communities vary in terms of the extent to which organizations within the community, especially the political and economic subsystems of the community, construct barriers to rights of gay people through discrimination, prejudice, and limits to full participation in community institutions. Increasingly, the health and social welfare subsystem in large urban areas has become more responsive to the needs of gay people, offering "support services for parents of gays and lesbians, work with teenagers, counseling for couples, services for the elderly, and help for people with sexually transmitted diseases" (Longres, 1995).

Communities of Persons with Disabilities

People with disabilities clearly constitute a community of identification, as evidenced by a movement on their part for social and economic justice, highlighted by the emergence of an Independent Living perspective and the passage of the Americans with Disabilities Act of 1990. As Mackelprang and Salsgiver (1996) have noted, "The birth of disability consciousness in the United States arose out of the turbulence of the 1960s. . .as significant numbers of people with disabilities demanded access to the mainstream of society." This movement for independent living "focused on societal responses and discrimination as the primary barriers to civil rights," not unlike the minority model of the civil rights movement for people of color. Under this perspective, people with disabilities have viewed themselves "not as patients or clients but as active and responsible consumers" who experience discrimination from the American culture.

One of the principles of the Independent Living perspective states that the greatest constraints on people with disabilities are environmental and social. People with disabilities live in a society and in communities with attitudes and behaviors that can be labeled "ableism"— a belief "that devalues people with disabilities and results in segregation, social isolation, and social policies that limit their opportunities for full societal participation" (Mackelprang & Salsgiver, 1999). For example, opposition to group homes for persons with disabilities comes in part from fears of neighborhood residents that these persons are a threat to society, and that the community needs to be protected from them, especially persons with mental disabilities. In response to ableism, "Out of adversity, a disability culture is being created, as are many disability-specific subcultures. Increasingly, disability is becoming defined as different, not bad; persons with disabilities are thriving, not just surviving." As a result, persons with disabilities are becoming a strong identificational community, developing a collective identity and actively participating in the political system as a social movement for civil rights and against discrimination. A sense of community is emerging as part of the self-help movement, especially as an avenue for advocacy on behalf of persons with disabilities.

Communities of Women

There is a lack of consensus as to whether or not women should be viewed as a community separate from the communities of place and identification in which they live and interact. Women form groups that meet our definition of communities of identification and interest, with gender being the major basis for the pursuit of women's interests, whether personal, interpersonal, or political. Feminism and the women's movement appear to support the idea that women constitute communities within American society, often distinguished by political ideologies, such as liberal, radical, or socialist (Nes & Iadicola, 1989). While there may be "no one feminist perspective," Hooyman and Gonyea (1995) contend that the "underlying bond among feminists is agreement that women's personal problems are affected by power inequities and injustices inherent in patriarchal structures and that women's oppression and subordination must be eliminated."

Given the immense feminist literature, the ties many women have to feminism and the women's movement, and the political activities engaged in by organizations of women, it seems reasonable to conclude that women form communities of identification and interest. The organizational context for women's groups at local and national levels is illustrated by political action groups, by collectives in support of health and human services for women, by regional and national associations in support of women's issues, mutual aid support groups, and by coalitions of women's groups. Examples of such groups are the Women's Business Conference, the National Association of Women Business Owners, and the Women's Economic Club. Such groups provide an organizational basis for women for networking and professional development in the business world (Cohn, 1999)

In their examination of postmodern feminism, Sands and Nuccio (1992) argue that "Postmodern feminism acknowledges that there is a multiplicity of women and women's movements representing diverse and divergent interests." This recognition poses a problem for some types of political activity among women's groups, as an emphasis on diversity of women may contradict the idea that women have "essentially" the same interests. It seems clear that there is no single voice for women, given differences among working-class, middle-class, and upper-class white women, and women of color, lesbians, or poor women. Still, there are many examples in which women form communities, such as women's sororities, religious orders of nuns, church women's mutual aid groups, women's colleges and alumni groups, women's professional groups, and lesbian women's groups.

Virtual Communities

Today there are many World Wide Web community sites "where people can find and then electronically 'talk' to others with similar interests" (Petersen, 1999). These community sites are offered by privately owned companies such as Tripod, GeoCities, Talkcity, and Yahoo! These sites begin by asking users to create online profiles of themselves by creating a Web page that is then placed within a "neighborhood" in keeping with their interests. Online communities allow users to socialize with their "neighbors" through "chat rooms" that permit users to "hold electronic conversations in real time" and message boards "where people can post notes to like-minded souls." An individual can also keep track of how many "visitors" view his or her site each day. The community site resembles "a virtual coffee shop, where people come and meet other people." In this sense, these sites become communities that focus on people who need people—"places to go when you want to feel right at home" (Petersen, 1999).

Is an online group truly a community? Galston (1999) contends that individuals forming groups on the Internet are members of "voluntary communities" that share common interests and goals. These communities are said to have "three defining conditions: low barriers to entry, low barriers to exit, and interpersonal relations shaped by mutual adjustment rather than hierarchical authority or coercion."

Examples of community Internet sites especially for women, described as "Places for Serious Sisterhood," include IVILLAGE: The Women's Network and Underwire, a weekly Web line on women's issues. IVILLAGE offers communities for different interests, such as parents of teenagers, potty-trainers, women with home-based jobs, stay-at-home moms, and fitness enthusiasts, as well as advice on health issues, child rearing techniques, and careers. Some two million women go to IVILLAGE's on-line communities "for women in search of kindred spirits" (IVILLAGE, 1999). Underwire provides advice on a range of topics, such as fitness and health, money, sex and relationships, as well as auto advice, questions on etiquette, book recommendations, and group storytelling.

Chapter 3 Review

Communities can be defined in terms of locality, identity, interest, and a combination of these dimensions. People belong to multiple communities of place, such as neighborhoods, municipalities, and metropolitan areas, as well as multiple communities of identification and interest. An individual's "personal community" denotes membership in a mix of communities in which a person engages in social interaction and obtains goods and services in order to promote social and economic well-being. Ecological and social systems perspectives serve as conceptual frameworks within which to examine locality-based communities. Examples of planned communities were presented in this chapter to illustrate the various social organizational dimensions of local communities of place, including the Disney community of Celebration, Florida, Old-Style Towns, and retirement communities. Communities of identification and interest were illustrated in terms of social class, color/ethnicity, white ethnicity, religion, sexual orientation, persons with disabilities, women, and virtual communities. Most people have multiple community identities and affiliations, and these communities often overlap with each other, especially in residential neighborhoods/enclaves with a high proportion of members of a particular ethnic, racial, religious, or lifestyle group.

4

Community Competence and Systems Perspectives

Two related ideas, a competent community and a good community, provide a context for using ecological and social systems frameworks to study locality-based communities. Systems perspectives help us assess the extent to which communities are competent and capable of achieving goals that promote community and individual well-being. Community competence is the capacity of a community to engage in problem-solving in order to achieve its goals. More specifically, a competent community may be defined as "one in which the various component parts of the community are able to collaborate effectively in identifying the problems and needs of the community; can achieve a working consensus on goals and priorities; can agree on ways and means to implement the agreed-upon goals; can collaborate effectively in the required actions" (Cottrell, 1983).

Community competence has two major dimensions. First, a competent community has the ability to respond to the needs of its membership, e.g., economic, educational, health, and social welfare. In this sense, the positive functioning of the community's subsystems, as well as the community as a whole, is a sign of community competence. Second, the residents of a competent community are able to create and/or use the resources available to them to solve daily problems of living (Barbarin et al., 1981). In a competent community, individuals, families, other groups and organizations are "able to identify with and find common cause with the community's way of life in order that their energies may be used to meet the community's needs" (Anderson, Carter, & Lowe, 1999).

In his development of the idea of community competence, Cottrell (1983) identified several conditions that enhance community functioning. Some of these conditions reside in individuals, while others are group attributes and behaviors. Community competence is influenced by the degree to which (1) residents have a commitment to their community; (2) there is a self-awareness among the various community groups of their own values and self-interests; (3) there exists a level of articulateness that allows for effective communication about community issues between the diverse segments of the community; and (4) residents participate in identifying goals and implementing them. Systems components often found in a competent community include procedures for handling conflicts between groups within the community, and the capacity for managing relationships between the community and the larger society while maintaining an appropriate degree of local autonomy.

What is a good community? Obviously, an important feature of a good community is a high degree of competence—the ability of its members and their representatives to "get things done" in the various subsystems of the community. One way of defining a good community is to identify the qualities that citizens value. For example, Martin Luther King, Jr. used the term "beloved community" to "describe an ideal town or city, which would flourish without racism, poverty, or violence" (Logan, 1993). Most Americans would agree with this view of a good community. Still, community qualities are value-laden in that they may not be regarded as "good" by all residents. It can be expected that people share some values and interests and differ with regard to others. However, basic rights and responsibilities of citizens must be recognized and practiced in a good community. Such a community seeks to promote social and economic justice and to reduce and eliminate barriers to justice that affect populations at risk of discrimination and oppression.

A long-standing list of values that have been associated with a good community are identified by Warren (1980) as follows:

- People should deal with each other on a personal basis.
- There should be a broad distribution of power within the community.

- The community should include a wide variety of different income groups, ethnic groups, and religious and interest groups.
- There should be a great deal of local neighborhood control.
- The community should encompass the greatest possible degree of cooperation in policy-making and the least possible conflict.

In identifying these values, Warren (1980) raises the caution that few communities possess all of these desirable qualities at the same time, nor do residents all agree on the degree to which these qualities should be fostered in a community. Thus, as people move to maximize the benefits of one community characteristic, such as autonomy, they may have to accept a reduction in benefits from other areas, such as extra-local, state, or federal funds. Similarly, broad decision-making involvement in a community, and strong neighborhood group control, may not be compatible with effective, efficient, and timely actions on the part of the community's political system. The small size of a community may allow greater opportunities for the formation of primary group relationships than would be found in large cities. On the other hand, a community's small size may limit its potential for diversity of community residents in terms of social class, ethnicity, race, or religious affiliation.

Consideration of the ideas of competent and good communities is important for human service professionals. These concepts are useful in assessing the needs of people and their communities, especially in terms of establishing goals and identifying barriers to their achievement. For example, human service professionals may consider a community to be competent when (1) its governmental officials determine priorities in conjunction with residents, such as controlling juvenile delinquency; creating new employment opportunities; creating safe neighborhoods and city streets; protecting the natural environment and (2) action is taken to fund and implement programs related to these goals. Thus, one measure of competence is the extent to which goals are actually achieved: Are social problems being controlled or reduced? Do United Fund campaigns and other voluntary giving projects for health and human services reach their goals? Are job opportunities created? Are occupational barriers for ethnic minorities, economically disadvantaged people, persons with disabilities, women, and gay and lesbian persons reduced or eliminated through community action?

BARRIERS TO COMMUNITY COMPETENCE

A number of identificational communities were discussed in Chapter 3, such as people of color; white ethnic groups; gay male, lesbian, bisexual, and transgendered individuals; and persons with disabilities. There is a significant set of barriers to community competence that come from the values, attitudes, and practices of citizens toward identificational communities. Many locality-based communities lack a fair and just response to the specific needs of such groups. Hence, human service professionals are called upon to give special attention to such barriers as they interfere with the competence of a community in achieving social and economic justice for all citizens. In this chapter we identify some of these barriers for selected "at-risk" identificational groups.

Barriers for People of Color

Racism is a major force that fosters a lack of community competence in local communities with regard to people of color. Racism appears in several forms, such as individual, institutional, and cultural (Germain & Bloom, 1999). Individual racism is based on prejudicial attitudes and beliefs toward people who belong to "races" different from one's own. Longres (1995) has noted in regard to institutional racism that "Racism can exist independent of the attitudes and beliefs of individuals. When it is built into the norms, traditions, laws, and policies of a society, racism is said to be institutionalized." Cultural racism focuses on prejudices based on cultural differences thought to be inferior to the practices of one's own cultural group.

Discriminatory policies and practices toward people of color are usually designated as racism and may be found in any of the subsystems of a community. Racism exists in many forms, e.g., economic discrimination, insensitivity to the special social and health needs of people of color, distorted characterization of ethnic minorities by the mass media, provision of inadequate or inferior services, and racial profiling of minorities by police.

Social workers need to recognize the barriers and limitations imposed upon people of color within a community, especially when these barriers occur in human service organizations. As Barbarin et al. (1981) have noted, improving community competence requires a twofold focus:

1. an awareness on the part of community agencies about the cultural diversity brought to a community by different minority groups;
2. a minimal level of sophistication on the part of minority group members concerning ways to access and to make systems more responsive to their needs.

Some communities possess both organizational awareness and individual sophistication. Those that lack one or both of these attributes can benefit from the efforts of citizens, especially human service practitioners, to improve community competence. It is possible to create communities that support cultural diversity and social support systems that respond to the needs of all cultural, racial, and ethnic groups.

Barriers for the Gay Community

Gay people are discriminated against in many locational communities and in the armed forces. Such discrimination is usually attributed to *homophobia*, defined as "an irrational fear or hatred of homosexuality or homosexuals" (Germain & Bloom, 1999). It is common for persons who are openly gay to be denied civil liberties, excluded from social participation, subject to violence and stigma, and restricted in employment opportunities and benefits. In many American communities gay men, lesbians, bisexual, and transgendered persons constitute populations at risk for discrimination, economic deprivation, and oppression (CSWE, 1992). As D'Augelli and Garnets (1995) have indicated, these groups "constitute a large disenfranchised population which has been rendered invisible, marginalized, and deprived of basic civil rights," a population faced with barriers to "identifying with and joining their communities." A "don't ask, don't tell" policy was initiated in 1993 to combat discrimination in the military, but as of March 2000, a Pentagon study showed continued widespread harassment of gay persons in the armed forces.

In some communities efforts are made to overcome discrimination against gay people through legal means, voluntary associations, and the media. However, in many communities individuals identified with the gay community are viewed as members of a deviant group whose lifestyles and behavior are deemed to be unacceptable. In such communities discrimination may be illegal, but discriminatory practices are common.

Violence is a major problem encountered by gay persons, as evidenced by reports required by the Hate Crime Statistics Act of 1990. Anti-gay hate crimes, that is, "words or actions that are intended to harm or intimidate individuals because they are lesbian or gay" are prevalent within American society (Herek, 1989). The consequences of such crimes are not only the "physical and psychological harm they inflict on the victims" but the fact that they "create a climate of fear in gay communities." An understanding of the causes and antecedents of anti-gay hate crimes in a geographic community provides a foundation for considering how human service professionals can participate in community organizing efforts to prevent and eliminate these crimes.

Barriers to full participation in community affairs by gay persons appear to be less problematic in some locational communities than others. Some communities, as well as some neighborhoods, have gained a reputation for being hospitable, accepting, and sensitive to the needs and rights of gay residents. Such cities and neighborhoods become known to gay people, especially those located in large cities and in vacation areas. At the same time, members of these communities recognize the diversity of the gay community, such as variations in social class, ethnic or racial identity, religious affiliation, and lifestyles. Some states have legislation that prohibits discrimination against gay people. For example, California has several gay-rights laws, including the prohibition of harassment of gay students and teachers in public schools and colleges, a domestic partners registry law, and a law prohibiting job and housing discrimination on the basis of sexual orientation (Associated Press, 1999e). In the year 2000 the state of Vermont approved a law establishing the eligibility of gay "civil unions" to receive nearly all the state rights and benefits of married people in areas ranging from child custody to probate law. At the same time, however, California banned same-sex marriages. In March 2000, California voters approved Proposition 22, an amendment to the state's Family Code stating that "only marriage between a man and a woman is valid or recognized in California." The state will not recognize same-sex marriages performed and legally recognized elsewhere. The states of Wisconsin, Massachusetts, and Connecticut have education codes that prohibit harassment and discrimination based on sexual orientation.

Disputes in religious congregations about the role of gay people in local community church activities have become prominent in recent years. The Central Conference of American Rabbis, representing about 1800 rabbis in Judaism's reform movement, has declared that its members may conduct gay "unions." National religious organizations have increasingly taken positions that discourage the membership of gay people in local religious congregations. However, increasingly there are local community congregations that have a reputation for being "gay-friendly" and for creating religious and social activities that include gay members.

Barriers for Persons with Disabilities

The special problems of persons with disabilities have been identified in the Americans with Disabilities Act of 1990 (Greenhouse, 1999c). Some of these problems come from discrimination on the part of individuals and the actions of social institutions. "Persons with disabilities face major life stressors from discrimination in the community that create destructive, unjust differences in the resources and life conditions" for these individuals (Germain & Bloom, 1999). The Act of 1990 noted that ableism—that is, discrimination against individuals with disabilities—persists in such crucial areas as employment, housing, public accommodations, education, transportation, communication, recreation, institutionalization, health services, voting, and access to public services. Some communities have demonstrated competence in removing some of these barriers by creating policies and programs directed toward assuring "equality of opportunity, full participation, independent living, and economic self-sufficiency for such individuals," including alteration in architectural designs, provision of special transportation arrangements and facilities, and development of job training programs (Germain & Bloom, 1999). These community efforts are supported by the ADA legislation of 1990, which also established equal employment provisions for persons with disabilities, an area in which local communities have had little influence in the past.

A major barrier for persons with disabilities involves housing, especially with regard to the location of community-based treatment centers and group homes. The devaluation of people with disabilities in local communities often "results in segregation, social isolation, and social policies that limit their opportunities for full societal participation" (Mackelprang & Salsgiver, 1999). Competent communities seek to overcome these barriers "through 'integration' of people with disabilities into the wider population, to the greatest extent possible, in the provision of public services" (Greenhouse, 1999b).

Barriers for Women

A number of special barriers for women in local communities have been identified in the feminist literature under the term *sexism*. These barriers are often identified as examples of discrimination against women. Using our definition of community competence as a frame of reference, some communities limit the recognition of women as significant members of the community. Often, women are not involved in the identification of community problems, and therefore problems of concern to women are not targeted for community action and change. Problems for women occur in all of the major social institutions of society and local communities. They include under-representation in the political system, lack of status and equality in the work force, and lack of services in the health and social welfare system. One response to the call for equal rights for women in education has been the enactment of Title IX of the Education Amendments to the Civil Rights Act in 1972. This legislation stated that "no person in the U.S. shall, on the basis of sex, be excluded from participation in, be denied the benefits of, or be subjected to discrimination under any educational program or activity receiving federal financial assistance." The part of this legislation that has received considerable attention has been provisions related to academic institutions and athletics, calling for resources to support athletic opportunities for female students.

Some groups of women face special problems in urban communities, such as the elderly, female heads of households, low-income and unemployed women, and women of color. The special issues regarding the lack of power in communities by women of color are discussed by Gutierrez and Lewis in their 1999 book entitled *Empowering Women of Color*. Some of the problems in communities for low-income and unemployed women are related to the geographic location of many women's households in inner cities. This location poses threats to safety from violence and crime, inadequate housing, and unavailable transportation to jobs and services. Low income and unemployment limit child care options and health benefits for women and children.

SYSTEMS PERSPECTIVES: AN OVERVIEW

No single conceptual framework for understanding communities provides an adequate basis for the practice of social work. Theories that contribute to the study of communities include human ecology and social systems theory. These different but complementary frameworks establish a basis for understanding the structure and processes of locality-based communities. Both perspectives are widely used in social work education to help students conceptualize social environments. Using these two perspectives broadens our awareness of ways in which social interactions of individuals, groups, and organizations are patterned within a community. These two perspectives are discussed in the next two sections of this chapter.

Community as an Ecological System

Human ecology provides an interesting theoretical perspective for examining the social organization of a locality-based community. From an ecological standpoint, community is defined as "a structure of relationships through which a localized population provides its daily requirements" (Hawley, 1950). This definition is grounded in Hawley's definition of ecology as "the study of the relation of populations to their environment." The focus of this definition is on the spatial organization of people and organizations, that is, "the distribution of people and services operating in a system of interdependence." This perspective emphasizes the importance of a "division of labor" within a community—the interaction of occupational groups and technology in a stratification structure, resulting in an interdependence of the parts of the community and between communities (Hawley, 1950; 1986).

The community as an ecological system operates at two levels, the biotic (subsocial) and the social. As in plant and animal ecology, a pattern of interdependence develops among humans who share a common habitat. These patterns or relationships at the biotic level are not considered to be deliberate or rationally determined, but are viewed as impersonal and symbiotic. Such patterns can be observed in the structure of communities as they develop.

One way of thinking about the ecological system of a community is captured by the acronym POET: population, organization, environment, and technology. An ecological perspective focuses on the population characteristics of a community (size, density, diversity), the social organization or structure of a community, the physical environment or habitat (land use), the social environment or social groups in the community, and the technological forces in a community, such as communication, transportation, means of production of goods and services (Norlin & Chess, 1997). The ecological perspective seeks to describe and explain changes in the salient features of population groups within geographic areas, such as social class, racial and ethnic composition, age structure, aspects of family composition, and division of labor within the community.

Viewing a community from an ecological perspective draws our attention to the interdependence of people, services, and their local environment and to community interactions with other communities and the larger society. Of particular interest is the physical environment, that is, patterns of spatial organization, such as the location of business and commercial areas, residential areas, health and welfare services, recreational areas and parks. An ecological perspective also helps to explain community changes, such as movements of population groups, patterns of migration and immigration, succession and segregation, and growth dynamics of communities. It provides a framework for judging when such changes are beneficial or detrimental to residents and the community as a system. From an ecological perspective, a competent community enjoys a productive balance between its inhabitants and their environment, a division of labor that produces goods and services that are essential for sustenance, and a process of change that is orderly and nondestructive.

There are a number of social processes that make up the ecology of a community. One major process is competition, wherein social groups and organizations within a community compete with each other for space, resources, and dominance. This process involves a symbiosis or living together, and often is represented by a cooperative competition, whereby the competing groups operate under commonly accepted rules. A major area of competition in communities involves the use of land, as individuals, groups, and social institutions seek an "advantage of place" for commercial, industrial, institutional, and residential purposes. Social units within the community are regarded as dominant when they have the power to control the use of the most valued land in a community.

In addition to competition, a number of other processes are associated with an ecological perspective of community. These include centralization, concentration, segregation, invasion, and succession (McKenzie, 1926; Poplin, 1979).

Centralization describes a clustering of institutions and services in a central location, such as a business district or a transportation or communication center. Historically, centralization in a central city, such as New York City, Chicago, Los Angeles, and Atlanta, led to the city's domination of the surrounding metropolitan area. Currently, many central cities have lost their dominance over the marketplace, with political and economic dominance moving to edge cities and suburban communities. The concept of decentralization describes a process by which individuals and organizations move away from the central city. The development of major company offices outside central cities, the creation of shopping malls and sports facilities in suburban areas, and the movement of health and human service agencies to suburban areas are examples of decentralization.

Concentration describes the influx of population groups, such as through immigration or migration, into an urban area, or the movement of businesses or recreational/leisure-time facilities into a confined geographic area. For example, legal services, federal and district courts, and related activities are often concentrated in the downtown business areas of large cities.

The process of segregation describes how individuals, groups, and institutions, distinguished by such characteristics as race, ethnicity, social class, or religion, gravitate to separate physical locations. Segregation is an ongoing process whereby groups isolate themselves from one another, as in the development of white suburban neighborhoods, Latino neighborhoods in inner cities, and underclass populations in inner-city neighborhoods of large cities.

When one group moves into an area occupied by a distinctively separate group, e.g., African Americans into formerly white neighborhoods, or young professionals into ethnic community areas in inner-city areas where gentrification is occurring, the process is called invasion. The term succession also is used to describe this process, especially after a new group has replaced the previous residents.

Early ecologists in the "Chicago School" at the University of Chicago, especially Park, Burgess, and McKenzie (1925), believed that ecological processes led to predictable patterns of land use, spatial distribution, and community organization. These patterns were described in terms of concentric circles or zones. Five zones were identified: central business district, zone of transition, zone of independent working men's homes, zone of better residences, and commuters' zone (suburban residential areas). Describing the spatial organization of a community in terms of zones or sectors highlights the heterogeneity and homogeneity of urban areas (Choldin, 1985). Some zones attract homogeneous population groups. Ecologists label these zones "natural areas." Examples include skid rows, Chinatowns, rooming house districts, industrial areas, and ethnic neighborhoods. These areas are seen as "natural" because they are unplanned and result from the process of selection and competition related to land use. Research on communities since the development of the concentric zone hypothesis indicates that most current growth in cities does not occur in a concentric zone fashion. Nonetheless, "natural" communities with common culture and concerns continued to form within the urban community. The works of Wilson (1996) in Chicago and Coulton, Pandey, and Chow (1990) in Cleveland describe the concentration of low-income and underclass population groups within inner-city neighborhoods, not unlike the early development of zones of transition near a central business district. Zones for homeless people are an example of governmental efforts to concentrate these individuals in specific areas of inner cities.

Social Mapping

Social mapping allows us to describe a community in terms of its spatial organization—that is, the distribution of people, organizations, and resources within the community. Through social mapping we are able to visualize the physical layout of the community, such as the location of residences, industrial units, commercial and business areas, services, churches, hospitals, recreational areas, social agencies, and schools. We can then observe changes in the use of space over time. Geographic information systems (GIS) are increasingly used in the human services to create maps for practice and administrative purposes (Queralt & Witte, 1998a, 1998b; Maguire, 1991). Geographic information systems are computer systems for capturing, storing, manipulating, analyzing, displaying, and integrating spatial (geographic or locational) and nonspatial (statistical or attributional) information (Queralt & Witte, 1998a). These information systems can be used to create maps pinpointing gaps in service delivery, areas of low service, transportation problems, and areas in need of services, so that "social services agencies can analyze services in relation to clients and to the community."

Excellent illustrations of the use of U.S. Census data and other sources of information in geographic information systems can be found in the work of Queralt and Witte (1998a), who use maps to "analyze and present results in a visually meaningful and appealing way." Illustrative maps are used to identify areas with high levels of child poverty and public assistance, child care center capacities in a given area, families receiving child care subsidies, and distance to work for families who need child care. These maps support the authors' assertion that "by mapping the location of problems of concern in specific localities, one can develop a service strategy that is sensitive to the needs of the community."

Another approach to social mapping is found in the work of Andrews and Fonseca (1995) entitled *The Atlas of American Society*. Maps are used to compare the states in relation to the social well-being of Americans with respect to population distribution in city and countryside, demographics of residents of the states, migration, mobility and population change, affluence versus poverty, ethnic and cultural diversity, health and disease, medical care and costs, lifestyle risks, education K–12, higher education, crime and violence, status of women, children, senior citizens, politics and religion. Data used in the maps are obtained from the U.S. Bureau of the Census and many private and public organizations. Data are displayed by use of computer mapping software.

Social mapping can be used to focus on the cultural characteristics of geographic areas of a community. For example, Suttles's (1968) classic study on *The Social Order of the Slum* uses maps of Chicago neighborhoods to show land use patterns in relation to ethnic sections of mostly segregated neighborhoods of Italians, African Americans, Mexican Americans, and Puerto Ricans. Green (1999), in *Cultural Awareness in the Human Services*, discusses the usefulness of social mapping as a step toward cultural competence. Green suggests that the social worker entering an unfamiliar community visit the community for the purpose of social mapping: "identifying and recording the cultural resources of a community." Mapping includes the production of physical maps and descriptive information about ethnic groups in the area, patterns of geographical and social mobility, and information on access and utilization of available human services.

The focus of ecological perspectives on the spatial organization and physical environment is illustrated by ways in which neighborhoods are defined as spatial units in a community. Individuals often use mental maps to "conceptualize and negotiate their movement through and relationship with their surroundings." Incorporated into these mental maps are physical elements of a city such as streets, bus routes, walkways, parks, landmarks, "factors that inform individuals' interpretation of space and the delineation of boundaries that order the physical world of the city and help guide their action within it" (Chaskin, 1997). Mental mapping usually includes dimensions of both physical space and social interaction, especially in drawing boundaries of neighborhoods. Formal organizations, such as social agencies, banks, city planning departments, and grassroots organizations, also engage in defining boundaries for areas within a city, boundaries based on social mapping that may not always coincide with the mental maps of residents.

COMMUNITY AS A SOCIAL SYSTEM

Social systems theory provides a useful perspective for understanding American locality-based communities. While the theory is unusually complex, its major concepts guide us in identifying the structural and functional attributes of a wide variety of community types. We begin with the idea that a social system involves the interaction of two or more social units, e.g., the interactions of individuals in social groups such as families, neighborhood groups, or peer groups, the interactions within and among other social groups and social organizations, such as schools, businesses, social welfare agencies, health agencies, and the interactions of the component parts or subsystems of a community. This book focuses on the community as a social system, how the parts of the system function, and how this system meets the needs of its members. We will identify the various subsystems within a community, such as the economic, political, educational, health, and social welfare systems. We are interested in examining the activities of the various social units that make up the subsystems in order to determine how well these units carry out their community functions. The major social units within each of these subsystems are formal organizations, such as governmental organizations, economic organizations, health care organizations, and social welfare agencies. A significant aspect of a community social system also involves the functioning of informal groups, including families and other social groups. Through community assessments we can evaluate how these groups contribute to the functioning of community subsystems, e.g., parents' activity in relation to schools, and residents' contributions to the community as a whole through civic involvement and voluntary associations.

An important aspect of a social systems perspective is specification of the boundaries of the system in relation to its environment. To illustrate, a central city or other municipality in a metropolitan area may be defined as a community system whose boundaries are likely to be both geographical and psychological. The environment includes other municipalities as well as state, regional, and national entities with which the municipal community interacts. One of the central functions of such a community system is boundary maintenance. A community engages in activities that will assure its continuance as a separate entity or social organization. Boundary maintenance is exemplified by physical boundaries and legal, political boundaries. Social boundaries may be established by people within a local, spatial community to other non-place communities, such as membership in communities defined by lifestyle, social class, ethnicity, or racial identification.

Another feature of a systems model concerns the interaction of the system with outside systems beyond its own boundary, such as other communities and society. This set of outside systems, especially the American societal system, is designated by Norlin and Chess (1997) as a *suprasystem*: a system that provides inputs into local community systems and receives outputs from them. The interaction between community systems and the suprasystem provides for inputs into the community system, such as money, material resources, and information. Outputs may be thought of as the results of the interactions with the suprasystem that result in achieving the goals of a community or its subsystems. These goals may be related to employment, health, safety and security, social welfare, education, housing, and other indicators of quality of life.

Social systems theory assists us in understanding how the interactions of the social units within a community are patterned. Classical social systems theory, particularly as developed by Talcott Parsons (1951), describes these patterns in terms of systems functions or pattern variables. Norlin and Chess (1997) provide an excellent and extensive discussion of these patterns, along with helpful examples. A simple way of understanding and applying these systems ideas to communities is to identify the major social units that carry out the functions of the community system. Social units having to do with the system's external activities serve "task functions" of adaptation and goal attainment through such community systems as the economy and the polity. "Maintenance functions" of integration and pattern-maintenance/tension management occur in such social units as the family, culture, and education. Integrative and pattern-maintenance/tension-management functions are viewed as internal activities, while goal attainment and adaptation relate to the external environment.

Further elaboration of these functions of a community system appears in the work of Norlin and Chess (1997). These educators use a Parsonian framework to illustrate the problems a community system must solve in order to maintain itself and to meet the needs of its citizens. These "four main problems or dimensions of system structure and process" fall along two axes: External/Internal, and Means/End. The external/end dimension is called "goal attainment"; the external/means function is "adaptation"; the internal/end function is "integration"; and the internal/means function is called "pattern maintenance and tension management" (Parsons, 1951). Thus, *adaptation* represents the activities of the local community vis-à-vis the external environment in reaching community goals. Norlin and Chess (1997) give as an example the efforts of a local community to adapt to and/or change state and federal laws in order to promote a community goal of economic development. *Goal attainment* involves the specification of desired outcomes—products and services—of the system and the activities required to satisfy the needs of community members. Achievement of this function serves to link the local community to other communities and to society. Examination of this function in local communities assists us in understanding the interdependencies of society and local communities, as discussed in Chapter 1 on the societal context of communities.

Pattern maintenance and integration functions of a community system contribute to the internal development and continuance of the community. *Pattern maintenance* involves activities that help manage conflicts and tensions within a community, through means such as community norms, social participation in community organizations, and promotion of civil order. Many of these activities serve to help the community system maintain its stability or equilibrium. The justice system within a community is a major source of integration, as it deals with conflicts of community members and resolves the community's political problems. *Integration* refers to the attachments individuals have to their community, usually developed through primary group relationships with members of their families, churches, neighborhood groups, and workplace groups, as well as ties to formal organizations such as civic groups.

APPLICATION OF A SOCIAL SYSTEMS PERSPECTIVE

The work of Roland Warren (1963) demonstrates how social systems theory can be applied to the functioning of locality-based American communities. Warren (1963) defined a community to be "that combination of social units and systems that perform the major social functions having locality relevance." These five functions are production/distribution/ consumption, socialization, social control, social participation, and mutual support. Our examination of these functions focuses on the subsystems, or social institutions that carry out community functions, including economic, political, education, health and welfare systems. These subsystems carry out community functions mainly through formal organizations, such as corporations, governmental units, schools, churches, medical care facilities, social welfare agencies, and voluntary associations. In addition to these formal structures in the community, there are numerous primary groups that engage in social activities on a daily basis and contribute to the performance of community functions. These primary groups include family and other household groups, friendship groups, kinship groups, neighborhood groups, peer groups, self-help groups, and informal social clubs. We now elaborate on the five community functions identified by Warren (1963).

Production/distribution/consumption activities in urban communities require a high degree of specialization of employment (division of labor), and the presence of complex bureaucratic organizations (e.g., business, industry), and consumption patterns (of goods, services, energy). The daily living of individuals is dependent on the performance of the economic subsystem.

Socialization of individuals and groups involves the impact of culture on personality, the learning of values and behavior, and the patterning of social roles. The family and the school are the most common social units contributing to socialization of community members, but other forces, such as friendship groups, kinship groups, television, radio, movies, newspapers, popular magazines, and books also influence socialization.

Social control involves a range of pressures on people to behave according to community and societal norms. These pressures come from a variety of sources, some internal to the individual and some from the social environment. A principal source of social control is the local government—law enforcement agencies, courts, and control arrangements such as stoplights, parking meters, and no-smoking signs.

Social participation occurs within both informal primary groups and formal organizations. Social participation includes a wide range of activities within and connected to schools, churches, political parties, social clubs, organizational memberships, recreational facilities, and fund-raising events.

Mutual support involves assisting people in need when the needs are beyond the capability of the individual, the family, or the household.

Mutual support occurs in relation to illnesses which require professional help, family problems requiring professional counseling, learning and behavioral problems of children requiring professional counseling, and economic problems requiring income maintenance programs and financial assistance. A primary source of mutual support consists of health organizations and social welfare agencies, but the activities of social workers providing mutual support are not limited to these organizations. Social workers are often involved in government and business sectors through social programs involving employment services, job counseling, money management, and job training; as well as court services, criminal justice systems, and legal aid services.

Communities interact with other communities, and these external relationships have important implications for the ways in which a particular community system maintains its boundaries and its equilibrium. But more importantly, community subsystems interact through their formal organizations with similar social units outside the community. These extracommunity relationships are identified by Warren (1963) as vertical, in contrast to the horizontal interactions within a community. These types of relationships are illustrated by Warren in regard to mutual support. An example of a typical community unit is a voluntary health association; a unit of horizontal pattern: community welfare council; a unit of a vertical pattern: National Health Association.

COMMUNITY AS AN "ECOLOGY OF GAMES"

An interesting use of concepts from ecological and social systems theory is provided in Long's (1958) classic discussion of community as an "ecology of games." Long views a local community as a territorial system within which structured group activities occur. Sets of these activities are viewed as "games," such as a banking game, a contracting game, a newspaper game, a civic organization game, an ecclesiastical game, and many others. The major games are similar to community subsystems. Long suggests that there is no overall coordination of the games in a community; rather, they relate to each other in a symbiotic manner. Thus, the subsystems of the community operate in an ordered but unplanned basis, with the general public deciding whether or not the games are being played well. Social order in the community is maintained because the games have expectations, norms, and rules for their players, not because there is an overall political game that dominates the community system. This idea of social order has been elaborated upon by Giamatti (1998) in his book *Take Time for Paradise: Americans and Their Games*. Giamatti compares communities to sports, noting that they are both deeply conventional, with established rules and social agreements. Giamatti maintains that when conventions are respected within communities, we have a city where people choose to live, just as people continue to watch or participate in sports in which the players adhere to the rules.

An important question arising from the games analogy is "What game or group links the various games together into the social order of the community?" Moving from a proposition that social order is unplanned, Long (1958) then suggests that the various games in the community, while competing with one another, are linked through social interaction of leaders in each of the games. Office holders and organizational executives have an interest in achieving their goals within their own games, and they recognize that interaction with the players in other games is important. The leaders in the various games are all influenced by the newspaper game, as it seeks to set the civic agenda, the topics, concerns, and ideas that people talk about, have an investment in, and expect the civic leadership to do something about. While the various games may contribute to the overall order of the whole community, Long contends that the social game may be the most significant game that integrates all the other games. The social game is played by leaders in the various subsystems (games) of the community, through activities such as overlapping board and club memberships, measures of social standing, and social activities.

The games analogy provides a creative way of thinking about the goals, functions, and activities of the organizations within the various community subsystems. It helps in assessing the extent to which each of the subsystems functions effectively in a community, using a "keeping score" approach to measuring community competence. The games perspective points to ways of understanding the leadership and power structure of the community. Taking the social welfare game as an example, each human service organization can be examined in terms of the part it plays in the social welfare game, what score it receives for services delivered and the effectiveness and attainment of social goals, how the organizational leaders within the social welfare field interact with each other, and how the organizations interact with welfare coordinating agencies and other subsystems.

Chapter 4 Review

This chapter opened with a discussion of community competence and an exploration of the question, "What is a good community?" For several populations at risk for discrimination, we identified barriers to full participation and equal opportunities. The basic features of an ecological perspective were identified in relation to locality-based communities. Social processes that make up the ecology of a community were discussed: competition, concentration, centralization, segregation, and succession. We saw that social mapping provides a way of describing communities in terms of their spatial organization, including distribution of people, organizations, and resources, along with an indication of how special populations in the United States face barriers to full participation and equal opportunities. In presenting the major elements of a social systems perspective, we identified four major problems of systems that must be addressed by the community: adaptation, goal attainment, pattern maintenance, and integration. These systems patterns provide a context for assessing how a community displays competence in responding to community systems problems.

The systems properties of communities direct our attention to the social organization of a community and the processes related to stability and change. The ecological perspective emphasizes the spatial properties of a community, the demographic characteristics of population groups, the social processes of the community, and the interdependencies that develop within and among communities to meet the requirements of daily living. The social systems perspective demonstrates how a community operates to perform functions for its members. Our principal focus will be the performance of subsystems, and their formal organizations, such as social welfare agencies, schools, churches, businesses, local governmental units. We explored Long's (1958) analysis of a community as an "ecology of games," which combines ecological and systems principles to assess the functioning of community subsystems and the community as a whole.

5

Demographic Development of Communities

Using an ecological systems perspective makes it easier to study the demographic characteristics of a population residing in a specific location, such as a metropolitan area, municipality, or neighborhood. The most commonly explored characteristics are population size, density, and diversity. The ecological perspective draws upon the science of demography to study factors such as increases or decreases in the size of population groups, their vital statistics, their location, changes in their territorial distribution through migration and diffusion, social and residential mobility, and diversity of community residents in terms of race, ethnicity, religion, and socioeconomic status.

A major source of data for understanding communities in demographic terms is the U.S. Bureau of the Census. The Bureau collects population information through a decennial census, and it also conducts surveys that serve as the basis for projections and estimates of population characteristics and changes that are published yearly as Statistical Abstracts. For the collection and analysis of census data, local communities are divided into geographic areas called census tracts—relatively small units for reporting numbers of residents and their social characteristics. Tracts are divided into census blocks that vary in size, depending on the density of population in a given area. The number of residents in communities is closely associated with the terms used to describe them: village, town, city, metropolis, and metropolitan area.

POPULATION SIZE

The U.S. Office of Management and Budget (OMB) reports population sizes, as determined by the U.S. Bureau of the Census, for metropolitan areas, cities, urbanized areas, and rural areas. A metropolitan area is defined as "a core area containing a large population nucleus, together with adjacent communities having a high degree of economic and social integration with that core" (U.S. Bureau of the Census, 1998). There are three major designations of metropolitan areas: Metropolitan Statistical Areas (MSAs), Consolidated Metropolitan Statistical Areas (CMSAs), and Primary Metropolitan Statistical Areas (PMSAs). Standards used to define each of these types of Metropolitan Statistical Areas are cited in the Statistical Abstracts of the U.S. Bureau of the Census (1998) as follows:

1. An MSA must include at least one city with 50,000 or more inhabitants, or a Census Bureau-defined urbanized area (of at least 50,000 inhabitants) and a total metropolitan population of at least 100,000 (75,000 in New England).
2. An area that meets these requirements for recognition as an MSA and also has a population of 1 million or more may be recognized as a CMSA.
3. The component parts (MSAs) of a CMSA are designated as PMSAs.

In 1998 the United States contained 256 MSAs and 18 CMSAs comprising 73 PMSAs, along with three MSAs, one CMSA, and three PMSAs in Puerto Rico. The title of "central city" is given to the largest city in each MSA/CMSA. Additional cities qualify as central cities if they meet specified requirements concerning population size and commuting patterns. The title of each MSA consists of the names of up to three of its central cities and the name of each state into which the MSA extends. MSAs in New England are established by somewhat different standards, as defined in the Statistical Abstracts published by the U.S. Bureau of the Census.

The entire territory of the United States is classified as metropolitan (inside MSAs or CMSAs: PMSAs are components of CMSAs) or non-metropolitan (outside MSAs or CMSAs). A distinction is made between urban and rural populations, with the urban population comprising "all persons living in (a) places of 2,500 or more inhabitants incorporated as cities, villages, boroughs (except in Alaska and New York), and towns (except in New England states, New York, and Wisconsin), but excluding those persons living in the rural portions of extended cities (places with low population density in one or more large parts of their area; (b) census-designated places of 2,500 or more inhabitants; and (c) other territory, incorporated or unincorporated, included in urbanized areas" (U.S. Bureau of the Census, 1998). An urbanized area comprises one or more places and the adjacent densely settled surrounding territory that together have a minimum population of 50,000 persons. In all definitions, the population that is not classified as urban constitutes the rural population.

The concepts of metropolitan, urbanized, and rural areas highlight the interrelationships among communities, as well as some differences between urban and rural areas. Communities within the same urban area often interact with one another. Residents of the land outside of a metropolitan area, e.g., those who live in the hinterland, the outskirts, or the rural-urban fringe, have connections with the metropolitan community, which in turn exerts influence over these non-metropolitan inhabitants. Communities adjacent to but outside the boundaries of a central city are described as suburban areas. These often include self-governing municipalities or townships. A community is defined as a suburb if it is an incorporated municipality within a metropolitan area and is not the central city. Suburbs are ordinarily thought of as being largely residential in nature, but they often include mixed land use ranging from almost total residential to almost total business/industrial.

The U.S. Bureau of the Census has established standard categories for population size, including communities with fewer than 2,500 residents, 2,500 to fewer than 50,000, 50,000 to fewer than 100,000, 100,000 to fewer than one million, and one million and over. An important factor to take into account when examining small communities (population under 50,000) is the nature of the surrounding area. For example, small communities may be adjacent to a central city in a suburban area, outside suburban areas but still in urbanized areas, in non-metropolitan areas, or in rural areas. The concept of a small community covers a rather broad range of population sizes, leading to a high degree of variation among these communities in terms of social organization, patterns of social relationships, and collective identity. People living in small communities located in non-metropolitan, rural areas, make up about 22 percent of the U.S. population, with most of this population living in the states of Idaho, Vermont, South Dakota, Wyoming, Maine, West Virginia, North Dakota, Arkansas, Alaska, and Iowa. These residential areas are often referred to as small or rural communities. In recent years a rural-to-urban shift in population has been followed by some movement out of suburban and central city areas to rural areas.

The work of Ginsberg (1998) is instructive with regard to the social and economic problems of small rural communities, such as unemployment, poor housing, lack of access to health care, lack of transportation, and lack of social services. Ginsberg's edited volume, *Social Work in Rural Communities*, gives attention to the problems of small and rural communities and provides discussions of special issues related to social work practice in these communities. For example, a generalist practice model is recommended for social workers in rural communities. Of central importance is the need for social workers in these communities to "spend time learning the community and its people and allowing the community to come to know them before they can be effective in carrying out their responsibilities" (Ginsberg, 1998). Readings relevant to the practice of social work in small towns and rural areas are also found in the edited work of Carlton-LaNey, Edwards, and Reid (1999), *Preserving and Strengthening Small Towns and Rural Communities*. This volume focuses on "romantic notions about rural life and the harsh realities that too often confront residents of small towns and rural communities," demographic information on these communities, issues such as the importance of families, developing exemplary services and programs, social diversity, and preparing social workers for rural practice.

Martinez-Brawley (1990, 2000), in *Perspectives on the Small Community* and in *Close to Home: Human Services and the Small Community*, provides some interesting perspectives on differences between large and small communities that are relevant to social work practice. Her presentation of theoretical frameworks for examining small communities is supplemented by the use of literary and journalistic sources. Martinez-Brawley (1990) illustrates some of the opportunities in small communities for the development of a sense of belonging, identification, and connectedness. Her discussion of power, influence, and leadership in small communities suggests the different ways in which these processes operate in communities of varied sizes. Locality and localism have special, traditional meanings for people in small communities, and population size appears to be an important factor in the creation of the small-town culture.

DENSITY IN COMMUNITIES

Population density refers to the number of people within a physical space, usually measured in terms of square miles. High population density has traditionally been associated with central cities and low density with suburban and rural communities. This pattern is demonstrated in the development of suburban communities, particularly after 1945. At the same time, Rusk's (1993) analysis of population changes in 522 central cities of the United States shows a 50 percent decline in density in these cities from 1945 to 1990. Some low-density cities were able to expand, resulting in an increase in density, due to the fact that there was room to grow by building on vacant land or annexation of adjoining land. In other communities, known as port-of-entry cities, density has increased through immigration, e.g., Hispanics moving into Miami, Florida and the surrounding area, Hispanics and Asians moving into the Los Angeles area, and a mix of immigrants entering the New York City area. Since 1990, more than 100,000 immigrants have entered New York City annually, offsetting any decline in the city's population through deaths and migration (Sachs, 1999b).

High density of population has usually been associated with negative factors of city life, such as "too much noise, too much dirt, too much pollution," and "an environment that is stress-producing" (Krupat, 1985). Crowding within housing arrangements, transportation, use of facilities, neighborhoods, and in the wider community is viewed as having negative effects on one's quality of life. Density and crowding are measured in various ways, such as household size, number of rooms, persons per room, number of households in a dwelling, and subjective feelings about being in a crowded area. In contrast to this negative view of density, some urban planners believe that central cities need to increase population density in order to improve the social and economic conditions of the city. Rusk (1993), for example, has promoted the idea that central cities must be "elastic" enough to increase their population size through development of vacant land and buildings, expansion of city boundaries, and/or collaboration of city/suburban governments or metropolitan government. The consequences for cities that are not "elastic" are lower tax revenues, lack of adequate public services, lower quality of education, fewer employment opportunities, and an increase in neighborhood segregation by race, ethnicity, and social class.

DIVERSITY IN COMMUNITIES

Data from the U.S. Census are used to describe the composition of metropolitan areas, municipalities, and neighborhoods in terms of a variety of demographic factors, such as social class, race, ethnicity, religion, family composition, age, and gender structures. The concepts of diversity, integration, segregation, and social stratification are helpful in describing the nature of geographic communities. These topics are discussed in a number of places in this book, including a discussion of demographics of American society in Chapter 1, demographic development of communities in this chapter, social stratification of communities in Chapter 6, and the emergence of social class and ethnic minority neighborhoods in Chapters 7 and 8.

In our discussion of metropolitan areas and central cities of large communities, heterogeneity of population in terms of race, ethnicity, and social class becomes apparent. While small towns and rural areas are often considered to be homogeneous, many of these communities have diverse population groups. For example, approximately 4 million African Americans live in rural areas, primarily in the South. Rural areas now include large numbers of migrant laborers and immigrants (Carlton-LaNey et al., 1999). Snipp (1996) has identified three types of areas in which minority groups are concentrated in rural areas: American Indian reservations, Latino *colonias* (settlements of Hispanic migrant workers throughout the rural West), and African American communities. These communities face challenges involving poverty and high rates of unemployment, health problems of community residents, and isolation from mainstream society.

Effects of Immigration

A significant change in the diversity of American communities has occurred in recent decades with the influx of new immigrants into the United States. Immigration may be viewed from several perspectives, such as the origin of immigrants, characteristics of immigrants' education, occupation, age, and family composition, time of arrival in the United States, and attitudes of long-time residents toward immigrants. A major contrast can be made between "older" immigrants and "newer" immigrants, with the older group represented mainly by white ethnics and the newer group by people of color, especially Asians and Hispanics. Based on patterns of immigration of racial and ethnic groups into the United States prior to 1924, the time of the National Origins Quota Act, the United States has been regarded as a nation of immigrants. The concept of ethnicity was closely related to the cultural and social processes of these immigrants, with Americanization for most coming through stages of biculturalism, acculturation, and assimilation. As we have noted earlier, barriers imposed by white society prevented many people of African American or Native American descent from being assimilated into the prevailing culture.

Between 1924 and 1965, entry of immigrants into the United States was drastically reduced. Still, the origins of immigrants remained pretty much the same as during the pre-1924 period. However, since the enactment of the new Immigration Act of 1965 (and succeeding amendments), there has been a dramatic increase in the representation of immigrants from Asia and Latin America, as well as an increase in the number of refugees from Third World countries. In response to concerns over illegal immigration and its effects on national and community economic systems, the Immigration Reform and Control Act of 1986 was enacted to control immigration and to allow some undocumented residents to become citizens (Finch, 1990).

Census data from 1990 display unusually large changes in the racial and ethnic composition of the United States from 1980 to 1990, with nearly one in four Americans being of African, Asian, Hispanic, or Native American ancestry in 1990, compared to one in five ten years earlier (Barringer, 1991). A significant part of this growth came from nearly ten million ethnic minority immigrants, especially in the Hispanic population. An equally dramatic change is the new diversity of the Asian population due to immigration, especially fast-growing groups of Vietnamese, Koreans, and persons from India. An important feature related to this growth in ethnic populations is the distribution of new immigrants. An analysis of 1990 census data by Frey (1993) shows that most immigrants are flooding into just a handful of states, while the rest of America is largely untouched by the new immigration. Of the seven "port of entry" states that received the most immigrants—New York, Texas, New Jersey, Illinois, Massachusetts, Florida, and California—the white, non-Hispanic population declined in all of these states except Florida. Approximately two-thirds of all immigrant growth took place in ten metropolitan areas, due in part to migration from these areas by less-skilled workers. These ten areas are Los Angeles, New York City, San Francisco, Chicago, Miami, Washington, D.C., Houston, San Diego, Boston, and Dallas. This change has led some demographers to believe there is a new "white flight" occurring, not just from central city communities, but from states and regions of the United States (Frey, 1993). Over the past decade, native-born, less-skilled workers have been moving away from high-immigration areas, especially "port of entry" states such as California and communities such as Los Angeles (Frey & Liaw, 1998).

As a result of recent immigration patterns in New York City, while there are still "immigrant neighborhoods," there is an increase in the diversity of neighborhoods in the five boroughs. City planners now predict that the non-Hispanic white population will decline in the near future to 35 percent of the city population, with the Hispanic population growing to 29 percent, non-Hispanic black population to 26 percent, and Asian population to 10 percent. In the past few years the largest groups of immigrants have come from the Dominican Republic, the countries of the former Soviet Union, and China, with fast-growing groups coming from Ghana, Nigeria, Bangladesh, and Egypt. As a result, neighborhoods in the boroughs have become much more diverse, with less concentration in old ethnic neighborhoods of the past, such as Asians in Chinatowns and Dominicans in traditional enclaves. These new immigration patterns have led to the conclusion that "New York City is ending the century as it began. . .oxygenated by immigrants. . .with the new arrivals coming from an increasingly diverse set of nations and settling over a broader swath of the city than ever before" (Sachs, 1999b).

The situation in Georgetown, Delaware, a small town of just over 4,000 people, illustrates how demographic changes caused by immigration can transform a community (Escobar, 1999). Since around 1995, there has been a large influx of Guatemalans into this community, drawn by the poultry industry's need for workers. By 1999 Georgetown had become a "modern-day company town," with more than a third of the population having been born outside the U.S. As the town's demographics changed, the size and diversity of the population grew. The density of the population increased, with the influx of new immigrants creating "a chaotic, competitive, and very profitable rental market." Overcrowded housing, along with housing code violations, led to more stringent housing ordinances.

As more and more Guatemalans took jobs in this community, many began bringing their wives to Georgetown, followed by an increase in the birth rates of the newcomers. Families tended to establish housing within a Guatemalan enclave, called Kimmeytown, to begin to purchase homes, and to build a community with its "own support network, its own rules, its own stores, its own churches, and most significantly, the only baby boom around" (Escobar, 1999). Two Spanish nuns, from the South Bronx and Washington, created a social agency and fostered attachments to the local Catholic Church. Several Pentecostal congregations were also established in the community. Rapid demographic changes, especially the new ethnic diversity, created "growing pains" for the community, especially for the "old-line" Georgetowners who saw "the familiar become foreign almost overnight" (Escobar, 1999). Longtime residents formed a Historic Georgetown Association to promote housing controls and to encourage the Perdue Farms poultry plant to help the new workers by providing access to bilingual medical care, a wellness center, and a child care center. Some longtime residents recognized that the local community's economic system benefited from the new immigrants, and began to see "the Guatemalan people as a tremendous asset" (Escobar, 1999).

PHASES OF URBANIZATION

Concepts such as ecology, social organization, and sociocultural lifestyle can be used to examine the process of urbanization. A common-sense definition of urbanization is an ecological one: population movement from rural to urban areas, leading to an increased proportion of the population in urbanized areas. Closely associated with these changes is that fact that the basis of work for most people shifts from agricultural to nonagricultural (industrial) employment, and hence to service occupations. As small towns become cities, small cities become larger cities, and new metropolitan areas develop, the social organization of these communities becomes more complex. Their interdependencies with other communities, and with state and national levels of government, are intensified. Sociocultural lifestyles, values, and social relationships of people change through urbanization, especially as secondary relationships increase and primary group social interactions decline.

A useful conceptualization of urbanization emphasizes the productive functions of communities and the ways in which changes in transportation and communication have facilitated the production of goods and services. Changes brought about by urbanization are attributed to technological advancement. From this point of view, urbanization has occurred in three major phases related to transportation and communication technology: the city-building phase (from the 1830s to about 1925), the metropolitan phase (from about 1920 to the present), and the diffuse phase (beginning in about 1950 and continuing to the present). The city-building phase was facilitated by developments such as the railway system, steam power, and ships, and the telegraph, all of which led to a pattern of urban settlements we now call central cities. During this phase, communities grew by migration, by natural growth, and from immigration. Major population redistributions took place, especially migration from rural areas to urban areas. Ecological factors strongly influenced the growth patterns of some major cities and the decline of others during this period, producing the development of close proximity between employment and residence and an increased division of labor in the work force.

The beginning of the metropolitan phase of urbanization around 1920 was marked by the fact that more than half of the total population lived in urban places. In this period the areas surrounding central cities showed increases in population through the process of decentralization.

This phase came about due to changes in short-distance transportation (motor vehicles) and communication (telephones), the extension of facilities such as water/sewer systems out from the central city, and new opportunities for residential housing in outlying areas. During this phase the proportion of white-collar jobs increased, with a growth in the scale of formal organizations. Large-scale organizations developed multi-level operations through branches, and new management-labor relationships resulted from the growth of labor unions. Urbanization in this phase, just after the end of World War II, involved a movement of industry out of the central city areas and a movement of people to "first-ring" suburban residential areas just outside the central city. This migration to nearby suburbs and beyond, which included high proportions of young families, whites, and people of high socioeconomic status, left in the inner cities many people of color, female-headed families, recent migrants from rural areas, immigrants from foreign countries, and people with low incomes.

During the metropolitan phase, with movement of people, businesses, and industry to outlying areas, major central cities continued to control and coordinate community functions within metropolitan areas. But the central cities became less dominant as a diffuse urbanization phase emerged. During this phase the zone of dispersion of people for residential purposes was broadened further, and business and industry continued to disperse, along with major entertainment centers such as superdomes, concert parks, national corporate offices, and hotels. As this decentralization occurred, the major expansion of job markets and employment opportunities developed in the outlying regions of large metropolitan areas, especially in middle-sized edge cities.

As suburban residential communities developed, an image of lifestyles and social interactions in these areas emerged. These communities appeared to be homogeneous in race (white) and social class (middle and upper), with similarities in housing designs (three-bedroom ranch tract houses), consumer habits, recreation, social status, and educational backgrounds. In recent years, however, some suburban communities have become more diverse in terms of social class, family composition, age structure, and ethnic composition. Older suburban communities, in particular, have become less segregated by race and ethnicity, so that by the year 2000 approximately 51 percent of Asians, 43 percent of all Hispanics, and 32 percent of African Americans lived in the suburbs. New immigrants, in particular, have moved into older suburbs, accompanied by the increase in ethnic businesses—e.g., Central Americans into the Long Island suburb of Hempstead, New York, and Latinos into the suburbs of the San Fernando

Valley in California (Kotkin, 2000). While there have been considerable changes in the older suburban communities, newer residential neighborhoods are likely to be highly segregated in terms of race and social class, especially in areas with extremely large homes built to suit the interests and lifestyles of increasingly wealthy, upwardly mobile families.

EDGE CITIES

The movement of businesses and people in the diffuse phase of urbanization has created "new" cities, popularly referred to as edge cities. These cities differ from the traditional suburban community in that they have taken on the functions and form of a central city, especially high-density office and retail development. Garreau (1991) has identified a large number of edge cities connected to some thirty-six major central cities in the United States, including areas of New York and New Jersey, Boston, Detroit, Atlanta, Phoenix, Dallas, Houston, Los Angeles, San Francisco, and Washington, D.C. The cities that have emerged within these metropolitan areas share many of the characteristics of the central cities. However, the architecture and use of space are considerably different, as are the transportation patterns and space for parking. As areas near "edge cities" develop, low-density office development turns these areas into "edgeless cities." What remains to be seen is whether or not these cities and their surrounding business and residential expansions will develop into communities—that is, will people identify with these places and engage in social interactions within their neighborhoods and the city areas? Will residents of these cities engage in social participation and civic life that leads to a sense of community? Or will these cities simply provide spaces for commercial and business activities, with little integration of workplaces with the functions associated with residence, such as school activities, religious affiliation, and participation in voluntary associations?

One of the principal problems for some people living in or near edge cities and newer suburban communities is a long commute to work. Census data indicate that an increasingly large number of people reside considerable distances from their jobs, that is, far from central cities and edge cities. This type of move generally brings with it a downside. Middle- and upper-class people who reside in communities at large distances from their jobs have less time with families, less time to enjoy their homes and their communities, and increased stress from highway driving. A major concern of parents who work far from home involves the care of their children.

Edge cities and other suburban communities provide a source of employment for central city residents, but transportation, both public and private, is often an obstacle to commuting to work. Transportation is especially problematic for people in the inner city and central city whose jobs take them far from home (Shellenbarger, 1993b). Special problems confront women who gain work skills through "welfare reform" programs and then find that many of the available jobs are a great distance from their homes. Thus, commuting to work has emerged as a challenge for women on welfare, along with obtaining child care. Studies continue to show a "spatial mismatch" between people on welfare, location of available jobs, and access to them. For example, available entry-level jobs are likely to require a commute by inner-city residents of more than one hour each way on public transit.

The federal government and some states have begun to address transportation problems through van pools, shuttle buses, car loans, car leases, and new bus systems. In Chicago and some other cities, a federal demonstration project, Bridges to Work, provides transportation to business parks. In areas such as Los Angeles, "welfare commuting" is a special problem due to the fact that a high proportion of all workers commute, resulting in traffic jams and congestion on the freeways (Bailey, 1997). Two possible solutions to the commuting problem—creation of new jobs in the central cities and relocation of residences—appear not to be able to overcome the problems of transportation for people on welfare.

Isolation is lessened when inner-city residents can find employment in suburban areas. This has been accomplished in some major American cities through the development of bus lines that link the inner-city poor with jobs in suburbia (Wartzman, 1993). With federal funds, cities such as Philadelphia, Chicago, Washington, Detroit, and Boston have shown interest in Mobility for Work initiatives, especially the creation of special bus lines to transport workers to jobs outside the inner city. An example of this kind of program is the 201 bus line in Philadelphia, which serves riders to and from jobs in communities near the central city. This bus line was developed to meet the workforce needs of suburban businesses, such as restaurants and manufacturing companies, and to facilitate employment of inner-city residents.

Another example of a strategy for connecting the urban poor to work comes from a study of the Detroit metropolitan area. Galster and Glazer (1998) note that even the booming economy of the 1990s was insufficient to overcome the problems of inner-city residents in gaining employment. These authors point out that labor markets are regional and inner-city residents must gain the skills to compete for jobs outside the central city. They recommend helping the urban poor through human capital development, especially better educational opportunities, improved schools, programs for early childhood development, and health care. A second area for development involves reducing economic segregation by opening up housing opportunities outside poorer residential areas.

URBAN SPRAWL

One of the consequences of the diffuse phase of urbanization and the emergence of edge cities has been urban sprawl, brought on by a lack of planned growth in many metropolitan areas. The federal government, together with some state and local governments, has responded to the increase in traffic congestion, gridlock, elimination of open space areas, and increased air pollution with proposals to contain urban sprawl and promote "smart growth." A number of suburban communities have placed growth initiatives on the ballot, supported by environmentalists who are in favor of preserving open spaces. Some local governments have initiated bond sales to purchase land for parks, preservation, and open space. The federal government has supported controlled growth with funding for preservation of parks, open spaces, protection of water supplies, and the development of abandoned industrial sites for commercial use (Janofsky, 1999). Vice President Gore's presidential campaign proposals for responding to urban sprawl included a call for federal agencies to cooperate in promoting planned growth. Under Gore's proposals, communities and regional areas would be encouraged to collaborate with each other to solve their urban growth problems.

The need for regional planning to address urban sprawl has been highlighted in a study by the Brookings Institution. The Brookings study reported that the Washington, D.C., region was "sharply divided, socially and economically, between its eastern and western halves," leading to the conclusion that "The problems of hyper growth on the one hand and social distress on the other are intertwined" (Cohn, 1999). The Report recommended that efforts be made to "bring more growth to the east (the District and Prince George's County, inner suburbs) where it is needed and less to the west (better-off communities), where it is causing problems" such as "worsening traffic jams, thousands of children attending classes in trailers, stagnant prices for some existing homes because so many new ones are on the market" (Cohn, 1999). One of the obstacles to a regional solution to these problems has been the difficulty of getting agreement on land use and other issues among District, Maryland, and Virginia governmental officials. There is also opposition from the building industry to attempts to stop residential neighborhood development in fast-growing affluent suburban areas.

An example of one state's response to urban sprawl is Georgia. In reacting to the sprawl created near Atlanta, the legislature of the State of Georgia passed a bill that created a transportation superagency "with broad powers to impose transit systems and highways on local governments, restrict development, and even put pressure on cities and counties to raise taxes" (Firestone, 1999). "Under the bill, if a county decides to build a shopping mall in an overly congested area, or an area without adequate transportation, a newly created Georgia Regional Transportation Authority could in essence veto the mall by refusing to issue permits necessary to tie it into the road system. The authority can plan and build new rail or bus systems or car-pool lanes, and if a county balks at paying required taxes, the authority can withhold vital state money until the county complies" (Firestone, 1999). This effort to contain urban sprawl focuses on regional approaches to planned growth and mass transit, something individual local governments have failed to develop.

An interesting way of curbing sprawl and promoting the vitality of the city core is found in Portland, Oregon (Hoover, 1999). Portland has become a national model for urban growth by establishing a growth boundary that involves the redevelopment of the core of the city. "A few miles outside the city, development abruptly stops at the urban growth boundary. Along the boundary, houses toe an imaginary line. On the other side, forest and farmland dominate the landscape. Nestled in the shadow of Mt. Hood and intersected by the Willamette River, Portland is seen by many as a national smart growth model. Its border rings in sprawl and forces economic redevelopment back to the city" (Hoover, 1999). In addition to establishing and maintaining a growth boundary, Portland controls growth in the following ways:

- A light rail system links workers and jobs.
- Design rules prevent blank walls at street level. Shops, artwork, and restaurants dominate the streetscape.
- Polluted sites are capped so developers can build on them, instead of requiring costly removal of contaminated land.

Another example of metropolitan Portland's attempt to control urban sprawl is an agreement between Washington County and the Intel Corporation. Along with the county government's agreement with Intel on a package of tax incentives, Intel agreed to pay a "growth impact fee" if it exceeded a ceiling of new manufacturing jobs in the area. In other words, Washington County wanted new jobs, but not too many, so that livability issues could be weighed against economic development, "new strains on schools, roads, utilities and many other services in the area" (Verhovek, 1999).

Houston provides an example of a city of sprawl. Houston "hangs onto its residents and its tax base the same way that Texas Rangers used to deal with outlaws. . .by hunting them down and capturing them" (Hoover, 1999). Houston uses an aggressive annexation polity to prevent uncontrollable decay, and has no zoning regulations to prevent growth. As a result of annexation, Houston has become a city of 617 square miles, has nearly doubled its population since 1960, and the metropolitan area has no separable suburban cities. At the same time, neighborhoods are involved in community problem solving through a Neighborhood Oriented Government program "which calls for city officials to solve problems with neighborhoods calling the shots." At the same time, the population of the inner city, bounded in a small area by Interstate 610, is increasing and is expected to quadruple by 2010.

Another approach to growth, with an emphasis on sharing, has occurred in the Twin Cities (Minneapolis–St. Paul) area. The Twin Cities have a plan for communities surrounding the Cities to benefit from growth, with communities in the area sharing 40 percent of new property taxes, so that of 186 communities, 137 have seen their tax base increase (Hoover, 1999). As these examples of governmental policies and programs to manage urban sprawl indicate, communities have varying "sprawl" problems and different solutions. In a 1999 report of the Sierra Club on "Solving Sprawl," states are rated in terms of such factors as land use planning and community revitalization. The report indicates that "States that are leaders in land use planning help local governments deal with sprawl by developing comprehensive growth management plans. The best states go beyond this by providing tools to local governments such as urban growth boundaries, which empower communities to coordinate growth and protect farmland and open space" (Thompson, 1999).

RURAL AREAS AND URBANIZATION

During the processes of urbanization many rural communities initially lost population, but more recently, some small towns and rural areas have realized considerable growth. Rural and small-town communities have taken on new socioeconomic functions, especially when companies have moved into these communities. There still remain some demographic differences between rural and urban areas regarding rates of fertility, age composition, family status, education, employment, and income. A key social organizational question is the extent to which rural communities have become part of a "mass society." Do bonds of local integration persist or change to vertical ties to the larger society? Most small rural communities appear to have developed vertical extracommunity ties that are linked to the larger urbanized society. Thus, in these small communities, local economic, educational, and governmental units have not been able to retain their customary high degree of autonomy. There seems to be little doubt that today few communities, even those resembling Garrison Keillor's fictional Lake Wobegon (Keillor, 1985), remain truly isolated from the larger society, since most small rural communities receive federal and state funding of social programs, education, and health services.

In the current phase of urbanization, does the quality of life differ for people in rural areas compared to that of people in urban areas? In the past, there have been significant differences in economic well-being, level of education, major health risks, health care, housing standards, and recreational opportunities. People in rural communities have been, and continue to be, less advantaged in these aspects but usually experience more safety, more family stability, higher environmental quality, and less pollution and noise. There are still some differences in the attitudes and behavior of rural and urban populations, such as religious beliefs, personal morals/vices, majority/minority issues, or political issues. However, continued urbanization seems to be progressively eradicating some rural/urban lifestyle differences, with rural America becoming "an exceedingly diverse place" in terms of "any social or economic attribute one wishes to choose. . .educational attainment, per capita income, occupation, and ethnic background provide examples. This diversity shapes both the public policies applicable to the countryside and the opportunities of rural communities and rural people" (Castle, 1993). Still, rural poverty remains "a significant factor in the lives of many rural individuals, families, and communities. . .In many rural communities, poverty shapes the problems and service needs of individuals and families. . ." (Fichen, 1998). Older adults in rural areas are more likely to be poor than are their cohorts in urban settings, especially the oldest-old, members of minority groups, and widows.

HUMAN CAPITAL AND RURAL COMMUNITIES

One of the major sets of differences between urban communities and rural communities is related to the work force, with people in small rural communities having deficits in educational attainment, worker skills, productivity, and earnings. One explanation for these deficits is the lack of investment in human capital on the part of these inhabitants, that is, the development of skills, knowledge, experiences, and abilities related to achievement in the work force (Beaulieu & Mulkey, 1992). Improvements in human capital investment involve education, job training, and health care programs, and are related to individual characteristics and aspirations, families, and communities. Human capital is associated with social capital, provided through family and community influence based on "the norms, the social networks, and the relationships between adults and children that are of value to the child while growing up" (Beaulieu & Mulkey, 1992; Coleman, 1988). When small rural communities do not provide social capital to support the development of human capital, students in rural communities are likely to have lower educational and occupational aspirations. This outcome suggests a need in these communities for improvements in the K–12 schools and in health care services, as well as improvements in the social and economic conditions and levels of social capital in families.

While it is clear that educational levels of people in rural communities are lower than for residents of urban areas, there have been considerable improvements and a narrowing of the educational gap between rural and urban residents. Nevertheless, there is a lack of jobs in rural areas that adequately utilize the available human capital of residents (Killian & Beaulieu, 1992). Residents in rural areas with a high school education still must compete with college-educated workers for jobs, while many of the college-educated workers either get the local jobs or migrate to urban areas, leaving the rural community with lower human capital resources.

The small size of rural communities appears to provide an occupational structure that negatively affects students' educational and career aspirations (Beaulieu & Mulkey, 1992). Low aspirations are linked to a lack of interest in efforts that would lead to higher incomes, such as formal schooling and/or job training experiences. Since rural areas are less involved in agriculture, mining, and manufacturing jobs than in the past, there is less incentive on the part of young people to stay in school, to graduate from high school, or to go on to college. As Wilkinson (1992) notes, "Jobs and income lead the list of obvious rural deficits. Without adequate economic resources, communities tend to wither and often die." Important as economic and service deficits are in these communities, Wilkinson (1992) has argued that they are only "surface manifestations of a more fundamental underlying problem of contemporary rural life, namely the problem of community deterioration." This problem is defined as one of rural communities not being able to "act"—that is, to engage in the steps that characterize the development of community competence, described in Chapter 4. One response to this problem has been strategies of community development: "the capacity of people in rural areas to shape their own future well-being." Important influences on such development are new forms of communications technology and the incorporation of local community development (social, health, educational, and economic) into a national rural development policy that provides resources from state and national governments.

One factor that has limited the economic viability of small towns has been geography—that is, the long distance from these towns to the nearest trunk lines for Internet connections. As a result, there is a very high cost of telephone lines in many rural counties due to the small number of people using the Internet connections. An example of a community with this problem is North Adams, Massachusetts, a "long-depressed former mill and factory town, cupped in the Berkshire Mountains in the remotest corner of Massachusetts" (Goldberg, 1999). Community business and civic leaders in Berkshire County have created a task force to develop business and technological plans and to seek public and private money to obtain a fiber optic cable that will support efforts to bring jobs to the region. The goals of the task force are supported by "a handful of tech upstarts" from Williams College in Williamstown who have sites on the Web, and the high-tech Massachusetts Museum of Contemporary Art in North Adams that offers computer courses and rents offices to technology-related companies.

DEMOGRAPHIC CHANGES IN THE INNER CITY

Studies of poor, inner-city neighborhoods illustrate the emergence of negative social, economic, and environmental conditions in these residential areas. Many inner-city neighborhoods display social features associated with high levels of poverty, physical decay, crime, and social disorganization. More often than not they have concentrations of nonworking poor and people of color. Residents, often labeled the "underclass," are socially and physically isolated from mainstream society through processes of segregation and hyperghettoization (Wacquant & Wilson, 1989; Wilson, 1994, 1996). Summaries of studies by Wilson (1994, 1996) in Chicago and Coulton et al. (1990) in Cleveland are introduced here to illustrate the relationship between demographic changes and the problems of residents in inner-city communities.

In his studies of inner-city neighborhoods in Chicago during the 1980s and 1990s Wilson (1994, 1996) found evidence of a "new urban poverty" characterized by "poor segregated neighborhoods in which a substantial majority of individual adults are either unemployed or have dropped out of the labor force." Thus, in 15 black community areas the employment rate in 1990 for adults was 37 percent, in contrast to a 54 percent employment rate in 17 other predominantly black community areas. Over the years since the publication of *Black Metropolis* by Drake and Cayton in 1945, and especially since 1970, many black inner-city neighborhoods have changed to areas of high poverty rates and high joblessness. In turn, many of these neighborhoods changed from areas with high levels of social organization to low social organization, as evidenced by weak social networks and a lower capacity to maintain social control.

Wilson (1994) identifies two major factors that account for joblessness and decline in social organization in these neighborhoods: changes in the economy, especially for young black males, and changes in the class and racial composition of these neighborhoods, due in part to the departure of working residents. Also significant in the development of new poverty areas have been policies of the federal government with regard to urban renewal, location of public housing, and decline in federal funding for urban programs. These policies and programs included "general revenue sharing, urban mass transit, public service jobs and job training, compensatory education, social service block grants, local public works, economic development assistance, and urban development action grants" (Wilson, 1994). With these changes, these neighborhood areas began to show "concentration effects" of poverty and joblessness on basic neighborhood institutions, such as churches, stores, credit institutions, restaurants, recreational facilities, community groups, and professional services. In contrast, neighborhoods with black working families remained stable and socially organized, with fewer social problems found in the ghetto poverty areas, such as violent crime, drug addiction, AIDS, and homelessness (Wilson, 1994).

The studies by Coulton et al. (1990) in Cleveland also illustrate the effects of demographic changes in large urban areas. These authors studied the concentration of poverty in Cleveland, Ohio, demonstrating the growth of high-poverty areas to the point that they cover one-third of the land area of Cleveland. The city is expected to have about two-thirds of its land as poverty areas in the year 2000. The Coulton et al. (1990) study used a mapping procedure to show that the traditional areas of poverty are adjacent to new areas, which in turn are linked to emerging poverty areas. Changes in the city were the result of more people becoming poor and more non-poor residents leaving the city. Some of the consequences associated with living in poverty areas included excessive rates of death, low birth weight, child abuse, infant deaths, delinquency, and teen pregnancy. The social and physical neighborhood environment in inner-city poverty areas displays a "fading inner-city family," increased racial antagonisms, limited social networks, lack of participation in community-wide organizations, lack of employment, high crime rates, deterioration of housing conditions and property values (Wilson, 1996; Coulton et al., 1990). The Coulton et al. (1990) study suggests implications for the practice of social work. "Social workers need practice models that combine their traditional approaches to service delivery with economic redevelopment. . .and mechanisms that re-establish connections between central city residents and distant, suburban job locations."

Demographic and social structural factors since the 1970s have resulted in neighborhood changes that include an increase in urban poverty neighborhoods and minority populated neighborhoods. Using data from the Panel Study of Income Dynamics, Quillian (1999) confirms the work of Wilson (1987, 1994) and Coulton et al. (1990). Quillian's findings demonstrate "(1) the migration of the non-poor away from moderately poor neighborhoods has been a key process in forming new high-poverty neighborhoods, although in the early 1980s increasing poverty rates were also important; and (2) African Americans have moved into predominantly white neighborhoods at a pace sufficient to increase their numbers there, but neighborhoods with increasing black populations tend to lose white populations rapidly."

An exemplary response to the barriers facing single women, members of minority groups, and new immigrants who want to become homeowners is a program initiated by the Fannie Mae company in March 2000 to reduce the gap in home ownership between these groups and middle-class whites (Shepard, 2000). Fannie Mae, formerly the Federal National Mortgage Association, is a government-chartered corporation that provides mortgage capital funding for middle- and low-income people. The corporation's program for underserved populations includes a commitment of $2 trillion over a period of ten years.

The demographic and social changes in inner-city neighborhood communities are associated with unavailability of various forms of capital, including financial, human, social, cultural, environmental, and political capital (Fellin, 1998). All of these forms of capital are in need of development in poor inner-city neighborhoods in order for residents to achieve economic security, health and well-being, civic participation, social interaction, and mutual aid. For example, studies of capital development suggest that neighborhood initiatives are

effective in creating social and cultural capital: positive bonds and relationships and social control among residents. Such initiatives may
include activities of block clubs, police-community programs, youth
programs, mutual help organizations, and churches. These initiatives
can be expected to create human capital, especially in the improvement of local neighborhood schools and the educational attainments of
young people in the community. Cultural capital, especially in communities of color, can be developed by increasing the power and capacity of informal networks of family, extended family kinship groups,
and friends, especially through the cultural strengths of residents that
help them respond to neighborhood violence, economic issues, and
environmental concerns. Social workers can play roles in inner-city
neighborhood capital development strategies that correspond to forms
of capital. These practice roles are found in programs for early childhood and family development (social and human capital), school-
based services (human capital), youth programs (social and human
capital), and economic development (financial capital).

CHANGES IN RESIDENTIAL SEGREGATION IN METROPOLITAN AREAS

Residential segregation by race continues in urban America, but studies of segregation patterns in metropolitan areas over time suggest that
there is some movement toward a more integrated society. A study by
Farley and Frey (1994) provides an illustration of how an ecological
perspective can be used to examine demographic changes and structural characteristics of cities and their influence on residential segregation. Farley and Frey (1994) make use of 1990 census data from 232
U.S. metropolitan areas that had substantial black populations. They
expected declines in segregation due to "reduced discrimination in
housing, economic gains among blacks, and more tolerant attitudes
among whites." Support for this expectation demonstrated considerable change from patterns that prevailed after World War II, when segregated white suburbs developed as a result of the following factors: (1)
mortgage lending policies were discriminatory; (2) blacks who sought
housing in white areas faced intimidation and violence similar to that
occurring during World War I; (3) after World War II, suburbs developed strategies for keeping blacks out; and (4) federally sponsored
public housing encouraged segregation in many cities (Farley & Frey,
1994). These factors changed to some extent in the 1960s and onward,
especially following the passage of the Fair Housing Law of 1968 and
the Community Reinvestment Act of 1977, as well as changes in the

racial attitudes of whites, new housing construction, and the growth of the black middle class.

During the 1980s modest declines in segregation of whites and blacks were found in most metropolitan areas, with the largest changes occurring "in young, southern and western metropolitan areas with significant recent housing construction." Population size of the metropolitan areas had an influence on declines in segregation, with small areas being less segregated than large ones. In looking to the future, Farley and Frey (1994) have concluded that "the American apartheid system may break down slowly, if at all, in the old, large metropolitan areas." Thus, residential segregation of blacks and whites was expected to continue, and to remain well above that for Hispanics and Asians. Federal housing officials believe that the major cause of this segregation continues to be unequal housing opportunities resulting from the actions of mortgage lenders, landlords, and others who discriminate against members of minority groups (Associated Press, 1998c).

Fair housing audits continue to show the presence of discriminatory practices in housing markets, demonstrating that these barriers remain significant (Quillian, 1999). At the same time, whites continue to avoid integration by moving out of transition neighborhoods and into all-white neighborhoods. Quillian suggests that the experiences of African Americans differ from those of other racial/ethnic groups in that "negative stereotypes about other racial and ethnic groups are often not as strong" and "there is less migration into black urban neighborhoods from international destinations than is the case for Hispanic or Asian neighbors." In 1998 the Department of Housing and Urban Development initiated a study of patterns of discrimination in the selling and renting of houses and apartments. At the time of the study, home mortgage denial rates were 26 percent for whites and 53 percent for blacks, even when income levels were taken into account. In March 2000, the U.S. Housing and Urban Development department responded to discrimination by establishing a policy to reduce segregation in government-sponsored housing. The policy requires the nation's 3200 public housing authorities to place tenants from different races and income levels in the same buildings.

GENTRIFICATION

During the diffuse phase of urbanization, some changes in land use within inner-city neighborhoods have been labeled "gentrification." This process has involved the rehabilitation of old dwellings for household use by individual investors and real estate developers. The concept of gentrification is borrowed from the British experience of "young professional people. . .the so-called gentry, buying and renovating small homes and row houses in several central districts" (Choldin, 1985). Gentrification in the United States represents a competition for use of urban land, often with replacement of poor elderly people, seasoned workers, and residents of single-room-occupancy hotels by working-, middle-, and upper-class individuals and families. As a result, some slum neighborhoods and deteriorated housing areas have become fashionable residential areas for young, upper-middle-class whites.

While there has been an increase in the number and scope of gentrified areas in large American cities, what may appear to be a back-to-city movement of population actually involves a relatively small number of people. At the same time, gentrified areas offer the central city an opportunity for revitalization of business and recreational activities. Gentrified areas illustrate a form of succession in which middle- and upper-class whites displace poor people, people of color, and the elderly from their housing. In some instances, however, housing and neighborhood rehabilitation has been carried out by low-income residents and ethnic minority groups, usually in neighborhoods in which the residents have been living (Whyte, 1988). These developments still leave a lack of affordable housing for people who usually live in rooming houses and single rooms, with housing for these individuals drastically reduced by gentrification.

Gentrification usually involves a change in the social class level of residents, higher-priced housing, and new business developments. An old Brooklyn, New York waterfront area known as Dumbo (for Down Under the Manhattan Bridge Overpass) is an example of this process (Sengupta, 1999). Some long-time residents, including many artists, have enjoyed "the area's modest rents, gritty solitude and tiny sliver of state park right on the river" and "are not happy about the possible changes." These proposed changes include "building a fashionable hotel designed by a fashionable French architect, along with a complex of shops, restaurants, movie theaters and a skating rink with glorious river views." Now the area has small printing plants and carpentry shops in old factory buildings, city agency offices, one-bedroom condominium apartments, loft housing units, row houses, a few restaurants, and no grocery stores or banks. Some of the current residents expect that the new real estate developments will increase the number of residents sixfold, as it becomes "a den of upwardly mobile comforts." At this point the neighborhood of Dumbo will have become gentrified.

A somewhat different example of gentrification can be found in the

North Kenwood section of the South Side of Chicago, where City Hall was instrumental in transforming a neighborhood "by knocking down eyesores, readying parcels and recruiting developers" (Johnson, 1999). The development of the Lake Park Pointe Shopping Center includes a supermarket, bank, real estate office, drugstore, dry cleaner, and eyesight clinic. This new "suburbiascape" in the inner city "is gentrification gradually extending its reach into neighborhoods that had been desolate," making North Kenwood a neighborhood "where there is the constant movement of people. It also helps give a community a sense of identity" (Johnson, 1999). The new development also includes gentrification of residential property with remodeling and new construction attracting new residents to the area, including affluent young black professionals.

Chapter 5 Review

In this chapter we discussed three major demographic characteristics of locality-based communities: population size, density, and diversity. The framework for collection of data on these factors by the U.S. Bureau of the Census was presented. We examined the role of immigration in creating cultural diversity in society and local communities. Viewing the phases of urbanization from an ecological perspective assisted the reader in understanding the demographic development of communities. Attention was given to the development of "edge cities" and urban sprawl. The impact of urbanization and suburbanization on rural communities was discussed, with consideration of the development of various forms of capital for residents of non-metropolitan areas. Changes in the demographic and social characteristics of residents in the inner-city neighborhoods, especially in the segregated residential areas of large cities, were identified. Finally, examples of the gentrification of sections of urban areas were presented.

6

Stratification by Social Class

A prominent feature of the social organization of a community is its patterns of social stratification. Social class groups differ in their access and control over resources related to life chances, lifestyles, and quality of life. In addition to social class, other forms of stratification involve characteristics such as race, ethnicity, and religion. Membership in these communities of identification often influences the location of individuals within the various social classes of American society and its locational communities.

Discussions of stratification systems can be found in a number of places in this book. In Chapter 1, social stratification was examined with regard to social groupings in American society. A brief presentation about social class communities was included in Chapter 3. In this chapter we will describe more fully the criteria used to classify and rank people and communities in terms of social class. Next, we will explore the ways in which opportunity structures permit upward social class mobility, constitute barriers to such mobility, or promote downward mobility. We will examine the ways in which groups stratified by race and ethnicity are also stratified according to social class.

113

THE MEANING OF SOCIAL CLASS

Stratification by social class refers to differences among people, often expressed as socioeconomic status (SES), family, social standing, and lifestyles. These indicators of social class are used by demographers and social planners to assign individuals and households to class groups and to describe the class structure of communities. Dimensions of social class also are used by individuals to determine their membership in a social class group, with social class groups serving as identificational communities. The major factors used, both individually and collectively, to determine social class membership include occupation, income, educational attainment, and lifestyle. These indicators of social class can be measured by quantitative means, such as the yearly income earned by an individual or household, the amount of education and academic or professional degrees an individual possesses, and the type of work one does. These indicators often carry with them some degree of status, that elusive term that involves prestige, distinction, and social standing, and is based on a mix of objective and subjective judgments of others as well as one's own self-evaluation.

Various terms characterize the strata or classes within a social class system, but they always carry status connotations. People are located in positions in the class structure that involve various degrees of status, prestige, or privilege. Social class usually involves social roles in the economy and the workplace, domination or subordination in authority structures, the nature of work (blue- or white-collar work), opportunities, and access to resources (Longres, 1995). The most popular designations of classes are names created in the classic studies by Warner and Lunt (1941) and Warner (1949), e.g., variations of upper, middle, and lower classes, such as upper-upper, upper, lower-upper, and so on. Class names from these studies have been modified over the years. For example, Jackman and Jackman (1983) used labels of poor, working class, middle class, upper middle class, and upper class to distinguish social classes from each other. A relatively new class term, underclass, has emerged to distinguish the lowest income group from groups such as the lower class, working class, and working poor.

Issues of classification become apparent as we examine the ways in which occupation, income, education, and lifestyle are selected and measured in order to create social class categories. A major issue involves establishing lines between classes—for example, determining at what point a person belongs to the middle class rather than the lower class. Class strata are not rigid, but are constructed by social scientists, social planners, and human services professionals through data on one or more dimensions of social class. These indicators of social class are identified in the annual Statistical Abstracts prepared by the U.S. Bureau of the Census.

OCCUPATION, INCOME, AND EDUCATION

The U.S. Bureau of the Census defines major occupational categories, with elaborate lists of occupations coded under each category, and makes these data available by census tracts. As a result, an occupational profile can be created for a metropolitan area, a municipality, a neighborhood, or a census tract or block. The major occupational categories are listed below:

- Managerial and professional
- Technical, sales, and administrative support
- Service occupations
- Precision production, craft, and repair
- Operators, fabricators, and laborers
- Farming, forestry, and fishing

Income levels of community residents can be measured in a variety of ways, such as the annual income of the head of the household, the combined income of household members, and/or the income of adults in a household. Income levels are usually presented in Census Bureau publications according to the following categories:

- Less than $5,000
- $5,000 to $9,999
- $10,000 to $14,999
- $15,000 to $19,999
- $20,000 to $24,999
- $25,000 to $34,999
- $35,000 to $49,999
- $50,000 to $74,999
- $75,000 to $99,999
- $100,000 and over

Level of education is measured in terms of highest grade completed. The major census categories are listed below:

- Less than 9th Grade
- 9th to 12th grade
- High school graduate
- Some college, no degree
- Associate degree

- Bachelor's degree
- Graduate or professional degree

Census Bureau data on occupation, education, and/or income make it possible to develop social class profiles of communities of place. A community social class profile may be based on a single variable, such as occupation, or some combination of measures of occupation, income, education, and lifestyle. Community profiles of social class illustrate ways of using aggregate data from the Census Bureau to determine the proportions of people in various social class levels in a given geographic area. It is important to recognize that social class structures of individuals or households may be influenced by other factors, most notably race, ethnicity, family background, and lifestyle. Individuals in racial, ethnic, or religious groups may construct a social class hierarchy through "subjective" rankings within their own specific group. The use of "objective," quantitative indicators of occupation, income, and education may also be misleading due to the arbitrary nature of drawing lines between population groups. In fact, the boundaries of the various social classes are likely to be fluid, as illustrated by the various ways in which city planners, governmental officials, and professional health and social welfare groups create social class profiles of communities and special population groups.

LIFESTYLE

It is reasonable to assume that some combination of occupational position, income, and educational factors influences the lifestyles of individuals and families. Although the correlation between social class and lifestyle may not be perfect, individuals classified as upper class or upper middle class are likely to differ from other classes according to the neighborhoods in which they live, the clothes they wear, the cars they drive, the foods they eat, and the churches they attend. While these behaviors are associated with social class, lifestyle alone is difficult to observe systematically and to measure in order to determine a person's social class position. A major exception is the value and location of a person's residential dwelling as a signifier of social class. Communities in a metropolitan area or municipality are often characterized by home values and the associated prestige. Home value appears to be associated with consumer spending patterns, club memberships, ownership of summer and/or winter homes, travel and vacation styles, types of automobiles, and choices of reading material.

Lifestyles are linked to the idea of prestige or status, concepts associated with behaviors made possible or restricted by income, occupational position, and education. Status or prestige appears to be conferred differently, depending on one's group or subculture. Thus, a recent appraisal of the basis of status noted that "in a socially fragmented, multicultured America, there is no one path to prestige" (*New York Times*, 1998). In a light-hearted article on status in different subcultures, status is defined in various ways:

- For Manhattan parents, a kid who curls up with the classics
- For retirement-villagers, a (still!) valid driver's license
- For long-haul truckers, millions of miles without a scratch
- For the 90's nouveau riche, getting what you want in a snap
- For middle-class 8-year-olds, a stay-at-home mom
- For sunbelt trailer-park residents, movin' on up
- For vegetarians, eating it all raw
- For gourmets, the coolest heat
- For surfers, a key to California's best private beach
- For psychiatrists, really getting inside a head
- For Washington pundits, the last word on absolutely anything
- For CEOs, having a networked secretary
- For Humanities profs, being post-Paglia

(*New York Times*, 1998)

As these formulations of status indicate, status is fluid, changes over time, makes distinctions on the basis of subjective criteria, can be empowering, can be gained and lost, has its symbols, labels, and logos. It may be attached to a pickup truck or a Lincoln Navigator. An example of a "status symbol" of upper-class people is the use of fine linens (Yazigi, 2000). In Manhattan, there is a current vogue of linen parties, where "status-conscious chatelaines fork over anywhere from $100 for a baby pillowcase to the $60,000 that a woman from River House spent on bedding in a single sitting. . . .Park-Avenue-perfect linens typically are traditional: whites and off-whites with two-color monograms and embroidery. Just like the matrons at the turn of the century, women pick out their colors (say, pink and green) from 200 possibilities and patterns (say, eyelash) that will be embroidered by hand. . .one-of-a-kind sheets to match their décor" (Yazigi, 2000).

An illustration of some of the features of status comes from workplace preparations to deal with potential glitches in computers at the beginning of Y2K. To be needed at work on New Year's Eve was considered by some as a symbol of job status. Thus, "an executive's importance in the corporate hierarchy" was attached to skills in dealing with technical problems that were highly unlikely to occur: "In an odd twist in the corporate power equation ... the most important people in an organization are the ones who will be working" (Steinhauer, 1999). In usual holiday seasons lifestyle was more likely to be a status symbol; for example, in New York City, "Power is measured by the number of smart party invites received and the relative coolness of one's vacation plans. Executives take calls from the office, but they do so on their cell phones from a trendy brasserie in Aspen" (Steinhauer, 1999).

One aspect of lifestyle that has traditionally been used to distinguish between the social classes, particularly to differentiate the upper class from other classes, is etiquette. In the words of the French author and art/wine connoisseur Guy de Rothschild (1985), "Class is an imponderable mixture of good taste, refinement, proper clothes and proper manners." "Class" is associated with the idea of "high society" or "the rich"—terms that refer to a social group usually distinguished by history of family background, marriage, manners, and money (Barron, 1990). From the time of the Mayflower until recent years, membership in "Society" has been restricted to people of white, Anglo-Saxon, Protestant ancestry. Recently these restrictions have loosened somewhat, as reflected in the Social Registers and membership rosters of social clubs located in large urban communities.

The lifestyles of members of the upper classes can be described in terms of where they "winter," where they "summer," where they shop, where they buy their jewels, who decorates their houses, who caters their parties, and who buries them (Barron, 1990). One of the problems for "old-timers" and year-round residents in summer places such as the Hamptons is the arrival of the "nouveau riche" who build bigger and more costly mansions that some call "eyesores" (Barstow, 1999a). Another sign of upper-class society is support for philanthropic organizations, such as contributions to the arts and related causes. To be accepted in some upper-class groups, the important thing is not how much money one has or how much one makes, but how much one gives "back to the community" in time and money.

Generally speaking, upward occupational and residential mobility has been associated with changes in lifestyle. At the same time, lifestyles associated with the upper classes, such as home furnishings, food tastes, recreational pursuits, and clothing styles have "trickled down" to the lower social class groups through outlet stores, K-Mart, and Wal-Mart, television shows by Martha Stewart, and fashions by Tommy Hilfiger, Nautica, and Nike.

There is some indication that members of social classes seek to reproduce themselves, especially within middle-class and upper-class families. An example of this process is examined by Thomas (1991) in his description of "young society" in Washington, D.C. These young professionals, "the nouveau WASP wanna-bes," are "well-to-do thirtyish professionals" who attended the "right" schools and colleges, are active in the same cultural and charitable organizations and social events. They appear at the same club-sponsored parties, have linkages to young socialites in New York and Boston, and have a high rate of marriage within the same social crowd. Members of this young society have a lifestyle that strongly resembles that of their parents, and in this sense, the upper class is reproducing itself.

SOCIAL CLASSES AS COMMUNITIES OF IDENTIFICATION

Americans tend to associate themselves with a social class. The basis for their identification may be one or more of the social class indicators discussed above. Most Americans who live in metropolitan areas reside in communities that are diverse in terms of social class. However, people usually reside in homogeneous social class neighborhoods, when class is measured by objective and/or subjective factors. Subjective concepts such as class consciousness, class awareness, class identification, and cognitive maps of class, have been used to describe the ways in which people consider social class as a basis for community identification.

The concept of social class appears to have considerable impact on the way people think of themselves. For example, using residents' reports on their subjective interpretations of social class, Jackman and Jackman (1983) found that "social class is a major source of group identity for most Americans." Of special interest is the Jackmans' finding that Americans perceive classes as "a graded series of social communities." Their research involved a national sample of respondents who identified themselves as belonging to one of five class categories: poor, working class, middle class, upper middle class, and upper class. Respondents used not only educational attainment, occupation, and income to determine their class position, but also cultural factors such as lifestyle and "beliefs and feelings" in making this judgment. Thus, class was observed to be of significance to respondents, and "class has a subjective meaning that transcends the economic sphere and incorporates factors normally associated with status groups," such as education, beliefs, lifestyle, and family. In regard to family, the occupation of the male had the most important influence on class identification, even in households in which women were employed outside the home. People indicated that they preferred to live in areas in which their neighbors belonged to the same class, and that they tended to have friends of similar occupational status. In this sense, the study's findings supported the idea that social classes are social communities.

THE UNDERCLASS

In recent years social scientists and human service professionals have given considerable attention to people who live in poverty, or move in and out of poverty, who are usually unemployed or employed on an irregular basis at low wages, and/or who are unskilled workers. This group has been labeled the underclass. Individuals and families in this group appear to be outside, or under, the traditional social class hierarchy. Members of the underclass are likely to be restricted by social and economic barriers from upward mobility into the traditional class structure. People in the underclass are likely to be confined to their position by a number of societal forces, such as the educational system, the economic system, and the health and social welfare system. The underclass includes people who reside mainly in dilapidated inner-city nonwhite and white neighborhood areas, in rental property, on the "streets" or in homeless shelters, or in poor rural communities. People in an underclass also reside in small and mid-size cities in census tracts where at least 40 percent of the residents are poor and at least two thirds of the residents are white.

Four themes have generally been used to describe the underclass: economic, social-psychological, behavioral, and ecological (Devine & Wright, 1993). Individuals and families in an underclass move in and out of poverty, and most poverty and underclass status is not intergenerational. At the same time, a high proportion of people in the underclass are chronically poor. Descriptions of people entrenched in the underclass usually emphasize the discrepancy between the values and norms of this population and the rest of American society. Negative orientations toward education and employment, coupled with alienation, social isolation, and negative perceptions of conventional society, are attributed to people in the underclass, sometimes without foundation. In terms of behavior, underclass people are pictured as displaying "antisocial, deviant, dysfunctional, or threatening behaviors; criminal activity, drug and alcohol abuse, welfare dependency, joblessness, teenage pregnancy, and so on" (Devine & Wright, 1993). Finally, people with the economic, social-psychological, and behavioral characteristics described above have become concentrated in central city neighborhoods and in rural poverty areas.

Understanding the plight of the underclass is particularly important for human service practitioners. Service workers participate in a variety of programs directed toward alleviating the problems of these individuals and in changing the conditions that keep them in a state of poverty. Housing programs, job training programs, and other social welfare programs have been developed to help underclass people move onto the traditional social class ladder. These programs have helped some of these individuals move into mainstream society, yet the presence of a substantial underclass group within urban and rural communities continues to be a major social and community problem.

SOCIAL MOBILITY

As already noted, placement of an individual or a household into a social class category is arbitrary because class groupings are constructed, not predetermined. Lines can be drawn, however, between groupings as a way of examining the extent to which class groups become larger or smaller over time. In recent years, some social scientists have maintained that economic conditions have favored the growth of the upper middle and upper classes. At the same time, many middle-class people have moved downward and out of the middle class. These two forms of class movement appear to have led to a shrinking of the middle class, with some people moving up and out, and others downward into a lower class.

Human services professionals are interested in social mobility from two points of view. First, is the American social class system an open system, or does it maintain barriers to upward mobility? Second, what can be done to facilitate the upward movement of individuals at the bottom of the social class ladder in order to improve their "life chances" and quality of life? A major goal of human services professionals is to help create an open class system by providing services and resources for people in disadvantaged positions in society, especially individuals living in poverty. Since this part of the population is disproportionately represented by people with ethnic minority status, social workers are expected to work toward elimination of racial barriers to opportunity in occupations, income, and education.

SOCIAL CLASS AND ETHNIC MINORITY GROUPS

Ethnic minority groups in the United States have been designated by the Equal Employment Commission, established by the Equal Rights Act of 1964, as African Americans, Asian Americans, Native Americans, and Hispanic Americans. These groups have minority status in a white majority society. Hence, in stratification terms, each group constitutes a non-dominant class location in relation to prestige, power, and privilege. At the same time individuals and households within these minority groups may be classified with regard to their position in the social class structure. Thus, there is an ethnic stratification system based on race/ethnicity that intersects with social class position in the society (Devore & Schlesinger, 1996). Generalizations about the social class of ethnic minority groups are problematic, since each of the major groups is made up of many specific groups that have diverse characteristics, especially with regard to culture, lifestyles, and social class location.

Longres (1995) highlights the fact that inequalities among ethnic minorities, in terms of the socioeconomic status of these groups, remain when comparisons are made to the SES levels of the white majority. Longres indicates that these inequalities are different for two groups of ethnic minorities. One group, comprising African Americans, Native Americans, Mexican Americans, and Puerto Ricans, appears to be disproportionately located at the bottom of the social class ladder. A second group, mainly of Chinese, Japanese, Filipinos, and other Asians, are somewhat higher on the ladder but face barriers to movement into the top rungs of the social class structure. Residential patterns reveal social class differences within these ethnic minority groups and between them and white majority groups. The first category of ethnic minority groups are more likely to live in poor ghetto neighborhoods and to be segregated from the white population. Members of the second category are more likely to live in middle-class residential areas, with a small proportion integrated into upper-class neighborhoods.

By using data from the Census Bureau to develop social class profiles for communities, we can depict the relationship between ethnic minority status and the class structure. For example, communities in a metropolitan area can be described in social class terms, and then data on race/ethnicity can be used to show the location of ethnic minorities in these communities. A similar type of analysis can be done for neighborhoods in a municipality. Analyses of this type tend to show a growing African American middle class, with some members integrated into white neighborhoods and others residing in mainly black middle-class suburban communities (Nathan, 1991). Similar patterns have been found in neighborhoods of Hispanic Americans in middle-class residential areas. Asian Americans tend to be the most integrated into middle-class and upper-class residential areas, although there is a growing representation of African Americans within these neighborhoods also.

African Americans and Social Class

The African American population in the United States encompasses more than 30 million people, approximately 12 to 13 percent of the total population. A small increase in the percentage of African Americans to 14 or 15 percent is expected by 2050. Studies of African Americans have focused on the discrimination and oppression that restricts social class mobility for members of this minority group. Special problems related to social class for African Americans in inner-city poverty areas have been identified by Wilson (1996) in his examination of the new urban poverty of the ghetto poor "when work disappears." Wilson observes that the "life chances" of African Americans have historically been influenced by a mixture of class and race factors, of racial discrimination and oppression, and class subordination, leaving them disproportionately located in the lower levels of the American class structure. At the same time, Wilson (1978, 1987, 1996) contends that as a racist society becomes less racist by virtue of changes in its policies and laws, the economic dimension of social class becomes equally important in determining the life chances of minority people. Under Wilson's formulation, old barriers to mobility within the class structure imposed by race continue, but there are new barriers created by the economic conditions of society, especially the disappearance of work in inner-city residential areas.

Even as economic conditions have influenced the social class location of inner-city African American residents, moving many into an underclass position, others have moved upward into the middle and upper middle classes. Occupational and income changes have often come about from increases in educational levels, leading to social mobility and residential movement out of the city into suburban communities. This movement is often attributed to the benefits of the civil rights movement in the late 1960s. New laws created a "climate" for advancement, so that about one third of African Americans have moved into mainstream, middle-class America (Queralt, 1996). Thernstrom and Thernstrom (1997) point out that the "rise of the black middle class" is most apparent from 1940 onwards, with both black men and women moving into middle-class occupations. Affirmative action programs have helped raise the percentage of African Americans within the middle class. Big gains have been made in "female-dominated" professions such as teaching, social work, and nursing (Thernstrom & Thernstrom, 1997). Dramatic increases have also occurred in the number of African Americans in law, medicine, college teaching, and engineering, and in government employment.

Surveys in 1996 indicated that about 40 percent of African Americans consider themselves to be members of the middle class, compared to about 70 percent of whites. This movement into a large black middle class still leaves a large group in the working class and a sizable group with incomes below the poverty level (Queralt, 1996; Thernstrom &

Thernstrom, 1997). A U.S. Census report for incomes in 1998 showed 26.1 percent of African American households below the poverty line of $16,655 for a four-person household, compared to 12.7 percent of the total population and 2.5 times greater than the rate for whites (Uchitelle, 1999b). The median income for African American households in 1998 was approximately the same as the 1997 figure of $25,400, with the median for non-Hispanic whites at $42,439 in 1998.

At the other end of the social class continuum, increasing numbers of African Americans meet the customary criteria for classification as members of the upper class. A separate social class structure composed solely of African Americans also can be identified. The emergence of a separate black upper-class group is dramatized in the work of Graham (1999), *Our Kind of People: Inside America's Black Upper Class*. Graham makes the case that over many years a small group of African Americans has emerged into an exclusively black "upper class" group. His evidence for his picture of a black upper class comes from examination of social organizations such as Jack and Jill for children, social groups such as the Boule and the Links, sororities and fraternities affiliated with educational institutions, and vacation enclaves such as Sag Harbor in New York and Oaks Bluff on Martha's Vineyard. Graham (1999) concludes that a group of prosperous black Americans "form an extensive and cohesive group with distinct traditions and a strong sense of identity" (Lee, 1999).

While there exists a group of African Americans with occupational, income, and educational status equivalent to upper-class status, this has not meant that members of the white upper class have viewed these individuals as belonging to the same social class. Only a very small group of African Americans appear to be regarded by members of the white upper class as belonging to the upper class (Williams, 1999). For example, black athletes, actors, and business owners may be wealthy, but they are not always accepted into upper-class white "society." This same phenomenon holds true for members of other minority groups as well as some members of white ethnic groups. In the minds of some people, membership in the upper class remains exclusively WASP.

Asian Americans and Social Class

Asian Americans constitute more than 3.3 percent of the total U.S. population, and by the year 2050 are expected to be nearly 10 percent. There are at least 29 subgroups in the U.S., with the three largest Asian groups being Chinese, Filipino, and Japanese (Lie, 1999). Asian Americans continue to be regarded by many people as a "model minority" group—one whose members have "made it" in this "land of opportunity" (Cheng & Yang, 1996). This is so because Asian Americans as a group have achieved higher economic and educational achievements than the average levels of the U.S. population. Census statistics demonstrate this success in terms of occupational status, income, and education, especially among the largest Asian groups. The U.S. Bureau of the Census reported that in 1998 the median income of Asian Americans was higher than that of other ethnic minority groups, as well as the non-Hispanic white population. Still, a report entitled "The State of Asian Pacific Populations: Transforming Race Relations" showed that "old stereotypes cause them (Asians) to be seen as perpetual foreigners" (Fletcher, 2000). Both of these facts overlook the ethnic and socioeconomic diversity of these groups and the economic and social problems of some Asian Americans, especially refugee groups. The success and assimilation of many Asians in American society obscures the problems faced by new immigrants.

The diversity of Asian American subgroups makes it difficult to generalize about their place in the American social class structure. This difficulty has become more pronounced as a result of the almost doubling of this group between 1980 and 1990 as a result of migration from mainland China, Taiwan, Hong Kong, Vietnam, Cambodia, Laos, the Philippines, Japan, South Korea, Micronesia, and the Indian subcontinent (Queralt, 1996). The different locations of these groups in the social class structure are illustrated in the case of Los Angeles, where two migration streams occurred between 1970 and 1990, one of highly educated Asian immigrants moving into professional and managerial positions, and the other of semiskilled and unskilled individuals in manufacturing and services (Cheng & Yang, 1996). By 1990 the Los Angeles region had the largest Asian American population (more than 1.3 million) in the United States. While at times confirming the model minority image, statistics from the Los Angeles region also show the considerable diversity among and within subgroups. Still, the occupational status, income, and level of education of the total group is higher than that of the white population. Data on occupational mobility also confirm the model minority thesis, even though some subgroups do not show upward mobility (Cheng & Yang, 1996). However, Cheng and Yang note that "discrimination still inhibits Asian American progress," especially for new immigrants and refugees.

Hispanic/Latino Americans and Social Class

Hispanic/Latino Americans made up approximately 9 percent of the U.S. population in 1990, and are expected to constitute approximately

25 percent of the population by 2050. The largest groups are Mexican American (64 percent), mainland Puerto Rican (10.5 percent), and Cuban American (4.9 percent) (Queralt, 1996). The length of time in the United States for this group varies from several generations to recent immigrants. Because the Latino population is composed of people from more than 20 different countries, and includes people identified as white, as mixed-race, and people of color, generalizations about the total group are usually not appropriate. Within Hispanic/Latino groups, the patterns of social class status for Cuban Americans tend to be higher than those of Puerto Ricans, whereas Mexican Americans in the Southwest tend to have better employment opportunities, and hence higher social class position, than most other Latino groups. In general, the Latino population is lower on all measures of social class, in terms of occupational status, income, and education, when compared to whites, African Americans, and Asian Americans (Queralt, 1996).

Native Americans and Social Class

Estimates of the size of the Native American population in the United States, which includes American Indians, Eskimos, and Aleuts, range from 1.4 to 1.9 million people, less than one percent of the total population. Approximately 542 American Indian tribes are represented in this major ethnic minority group. There is considerable variation between tribes in terms of culture and language, with the largest groups being the Cherokee, Navajo, Chippewa, and Sioux (Longres, 1995). Less than one third of the Native American population resides on reservations, with about half of the total group living in rural areas and the other half in urban areas. While there is evidence of improvement in socioeconomic status of Native Americans, especially since the 1960s, they continue to be the most disadvantaged group in American society (Queralt, 1996). A high proportion have low educational levels, a low standard of living, high rates of unemployment, poor housing, absence of capital assets, and incomes below the federal poverty line (Locke, 1992).

Chapter 6 Review

As discussed in this chapter, stratification by social class is a prominent feature of communities throughout the United States. The examination of the social class patterns in a local community can assist us in developing an ecological perspective. The meaning of social class in the United States was explored, highlighting the inequalities among people in terms of socioeconomic status and lifestyles. Classification of people and communities by occupation, income, and education provides a basic foundation for determining social class levels. These factors, in turn, are associated with lifestyles and social mobility, with social class serving as a major source of group identity. Finally, the special impact of social class factors on people of color was discussed, setting the stage for the examination in Chapter 8 of the emergence of social class and ethnic minority neighborhoods.

7

Neighborhood Communities

A neighborhood is a community of place within a larger community, usually a city or other incorporated area. Residential housing is
the most prominent feature of a neighborhood. As spatial units, neighborhoods may also have other physical features, such as parks, schools,
churches, recreational facilities, service facilities (police and fire stations), or businesses. When neighborhoods have some of these physical and social features as well as residential housing, they may be
referred to as "enclaves," especially if the residents share a distinctive
lifestyle (Abrahamson, 1996).

Neighborhoods are regarded as communities because the residents
constitute a social group involved in some level of social interaction—
some "set of connections" such as "social connections (as in kin, friend,
and acquaintance networks), functional connections (as in the production, consumption, and transfer of goods and services), cultural
connections (as in religion, tradition, or ethnic identity), or circumstantial connections (as in economic status or lifestyle)" (Chaskin,
1997). These social interactions and connections provide a basis for
creating primary group relationships, for establishing organizations,

for obtaining resources for daily living, and for maintaining a collective identity and sense of community. As a result, neighborhoods usually are not only locational communities but also identificational/interest communities.

Neighborhood communities form a significant part of the social environment of individuals, families, and other small groups, and they influence human behavior in important ways, such as child and family development, socialization, education, and social control. Developing an understanding of neighborhood communities contributes to our knowledge of bio-psycho-social development of individuals and families necessary for generalist and interpersonal social work practice. Neighborhoods also provide an important context for social work practice at community and organizational levels, especially with regard to community building—that is, "activities, practices, and policies that support and foster positive connections among individuals, groups, organizations, neighborhoods, and geographic and functional communities" (Weil, 1996). Community building involves practice strategies of social planning, social and economic development, community organizing, social action, and empowerment practice. All of these require an understanding of the structure and processes of neighborhood communities. Increasingly, neighborhoods are the locus for community-based services for people with special needs, such as people with developmental disabilities, mental and physical disabilities, people in poverty, and older adults.

NEIGHBORHOOD BOUNDARIES AND SOCIAL MAPPING

The physical boundaries of neighborhoods may or may not be precise. Boundaries are determined by various groups of people, including professional planners, political parties, health and social service agencies, educational systems, and neighborhood residents. Boundaries of neighborhoods establish a basis for using census tract data. Using such data, neighborhoods can be described in terms of size and density of the population, ethnic and/or racial composition, level of employment, age structure, family composition, income, and educational levels of residents. In large cities such as New York City, Chicago, or Los Angeles, several neighborhoods are likely to be grouped into large districts or areas that may also be called neighborhoods. An important aspect of neighborhoods, therefore, is the size of the spatial area and the number of residents living within a defined geographic area.

Professional service providers and governmental agencies usually define neighborhoods by grouping together a number of census tracts, guided by the boundaries of a local school, a political district, a sub-division, and/or a service area. Social agencies, in particular, define the boundaries of a neighborhood for service purposes. These agencies seek to establish target populations for neighborhood services, to gain legitimacy within the neighborhood, and to create linkages to formal organizations and resources in the broader community (Chaskin, 1997). Studies by Queralt and Witte (1998a, 1998b, 1999) establish neighborhood boundaries by census tracts in order to identify the supply of center-based and family child-care services, to study socioeconomically distressed neighborhoods in relation to child-care services, and to map areas in terms of unmet needs. Census tracts are considered areas that most closely approximate residential neighborhoods, since tracts are "small, relatively permanent statistical subdivisions of a county...designed to be homogeneous with respect to population characteristics, economic status, and living conditions" (Queralt & Witte, 1998b).

After neighborhood boundaries have been identified by health and welfare agencies, especially in low-income neighborhoods, service providers may use community asset mapping to obtain "a geographically organized catalog of the resources and assets of a community in relation to the community's needs" (O'Looney, 1996). Three categories of maps have been used by O'Looney to assess neighborhood community needs and assets:

1. Maps that outline the needs and deficiencies of communities
2. Maps that outline the strengths and capacities of communities
3. Maps that outline the cautionary history of community figures

The first category represents a deficit approach: a ritual of needs assessment and deficit mapping traditionally used to allocate social service resources. This "deficit" approach typically emphasizes needs and allocates resources without attention to or use of the strengths and assets of communities. An example of a deficit approach is Queralt and Witte's (1999) demonstration of the use of Geographic Information Systems to "map 'deficit' scores to identify geographic areas of unmet needs or service deficits in relation to child care." These investigators do, however, also focus on strengths of neighborhoods in terms of child-care supply and socioeconomic conditions, e.g., level of socioeconomic distress.

The second category of maps is similar to the strengths perspectives developed in the works of McKnight and Kretzmann (1993) and Saleebey (1997). McKnight and Kretzmann emphasize "capacity-focused" community development based on mapping the assets of individual residents, local associations, and formal institutions. O'Looney's second category of mapping focuses on the collection of data on the following assets:

- The number and types of places where people gather for fun or good works;
- The number and locations of people who have skills that are being underutilized;
- The existence and location of businesses that play positive roles in the community;
- The number, type, and location of community volunteers;
- The number and type of civic groups, clubs, and neighborhood organizations;
- The number and location of people who are willing to exchange services with others.

As O'Looney (1996) notes, "At the public level of neighborhood development, taking a strengths perspective has practical implications for the way neighborhoods attempt to engage outsiders in their cause and the way outsiders attempt to support neighborhoods." From this perspective, a strengths-focused approach can use maps to locate the following:

- Residents who could potentially act in the capacity of resident service workers, and who are identified as being from within a community rather than from outside;
- Residents who could contribute to the governance of human service agencies;
- Residents who could engage other natural helpers in the delivery of services;
- Existing neighborhood facilities and organizations for neighborhood-centered delivery of services;
- Areas where support of new or emerging neighborhood organizations is needed.

The third category of maps is most closely related to the idea of stories turned into maps. Maps of this sort attempt to "tell the tragic stories of a community," indicating historical landmarks, places where mishaps and misunderstandings have occurred, where buildings have been destroyed, and sites of events whose memory produces a "sense of tragic loss." Some examples might be Columbine High School in Colorado, the Federal Building in Oklahoma, the house where Elian Gonzales lived in Little Havana, Miami, Florida.

Maps of neighborhoods often have boundaries determined by residents. These neighborhoods tend to vary from a small area of one or a few blocks (an immediate or nuclear neighborhood) to an extended or community neighborhood encompassing a large number of blocks. Sometimes residents define the boundaries established by the city and other formal organizations, but often, boundaries of a neighborhood may be defined subjectively and guided by the "mental maps" of individuals. A person may define a neighborhood as a small spatial area when referring to social relationships, and a larger area when referring to social institutions. These mental maps are usually formed by reference to physical space as well as a resident's view of the social institutions in the area, such as schools, churches, neighborhood associations, and/or the area in which social interactions occur, such as neighboring and other social activities. An individual's mental map of a neighborhood may also include negative "images of crime and violence, of joblessness and welfare dependency, of gangs and drugs and homelessness, of vacant and abandoned land and buildings" (McKnight & Kretzmann, 1993).

Chaskin's (1997) review of the literature on factors that influence an individual's definition of neighborhood boundaries provides insights that can enhance our understanding of neighborhoods. Residents are likely to define neighborhoods and the area of their social relationships in terms of mental maps that are related to "who they are" within the neighborhood, the community, and society—e.g., African Americans, older people, unemployed persons, unmarried persons, and long-term residents. People in urban neighborhoods tend to define neighborhoods as smaller areas than individuals in suburban areas, as do women with small children and long-term residents. The significance of the relationships of residents in a neighborhood to the broader community in defining boundaries is illustrated in studies of Hispanic and African American groups in Los Angeles (Chaskin, 1997). These ethnic minority groups, when compared to non-ethnic upper-class residents, have been found to possess detailed perceptions of their immediate neighborhoods and restricted, less detailed images of the broader community.

NEIGHBORHOOD APPEARANCE

Neighborhoods differ not only in spatial area and population size, but also in architecture and appearance, type of residential dwellings (single, multiple), and presence of nonresidential buildings, such as schools, churches, stores, service facilities, and offices. Physical features of neighborhoods take on meaning when outsiders and/or residents use them to describe a neighborhood in positive or negative terms. Thus, people often identify neighborhoods in terms of their physical appearance, characterizing them as run-down, well kept, beautiful, nice, fancy, old, new, clean, or dirty. These descriptions are images people have of their own neighborhoods, as well as outsiders' views from walking or driving through a neighborhood.

In some cities, residents attempt to maintain the appearance of their neighborhood by enforcing municipal rules, such as ordinances requiring mowing or cutting of weeds; by enacting zoning laws involving modification and construction of buildings; and by enlisting the help of homeowners' associations or organized voluntary groups to clean up the neighborhood. Other neighborhoods, especially areas described as slums, are marked by litter, broken glass, and boarded-up abandoned dwellings that leave an impression that no one cares about the neighborhood. In these areas there appears to be a strong association between physical deterioration, low levels of personal safety, and high crime rates.

Location is a distinguishing feature of a neighborhood. Traditionally neighborhoods have been categorized as being located in rural, suburban, or urban areas, in central cities or suburban communities, in inner-city or transitional areas, in areas adjoining central cities, or in small towns or villages. Neighborhoods often take on a reputation and a name in keeping with their location as well as characteristics of the residents, such as social class, religion, and race or ethnicity.

NEIGHBORHOOD AS PRIMARY GROUP

Most people residing in neighborhoods engage in some level of social interaction and develop social relationships that make the neighborhood a primary group for its members. A neighborhood may be viewed as a special kind of primary group, while having properties similar to other primary groups, such as the family and other small groups. These properties include face-to-face, relatively permanent, diffused, affective, and non-instrumental relationships. Individuals engage in different levels of primary group relationships in neighborhoods, ranging from the isolated individual with limited or no social interaction with neighbors, to the socially active individual who engages in both informal and formal social activities. Neighborhoods provide opportunities for different kinds of interpersonal networks and group interactions that are primary in nature, such as parent groups, peer age groups, gangs, social club groups, athletic groups, or neighborhood tavern groups. Members of some of these groups congregate at particular locations, such as parks, drugstores, coffee shops, or schools. These primary groups usually draw their membership from people living in the neighborhood.

Neighborhoods as primary groups can be characterized in terms of various levels and types of social interaction. In some communities, neighbors may serve as good friends, providing for intimate, close, intense, and frequent social relationships. Or neighbors may be friendly, helpful, good neighbors, and yet not fulfill the roles played by friend or kinship groups. There are usually clear distinctions in social roles among neighbor, friend, and kin, although sometimes these roles overlap. Examples of neighboring including visiting, dining together, borrowing tools or food, celebrating holidays or other events, holding block parties, exchanging services such as baby-sitting or help with household tasks, driving, and giving advice and information. Residents often establish informal rules or expectations about how neighbors should behave. These rules, or norms, appear to differ among social class levels and among cultural and ethnic minority groups.

The nature of interpersonal networks and relationships in neighborhoods is influenced by factors such as gender, age, ethnicity, religion, family composition, and socioeconomic status. In addition, residential stability is associated with friendships and social interaction within neighborhoods, in contrast to low levels of interaction in transitional, high-mobility neighborhoods. Ethnic enclaves as neighborhoods often lead to high social interaction among segregated groups and high levels of local neighborhood identification and attachment (Chaskin, 1997). The extent to which individuals are integrated into the larger community and society appears to affect the intensity of local neighborhood interaction. Thus, residents who are most integrated into the broader community, such as people belonging to a high social class, may have larger, but less active, neighborhood social networks. Chaskin's (1997) study of neighborhood social interaction found that African Americans "tend to have neighbor networks that are both more 'spatially proximate' and stronger in that they are more intimate, have endured longer, and are characterized by more frequent contact."

An emerging form of neighborhood social interaction is based on the use of e-mail (Kugel, 1999). An example is a neighborhood in Cambridge, Massachusetts, in which a newcomer visited neighbors and created a spreadsheet with everyone's name, street address, and e-mail address. As a result, neighbors began communicating with each other about topics such as getting rid of bats, finding a car mechanic, fund raising, and training pets. The functions of neighborhood watch groups could be incorporated into such e-mail neighborhood groups. In the case of the Cambridge neighborhood group, a member states that "We're a community in a whole new sense—one that solves problems and shares news, both good and not so good" (Kugel, 1999).

NEIGHBORHOOD FUNCTIONS

Neighborhoods serve a number of community functions, providing for a set of "connections" that involve social interaction, social relationships, and social networks. These functions make the neighborhood a sociability arena by virtue of opportunities for visiting/neighboring, avenues for gaining information, advice, mutual aid, and social participation. Mutual aid is available in neighborhoods on an informal basis, usually not requiring payment for goods and services, but on an exchange basis. Thus, neighborhoods may provide resources not otherwise so readily or immediately available, such as responses to emergencies. Of course, residents in local neighborhood communities vary in the extent to which they utilize resources from informal sources, such as neighbors, in contrast to the purchase of services from formal organizations. Communication patterns vary in neighborhoods. The neighborhood often provides opportunities for exchange of information and resources between neighbors and provides a basis for mutual aid. Neighborhoods often serve as a basis of social identity and status for their residents. Names given to neighborhoods convey an identity to outsiders as well as residents, an identity that may indicate some level of socioeconomic status, religious identification, or ethnic group status. Neighborhoods often acquire their names from elementary schools, religious congregations, real estate developers, political precincts, or parks.

Increasingly, social service and governmental agencies as well as the private corporate sector, such as bank and real estate organizations, look to neighborhoods as an organizational base. Neighborhood block clubs and associations are a prime example of voluntary associations based on neighborhood residence. These groups have formal and informal leaders that assist the neighborhood in acting on its own behalf and linking it to the resources of the wider community. These groups form the basis for empowerment of residents, especially in connecting them to organizations in the broader community, including governmental agencies, private businesses, and religious congregations. Neighborhoods serve as the social context for membership in voluntary associations such as interest groups, social-movement groups, client organizations, tenant organizations, parent-teacher associations, and political groups. Many private- and public-sector organizations use neighborhoods as the social units for communication, as sources of volunteers for social programs, and as providers of input and social support. For example, banks, social agencies, and hospitals create voluntary neighborhood groups as links to their formal organizations and as a basis for legitimization and support.

An important function of many neighborhoods is socialization based on *social organization*—that is, "the extent to which the residents of a neighborhood are able to maintain effective social control and realize their common values" (Wilson, 1994). Neighborhood social organization concerns "the prevalence, strength, and interdependence of social networks and the extent of collective supervision that the residents direct and the personal responsibility they assume in addressing neighborhood problems" (Wilson, 1994). Social organization in neighborhoods is sustained by formal organizations, such as law enforcement, churches, and neighborhood associations, and by informal social controls, such as friendships, social networks, parental supervision and involvement, and social cohesion. Safety in a neighborhood is of primary concern to residents of inner-city ghetto poor neighborhoods, with major challenges to the social organization of a neighborhood coming from violent crime, drug addiction, family instability, joblessness, and decline in social institutions, social and health services, and economic opportunities (Wilson, 1994). One response to these problems has been community development programs that seek to improve the institutional supports and informal family and neighborhood supports for these neighborhood communities.

In middle- and upper-class neighborhoods the function of social control has been enhanced by the creation of "defended neighborhoods" with increased law enforcement, gated communities, neighborhood watch groups, and parental involvement in regulating behaviors in the neighborhood. Studies of "defended neighborhoods" support the idea that when these neighborhoods are mostly white and experience an in-migration of members of ethnic minority groups, this demographic change predicts racially motivated crime directed at minorities. Thus, a study of white "defended" neighborhoods in New York City found that "victimization of blacks, Asians, and Latinos tends to be higher in areas where whites have long been the predominant racial groups, particularly when these areas experience significant growth in minority population" (Green, Strolovitch, & Wong, 1998).

One explanation for the variations found in neighborhoods with respect to criminal violence has been the influence of low socioeconomic status and residential instability of neighborhoods in creating high levels of violence. A study by Sampson, Raudenbush, and Earls (1997) explored the question of why a concentration of poverty and instability leads to high levels of violence. These authors found that neighborhoods with collective efficacy—that is, neighborhoods whose residents share common values and are able to maintain effective social control—have lower levels of violence. Thus, when neighbors use informal mechanisms, such as conditions of mutual trust, solidarity, and social cohesion, to regulate the behavior of people in a neighborhood, collective efficacy is created and the risk of violence reduced. Residential stability and home ownership are conditions that lead to social control. While informal social controls help reduce violence, the activities of formal organizations, such as community policing, as well as improvements in the economic conditions of residents, are important forces that promote safety and reduced crime and violence in neighborhoods.

NEIGHBORHOOD TYPES

A number of dimensions of neighborhoods involve the behaviors of individuals, families, and small groups engaged in social interaction and social participation in informal social networks and in formal organizations. We have identified some of the primary group characteristics of neighborhoods in terms of the kinds of social relationships that may occur within this geographic area. We have also specified some of the population characteristics and organizational factors that can be used to describe neighborhoods, such as social class and racial composition. Other dimensions of neighborhoods include residents' identification with and attachment to the neighborhood, informal networks and formal organization as sources of social and economic resources, linkages of individuals and organizations in neighborhoods to the broader community, the stability/mobility of neighborhoods in terms of population turnover, values held by residents, economic levels of neighborhood residents, and segregation/integration in terms of race and ethnicity. Each of these dimensions can be used singly or in combinations to distinguish one neighborhood from another, thus delineating types of neighborhoods. For example, the average level of social interaction in a neighborhood can be used to "type" a neighborhood as one with high, medium, or low social interaction. Neighborhoods can also be typed by racial composition in terms of segregated or integrated neighborhoods.

The following models represent some major "ideal" types of neighborhoods developed in the social sciences and social work, using various combinations of neighborhood dimensions.

MODEL ONE: SOCIAL IDENTITY, SOCIAL INTERACTION, AND LINKAGES

This model distinguishes neighborhoods on the basis of social identity, social interaction, and linkages to the wider community.

People develop a sense of identification with their place of residence that can be measured along a continuum from negative to neutral to positive (minimal to high). Identification with a neighborhood may be expressed through the concepts of community attachment and social integration. Individuals also vary in terms of the degree and type of social interaction with neighbors, and again, this factor can be measured on a scale of low to high levels of interaction. Both individuals and organizations in a neighborhood may engage in activities beyond the neighborhood in order to gain external resources, to establish connections with other community groups such as the local community government, and to help solve neighborhood problems. The neighborhood types constructed by Warren and Warren (1977) through reference to social identity, social interaction, and linkages continue to provide a useful framework for assessing neighborhoods for social work practice. Six neighborhood types are identified: integral, parochial, diffuse, stepping-stone, transitory, and anomic.

Neighborhood communities in which residents have a high level of positive identity with their neighborhood, high level of social interaction, and strong linkages beyond the neighborhood are labeled integral neighborhoods. Parochial neighborhoods are those with high identity and social interaction but low level of linkages. Integral and parochial neighborhoods are classified as traditional neighborhoods. A second set of neighborhood types, called mobile neighborhoods, includes stepping-stone neighborhoods with low identity, high social interaction, and high linkages, and transitory neighborhoods with high linkages, low identity, and low social interaction. A third set of neighborhoods, called mass society neighborhoods, includes diffuse neighborhoods with high identity but low interaction and low linkages, and anomic neighborhoods that are low on all dimensions. Some of the benefits and limitations of these neighborhood types are described below.

Traditional Neighborhoods

1. The integral neighborhood has a high capacity to identify its problems and to take action because of its internal organization and its links to the outside community. While this type of neighborhood may be easier for the higher social classes to create, it can be found not only in white-collar suburbs but also in inner-city areas and blue-collar industrial communities.
2. Due to its strong group identity, based on factors such as race, social class, age, and physical isolation, the parochial neighborhood

has social integration, strong commitment to the locality, and a capacity to get things done without outside help. On the negative side, its functions for residents may be limited in resource procurement by the lack of linkages to the larger community.

Mobile Neighborhoods

3. Stepping-stone neighborhoods are areas in which people are highly mobile occupationally, socially, and residentially, and hence, not strongly committed to their current neighborhood. They anticipate relocation connected with career moves. A special concern for this neighborhood type is fulfilling the needs of individuals who do not move and look to their neighbors to establish long-term friendships.
4. Transitory neighborhoods have high membership turnover and no mechanisms for dealing with change. People may use the broader community as a point of reference.

Mass Society Neighborhoods

5. The diffuse neighborhood has a high degree of collective capacity to act but does not exercise it. In this residential setting, people feel they do not need the neighborhood for help or social interaction, but still identify with their place of residence. Examples of these neighborhoods include some upper-class suburban housing areas and high-rise luxury apartment dwellings.
6. The anomic neighborhood, with low levels of identity, interaction, and linkages, appears to be a non-neighborhood. This type of neighborhood is usually associated with low-income public housing projects and skid-row neighborhoods. This type of neighborhood seems to have no capacity for collective action, but there may be higher levels of identity, attachment, and social interaction than are apparent at first glance.

The grouping of these six neighborhood types into three categories—traditional, mobile, and mass society neighborhoods—emphasizes two important dimensions of neighborhood primary groups: (1) the level of mobility or turnover of residents and (2) the capacity to retain primary group cohesion/social integration (Litwak, 1985). Traditional neighborhoods have stability of membership but are not well suited for integrating newcomers into a community. Mobile neighborhoods have a high turnover of residents but possess mechanisms for quickly integrating new residents and for retaining neighborhood cohesion. Mass neighborhoods have high mobility of residents and little capacity for integrating newcomers or retaining cohesion.

Litwak (1985) demonstrated the usefulness of this typology in identifying the service needs of older adults. The traditional neighborhood offers these individuals the most readily available resources, as this neighborhood has some of the features of an extended family. Older adults have the most difficulty in mass society neighborhoods, especially if they are in ill health and cannot handle daily living tasks. The nature of these neighborhood contexts is important when older adults consider making a residential move. Thus, persons with good health might benefit most by moving into a mobile neighborhood, where some resources are available and where quick integration and acceptance is the norm. The mass neighborhood would not be a good setting for older individuals with health care needs, as it does not provide informal help from neighbors. Familiarity with these neighborhood types is helpful in matching a resident's service needs with neighborhood features such as mobility of residents, presence or absence of means of rapid social integration, and the availability of informal help from neighbors versus more formal services from health and welfare organizations.

MODEL TWO: ORGANIZATIONAL AND VALUE DIMENSIONS

The next categorization of neighborhoods focuses on organizational, value, and change dimensions of neighborhood primary groups (Fellin & Litwak, 1968). The organizational base of neighborhoods may be identified in terms of the associational structure of informal contacts and local formal organizations such as voluntary groups. Neighborhoods can be classified in terms of their level of organization and their capacity to implement their values. Values, then, provide a second major dimension for classifying neighborhoods. Neighborhood values, such as orientation toward education, social order, and good citizenship, may be viewed on a positive-negative continuum. Neighborhoods vary in regard to whether the values of a neighborhood group are consistent with those of the general society. Combining these dimensions of organization and values leads to four types of neighborhoods: (1) positive values, organized; (2) positive values, unorganized; (3) negative values, organized; and (4) negative values, unorganized.

Most "traditional" and "mobile" neighborhoods, such as middle-class suburban neighborhoods and stable working-class neighborhoods in central cities, illustrate the first neighborhood type. These neighborhoods are organized to implement positive values regarding education, participation in community life, community improvement, and maintenance of social order. The second neighborhood type is found in "mass" neighborhoods such as transitory neighborhoods of working-class residents in rental homes and apartments. The third type is represented in neighborhoods with high crime rates and many youth gangs, resembling the anomic neighborhood. The fourth type is found in inner-city skid-row and rooming house neighborhood areas, as well as many high-rise, low-income urban housing projects.

Burns Street, a neighborhood in southeast Washington, D.C., is an example of a residential area organized to implement positive values. Some twenty years ago the residents of this neighborhood formed a Neighborhood Watch group, with neighbors creating "a network where it seems everyone knows everyone and takes pride in working together to create a common bond" (Wilgoren, 1999c). Residents are now mostly retired, but continue to keep their residentially stable neighborhood the way they want it—peaceful, tidy, free of crime, trash, and abandoned cars. They use their neighborhood organization to hear police reports and to press city officials for better services, and they use informal communications, porch lights, and phone calls to each other and to the police to keep the neighborhood safe and to help each other.

MODEL THREE: POPULATION AND ORGANIZATIONAL FACTORS

This model is guided by a mix of population factors, poverty and mobility, and organizational factors, networks, and external links. Informal networks include ties to kin, friends, and informal groups, and secondary formal networks refer to schools, recreational centers, church groups, and similar organizations. External links involve ties to support and resources outside the neighborhood. Figueira-McDonough (1991) has used an ecological perspective to construct these community types, drawing on some of the dimensions used in Model One. Four "ideal types" of communities, adapted here to refer to neighborhoods, are created in this model: (1) stepping-stone community (non-poor and mobile, with low primary networks, high secondary networks, high external links); (2) established community (non-poor and stable, with high primary networks, high secondary networks, low external links); (3) disorganized community (poor and mobile, with low primary networks, low secondary networks, low external links); and

(4) parochial community (poor and stable, with high primary networks, low secondary networks, low external links). As noted above, the extent of primary and secondary networks and external links to the broader community vary among these community types.

The stepping-stone community described in this model is similar to the stepping-stone neighborhood of Model One. The informal networks are weak, but there is high use of formal networks and strong external links. The established community, being high in primary and secondary networks and low in external links, is similar to the parochial neighborhood of Model One. Since the disorganized community has difficulty creating and maintaining primary and secondary networks, as well as external linkages, it is similar to the anomic neighborhood in Model One. Finally, the parochial community, with high primary networks and low secondary networks and external links, resembles the parochial neighborhood of Model One.

This typology emphasizes sources of resources by taking into consideration features of individual households (poverty), and of other members of the community (networks and external links). Hence, this typology has particular relevance to social work practice at both the "micro" and "macro" levels, since it points to the need for assessment of the level and source of social supports available to clients. This framework has been used to guide research on the relationship of community types to social problems. Figueira-McDonough (1991) used her framework to show the relationship of neighborhood types to rates of delinquent behavior. She found the highest delinquency rates in the disorganized neighborhoods, followed by the stepping-stone and parochial neighborhoods, with the established communities having the lowest rates. The policy implications of this research suggest that "an effective response to the problem (of delinquency) requires interventions that will strengthen the organization of communities...and that such interventions have to be tailored to the communities' characteristics and must take into account the demographic preconditions of organization" (Figueira-McDonough, 1991).

MODEL FOUR: ECONOMIC LEVEL, MOBILITY, SEGREGATION

In developing this model, Figueira-McDonough (1995) continued to focus on ecological factors such as economic levels and mobility/population turnover. In addition, she introduced the factor of ethnicity by focusing on residential concentration of minority groups—that is segregation/integration levels—in an effort to more fully understand the social disorganization of underclass communities and the extent of neighborhood resources (personal, organizational, and economic) in poverty neighborhoods. The types she creates are based on the proposition that "poverty is expected to jeopardize a community's ability to foster and maintain formal organizations and mobility is expected to limit the viability of primary groups."

Census tract data from neighborhood communities in Phoenix are used to apply neighborhood types to the study of propositions regarding residential poverty, segregation, school dropout rates, levels of social disorganization, population mobility and primary networks, and formal local organizations. These neighborhood types are listed below:

1. Well-off/mobile
2. Well-off/stable
3. Middle economic level/mobile
4. Middle/stable
5. Poor/mobile
6. Poor/stable
7. Very poor/mobile
8. Very poor/stable

Using this model of analysis, Figueira-McDonough (1995) found school dropout rates to be highest in the very poor neighborhoods, decreasing as one moves up to higher economic level communities. Mobility made a difference in dropout rates at the highest and lowest economic levels. These neighborhood types were also used to investigate the relationship of economic level and mobility to primary networks and formal local organizations. Findings indicated that well-off neighborhoods were better able than poor neighborhoods to maintain local organizations that offered recreational and social activities.

In a variation of this model of neighborhood types, Figueira-McDonough combined the factors of economic level, segregation, and mobility of residence into five types that could be assessed in relation to youth-related formal and informal organizations. The five types are listed below:

1. Very poor, very segregated, very stable neighborhoods;
2. Very poor, very segregated, moderately stable neighborhoods;
3. Poor, moderately to highly segregated, moderately to highly stable neighborhoods;
4. Middle-class, minimally to moderately segregated, moderately stable neighborhoods;
5. Well-off neighborhoods with a minimal minority presence and varying stability.

Using this typology, the mix of poverty, segregation, and mobility of residence is associated with a lack of organizations and informal activities for young people. Thus, the limited internal resources of poor, segregated, mobile neighborhoods exacerbate school dropout rates and social disorganization.

One of the major implications of this model for social work practice at the community level is the need to recognize differences between neighborhoods in regard to availability of informal and organizational resources for youth. This model of neighborhood types guides the social worker involved in community organization practice in assessing the extent to which such resources exist in underclass poverty neighborhoods. For example, since most poor neighborhoods need both formal and informal resources, the schools and churches in these areas provide a basis for development of local services. Figueira-McDonough draws from her categorization of neighborhood types and her research findings to recommend practice strategies that involve collaboration between organizers in a number of underclass neighborhoods. These strategies focus on finding and utilizing resources, developing human and social capital among residents, and using empowerment practice focused on community development.

NEIGHBORHOODS AS ENCLAVES

The term *enclave* may be used to describe self-contained neighborhood communities that include distinctive clusters of residents as well as "specialized commercial enterprises and institutions that support the inhabitants' special ways of life" (Abrahamson, 1996). Abrahamson (1996) describes an enclave as "a geographic entity and as a space with social meaning" as it "tends to be an object of residents' attachments and an important component of their identities." While racial or ethnic concentrations are often the basis for the development and maintenance of enclaves, some enclaves are grounded in religion, lifestyle, social class, sexual orientation, immigration status, or some combination of these factors. The concept of enclave directs our attention to the neighborhood as an identificational community, involving "a special relationship between a distinctive group of people and a place"— a relationship that resembles a subculture (Abrahamson, 1996). As Abrahamson notes, an enclave differs from our customary definition of a neighborhood community in that it also focuses on "specialized stores and institutions that provide local support for the residents' lifestyle." The growth and development of enclaves in central cities and suburban communities is illustrated by Abrahamson (1996) in his discussions of an elite social class enclave (Boston's Beacon Hill); a working-class enclave ("Back of the Yards" Chicago); racial/ethnic enclaves in Detroit, Michigan, Chinatown in San Francisco, Little Taipei in suburban Los Angeles, and Miami's Little Havana; gay enclaves in San Francisco's Castro and Mission Districts; and a religious enclave of Hasidic Jews in Brooklyn. These discussions provide a useful extension of our consideration of the emergence of social class and ethnic/cultural neighborhoods in Chapter 8.

SLUM AND GHETTO NEIGHBORHOODS

Models of neighborhood types may be examined in the context of social class and ethnic minority communities. As highlighted in the next chapter on the emergence of social class and ethnic minority neighborhoods, these classification systems are the most common ways of identifying neighborhoods. There is often an overlap of social class with race and ethnicity. A brief discussion of slum and ghetto neighborhoods assists in the understanding of this overlap. All large U.S. cities have slums and ghetto neighborhood communities. The label of slum is usually applied to poor neighborhoods distinguished by their physical environment: deteriorated housing; evidence of filth and unsanitary conditions; blighted condition of streets, alleys, parks, and business buildings; and boarded-up and unoccupied structures. The atmosphere of the slum is created by these undesirable physical conditions, reinforced by conditions of poverty, health problems, family disorganization, high crime rates, and lack of safety. Because of residents' lack of positive identification with the neighborhood, low levels of social interaction, high turnover, and lack of informal and formal organizations and linkage to the wider community, slums are usually classified as anomic or disorganized neighborhoods. They are highly segregated by social class, with a high proportion of residents consisting of unemployed members of an underclass.

While it is common to associate slums with ghetto neighborhoods, such an association is misleading, as many ghetto poor areas do not have the physical and social environments associated with slums. Ghetto neighborhoods (often referred to as "the hood" by residents), are usually distinguished by residents who have little choice of living elsewhere. Thus, ghetto neighborhoods, sometimes called ethnic enclaves, are often associated with race or ethnicity, with the term most commonly applied to areas with high proportions of African American or Hispanic American residents. The term *barrio*, a positive term, is often used rather than ghetto by Latino/Hispanic Americans to refer to their neighborhoods. Ghetto and barrio terms carry with them connotations of a poverty area, as well as cultural area, since many residents in these neighborhoods develop their own cultural patterns of social interaction, social control, and relationships to the larger community.

Residents in these ethnic neighborhoods often have "ethnic capital" that serves to bring about social mobility for themselves and their children. As Borjas (1999) observes, "These neighborhoods provide a close-knit and geographically compact community where members of the same ethnic group interact closely and frequently, influencing one another's behavior, marrying one another, and transmitting valuable information about economic opportunities through the social web that makes up the ethnic network." Under these conditions, Borjas suggests that ghettos can be good, providing "a terrific head start in the economic race." On the other hand, ethnic ghettos may be bad for their residents. Ghettos become problematic when negative neighborhood effects become prominent, such as joblessness, increases in welfare dependency, decreases in social organization and social control, and increases in crime and violence. Residents of these ghettos may find themselves in "socioeconomic traps" characterized by restricted social mobility for families and children.

Another view of ghetto poor neighborhoods is provided by Suttles (1968) in his study of Chicago slums. In *The Social Order of the Slum*, Suttles demonstrates that slums, rather than being disorganized, may have a social order of their own. His study of the Addams area in Chicago demonstrated that an order emerged from the fact that most residents followed conventional norms of behavior. Even deviants developed a system of control and organization that resulted in social order. The neighborhoods Suttles studied contained populations of African Americans, Puerto Ricans, Italians, and Mexican Americans. Suttles found that these groups used an "ordered segmentation" to guide their social relations with one another—that is, these groups established informal territorial, institutional, and communication arrangements to handle conflicts and to maintain social order.

Ghettos, while often associated with ethnic minority populations, may be composed of mostly white residents. Lower Price Hill in Cincinnati, Ohio, is an example of a white ghetto neighborhood (Tilove, 1995). Lower Price Hill is a community of poor white people, including many who have migrated to Cincinnati from poor Appalachian communities. These residents are "stereotyped as lazy and stupid, people with bad genes, bad teeth and bad English, whose lives are circumscribed by the highway, the waste-blackened creek, the sewage plant and the ugly assortment of air-fouling industries that hem them in. The residents are viewed by outsiders as 'white trash,' hence ignored or belittled, with their neighborhood conjuring up images of dirt yards arrayed with junked cars, kids and dogs." Insiders in Lower Price Hill feel "dumped on" by the wider community and identify their neighborhood as low-income, stable, with low crime rates, with people living there by choice. The neighborhood has a Community Council that has been active in improving the environmental conditions of the neighborhood, and which contends that the people of Lower Price Hill look out for each other and cherish their homes, families, and neighborhood.

It is instructive to refer to the neighborhood types in our models to consider how ghetto and barrio neighborhoods can be classified. An outsider's view of Lower Price Hill in Cincinnati could lead to its classification as an anomic, disorganized neighborhood. In contrast, the description of the neighborhood by the Community Council would classify it as a parochial or integral neighborhood. With regard to other neighborhoods around the country, such as parts of Harlem in New York, parts of the South Side of Chicago, and some areas of East Los Angeles, these ghetto/slum neighborhoods would likely be classified as anomic, transitory, and/or disorganized. Other ethnic minority poor neighborhoods resemble parochial neighborhoods, with strong resident identification with the area, high levels of social interaction, residential stability, but few links to the larger community. These neighborhoods usually have more employed persons, a stronger presence of formal organizations such as schools, churches, and block clubs, and mechanisms of social control and social order, than do poverty areas.

A number of public housing projects in U.S. cities have become ghettos and slums—that is, they have become segregated by race, by the presence of unemployed welfare families, and by slum social and physical conditions. The Robert Taylor Homes housing project in Chicago is an example of a ghetto/slum created by the Federal Government and now being razed under a Federal program called Hope VI (Belluck, 1998). The Robert Taylor Homes project has been called "the nation's largest housing project, much of which is "considered the worst slum area in the United States" according to its landlord, the Chicago Housing Authority. This housing project originally included 28 high-rises with more than 4,000 apartments, with a population of more than 11,000 people, 99 percent of whom were black, with 96 percent of the adults being unemployed.

Three high-rise buildings called the Hole, the most oppressive section of the Homes, were razed in 1998, revealing numerous problems in the resettlement of its residents. The city housing authority spent some of the federal money from Hope VI on social services in response to the unemployment problems, "trying to place as many residents as possible in high school equivalency courses, training programs, and jobs." Relocation specialists were faced with the fact that "One of the toughest questions facing housing officials is how to deal with intensely troubled families. Their problems could not only cripple their adjustment to a new home but could also harm their new neighborhoods." These problems include drug abuse, child neglect, and welfare dependency, and the need for intensive counseling from the housing authority's social services department. At the same time, because of a shortage of affordable housing and limited Section 8 certificates, relocation sometimes means moving to run-down, poor, unsafe neighborhoods. Still, the goal is "to disperse the project's concentrated poverty without introducing or aggravating social problems in new neighborhoods. Success will require communities to accept as neighbors people they have long been happy to have out of sight" (Belluck, 1998).

Chapter 7 Review

Neighborhoods can be viewed as geographical areas that provide sets of connections for residents, such as social, functional, cultural, and/or circumstantial relationships. Boundaries of neighborhoods are defined by local governmental units, by professional service providers, and other groups outside the neighborhood. Boundaries are used in the creation of social maps of neighborhoods, especially with regard to their deficiencies and unmet needs, and their strengths, assets, and capacities. Boundaries may be established in a subjective way by residents. Neighborhoods are also defined as personal arenas wherein the neighborhood boundaries are created by "mental maps" and where the residents constitute a primary group, with neighboring and personal relationships determining the boundaries.

The major focus of the chapter was on models of neighborhood types developed through use of several dimensions of community, such as identification, social interaction, linkages to other areas, residential mobility and stability, economic level, segregation and integration, and type and use of social networks. Examples were included to show how these neighborhood models can be used to assess neighborhood resources. In addition, neighborhoods were examined in terms of "enclaves," slums, and ghettos. The next chapter extends the consideration of neighborhood types through a focus on social class and ethnic/cultural neighborhoods, exploring their emergence, maintenance, and change in American communities.

8

Social Class and
Ethnic/Cultural Neighborhoods

The most common criteria used for classifying neighborhoods are social class, ethnicity, and culture. Neighborhoods may be distinguished by social class through the use of census data regarding occupational status, household income, education, and lifestyle. Residents usually refer to one or more of these factors in assigning social class names to their neighborhoods. Class names include terms such as wealthy, middle-class, working class, poor, underclass, and skid row neighborhoods. Names for ethnic neighborhoods include those of white ethnic groups, religious ethnic groups, and ethnic minority groups. Use of ethnic/cultural labels for neighborhoods usually indicates that members of a specific group are over-represented in relation to the general population, such as an African American neighborhood or a Hispanic/Latino neighborhood. Religious or white ethnic labels are usually used when a substantial portion of the population, even if not a majority, are members of a specified group, such as Jewish, Catholic, Italian, Polish, or Irish neighborhoods.

The term *integrated* is often applied to neighborhoods that are predominantly white, but have some residents who are people of color.

149

The label *segregated* is usually applied to neighborhoods in which more than half of the residents are nonwhite. The terms integrated and segregated are usually not used to describe the composition of social class neighborhoods. More often, terms such as wealthy, middle-class, mostly middle and working class, or poor will be used to describe diverse social class neighborhoods. The composition of neighborhoods by social class and ethnicity is not static, with some changes occurring naturally and other changes brought on by planned interventions. The major focus of this chapter is on the paths of neighborhood change—the ways in which neighborhood patterns based on social class, ethnicity, and culture emerge and are maintained or changed.

SOCIAL CLASS NEIGHBORHOODS

Home values and percentages of home ownership are the most visible signs of social class in neighborhoods. The value of a home is a manifestation of what residents are able to afford and/or are willing to pay for a home. Home ownership is usually linked to some combination of occupational status, household income, and educational level of members of a household. Homes are a proxy for the lifestyle of residents in a neighborhood, and the value of homes is a useful measure of social class. Why do people live where they live? Some people choose a neighborhood because of the features of the home they prefer. People also may view their home as a status symbol and choose to live in as high a social class as they can afford. Most people choose to live in places where they feel comfortable. Comfort may involve perception of safety, interaction with people with similar lifestyles, and living with people of "one's own kind." Some people have little choice concerning where to live, because of discriminatory mortgage lending and real estate practices. Thus, the location of a home, the actual physical appearance and features of a home, the social and economic characteristics of people in a neighborhood, and the prevailing business practices all influence why people live where they live.

Real estate salespeople and developers are fond of saying that the value of a home depends on three factors: "location, location, and location." A neighborhood is likely to have advantages or disadvantages of place because of the social class level of the residents. Middle-class and upper-class neighborhoods, particularly those in suburban communities, have advantages of high-quality schools, protective zoning, public resources devoted to safety, and parks and recreational facilities. In contrast, high-poverty neighborhoods have poor public services, schools of poor quality, high unemployment rates, few adult role models, high crime rates, and deteriorated physical conditions.

Neighborhoods with high poverty levels have been called ghetto poor, with 40 percent or more of households in these neighborhoods having incomes below the federal poverty line. In his studies of African American poverty neighborhoods in Chicago, Wilson (1994, 1996) observed that these inner-city segregated neighborhoods have become part of a "new urban poverty" in which a substantial majority of the adults are not working. As a result, a large number of families are "on welfare," leading to a designation of these areas as ghetto poor, underclass, or "welfare neighborhoods." An example of a welfare neighborhood in Brooklyn, New York is Southside in the predominantly Hispanic community of Williamsburg (Sexton, 1997). In this neighborhood the median household income is slightly higher than $14,000, with 45 percent of the residents living below the poverty level and 49 percent receiving public assistance. The broader community of Williamsburg is home to a substantial number of Hasidic Jews, with an estimated 30 percent receiving public assistance. There are also a large number of legal immigrant families in this community who do not have citizenship.

Families and individuals in welfare neighborhoods such as Southside in Brooklyn have had to deal with the effects of changes in welfare programs resulting from welfare reform legislation passed in 1996. This legislation included new rules for providing assistance to families and children, work training requirements, food stamp eligibility restrictions, changes in Supplemental Security Income benefits, and new standards for establishing disability of children. The economic effects of welfare reform have had implications not only for individuals and families, but for the neighborhood of Southside as a whole, including schools, churches, businesses, that have functioned "on welfare money." The immediate effects appear to be negative for the neighborhood economy and some of the neighborhood institutions, such as strains on the day care system. But the new legislation holds hope that the residents of Southside "will reclaim their independence, find work, give up the corrosive burden of welfare. And its economy, despite short-term damage, will emerge as an authentically healthy engine" (Sexton, 1997). In the meantime, a mother on welfare raised the concern that "Maybe the neighborhood now goes down the drain. Welfare has been a kind of security for the neighborhood."

DIVERSITY IN SOCIAL CLASS NEIGHBORHOODS

Neighborhoods have not always been class-linked, with most residents having similar social class characteristics. In the past most residential areas in large cities had a diversity of people of different social classes, particularly in white ethnic and religious-related neighborhoods, as well as African American and Latino neighborhoods. For example, black neighborhoods in Chicago before 1960 usually had a mix of residents of middle- and working-class levels (Wilson, 1994, 1996). Studies of Detroit have shown similar patterns in past years for African American neighborhoods, with a blurring across class lines and considerable heterogeneity in their composition (Warren, 1975). Residents in these neighborhoods displayed a diversity of values, economic, educational, and lifestyle differences.

Other examples of neighborhoods that have had heterogeneous social class levels come from studies of central city communities with high proportions of Jewish, Catholic, Polish, Italian, or Irish populations. In these cases, individuals who had a higher social rank than most area residents often chose to reside in these neighborhoods because of family, ethnic, and/or religious affiliations. By the 1990s most ethnic minority and white ethnic neighborhoods were no longer heterogeneous in terms of social class, especially in inner-city sections of large metropolitan areas (Rusk, 1993; Wilson, 1996). Some of the demographic and economic changes that led to class homogenization within ghetto poverty areas in cities such as Chicago included discrimination in housing markets, changes in age structure and family composition, an increase in single-parent households, and departure of working- and middle-class persons to the suburbs. Suburbanization has been the major process leading to white and nonwhite flight from central cities to suburban communities.

The Mount Morris Park neighborhood in Harlem provides an example of how "urban pioneers," community groups, governmental agencies, and private development corporations have restored a deteriorating urban neighborhood and the area around it (Rozhon, 1998). Historically, rows of brownstones were constructed in about 1885, with a process of succession involving white Protestants occupying the area first, followed by Eastern European Jews, and then African Americans in the 1920s. During the 1990s, as a part of the process of housing and business development, the social class composition of the neighborhood area changed. Middle-class professionals began buying brownstones. With the support of HUD, the State of New York, and private developers, three-family row houses were built for low- and moderate-income residents. Co-op apartments for buyers with varied incomes were built, with retail complexes included in the buildings. Luxury condominiums were built in the neighborhood in an area called the Ruins—state-owned houses in an old urban renewal area that never got developed. The city's Department of Housing Preservation and Development has supported the renovation of more than 1,300 houses in the neighborhood. Prior to these housing projects, the neighborhood had one of the lowest home ownership rates in New York City and the country: 6.5 percent, compared with 29 percent citywide and 48 percent nationally. The Mount Morris Park Community Improvement Association, and other community groups, now have high hopes that the new home-ownership development and retail projects will result in a "renaissance of Mount Morris" as a part of a "second Harlem Renaissance" (Rozhon, 1998).

Described as a model of urban blight, the Cecil B. Moore neighborhood of lower North Philadelphia has over the past few years changed from a community with "dilapidated houses, boarded storefronts and lots strewn with garbage and glass" to a "neighborhood reborn" (Janofsky, 1998). Formerly an area with a declining population and dangerous blocks due to illegal drug trafficking, the neighborhood has become a residential and commercial area with new and rehabilitated housing and businesses. The change has occurred through investments made by churches, together with funds from city and federal government. Many of the housing and neighborhood improvements were the result of planning by the Cecil B. Moore Home Ownership Zone that supported purchase of homes by working-class families. Changes in this neighborhood community were brought about in part by money from the Federal Empowerment Zone of Philadelphia and support from local institutions such as Temple University. Temple University built an arena, a student center, a technology center, dormitories, a theater and a library, while encouraging the building of low-to-moderate-income housing around the arena. The University hoped to "blunt the image of lower North Philadelphia as a dangerous, crime-ridden area" (Janofsky, 1998). According to the pastor of a local church, residents are optimistic: "There is a great desire here to improve neighborhoods.... [People] are tired of running. They are ready to dig in and take responsibility for their neighborhood."

CHANGE IN SOCIAL STATUS OF NEIGHBORHOODS

Given the mobility of Americans within and between communities, the question arises as to whether neighborhoods maintain their social status over time. Studies of inner-city poverty areas show a decline in status in these neighborhoods, due to the decline in employment and increase in welfare dependency among residents, as well as the departure of upwardly mobile individuals and families (Wilson, 1996). At the same time, many working- and middle-class ethnic minority neighborhoods have been able to maintain their status because of residential stability and strong institutional supports from schools, churches, medical and social service institutions, and neighborhood voluntary organizations. Many urban neighborhoods that have become more integrated racially have managed to maintain their class status through institutional and voluntary group efforts that support integration.

Although suburban neighborhoods tend to maintain their social status over time, many show a slight decline in social class after two or more decades as residents grow older or move away. However, the local governments in suburban communities assist residents in maintaining the status of their neighborhoods. Legal restrictions, especially zoning laws, are used to assure neighborhoods the advantages of place and class status. Thus, homes are not just places where people live, but are also status symbols that contribute to the status of the local community. While older suburban communities have limited opportunity for expansion of housing, and hence, for status improvement, newer communities are able to attract people of higher social class by building expensive homes. Upper-class, affluent neighborhoods in central cities and suburban communities tend to maintain their status over time, but must compete with new housing developments designed for persons of high social class status.

ETHNIC NEIGHBORHOODS

Ethnic neighborhoods are found in central cities of most large urban areas. These neighborhoods are usually referred to as "communities" based on the ethnicity, culture, nationality, or religion of many of the residents. Such communities can also be characterized in terms of heterogeneous or homogeneous social class composition. Studies of large urban areas show an increase in the number of neighborhoods identified with people of color, particularly African American or Latino/ Hispanic neighborhoods, and in some instances, by people affiliated with a religious/cultural group. Many of the older white ethnic and religious neighborhoods have changed into communities of color through the process of succession. At the same time, some religion-based neighborhoods have emerged and flourished.

An example of the emergence of a new "Old World," religion-based, and mixed social class neighborhood is Borough Park in Brooklyn,

New York (Sontag, 1998). This is an ultra-Orthodox Jewish neighborhood community with a nucleus of "Yiddish-speaking and strictly religious Hasidim of various sects" that has grown into a religious enclave that is diverse in social class. A house-building boom in this neighborhood since 1992, especially of additions to present housing, has resulted in extremely large homes, two-family homes, single-family homes, and apartments, with a wide range of home sizes and prices. Yet, "you have people of vastly different incomes not just tolerating each other but actually mingling" and "rich, working class and poor not only live side by side, but pray together and send their children to the same schools" (Sontag, 1998). The neighborhood has a commercial center, 13th Avenue, "with its aromatic bakeries, kosher pizzerias, and Judaica barns," along with many yeshivas and synagogues "from holes-in-the-wall, called shtiebels, to vast, tiered shuls."

Most Native Americans who are not residing on reservations or in rural communities live in central city neighborhoods. The U.S. Census of 1990 counted approximately two million Native Americans in the United States, with about two thirds residing in off-reservation areas. Edwards and Egbert-Edwards (1998) have noted that "whether residences are maintained in rural reservations or urban areas, Native Americans are influenced by strong cultural ties to their native identity." As Native Americans have relocated from reservations and other communities, they appear to seek out neighborhoods where other Native Americans already reside and where there are Native American social institutions, such as health centers and recreational centers. Native Americans in urban areas usually live in inner-city neighborhoods with other people of color and often encounter problems involving housing, employment discrimination, and lack of social services. Although these neighborhoods include other ethnic minorities, especially African American and Hispanic/Latino Americans, Native Americans traditionally have had low levels of social interaction with other neighborhood residents. They are likely to interact informally with other Native Americans in their homes, in Native American centers, and in church-related programs.

Asian Americans are more likely to be integrated into middle- and upper-class neighborhoods than are members of other ethnic minority groups, but there are still Asian neighborhoods in many central cities. Recent changes in immigration patterns have led to an influx of Asian Americans into large cities and a resulting increase in Asian American neighborhoods, especially in the cities of Los Angeles and New York City. Asian Americans have also formed their own neighborhoods in suburban communities. A similar pattern has occurred for other communities of color, as they have moved into neighborhoods identified as "zones of emergence" (Nathan, 1991). Such areas include the Buck-eye-Woodland neighborhood in Cleveland, where a mostly Hungarian population has been replaced with a large group of African Americans. Another such area is the Sunset Park neighborhood in Brooklyn, New York, with a high proportion of Puerto Ricans moving into this community. Areas with increasingly high proportions of working-class and middle-class African Americans and Hispanics include the New York City communities of Queens, Brooklyn, and the Bronx; the Hickman Mills area of Kansas City, Missouri; and Aurora, Colorado.

An interesting "port of entry" concept helps explain suburbanization of ethnic minority groups. This idea was developed by Rose (1976) in a study of fifteen communities in which African Americans had moved into predominantly white suburban areas. In some of these communities residents of central city ghettos had moved to contiguous suburban areas through a "port of entry": a housing area located just across the border between the central city and an older suburban community. Thus, some blue-collar, lower-class, and middle-class African Americans were able to move from the central city to inner suburbs that then became racially mixed. From these areas, some middle-class residents in these neighborhoods were then able to move on to outer suburbs with lower percentages of minorities. The history of the movement of people of color to suburban communities suggests that areas that have attracted ethnic minorities tend to include:

1. Older, densely settled suburbs that often contain, or are located close to, centers of employment. Members of minority groups move into these white neighborhoods because they can afford the housing, which is available because whites have moved on to newer suburbs.
2. New suburban developments built to attract minorities, and some new, purposely integrated communities.
3. Low-value homes in suburban neighborhood areas and some public housing developments.
4. Middle-class communities in "zones of emergence."
5. Upscale, upper-class neighborhoods that attract people in professional occupations (Farley & Frey, 1994; South & Crowder, 1998).

SPATIAL AND SOCIOPSYCHOLOGICAL COMMUNITIES

Ethnic neighborhoods usually display characteristics of both locational and identification/interest communities. Thus, for many ethnic groups, including those based on ethnicity, culture, and/or religion, the neighborhood is a spatial community as well as a sociopsychological community. A useful framework for examining these types of neighborhoods has been developed by Taylor (1979) in regard to the development of black ethnicity in urban communities in the northern part of the United States. This conceptual framework is applicable to the assessment of all ethnic groups when there is an overlap of residential community and community of interest. Taylor examined black ethnicity in relation to segregated residential patterns. According to Taylor's thesis, as southern blacks migrated to large northern cities, they faced "severe racial discrimination and structured inequality" and settled mainly in segregated residential neighborhoods. As a result, "specialized black institutions and services, newspapers, churches, bars, cafes, developed...and promoted internal bonds and cohesion among older and more recent black residents in northern cities." This form of neighborhood development has been referred to as *gemeinschaft* or neo-*gemeinschaft*, indicating ethnic minority relationships that are "personal, informal, traditional, gender, and sentiment based" (Rivera and Erlich, 1998). These segregated neighborhood communities provided residents with the essential social and cultural resources to cope with the problems of urban society. Wilson (1996) has documented the presence of socially organized neighborhoods of working-class African Americans in Chicago prior to the 1960s. Thus, the segregation of African Americans into innercity neighborhoods is said to have had a major influence on the development of the contemporary urban black residential area as both a spatial and sociopsychological community.

Taylor's (1979) framework for understanding these minority communities focuses on four segments identified according to residence and patterns of identification. Segment A comprises a majority of urban blacks who reside in areas with a black resident majority and have a positive identification with the black community. Segment B is formed by blacks living in integrated white communities but retaining identification with the black community through involvement in black organizations and social contacts with residents of black areas. Segment C includes blacks who live in areas with a black majority but do not identify with or participate in the black community. The smallest segment, Segment D, includes individuals who neither reside in a black spatial community nor identify in a sociopsychological way with the black community. While Taylor's work focuses on African Americans, his framework can be used to examine spatial and psychosocial aspects of other ethnic minority communities as well as white ethnic and faith-based communities.

SEGREGATION IN NEIGHBORHOODS

The presence of neighborhoods of people of color, particularly African American and Hispanic/Latino, persists in U.S. society for a variety of reasons. Some members of ethnic minority groups prefer to reside in neighborhoods populated mainly by members of their own group. These individuals fit into Taylor's (1979) Segment A: people who reside in and are positively identified with the minority community. These neighborhoods also receive people who are unable to move into other neighborhoods due to economic factors and/or discrimination in housing. There is strong evidence that societal and community barriers to residential mobility prohibit some persons from "leaving the 'hood" and becoming a part of Segment B. These barriers include not only financial constraints and housing discrimination, but obstacles imposed by suburban communities to new arrivals from minority groups, such as restrictive covenants and zoning ordinances.

Classification of neighborhoods as integrated or segregated is an arbitrary process. Although the concepts of segregation and integration are useful in describing neighborhoods and communities, measurement requires some demarcation of percentages of ethnic minority and white residents required for classification. Residents also have their own perceptions of how integrated or segregated a neighborhood is, based on their own criteria and observations. For example, a study in Chicago by the Woodstock Institute indicated that "As blacks become 20 percent of the residents, whites no longer call a neighborhood integrated. To many whites, such a neighborhood is black" (Dedman, 1999). In some studies of white and nonwhite residential areas using census tract data, a neighborhood is designated as predominantly black if it has a population of more than 89 percent black, predominantly white if the population is less than 10 percent black, and racially mixed if the neighborhood has a population between 10 percent and 89 percent black (South & Crowder, 1998).

A rather sophisticated measure of residential segregation developed by Taeuber and Taeuber (1965) has been used by demographers to examine changes in segregation patterns of people of color. This measure is an index of dissimilarity: the extent to which any two groups are separated from each other. The index of dissimilarity "captures the degree to which blacks and whites are evenly spread among neighborhoods in a city. Evenness is defined with respect to the racial composition of the city as a whole. If a city is 10 percent black, then an even residential pattern requires that every neighborhood be 10 percent black and 90 percent white. Thus, if a neighborhood is 20 percent black, the excess 10 percent of blacks must move to a neighborhood where the black percentage is under 10 percent to shift the residential configuration toward evenness. The index of dissimilarity gives the percentage of blacks who would have to move to achieve an 'even' residential pattern...one where every neighborhood replicates the racial composition of the city" (Massey & Denton, 1993). An illustration of the use of the index of dissimilarity is found in a study by Harrison and Weinberg (1992), with 1990 census data showing segregation patterns for African Americans to be much higher than for Hispanic, Asian, and Native American groups.

In another study of changes in residential segregation, Farley and Frey (1994) used the index of dissimilarity to study the emergence of segregated suburbs and the segregation patterns of 232 U.S. metropolitan areas with substantial black populations. They used an ecological model of analysis to show that segregation decreased from 1980 to 1990 in most metropolitan areas, especially in young, southern, and western metropolitan areas with significant recent housing construction. They noted that "because the black population continues to migrate to such areas, residential segregation between blacks and whites should decline further, but remain well above that for Hispanics or Asians." These "small steps toward a more integrated society" were attributed to four developments: "changes in federal housing policies, liberalization of white attitudes toward blacks, growth of the black middle class, and substantial new housing construction."

WHITE FLIGHT

An increasing number of large American cities have more than one half of their population represented by people of color, many of them living in segregated neighborhoods. Changes in patterns of neighborhood residence in the United States, as illustrated above in the study by Farley and Frey (1994), provide examples of the ecological processes of segregation and succession. In the period following World War II, from 1945 onward, there was a dramatic movement of whites to suburban residential areas, a movement usually referred to as "white flight." This development can be attributed to a combination of racial and nonracial causes. Racially related causes for the movement of whites from central cities to mostly segregated white suburban communities include white prejudices against living in neighborhoods with ethnic minorities, increases in racial disorder within the central cities of large metropolitan areas, attempts to desegregate city schools, discriminatory housing practices, and increases in the numbers of ethnic minorities migrating into central cities.

Non-racial causes for white flight include the following "pushes" and "pulls":

- the need for larger houses by white families in central cities;
- accessibility of new suburban housing;
- an economy that supported upward social, occupational, and residential mobility;
- availability of low-interest home loans from private and public sources, such as V.A. loans;
- new employment opportunities in suburban areas;
- lower property taxes in the suburbs.

An additional reason for the movement of whites to the suburbs was a growing perception of central city problems such as rising taxes, crime, declining quality of education and of municipal services, and a deteriorating physical infrastructure. By all accounts, many of these racial and nonracial causes continue to assure segregated neighborhood areas in the central cities, a decline in population growth, and an increasing proportion of minority group residents. At the same time, more people of color have been able to enter the first ring of suburban communities, with some of these older suburban areas populated mostly by middle-class members of minority groups.

SUCCESSION

The ecological concept of *succession* is particularly useful in understanding changes in neighborhood residential populations. Succession involves the replacement of one group by another, usually in terms of race, ethnicity, or religious affiliation. Historically, neighborhood residential areas in central cities have changed through succession, the replacement of one immigrant group by another. This type of succession, involving white European immigrants, has been regarded as the customary, orderly process of social change in residential patterns. In recent years, population groups characterized by their color, especially new immigrants and refugees, have been involved in a process of succession. The most dramatic example of succession continues to be the movement of African Americans into white residential neighborhoods, especially in the central cities and contiguous suburban communities of large metropolitan areas.

The process of succession usually involves a first phase of a new group entering a neighborhood occupied by an established group. A key element of this phase is the fact that the established group, usually white, takes advantage of housing opportunities available to them elsewhere, leaving housing available to an incoming group. A second phase of the process moves from a normal replacement rate to a "tipping point" at which whites begin to move out rapidly because they perceive the area as "too integrated" or too "racially mixed." Historically, reaching the tipping point and moving to a turnover in population has occurred with the active participation of the real estate industry. The assumption is that the process of succession continues to the point of almost complete, or complete, turnover of population.

An example of complete succession is described in the work of Levine and Harmon (1992), *The Death of an American Jewish Community*. Between 1968 and 1970 the Boston communities of Roxbury, Dorchester, and Mattapan changed from an area with 90,000 Jews to one with a majority of African American residents. Levine and Harmon contend that a combination of bankers and brokers, along with federal agencies, were responsible for the collapse of the Jewish community in this area. Rapid turnover of the neighborhood population was attributed to blockbusting, "scare tactics used by commission-hungry real estate brokers to force the quick sale of homes."

An example of succession in process is the Ashburn neighborhood in Chicago. Formerly an Irish Catholic neighborhood, with Germans and Swedish residents making it ethnically diverse, in the 1990s Ashburn attracted young black families as home buyers. A study by the Woodstock Institute showed that "Ashburn is now about 60 percent black, and tipping fast," with a restaurant owner observing, "In five years it'll be all black" (Dedman, 1999). Community groups have sued real estate companies, "accusing them of frightening whites out of the area to increase business," with the companies agreeing to pay monetary settlements. Thus, in this instance, because of factors such as racial steering, the increase in opportunities for home ownership among blacks has not led to an integrated neighborhood but rather to increased segregation. Ashburn illustrates the fact that the goal of the Fair Housing Act and the Community Investment Act to achieve "stable, integrated neighborhoods remains elusive" (Dedman, 1999). The Woodstock Institute study noted that "in Chicago, integrated neighborhoods do not stay integrated very long" (Dedman, 1999). Describing a neighborhood as integrated if it had between 10 and 50 percent black residents, researchers noted that in the early 1990s 110 of 1,169 neighborhoods in Chicago and its suburbs were integrated, but by 1995 only 27 of the 110 remained integrated (Dedman, 1999).

A number of social consequences have been observed in neighborhood residential areas that have been involved in the process of succession. Community-based groups and voluntary organizations associated with the established group decline or relinquish control to members of the incoming groups. In many cases new organizational memberships emerge among the incoming group. Social interaction of residents, such as neighboring, may change in these areas, but the nature of the new patterns of interaction is not well established. When these areas change from white to nonwhite populations there is often a change in ownership of small businesses. Property values of houses and business buildings often decline and eventually stabilize, but they may never rise to the extent they might have risen without succession of population in the neighborhood. A review of property values related to racial composition shows that "property values drop when black families move in" (Farley & Frey, 1994). In a study using data from the Panel Study of Income Dynamics, Harris (1999) found "clear evidence of lower property values in neighborhoods with relatively high proportions of black residents.... Housing loses at least 16 percent of its value when located in neighborhoods that are more than 10 percent black." While attitudes toward race may determine property values, social class factors are found to have a stronger influence on property values: people prefer to live in areas with high SES, which continues to be more common among whites than blacks. (Of course, racism is *still* a factor, as it fosters economic conditions that are unfavorable to high SES among blacks.) Neighborhood areas in which housing units are owner-occupied still have lower property values if the racial composition is at least 60 percent black. White flight often occurs in areas of succession, due in part to the assumptions of whites that the incoming nonwhite groups will be accompanied by an increase in the density of population (conversion of single to multiple dwellings), changes in the composition of households (to include extended family and friends), in the character of local institutions (more businesses owned by nonwhites), and in the development of strained relationships between long-time residents and newcomers.

Neighborhood change in some white and religious ethnic groups has some of the characteristics of the processes of succession, integration, and segregation. An example is the transformation of the Riverdale neighborhood in the Bronx borough of New York City into a vibrant Orthodox Jewish community (MacFarquhar, 1997). Riverdale consists of approximately 100,000 residents, about 35 to 40 percent of whom are Jewish. Many middle-class Jewish residents moved to the area from the 1960s onward, with a mixture of Orthodox, Conservative, and Reform congregations. The transformation has come about with a dramatic increase in the past few years of Orthodox Jews to about 20 percent of the Jewish population. While there is some tension between Orthodox and non-Orthodox community residents, there is also evidence of cooperation between rabbis of Orthodox, Conservative, and Reform congregations.

CREATION AND MAINTENANCE OF RESIDENTIAL INTEGRATION

Some communities make special efforts to create and/or maintain racial and ethnic diversity in their neighborhoods. Two major approaches to achieving and maintaining integration goals and countering the forces creating residential segregation have been (1) governmental programs involving legislation and fair housing enforcement, and (2) community-wide efforts carried out through local governmental units and voluntary private-sector groups. Federal, state, and local governmental fair housing laws have not resulted in the elimination of discrimination in housing or in the achievement of residential integration. This conclusion has been supported over the past several decades by housing studies and in various social policy statements, such as a report on "The Costs of Discrimination and Segregation" (Tobin, 1987). Housing analysts continue to fault federal, state, and local governments for not achieving housing integration goals and for creating and perpetuating segregated housing in the past. In response to these concerns, during the administration of President Clinton, the secretary of Housing and Urban Development, Andrew M. Cuomo, has actively supported governmental programs to overcome housing discrimination and promote integrated neighborhoods. These programs have as a goal of public policy that "all levels of government should actively strive to desegregate racially isolated communities and encourage stable, racially diverse ones" (Galster, 1992).

A second approach to residential integration has involved local community groups and initiatives. Achievement and maintenance of residential integration have become goals for an increasing number of local communities, with activities directed toward specific objectives, stated in terms such as achieving a racial balance, achieving integration, integration maintenance, and reduction of segregation. The most common examples involve attempts to attract African Americans into white neighborhoods and to retain whites in integrated areas to avoid resegregation. Examples of efforts toward creation of integrated communities include Oak Park, Illinois (Klibanoff, 1984); Park Forest, Illinois (Hayes, 1990a); Southfield, Michigan (Jones, 1990); New Rochelle, New York (Berger, 1998); Shaker Heights, Ohio (Pepper, 1990); Oakland County, Michigan (Dozier, 1993); and Columbia, Maryland (Hirsch, 1992).

Challenging questions have been raised regarding the goals and programs of these communities to promote and maintain residential integration. What kind of process will result in achievement of integration goals? What is a desirable level of integration, in terms of percentages of whites/nonwhites, of distribution of households by race or ethnicity in a given community or neighborhood? Who defines the level of desirability—the white population, the ethnic minority population, or both? Can a neighborhood or community become "too integrated"? Are programs that involve affirmative marketing through stimulation of white housing demand or ethnic minority demand racist and discriminatory? Galster (1992) and Saltman (1991) provide useful insights into how to answer these questions.

Galster (1992) makes a case for racial integration by proposing that a "stable integrative process" be established in all metropolitan areas. This process is one "in which homeseekers representing two or more races actively seek to occupy the same vacant dwellings in a substantial proportion of a metropolitan area's neighborhoods over an extended period." The desired outcome is not viewed in terms of reaching specific percentages of various groups, but rather as engaging in a process that "would tend to desegregate racially homogeneous neighborhoods and promote racially diverse neighborhoods." This approach is based on the proposition that segregation is limiting for nonwhites and white—e.g., for African Americans it limits "access to appropriate public education, health, and social service resources," to employment information and access to jobs, to accumulation of assets, and to economic security. Equally important is the idea that a process leading to integration in housing should address both "dwelling and neighborhood attributes"—not only housing choices outside ghetto neighborhood areas, but also creating a "suitable living environment" that has "neighborhood characteristics like schools, public services, physical environment, proximity to employment, and presumably, racial composition" (Galster, 1992). Galster (1992) argues that a stable integrative process is likely only when there are aggressive, coordinated public policies. Such policies are apparent in some of the illustrative examples presented in this chapter.

Saltman (1991) sought to answer some of the questions cited above through a study of 15 urban communities throughout the United States that had engaged in neighborhood integration maintenance efforts. Neighborhoods in the study were grouped into three categories:

1. Success: live neighborhood organization; stable, racially diverse neighborhood;
2. Failure: dead organization; mostly black neighborhood;
3. Conditional: live organization; transitional or mostly black neighborhood.

Based on this study, Saltman (1991) formed the following hypotheses concerning the success or failure of integration-maintenance programs:

The probability of. . .achieving a stable, racially diverse neighborhood. . . is greater:

1. the greater the amenities of the target neighborhood,
2. the more supportive the role of the city,
3. the more comprehensive a school desegregation program,
4. the more deconcentrated the location of public housing,
5. the more extensive an affirmative-marketing program,
6. the more effective a regional fair-housing program,
7. the greater the regional housing supply for all income levels,
8. the earlier the timing of the movement effort (e.g., before the target neighborhood is racially definable),
9. the more securely and adequately funded the neighborhood movement organization is.

Saltman concluded that racially diverse neighborhoods are maintained only with enormous difficulty. Keep these hypotheses in mind while reading the following examples of community efforts to create integrated neighborhoods.

EXAMPLES OF DIVERSE NEIGHBORHOODS

Oak Park, Illinois, and Park Forest, Illinois

One of the first communities to seek a racially diverse community was Oak Park, Illinois (Klibanoff, 1984). The local government led efforts to establish an open-housing ordinance in 1968, when the percentage of African American residents in this community was 0.2 percent. By 1984 the percentage had increased to 13 percent in response to a written local government policy to assemble "a mixture of racial and ethnic groups throughout the village." Financial incentives were offered to apartment building owners and tenants in order to increase residential integration, along with guarantees related to sale of single housing units. Coordination of these efforts came from a Housing Center.

Similar approaches were followed in Park Forest, Illinois, a middle-class community of approximately 24,500 residents, of which 10 percent were African American in 1978 and about 20 percent in 1990 (Hayes, 1990a). This community used affirmative marketing as its major method for attracting African Americans to reside in the community and attracting whites in order to maintain integration. The program also involved steering, through which African American home buyers were directed to housing options in other white neighborhoods, housing counseling was provided, for-sale signs were banned, and a fair-housing review board was established.

Southfield, Michigan

Southfield, Michigan, with a population of more than 75,000, has a goal of "integration maintenance" (Jones, 1990). The change in composition of the community from 9 percent African American in 1980 to 30 percent in 1990 created the perception among some whites that the community might become "too integrated" as a result of the high demand for housing by African Americans. Thus, efforts were made by the local government to stimulate white housing demand through a multiracial citizens' board, a Housing and Neighborhood Center, joint efforts with surrounding Oakland County, and collaboration with the local Jewish community. The Jewish community participated in efforts to foster integration by organizing to attract and retain Jewish families to the community.

New Rochelle, New York

This community of about 67,000 people has been described as "a city that has developed a culture of tolerance due to neighborhoods like Glenwood Lake and Rochelle Heights, where blacks and whites, Christians and Jews have lived side by side for decades" (Berger, 1998). In order to avoid white flight from Glenwood Lake, an association was formed to work with realtors to help maintain integration, as well as to help people get to know one another. School programs, such as a magnet school that draws students from outside the district, have been used to help maintain a racial balance in the school system. The city of New Rochelle has drawn a racial mix of middle- and upper-class professionals to all its neighborhoods, but there are still some areas that are less integrated than others: "leafy upper-crust areas tend to be more white, fraying neighborhoods nearer downtown more black and Hispanic. Jews, and increasingly Orthodox Jews, cluster in the north, while Italians and Irish are more prevalent south and west" (Berger, 1998).

Shaker Heights, Ohio

A somewhat different model of integration maintenance is illustrated in the community of Shaker Heights, Ohio, within the Cleveland metropolitan area (Pepper, 1990). In this community of 32,000 people, of which 29 percent are African American, the major goal has been integration maintenance through programs to stimulate white demand and to open up housing options for African Americans within other suburbs in order to slow down their migration into Shaker Heights. The Shaker Heights programs have focused on two levels, white suburbs in the metropolitan area and white neighborhoods within Shaker Heights. As a result, efforts were made to steer African Americans to other white suburbs and to direct African Americans into neighborhoods of 85 percent or more white residents.

ESTABLISHING INTEGRATION OBJECTIVES

In the preceding examples, local governments and community groups have taken the initiative to create and/or maintain integrated communities, mainly with respect to whites and African Americans. In communities where the presence of African Americans has reached approximately one-third of the population, programs seek to maintain integration but restrict further nonwhite population growth, that is, to stop the process of succession and resegregation. Maintenance of property values appears to be an important motivating factor in all of the programs devoted to the prevention of resegregation. All programs avoid setting specific quotas for the representation of ethnic minority groups in a community. However, one approach to determining proportions or mixes of population has been established by the Center for Open Housing in Oakland County, Michigan (Dozier, 1993). This county established a loan program with the purpose of facilitating integration. Under the program, "pro-integrative" moves are supported, defined in terms of the ethnic minority population of the County. Thus, with the county population at 9 percent minority, 10 percent is added, creating a figure of 19 percent as a guide for eligibility for a loan. If a white family moves into a neighborhood in which 19 percent or less of the residents are white, the move is defined as "pro-integrative," whereas a move is "pro-integrative" when an African American family moves into a neighborhood with 19 percent or less African American.

Community integration goals usually address the proportion of white and nonwhite people living in an area. It is generally assumed that social interaction between different racial and ethnic groups will occur as soon as the population is more diverse. However, some evidence suggests that racial and ethnic balance can be attained and maintained, but that "intermingling" or social interaction of residents may not accompany this balance. Racial integration and assimilation was one of the primary goals in the development of the planned community of Columbia, Maryland, during the 1960s (Hirsch, 1992). Residential and school integration has been achieved in this community of about 73,000 people, yet there has also been an emergence of separate social activities and social institutions, representing a "withdrawing into separate worlds" by many residents. These developments suggest that an important dimension of integrated communities is the nature of social interaction and identity on the part of residents with members of their own racial/ethnic/religious group. The example of Columbia suggests that various types of social interaction, some integrated and some separate, are likely to be found in communities that have achieved residential integration goals.

The issue of how much social interaction occurs in racially and ethnically diverse neighborhoods may be raised in regard to affluent suburbs. For example, the Oak River subdivision in Troy, Michigan consists of "upwardly mobile families from the Philippines, India, Egypt, Argentina and China...along with Jews, African Americans and plenty of WASPs...all going through the paces of modern life, house by house, side by side" (Stern, 1995). In this affluent, diverse community, many residents leave the neighborhood to participate in social, religious, and family events. There appears to be little social interaction within the Oak River neighborhood, due in part to the "densely scheduled lives" of people there, with many of the children attending private schools and few mothers at home during the day. Thus, many residents "self-select their social spheres...often along racial or ethnic lines and centered far from the neighborhood" (Stern, 1995).

SETTLEMENT OF NEW IMMIGRANTS

There seems to be no systematic way to describe the residential patterns of a widely diverse population of new immigrants. However, the categorization of community types developed by Hernandez (1985) can be used as a starting point. Hernandez suggests that immigrants are likely to enter one of several types of neighborhoods or move from one type to another over time. This typology was developed on the basis of residential patterns observed among new immigrants in Chicago and New York neighborhoods. The neighborhood areas include the following:

1. The ghetto or barrio, which generally includes a mix of ethnic and racial groups with a predominance of a single group.
2. The heterogeneous new immigrant district in which no single minority group predominates. It is more cosmopolitan and has better housing and other services than the ghetto or barrio.
3. The multiethnic, multiracial area distinguished by its instability and eventual succession by white middle-class settlement in the gentrification process. This is the kind of area to which young white urban professionals move.

4. The older neighborhoods of certain satellite cities. These are generally cities in the metropolitan area, beyond the suburban municipalities.
5. Scattered suburban settlements whose residents range from lower- to upper-middle-class social status. In this type of community, immigrant elites can mix with other suburban residents.

A number of observers have commented on housing patterns of immigrants during the 1990s. For example, Levine (1990) has noted that in New York City immigrants from the Caribbean, Latin America, Asia, and Africa have "revived bleak sections of the Bronx and Brooklyn and built two new Chinatowns" and rebuilt whole neighborhoods such as Kingsbridge in the Bronx, Washington Heights in Manhattan, Elmhurst in Queens, and Sunset Park in Brooklyn. New immigrants, especially from the Dominican Republic, have entered Hispanic neighborhoods, such as El Barrio, and this has caused tensions and rivalry between the Dominicans and the Puerto Rican residents (Gonzalez, 1992). Although these two groups have much in common in terms of ethnicity and language, the new Dominican community leaders seek representation in the political structure of the community, sometimes bringing about political feuding. At the same time, Puerto Ricans are concerned about losing their neighborhood identity due to the influx of new immigrants. At the beginning of 2000, new immigrant settlement patterns were being established in New York City. The tight housing market had led immigrants to seek housing all over the city, not just in traditional ethnic enclaves. For example, many immigrants from Asian countries were moving into neighborhoods outside the city's three Chinatowns (Sachs, 1999b).

These examples highlight the diversity of residency patterns among new immigrants. The integration and segregation patterns described by Woolbright and Hartmann (1987) differ among various Asian and Latin American groups. Recent immigrants from Asian countries have resided mainly in metropolitan areas, often within suburban neighborhoods. The one exception is Chinese immigrants, who are as likely as African Americans to reside in segregated areas of central cities. Filipinos and Koreans are likely to rank higher in social class than other Asian groups, are not likely to live in segregated areas, and are likely to live in suburban neighborhoods. Southeast Asians, such as Vietnamese, Laotians, and Cambodians, have had the most difficulty in assimilating, and those at the lower socioeconomic levels are likely to live in segregated areas. Hispanic groups vary in that Cubans are most likely to live in the suburbs, Puerto Ricans in central cities, and Mexicans in rural areas. Mexican Americans in both urban and rural areas are likely to have members in all the social classes and to be assimilated into a broad range of neighborhoods. They are more likely than African Americans to be able to enter any neighborhood they can afford. On the other hand, Puerto Ricans are likely to belong to a lower economic class, and to live in segregated neighborhoods within central cities. Cubans are most like whites in relation to socioeconomic status and less likely than other Hispanics to live in segregated neighborhoods.

The development of the community of Manassas in Prince William County in the Washington, D.C., region illustrates the creation of new ethnic neighborhoods of immigrants from Mexico (Moreno, 1999). Manassas is an example of an immigrant community located outside a large city, a community that has attracted Latino workers since 1986, "when a new federal law gave amnesty to millions of illegal immigrants, allowing them to legalize their status, move around the country freely and bring in relatives." Thus, between 1990 and 1996 the number of Hispanics grew by about 50 percent in Manassas and Manassas Park and by more than 50 percent in Prince William County. These residents from Mexico maintain close relationships related to their hometown ties to Mexican communities, their work associations in the construction industry, and their membership in the local Catholic parish in Manassas.

The entry of immigrants into suburban communities has been conceptualized by urban ecologists as a "spatial-assimilation" phase of residential and social mobility. In this phase immigrant minorities move away from central city ethnic enclaves or directly to suburban ethnic enclaves. As Alba et al. (1999) have noted, as increased numbers of immigrant groups reside in the suburbs, "it becomes easier for new arrivals to settle there, since the networks and infrastructures exist to meet their needs." The suburbanization of new immigrants is most apparent in the inner suburbs of Washington, D.C., such as communities in Arlington, Fairfax, Montgomery, and Prince George Counties (Bredemeier, 1999). According to the 1990 census, seven times as many immigrants lived in the Washington, D.C., suburbs (425,562) as in the District itself (58,887). Ethnic enclaves in these suburbs tend to attract residents from the same country, accompanied by ethnic-oriented shopping centers with numerous residents involved in small business ownership. Some of the older shopping centers in these communities "have been transformed into veritable international bazaars of goods, services, and restaurants." For example, "When an American closes another store, Vietnamese, Korean, Chinese, Arabs, Pakistanis, foreign people take over and make businesses" (Bredemeier, 1999). In a shopping center near the Fairfax-Arlington border, "a mixture of cultures has taken hold," including a photo shop run by a Chinese immigrant, an Indian vacuum-cleaner shop, an Iranian market, a Thai restaurant, a Chinese and Vietnamese grocery store, a Vietnamese toy and curio shop, a Salvadoran international-courier business, and an Afghan-run dry cleaner.

An interesting pattern of residential and business assimilation of new immigrants has occurred in Flushing, New York, a community that has attracted many Asian immigrants (Wysocki, 1991). Reflecting their success in business and related activities, the new Asian immigrants have moved into old neighborhoods, causing some resentment on the part of African Americans and whites. Another pattern is found in California, with new Mexican immigrants moving into barrios with poor living conditions and high rents. Due to anti-immigrant attitudes, some long-time Mexican American residents of the barrio have moved away from their old neighborhoods and into new communities (Montana, 1986). Others remain in their old neighborhoods but believe that community problems such as crime and deterioration of residential property are a result of the entry of illegal workers into their neighborhoods (Ferguson, 1992). In many of the neighborhoods to which immigrants are moving, their housing patterns appear to be representative of the traditional process of succession, resulting in ethnic neighborhoods being repopulated by new and different groups of people.

Another illustration of housing patterns of new immigrants is found in Brighton Beach and Manhattan Beach in Brooklyn, New York (Yardley, 1998). Many immigrants from the former Soviet Union settled in Brighton Beach, a residential community with Russian groceries, restaurants, and other businesses. By the end of the 1990s an increasing number of Russian immigrants had gained the means to move from Brighton Beach next door to Manhattan Beach, traditionally a "quiet, mostly Jewish enclave of old money and oceanfront houses." The "Russianization of Manhattan Beach" has involved the purchase by Russian immigrants of old homes, and the building of expensive new ones, in order to enjoy "suburban-type living," and a "very prestigious location," while remaining close to the "city" (Brighton Beach, not Manhattan).

GAY COMMUNITY NEIGHBORHOODS

Changes continue to occur in the residential patterns of members of the gay community. In the past the major pattern has been one of gay men and lesbians residing in locations identified as "gay ghettos"— gay neighborhoods, or gay enclaves, located usually in the central cities of large metropolitan areas (Mendelsohn, 1995; Abrahamson, 1996).

At the same time some gay people lived in scattered locations of central city neighborhoods and in suburban communities. A prominent feature of traditional gay neighborhoods is that they are places of residence as well as the location of social and business places such as gay restaurants, bars, clubs, bookstores, and parks. Thus, they have the characteristics of enclaves in that the gay residents live in the area, share a status important to their identity, and have specialized stores and institutions that support their lifestyle (Abrahamson, 1996). This enclave model of gay neighborhoods continues at present, in cities such as New York City, Washington, D.C., San Francisco, San Diego, Los Angeles, Detroit, and Minneapolis–St. Paul. However, an increasing number of gay people have been moving to suburban communities in recent years, some establishing new gay neighborhoods and enclave areas and others mixing into traditional neighborhoods of straight people.

Living in these suburban neighborhoods represents a suburbanization of gay life, "a move away from the very notion that for gay people, sexuality alone shapes identity. This movement suggests that issues once almost exclusively associated with 'mainstream' life...monogamy, family, children...are becoming increasingly important for gay men and women..." (Mendelsohn, 1995). The situation is somewhat different for older gay men and lesbian women, especially as they move into retirement. Some are concerned about the implications of their sexual orientation if they move into retirement housing developments for the general aging population. As a result, in communities such as Miami, Fort Lauderdale, Boston, San Francisco, and Atlanta developers are planning retirement communities and assisted-care complexes for gay people (Bragg, 1999).

An example of the shift in gay demographics is found in the movement of Detroit's gay community, once located in the Palmer Park area, north along Woodward Avenue to nearby suburban communities (Jeffrey, 1993). Thus, the city of Royal Oak has become a place "where a happy harmony between gay and straight seems to have been struck," still having some of the features of a "new gay ghetto." Here gay people buy homes, mix comfortably with their neighbors, and have access to gay businesses as well as to those with mixed crowds. In other communities such as San Francisco, while there is a movement to more mixed city neighborhoods and suburban communities, the Castro area continues to be a gay ghetto, with an identity "as a tight-knit, resourceful gay community." Still, it "has never been very welcoming to either lesbians or black homosexuals" and has become gentrified "and gone upscale, jammed with trendy restaurants and shops" (Duffy, 1998). Azalea Park in San Diego provides yet another example of changing residential patterns of gay people. In this neighborhood there was an active recruitment of gay people to be homeowners in a formally all straight, run-down, "bad" community. Hence, this neighborhood has become "a place where one's gay identity can coexist with...the 'root values' implicit in the American desire to own a home" (Mendelsohn, 1995).

Gay neighborhoods are sometimes identified mainly by the fact that they include commercial areas that attract gay people. The North Halsted area in Chicago is such a neighborhood/enclave, now given official recognition by the city, with "its own special symbol: towers ringed with the universal colors of the gay pride rainbow" and murals celebrating gay culture, such as one that decorates the front of the Jane Addams Center/Hull House. At the same time, since the North Halsted neighborhood has become so prosperous many gay people can no longer afford to live there. As a consequence, there has been a movement of some gays further north along Lake Michigan to Andersonville, making this area "the hottest neighborhood for gay men and women" (Johnson, 1997).

Chapter 8 Review

Neighborhood types have been presented in terms of social class, race, ethnicity, and patterns of identification with spatial and sociopsychological neighborhoods. As a general background for understanding social class and ethnic neighborhoods, attention was given to the ecological processes of white flight, black middle-class flight, segregation in central city and suburban neighborhoods, new patterns of integration, and new waves of succession. These concepts allow for the examination of changes in residential neighborhoods over time. Special attention was directed to efforts to create and maintain residential integration among whites and ethnic minority groups. Examples of diverse neighborhoods were provided. The settlement patterns of new immigrants, especially from Asian and Latin American countries, were described in terms of segregated and integrated living and in regard to residence in central-city or suburban neighborhoods. Finally, the changing residential patterns of members of the gay community were noted, especially the enclave model of gay neighborhoods and the suburbanization of gay people.

9

Community Social Welfare and Health Care Systems

Social welfare and health care services are provided to community residents through a combination of formal organizations, informal groups, and individuals. These services are offered in response to problems and needs within a local community by professionals in several fields, including social work, medicine, psychology, teaching, and nursing, and by volunteers, friends, kin, and neighbors. The professional activities of social workers are usually organized within a range of "fields of service" such as child and family welfare, criminal justice, physical and mental health care, leisure time and youth services, income maintenance/job training/employee assistance, substance abuse, and private practice (Garvin & Tropman, 1998; Johnson, 1998). Formal organizations within these "fields of service" are a part of a community system whose major function is the provision of social welfare and health care. Service "fields" are often referred to as systems, such as the child welfare system, the criminal justice system, the health care system, or the public welfare system. Each of these systems is made up of a number of formal organizations, such as social agencies, hospitals, clinics, community centers, welfare departments, courts, and centers for older adults.

Using a systems perspective, the organizations within the community social welfare and health care subsystems are viewed as interacting with each other and with other systems within the community, such as educational, economic, and political systems. While we refer to social welfare and health care as parts of a community system, it is useful at times to treat them as two subsystems. The organizations within these community subsystems are usually connected to one or more service sectors: public/governmental, private/voluntary, or business/corporate. Public-sector federal programs of the U.S. welfare state are delivered at the community level by governmental agencies, for-profit businesses, or nonprofit voluntary organizations. Voluntary and business sectors include programs in all of the "fields of service" briefly described in this chapter. Human service organizations in these fields operate in organizational environments that are usually structured around three types of services: (1) direct services; (2) community organization, planning, and social policy development; and (3) self-help and social support groups.

SERVICE SECTORS

Local community social welfare and health care service sectors mirror those of American society: public/governmental, business/corporate, and private/voluntary sectors. The boundaries of organizations within these three major sectors are not always clear, and there is usually some mix and overlap between them. Our focus in this chapter will be on the functions of the public and private service sectors in local communities, especially the changing responsibilities of these sectors for policy making, funding, program development, and delivery of services. The business/corporate sector, while providing some social welfare and health care benefits within business organizations, usually relies on outside nonprofit and for-profit social agencies and health care organizations for service delivery within the local community. The business sector includes for-profit organizations that provide social and health care services under contract from the public/governmental sector. These organizations will be examined in light of the changing roles of governmental agencies vis-à-vis for-profit and nonprofit organizations. Public/governmental programs at the national level are closely linked to service delivery agencies, offices, and organizations at the local community level. For example, offices are established in local communities to serve Social Security recipients, people eligible for public welfare programs, and people in need of health care services. These offices are linked to state departments, such as Departments of

Community Health, Departments of Social Services, Departments of Corrections, and Departments on Aging.

The private/voluntary sector provides community-based services to local residents through human service organizations, including direct service agencies, such as child and family services, emergency housing programs for homeless people, youth service and recreational programs, counseling agencies, mental health programs, hospitals and clinics. These organizations have governing policy-making boards of local citizens, and are often linked to state and/or national organizations for accreditation purposes and sponsorship. Voluntary, private service organizations are divided into two major groups, sectarian and non-sectarian. Examples of sectarian agencies include Catholic Social Services, Jewish Family and Children's Service, and Lutheran Social Services. The private sector also includes social service programs operated through faith-based communities, such as Catholic parishes, Protestant religious congregations, Jewish congregations, Islamic and other religious groups. The sectarian service field also includes community organization, advocacy, and planning/social policy-making organizations, such as Jewish Federation, Catholic Charities, and Lutheran Social Services, which are often affiliated with state and national organizations.

HUMAN SERVICE ORGANIZATIONS

Social welfare services are usually classified in terms of the major type of service provided at the local community level—that is, as direct service organizations and community/social planning/social policy organizations. All direct service agencies include a component of community work, social planning, and policy making, but their major goals are to provide direct services to a specified clientele, such as persons in need of marriage counseling, child welfare services, employment training, or income maintenance entitlements. The professionals in these agencies have direct contact with clients in assessing needs and providing services. Community, planning, and social policy organizations have as their major function the determination of social welfare needs within a community, the organization of services to meet these needs, and the coordination and allocation of resources for the delivery of services. Some voluntary associations, such as self-help and support groups, faith-based groups, and advocacy groups, are closely related to direct service and planning organizations in that they provide services and/or ways of communicating with consumers of services. Voluntary associations, such as client organizations, social-movement groups, and interest groups, take on advocacy roles and often seek to influence the goals and operations of formal social welfare services and planning organizations.

Direct Service Organizations

Direct social service agencies are established in a community to meet a range of social welfare needs of residents. The major focus of these agencies is on helping individuals and groups in their social functioning. These goals may be achieved through personal counseling, assistance in acquisition of resources, the development of problem-solving skills, and the generation of personal and social empowerment. Direct service agencies are usually specialized in terms of organizational purpose (e.g., vocational rehabilitation), skills (e.g., counseling), clientele (e.g., children, families, older adults), auspices (e.g., government, voluntary/private), and geography (e.g., boundaries of service areas), social problem (e.g., poverty, juvenile delinquency, homelessness), cultural, ethnic, or gender perspective (e.g., groups at risk for discrimination).

Direct service agencies can usually be identified in terms of fields of service. These fields constitute an organizational environment, or network, for the specific agencies within a particular service area. Agencies within a field of service relate to one another as well as to organizations in other fields of service through interorganizational exchanges. Interorganizational relationships are most apparent in agency efforts to obtain clients and develop material and personnel resources. In order to carry out these tasks, agencies are usually involved in referrals of clients, agreements on fees, reciprocal agreements on use of staff and facilities, and interagency case conferences. Various procedures may be involved in the development of these exchange arrangements, such as competition, bargaining, co-optation, cooperation, and coalition. The concept of environment is inherent in these interorganizational exchange relationships (Hasenfeld, 1983).

Community Organization and Planning Agencies

Community organizations are involved in community building through community and organizational change activities. Some organizations focus on direct community work within neighborhoods and local communities through "social planning, organizing, social and economic development, and social change directed toward expanding social justice" (Weil, 1996). Other organizations focus on interorganizational tasks, such as inter-agency planning, fundraising, and resource development and coordination to provide services to a community or a region. Social workers are active in both direct community and interorganizational work through such practice models as neighborhood and community organizing, organizing functional communities, community social and economic development, social planning, program development and community liaison, political and social action, coalitions, and social movements (Weil, 1996).

Traditionally, social workers have been engaged in community practice as change agents. However, as Ewalt, Freeman, and Poole (1998) have noted in *Community Building: Renewal, Well-Being, and Shared Responsibility*, "Today, greater emphasis is placed on encouraging community members, including youths, to participate and assume leadership roles in all phases of community capacity development," resulting in a "realignment of roles" and a "shift from 'community organizing' directed primarily by professionals to 'community building' directed primarily by community members." These social work educators urge professionals and community members to engage in efforts to "define community interests; define assets that already exist; define assets that are required; develop community capacity in governance; strengthen mutual helping processes toward shared responsibility; identify and strengthen local leadership capabilities; improve participation of all populations, including youths, women, and people of color, in decision-making." Such activities help in the identification and determination of "improvements needed in the physical environment, housing, economic opportunity, safety, education, and health care."

Organizations involved in community work seek to create, maintain, coordinate, and/or influence the organizations that deliver direct services. These local organizations are most often found in the private/voluntary sector and link their members to the local community through activities related to goals such as "neighborhood preservation and development, cultural understanding, social and economic development, and liberal and radical social reform" (Wenocur & Soifer, 1997). An important way in which this linkage occurs is through activities related to social welfare and health care issues at the "grass roots" level of a community. Organizational forms of these voluntary associations include interest groups, client consumer groups, parapolitical groups, social movement groups, local neighborhood groups, tenant organizations, environmental groups, and ethnic minority groups (Wenocur & Soifer, 1997). Members of these organizations, especially advocacy groups such as welfare rights, gay rights, and civil rights groups, are active in opposing or proposing actions of local voluntary groups and/or the local government. They often begin with "protest" and other social action agendas and become involved in planning activities related to the political, social, and economic development of the community.

Ideally, there is collaboration between local private-sector community groups, governmental units, and the business sector. This type of community collaboration is exemplified by the community development corporations (CDCs) that began in the 1960s. These organizations are nonprofit, controlled by community boards, focused on low-income geographical communities, and involved in economic development, "such as housing rehabilitation, construction and management, starting businesses, creating jobs for local residents, and/or operating services...all with the aim of sustaining and regenerating the social, physical, and economic life of the community" (Wenocur & Soifer, 1997).

Examples of community organizations related to social welfare are found in communities of color, where groups based on "community of interest" are formed around development of ethnic/racial solidarity and issues specific to the group (Wenocur & Soifer, 1997). An illustration of this type of community development is an organization in Seattle, People of Color Against AIDS Network (POCAAN). According to Gutierrez, Parsons, and Cox (1997),

> POCAAN describes itself as an organization that seeks to make fundamental change through community participation and leadership. Community members are active participants in the governance of the organization, in the staffing of projects, and in the planning process. In this way communities have considerable power regarding the methods and goals of organizing....POCAAN has developed methods of education that are based on the understanding and experience of community members. Because it is a multiethnic coalition, this has meant tailoring prevention education to the realities of different communities and subcommunities. This was most effectively done by facilitating the development of programs within specific communities to reach their own members. Educational efforts combine consciousness raising about AIDS with information about HIV transmission and prevention.

This community organization provides an example of how multicultural organizing takes place, and how public/private partnerships evolve. "It is based both on working within communities to provide education and support for AIDS/HIV prevention and on mechanisms to bring communities together to advocate for larger system change. Building strong, culturally relevant organizing efforts within specific ethnic and racial communities has been seen as providing a base for engaging other communities" (Gutierrez et al., 1997).

Community planning and social policy making agencies strive to identify the social service and health care needs of residents in the community; develop interorganizational relationships that respond to these needs; generate and improve resources in the community; allocate these resources to community agencies; and promote social policies. Examples of planning/policy organizations include United Way, Health and Welfare Councils, sectarian federations, children's services planning groups, and local health and mental health planning organizations. The major functions of some of these organizations are to raise money, assess needs, establish priorities of need, allocate funds, and influence social policies. Some organizations set minimum standards of service for affiliated agencies, coordinate services and programs, support agencies in the delivery of new services, and engage in social program evaluations and long-range planning.

SELF-HELP AND SUPPORT ORGANIZATIONS

The human service organizations described above are part of a community's formal helping network, with services provided by professionals in complex social and health agencies. Self-help and support groups also belong to the health and human services subsystem of a community, but they are less formal and less complex in their organizational structure than agencies (Powell, 1987, 1990). Self-help groups are sometimes distinguished from support groups, but they can also be viewed as parts of a continuum of informal helping. Self-help groups have a mission "of helping members to change some aspect of themselves" (Kurtz, 1997). Group participants have a problem or circumstance in common with other members, and professionals usually do not play active and ongoing roles in these groups. Support groups have a goal of "giving emotional support and information to persons with a common problem" (Kurtz, 1997). They are likely to use professionals as facilitators and to be linked to a health or social service organization, with members who are clients of the sponsoring agency. Although self-help groups and support groups share similar goals and organizational structures, self-help groups are more clearly focused on personal change.

Self-help and support groups serve their members as communities of interest and identification and, as such, respond to the needs of individuals for personal identity and sense of community. Self-help and support groups are empowering, as members join together for common purposes in order to exercise control over their own lives. Empowerment may extend beyond helping oneself to activities that involve members in larger community and political issues. The relationship of self-help and support groups to empowerment is illustrated in the tradition of mutual aid in African American and Hispanic American communities.

In their review of the self-help tradition of African Americans, Neighbors, Elliot, and Gant (1990) note the importance of black churches, fraternal organizations, and black women's groups in organizing self-help efforts and in promoting economic development and political empowerment. These authors broaden the concept of self-help to include the activities of social institutions, particularly black churches, schools, and business organizations. Thus, mutual aid and social support are viewed as important elements in the black self-help tradition, which includes advocacy, empowerment, a tolerance for diversity in membership, racial consciousness, and a broad definition of self-help. Implicit in these elements is an emphasis on "personal responsibility for advancing oneself as well as the group." This leads to the observation by Neighbors et al. (1990) that "empowerment is one of the most critical and highly valued benefits that members of the black community can attain by participating in self-help organizations."

Empowerment at personal, interpersonal, and political levels is also emphasized in a review of self-help in the Latino community by Gutierrez, Ortega, and Suarez (1990). Self-help organizations are seen as an ideal way for Latinos to gain power and control to overcome personal as well as group problems. As with African American self-help organizations, Latino organizations have emphasized mutual aid and have minimal levels of participation in "mainstream" self-help groups. Cultural factors have had a strong influence on these membership patterns, as "self-help is philosophically compatible with the Latino culture"—a culture associated with extended families, religious institutions, and social clubs (Gutierrez et al., 1990).

Another form of self-help is found in agencies run by clients or consumers. For example, a number of states sponsor consumer-run mental health agencies. The distinguishing characteristics of self-help agencies have been described by Segal, Silverman, and Temkin (1993). These agencies have an overriding goal of empowerment of consumers "within the organizations through exercising control over their collective experiences." In these agencies empowerment at individual, organizational, and societal levels is a major objective of clients. As Segal et al. (1993) note, clients work together to obtain resources, develop coping skills, enhance self-concepts, and reduce stigma, and they are encouraged to become actively involved in governance, administration, service delivery, and social policy making.

These features of self-help agencies are similar to those of independent living programs and different from those of traditional psychiatric rehabilitation programs.

In their study of four self-help agencies in the San Francisco Bay area, Segal and his colleagues (1995) concluded that "self-help agencies, in combination with community mental health agencies, can serve a poor, primarily African American and often homeless population. . . .subgroups that are traditionally less well served by the mental health system." Of special note was the fact that self-help agencies were able to reach mental health consumers who otherwise might not use services, and these agencies were able to connect people with mental health agencies for medical and psychotherapeutic care. Consumer-run agencies are also illustrated in the work of Mowbray et al. (1988). Examples of agency programs studied by these researchers include a project employing advocates to assist patients in their transition to the community; a program in which volunteers help clients practice social skills and engage in normal social activities; a program directed toward helping clients remain independent in the community; and a drop-in center for social activities and mutual support. Evaluation of these programs led to the conclusion that they were successful, "indicating the productivity and diversity of services possible from consumer groups."

Relationships between self-help and support groups and formal service organizations in the community are often complex. As Hasenfeld and Gidron (1993) have observed, these relationships are "an important issue of study because these two social organizations represent major systems of help and support to people in need." Both organizational and interorganizational perspectives are necessary in examining the relationships of these types of social organizations. An important task is to use these perspectives to develop ways of linking the two types of organizations. One such coordination model developed by Hasenfeld and Gidron (1993) focuses on various kinds of exchange relationships that can occur between self-help and support groups and human service organizations. These authors recognize two patterns of interaction: competition and cooperation. These patterns are said to depend on the nature of the self-help group and the human service organizations: their domain and mission, dependence on external resources, service technology, and internal structure. In the health and mental health systems, in particular, there is a continuing need to reduce the tensions between service agencies and self-help/support groups and to promote positive interrelationships. One feature of these efforts is to provide educational programs on self-help and support groups to professionals in formal organizations.

PRIVATE PRACTICE OF SOCIAL WORK

The health and social welfare system of a community includes professional social workers engaged in private practice. These individuals "are employed by their clients, maintain their own facilities, determine their own intervention methods, and base their activities on the norms of their profession rather than the requirements of social services agencies" (Barker, 1992, 1995b). Private-practice social workers usually engage in clinical practice with individuals, families, and small groups in forms of therapy and counseling, but some are involved in consultation and program evaluation with organizations in the community. Sometimes private practitioners contract to provide services in nonprofit and for-profit social service and health care agencies in the community. Although social workers in private practice do not work under the jurisdiction of formal human service organizations, they must adhere to the ethical standards of the profession. They are required to meet licensing or credentialing standards imposed by the laws of state and/or local governments. Private practitioners in many states may receive third-party reimbursement for their services through health maintenance organizations.

The profession of social work, as represented by the National Association of Social Workers, has accepted private practice as a valid method of social work practice, establishing minimum standards for this practice in 1964. Private practice in social work is strongly associated with "clinical practice" and psychotherapy, and the number of social workers in private practice has increased dramatically over the past several years, especially in relation to areas of mental health and mental illness. Specht and Courtney (1994) provide an interesting and provocative review of the development of private practice in social work, suggesting that this practice contributes to a move of the profession away from its mission to aid and serve the underprivileged through community-based social care.

COMMUNITY ORGANIZATION—ENVIRONMENT RELATIONSHIP

Both direct service social service agencies and community organization and planning agencies of a community operate within organizational environments. All organizations within the social welfare field are influenced by the general environment of a community and the particular task environment of the social agency (Hasenfeld, 1983). The general environment includes factors such as economic, demographic, cultural, political-legal, and technological conditions that affect all organizations in a community. For example, demographic characteristics, including distribution patterns of age, race and ethnicity, religion, gender, family forms, and socioeconomic status, influence how social agencies develop and deliver their services. An important factor in regard to utilization of services is the location of the service agency in terms of distance to be traveled by clients, access by public transportation, and accessibility for persons with disabilities.

The task environment refers to a group of organizations with which a specific agency routinely interacts, exchanges resources, and collaborates in the delivery of services. This environment includes agencies within the same field of service, but it may also involve agencies in other sectors of the community. The first step in identifying the relevant task environment of an organization is to determine the organizational domain: that is, "the claims that the organization stakes out for itself in terms of human problems or needs covered, population served, and services rendered" (Hasenfeld, 1983). Understanding the task environment means mapping the environment by taking into account service sectors, which include providers of fiscal resources, sources of legitimization and authority, providers of clients, providers of complementary services, consumers or recipients of an organization's products, and competing organizations (Hasenfeld, 1983). Human service organizations must relate to all these sectors, remaining aware of how each is influenced by general environmental conditions. Of equal importance is an understanding of "organizational networks" related to the development of interorganizational change strategies that maintain and strengthen an agency or provide effective services to community residents.

The organizational environment encompasses relationships that extend beyond the local community. These patterns are vertical: structured and functional relations of community social organizations to their extra-community systems. Private voluntary agencies and public, tax-supported agencies differ from one another in their vertical relationships to extra-community units. Public agencies often operate with close connections to state and federal governmental units. Local public agencies may be operated solely by county-wide governmental units but often are connected through funding sources to departments at state and/or federal levels. In many states, for example, the state department of social services operates branch offices that serve counties through a county departmental structure connected to county and federal governments for funding. Many community mental health agencies operate in this joint sponsorship pattern.

Many private voluntary associations are relatively autonomous, operated by their own boards of directors and financed through voluntary giving. Yet, these voluntary associations may have vertical relationships to professional accrediting bodies at the state and/or federal level. An example of this type of vertical pattern is a local community family service agency affiliated with the Family Service Association of America and/or the Child Welfare League of America, both of which are national standard-setting organizations. Other examples of vertical patterns among private agencies are sectarian agencies, such as Lutheran, Catholic, or Jewish family services connected to religious organizational structures at state and federal levels.

FIELDS OF SERVICE

A "fields of service" perspective is helpful in categorizing service agencies (Garvin & Tropman, 1998; Johnson, 1998). Brief descriptions of several fields of service are presented below. The reader should consult textbooks on the social services for an in-depth understanding of current and historical social welfare policies, programs, and service delivery systems in each of the fields. The fields of service usually include agencies from both public and voluntary sectors, and there is likely to be some overlap in services from one field to another. For example, services to children and families may be provided by public and private agencies in several fields of practice. A principal way of assessing the structure of the social services subsystem in a community is to identify the major formal and informal organizations that deliver services in each field.

Public Health and Welfare Programs

The organizations in this field of service provide health and income benefits and services through public welfare entitlements enacted by legislation and determined by eligibility criteria. Such programs include public assistance for elderly or blind people, families with dependent children, and persons with permanent and total disabilities (Johnson, 1998). This assistance is intended to supplement the programs provided through the Social Security System. Health benefits are provided through the Medicare and Medicaid programs of the Social Security System. For individuals not covered by the provisions of Social Security, "general assistance" consisting of money and services may be provided through a state or local community's social welfare program. Public welfare programs are administered by state and local community social agencies and seek to meet the food, shelter, clothing, and medical care needs of community residents.

Services for Families and Children

This field of service includes child welfare programs designed to deal with unmet needs of children, as well as more general services to entire families. These services, which are offered in both private and public agencies, include child protective services, adoptions, marriage counseling, parenting education, and homemaker services. Services in the voluntary sector are offered through child and family agencies, such as Catholic Family Service, Lutheran Family Service, Methodist Children's Home Society, and Jewish Family Service, as well as by family agencies and child guidance agencies sponsored by the local community. Other children's services are provided outside the home—for example, in foster care, day care, group homes, and residential treatment centers.

Criminal and Juvenile Justice Systems

This area of service is sometimes called the "correctional" field. It provides services for individuals involved in crime and delinquency. Services are usually divided in terms of age and gender and between services in community-based programs and services in institutions such as prisons, jails, juvenile detention centers and juvenile homes. The major components of this system are law enforcement (police), judicial (courts), and correctional (institutions) (Johnson, 1998). Social workers in this field are most likely to be employed in service agencies for youth, on the staff of juvenile courts, and in correctional institutions.

Physical and Mental Health

Social services related to physical health, mental health, and developmental disabilities are provided through a variety of organizations in the local community. These include hospitals, outpatient clinics, community mental health centers, family agencies, schools, aftercare programs, day care programs, health maintenance organizations, and hospice care organizations. Further description of health services is provided later in this chapter in a section on the health care system. Of particular relevance to this field of service is federal legislation related to health, especially the Americans with Disabilities Act of 1990, which establishes requirements for care and facilities at the local community level for persons with disabilities. Another major influence on health services is the Mental Health Parity Act of 1996. This law established regulations for insurance companies and employers in regard to extension of health care coverage for mental illness.

Services in the Educational System

Preschool, elementary, and secondary schools are settings for the delivery of social services (Allen-Meares, Washington, & Welsh, 2000). Social workers assist in carrying out the mandates of federal laws related to children with disabilities, such as the Individuals with Disabilities Act of 1990. Preschool programs such as Head Start serve as a locus for providing social services to children of low-income families. Social workers in many states comply with a certification process in order to work in the educational system with children and families. This area of practice is elaborated upon in Chapter 10, which focuses on the educational subsystem of the community.

Occupational Social Work

A variety of social services are provided in the workplace under the auspices of an employer or a union. These services are often provided as fringe benefits, such as employee assistance programs, substance abuse programs, day care, health care programs, medical leave programs, and mental health counseling (Rooney, 1998). These programs focus on areas such as absenteeism, alcohol and substance abuse, mental disorders, employee relations, family problems, and retirement counseling. Employers sometimes operate social service and health programs within the workplace, but often contract out the services to mental health centers, family service agencies, and health maintenance organizations. A number of services have been developed as a result of the Family Leave and Medical Act of 1993, many of them targeted to women in the work force.

Services for Older Adults

An increasingly large number of organizations provide services to older adults in local communities (Mann, 1998). Examples include nursing homes, hospice organizations, senior centers, adult care centers, mental health centers, assisted care homes, governmental programs of Medicaid and Medicare, family agencies, retirement villages, housing organizations (such as HUD's Supportive Housing for the Elderly Program), Area Agencies on Aging, employment and chore services agencies. Social services for older adults were a significant part of the Older Americans Act of 1965, which not only established new service programs but also created a system of Area Agencies on Aging to coordinate these services. Many of the services were available to all adults over 60 years of age, regardless of means.

Overview of Fields of Service

Human service organizations are generally organized in terms of "fields of service" that make up the health and social welfare system of a local community. Several steps may be taken in order to understand how this system functions. First, social workers need to become acquainted with the services offered by the agency in which they are employed. Second, they can develop an understanding of the functions and goals of their own agency/organization in relation to those of other community organizations in the same field of service. This involves exploring the nature of these other organizations and discovering what kinds of relationships they have with one another. Third, social workers may then focus on the relationship of agencies in their field of service to related organizations in other fields. Obviously, undertaking these steps requires time and effort, but these assessments are necessary in order to provide appropriate services and to more fully understand how well the health and social welfare system is operating in a given community. Finally, social workers need to become aware of emerging fields of practice, such as services related to housing and environmental concerns, geriatric needs, continuing and higher education, programs for immigrants and refugees, and programs that address the specific needs of women, ethnic minority groups, gay and lesbian persons, and persons with disabilities.

TRENDS IN COMMUNITY SOCIAL SERVICES AND HEALTH CARE SYSTEMS

The local community health and social welfare system is influenced by changes at the state and national levels of the welfare state. Some of these forces that have an impact on the local community include "the devolution of federal programs to the state and local levels; the blurring of lines between nonprofit and for-profit organizations; the changing distributions of income; major new wealth and its concentration; a revived interest in community and civil society; the evolution of religion and religious institutions; globalization; tax and other regulatory reform; and a retreat of government from various policy areas and the rise of privatization and market models" (Clotfelter & Ehrlich, 1999). A number of issues related to these forces were discussed in Chapter 2, and they underscore the interdependence of the public/governmental, private/voluntary, and business/corporate sectors of the welfare state.

Changes in the structure of the welfare state often start with changes at the federal level involving social policies, social welfare spending, and the delivery of services. For example, while historically the role of government in social welfare has increased over time, the federal governmental policy of devolution has changed the relationship of the federal government to other levels of government. Devolution places more responsibility, power, and resources in the hands of states and local communities in determining use of funds and in developing welfare programs in response to social problems. These policy and programmatic changes within governmental units have been accompanied by changes in the relationship of the public sector to the private/nonprofit sector.

The voluntary sector is made up of a mix of tax-exempt organizations that operate at the local community level, ranging from "charitable" nonprofit agencies to museums, colleges and universities, and religious congregations. Of these organizations, political debate most often centers on those with social welfare and health service functions (Boris, 1999; Brilliant, 1997). From the time of the Reagan presidency there have been efforts to move welfare programs from federal responsibility to the states and also to the nonprofit sector. As a result, "Nonprofits were viewed as inexpensive substitutes for government programs. They operated closer to the problems, used volunteers and non-unionized labor, collected donations, and were flexible and non-bureaucratic" (Boris, 1999). At the same time, as Kramer (1994) has observed, there has been a dramatic increase in recent years of purchase of service contracting, usually called privatization, "as the primary method for the delivery of the personal social services in the United States" by governmental social welfare programs. This movement illustrates the development of the U.S. welfare state as an "enabler" with public responsibility for "policy and planning, financing, regulating, monitoring, and audit, whereas non-governmental providers. . .are increasingly used to deliver a growing number of social services."

New Roles for Religious Groups

Social and health care services in the voluntary sector have traditionally been provided through religious congregations and religiously affiliated service organizations (Cnaan, 1997). These local organizations usually receive funding from voluntary philanthropic giving, from faith congregations, the general public, and religious organizations at state and national levels. Opportunities for funding from governmental units have increased through a "charitable choice" provision (Section 104) of The Personal Responsibility and Work Opportunity Reconciliation Act of 1996. As a result, faith-based social welfare agencies have become more involved in providing direct services at the community level in programs for homeless people, children's day care, emergency food assistance, new immigrant and refugee services, housing and other services for the poor and the elderly, orphanages, and hospitals. Direct service agencies that have limited funds and depend on volunteers for a substantial part of their work force have benefited from federal, state, and local public funding. While nonprofit organizations, including faith-based agencies and programs, are dominant within the voluntary sector in the delivery of social services, in recent years they have been challenged by the emergence of for-profit organizations that provide social services and health care through contracts with state and local community governmental units.

For-Profit Social Service Organizations

Traditionally, nonprofit organizations have competed with each other for governmental funding in order to deliver social services and health care mandated by governmental policies. Currently, the entry of for-profit organizations into the competition has changed the nature of the community welfare system through a process of "marketization" of welfare (Salamon, 1993). Thus, the community has become a "market" for human service organizations, as they seek financial support from government, from fees for service, from reimbursement from third-party payors, from philanthropic giving, and from community and private foundations. Under these conditions, "Nonprofits are no longer considered automatically entitled . . .or even best qualified. . .to provide social services in the United States" (Ryan, 1999). Ryan's (1999) discussion of "The New Landscape for Nonprofits" identifies for-profit companies that have moved into the social services delivery system, such as Lockheed Martin (case management, skills training, job placement); America Works (job placement, workplace support); Children's Comprehensive Services (treatment and education for at-risk youth); Maximus (job training, welfare-to-work programs); and Youth Services International (programs for juvenile offenders, reform schools).

Ryan (1999) attributes the growth of the nonprofits in delivery of social services and health care to four interdependent factors: size, capital, mobility, and responsiveness. Nonprofit service agencies are usually small organizations with limited budgets. In contrast, for-profit organizations entering the social welfare business are large, backed by sufficient capital to allow them to enter new markets. Nonprofit agencies are usually bound to a local geographic area and committed to serving the local community. In contrast, for-profit organizations are mobile and therefore able to move to new markets that are profitable. Finally, for-profit organizations respond quickly to requests for proposals from governmental agencies and are able to create new programs quickly. Nonprofit agencies, on the other hand, may be less responsive, especially if they are bound by agency mission and policy commitments. In the light of these organizational conditions, for-profit organizations have joined nonprofit organizations as a part of the voluntary/private sector of the social welfare and health care subsystems of local communities. Sometimes the for-profit organization is a competitor with the nonprofit agency for funding from local, state, and federal governments. At other times, nonprofit agencies collaborate with for-profit organizations in providing community services.

As nonprofit agencies seek to adapt to a new organizational environment, a number of questions can be raised about the effect of these changes in the voluntary sector on the local community and on society. While the question of who provides better service remains unanswered, the nonprofits make the case that they are better connected to the local community and offer services grounded in professional values, rather than in productivity. Nonprofit agencies claim they provide more unsubsidized services to their clientele through the use of volunteers and private voluntary giving. Related to this characteristic of the nonprofit agencies is the argument that they offer local residents opportunities for participating in the social welfare system though boards, volunteer services, and the like, thus contributing to a civil society. Finally, nonprofit agencies see themselves as advocates for disadvantaged people, and therefore have a policy agenda that involves advocacy and lobbying for improved services for their clientele—a goal not usually suited to for-profit organization (Ryan, 1999). Still, many human service professionals predict that the federal government will continue to restructure its roles, responsibilities, and funding patterns vis-à-vis the state and local governments, and will increase the privatization of public services through both nonprofit and for-profit organizations in the voluntary sector.

Provision of Emergency Services

As social problems emerge or expand, governments often take responsibility for the funding of new social welfare programs. At the same time, governments have tried to avoid creating public-sector service agencies to provide the new services by treating social problems as emergencies, e.g., hunger, homelessness, and domestic violence (Lipsky & Smith, 1989). With this perspective, government agencies make "purchase of services" arrangements that involve the funding of nonprofit or for-profit organizations. In these instances, governmental agencies contribute to the meeting of emergency needs of people, but they avoid making a permanent commitment to help those in need. Increasingly, however, the various governmental social welfare and health care organizations have gone beyond their limited response to emergencies by making commitments to the funding of private and public agencies to provide a range of ongoing services.

One form of privatization has been "contracting out" services: funding of private social agencies, both nonprofit and for-profit, to deliver services that are viewed as the responsibility of local, state, and federal governmental units. When emergency services are needed, contracting out seems to have several advantages for the public agency. These advantages include more rapid response to the problem through already established programs in private organizations, positive public relations from supporting the private sector, less commitment to provide future services, more options for changing service direction, and decreased expenses as a result of the ongoing operation of the organization (Lipsky & Smith, 1989).

There are some potential problems with treating social needs as emergencies. This kind of response by the public sector leaves unresolved the question of how the problems will be handled on a long-term basis. There is an assumption that the problems can be handled on a short-term, emergency basis. For example, emergency shelters for homeless people, first developed by the private sector through voluntary financial support, and followed by local community governmental support, did not deal with the need for affordable housing for poor people who are homeless or at risk of becoming homeless. In this example, the persistence of the problem led governmental units at federal, state, and local levels to participate in the funding of services and to develop systemic solutions and institutional commitments to deal with housing problems. Another issue concerns eligibility and criteria for emergency services. Such eligibility criteria for services by private agencies are often subjective, creating the possibility of unfair distribution of resources and treatment for those in need. On the other hand, agencies that provide emergency services can avoid some of the time and eligibility restrictions and move quickly to respond to individual problems. Perhaps the most important issue related to emergency services has concerned the length of time governmental agencies have been willing to fund such programs and to become involved in long-term solutions.

ETHNICITY AND THE SOCIAL SERVICES SYSTEM

Thus far, our discussion of the various types of social service and health care organizations has focused on mainstream, traditional, conventional services provided through formal organizations. However, as Iglehart and Becerra (1995) note, "Ideally, human services organizations would seek to provide services to all who need them within a community, but, in reality, many minority groups are unserved, underserved, or inappropriately served by the established human services system." In response to this situation, ethnic minority communities have created mutual aid and self-help groups, associations, and ethnic agencies to meet their special service needs. The most prominent organizational forms for the delivery of these special services have been ethnic agencies and faith-based voluntary service groups. Services that are provided in specific geographical areas of a community through neighborhood-based associations include direct services, community organizing, community development, and social action activities.

What is an ethnic agency? Examination of this question by Iglehart and Becerra (1995) highlights some of the organizational issues related to ethnic minority services, providing illustrations of ethnic agencies in local communities. These authors conclude that "The ethnic agency does not represent a monolithic entity; rather, it covers a range of agencies that provide a variety of services to a spectrum of ethnic groups. . . . Thus, there is no single model that defines the ethnic agency." Still, identifying some common characteristics of ethnic minority agencies assists us in understanding this model of service delivery to communities of color. The classic study by Jenkins (1981), *The Ethnic Dilemma in Social Services,* conceptualized the ethnic agency in terms of its special characteristics. In this study of child care agencies serving a high proportion of ethnic minority clients, such as day care centers, foster care/adoption agencies, residential centers, and youth services, Jenkins associates an ethnic agency with the following features: "(1) it serves primarily ethnic clients; (2) it is staffed by a majority of individuals who are of the same ethnicity as the client group; (3) it has an ethnic majority on its board; (4) it has ethnic community and/or ethnic power structure support; (5) it integrates ethnic content into its program; (6) it views strengthening the family as a primary goal; and (7) it maintains an ideology that promotes ethnic identity and ethnic participation in the decision-making processes."

Jenkins (1981) found that one of the principal features of ethnic agencies was their ability to incorporate some of the features of primary groups into formal organizations, thereby facilitating the agency's links to families and neighborhoods and increasing utilization of services. Thus, the organizational climate is structured in an informal way, and personal relationships are developed between clients and staff. There is "a relaxed and friendly climate," a lack of red tape, and a debureaucratization of the agency. These agency features assist in avoiding the underutilization of services that often occurs with mainstream, traditional agencies because of cultural barriers between clients and staff.

Iglehart and Becerra (1995) identify other features of the ethnic minority agency, stating that it "attempts to foster client empowerment in the agency" by providing information on how to utilize other helping systems, by emphasizing client participation in decision-making about services, and by seeking to empower the ethnic community. The agency has a commitment to the ethnic community: "The ethnic agency belongs to the community and is accountable to its community constituency." Since ethnic minority agencies are a part of the community's health and social welfare system, it is important to understand the nature of the interorganizational relationships between these agencies and other agencies in the private and public sectors. Iglehart and Becerra (1995) provide a set of propositions that "describe those factors that influence the ethnic agency's relationship with organizations external to the ethnic community," namely:

- *Proposition 1.* Ethnic agencies are not in competition with mainstream social services for clients.
- *Proposition 2.* In an interorganizational relationship, the ethnic agency is of importance because of its access to a particular ethnic population.
- *Proposition 3.* The refining of approaches to service delivery may promote interorganizational relations that include ethnic agencies.
- *Proposition 4.* As privatization increases, the ethnic agency will be called upon to extend services to its special population.
- *Proposition 5.* Interorganizational relationships are more likely to develop between public agencies and the ethnic agency rather than between mainstream agencies in general and the ethnic agency.
- *Proposition 6.* Changing federal funding requirements are developing partnerships between mainstream agencies and ethnic agencies.
- *Proposition 7.* The ethnic agency's interface with mainstream agencies is predicated on the availability of funding to support that interface.

- *Proposition 8.* In the ebb and flow of the fiscal environment, ethnic agencies are particularly vulnerable.
- *Proposition 9.* Ideological conflicts can occur between the ethnic agency and the mainstream agencies.
- *Proposition 10.* The problems of race relations that exist in the larger society permeate the dynamics of the relationship between ethnic agencies and mainstream agencies.

Community organizing and community development in poor ethnic minority communities needs to be a significant part of the community social welfare system. The edited work of Rivera and Erlich (1998), *Community Organizing in a Diverse Society,* makes an important contribution to our understanding of "the history, oppression, social problems, organizing, and community development experienced" by people of color. In this volume, a number of experts representing a range of communities of color provide discussions and illustrations of tactics and strategies of community agencies and associations that serve these communities. Such communities include Native Americans, Chicanos, African Americans, Puerto Ricans, women of color, Chinese Americans, Japanese Americans, Filipino Americans, Central American immigrants, and Southeast Asian immigrants to the United States. The authors writing about these communities focus on factors affecting agency outcomes. Central to these discussions is a "meta approach" introduced by Rivera and Erlich, one that focuses on a three-tiered process of contact intensity and influence in ethnic minority communities that involves primary, secondary, and tertiary levels of community development. The primary level of involvement "requires racial, cultural, and linguistic identity" involving "full ethnic solidarity with the community." The secondary level deals with liaison to the outside community and institutions by people with expertise and knowledge of the culture of the ethnic community. A tertiary level includes "working for the common interests and concerns of the community," working with the outside infrastructures as an advocate and broker for communities of color. Within this context, Rivera and Erlich (1998) identify practice elements for successful organizing—that is, qualities related to knowledge, skills, attributes, and values:

1. Similar cultural and racial identification
2. Familiarity with customs and traditions, social networks, and values
3. An intimate knowledge of language and subgroup slang
4. Leadership styles and development
5. An analytical framework for political and economic analysis

6. Knowledge of past organizing strategies, their strengths and limitations
7. Skills in empowerment strategies
8. Skills in assessing community psychology
9. Knowledge of organizational behavior and decision making
10. Skills in evaluative and participatory research
11. Skills in program planning and development and administration management
12. Self-awareness, including knowledge of personal strengths and limitations

HEALTH CARE

Because social workers are employed in such a wide range of health service organizations, and there is a close interrelationship between the social and health functioning of individuals, the health care system is often considered to be interconnected with the social services system of a community. Within the federal government, health and human services are combined at the Cabinet level. Within local communities, the health care system is usually viewed as related but not a part of the social welfare system. Ideally, local community health care is provided through a system that involves "a complex, comprehensive, interdisciplinary network of services comprising diagnosis, treatment, rehabilitation, health maintenance, and preventive intervention for people of all ages and circumstances" (NASW, 1982). The areas of physical health and mental health are often divided into two systems, but there is a view that neither is "so much a system as it is the outcome of responses to different health needs" (Jensen, Cayner, & Hall, 1998). In local communities, there is an overlap in public health, physical health, and mental health services, as well as considerable interdependence between the organizations in each of these areas. Our use of the term *health care* encompasses the policies, programs, and services offered through the public health, physical health, and mental health systems of a community.

The structure and functioning of the health care system in a community can be examined by applying many of the concepts used to understand the social welfare system. Thus, the local community health care system provides services through complex bureaucratic organizations such as hospitals, rehabilitation centers, psychiatric hospitals and clinics, mental health centers, nursing homes, and through the private practice of professional health service providers. These providers include physicians, psychiatrists, psychologists, social workers, nurses, occupational therapists, and physical therapists. Services in the mental health system include not only treatment of mental illness but also the provision of other social services, such as supportive services involving housing, financial assistance, and job skills training. As a result of the movement of patients from hospitals to local communities, services have increasingly become "community-based," especially through programs that focus on preventive services and psychosocial rehabilitation and are coordinated through case management and behavioral managed care organizations.

Health care organizations are dependent on community legitimization and sanction. They have both horizontal and vertical patterns of organizational relationships with their environments, and may be involved in either direct service or planning functions or both. They draw heavily on private, corporate, and public funding at local, state, and national levels. Health care organizations interact with other subsystems of a community, particularly with the political, economic, and social welfare systems. In examining the health care system of a community, it is important to identify the boundaries of the relevant communities. For example, the components of health care systems will vary in relation to their host community (metropolitan area, municipality, or neighborhood). The size of the community affects the extent to which health care services, especially specialized services, are available and accessible.

The diversity of a community, in terms of ethnicity, race, and social class, has an impact on the nature of the health services offered, so that in many communities there has been a development of ethnic minority health care programs. For example, the state Office of Mental Health in New York has established a "special system for treating patients with mental illness who speak only Chinese dialects or Korean" (Fein, 1998). In this program, these patients are placed on units at two state hospitals in New York City that are staffed by nurses, doctors, social workers, and psychiatrists who speak Mandarin, Cantonese, or Korean. This program seeks to assure that patients receive appropriate care, since "the inability to communicate in the same language makes diagnosis and treatment nothing more than a guessing game" (Fein, 1998). A similar program had been established previously, establishing psychiatric units for patients who speak only Spanish. In both programs, there was recognition that better linguistic services were necessary in hospital emergency rooms, where mental health patients most often enter the health care system.

Major criticisms of the health care system include concerns about a lack of coordination and cooperation between physical and mental health organizations, between private, business, and public service sectors, and between the service units and professionals within each subsystem. This inefficiency has led to the charge that a number of consumers, patients, or clients get "lost between the cracks" in attempting to obtain health care services. Disorganization in the health care system has negative effects on all persons in need of health care, but especially disadvantaged and ethnic minority persons. The most neglected and underserved population group is the nation's two million Native Americans. Michael H. Trujillo, Assistant Surgeon General and director of the U.S. Indian Health Service, has brought these health care needs to the attention of the Congress in an effort to gain funds to raise "Indian health care up to acceptable levels" (Claiborne, 1999b). Native Americans are entitled to free health care under treaties signed with the federal government, but studies show that American Indians are much more likely than the general population to suffer from tuberculosis, liver disease, and diabetes. "Only 15 of the 515 Indian health facilities nationwide are equipped to handle tertiary-level care, and the chair of the National Indian Health Board has noted that "Indians are routinely denied hospitalization and specialized care until their illness becomes unbearably painful or life-threatening" due to low levels of Indian Health service spending (Claiborne, 1999b).

Another indicator of the lack of health services for ethnic minority groups comes from a 1999 survey conducted by the Centers for Disease Control and Prevention (Brown, D., 1999). This study of adults aged 65 years and older on Medicare indicated that "inadequate vaccination against influenza and pneumonia is a public health emergency," with vaccination rates for whites of 68 percent for influenza and 48 percent for pneumonia; for blacks of 46 percent and 25 percent; for Hispanics of 53 percent and 36 percent. In response to these study findings, Surgeon General Satcher stated that "an especially high priority is increasing vaccination rates in minority communities."

A major initiative for improving the system of health care within the nation and its communities was launched in 1993 by the Clinton administration under the leadership of the First Lady. This initiative did not lead to health care reform, but there has been a concerted effort from the government and business to curtail the cost of health care services, especially through various forms of managed care. It is clear that the operation of the health care system in metropolitan and municipal communities is highly dependent on state and federal programs for funding and on public and private health insurance for coverage and financing. Thus, understanding the health care system of local communities requires knowledge about the particular community, its health care organizations and professionals, and the horizontal interorganizational arrangements for care. It also requires knowledge about the general health care environment of private and public policies, organizations, and programs at state and federal levels. Recent trends and health care system issues will now be discussed in relation to health insurance, managed care, parity in mental health care, and patients' rights.

TRENDS IN THE HEALTH CARE SYSTEM

Health Insurance

One of the most challenging problems in the health care system is the lack of health insurance coverage for more than 43 million people in the United States, approximately 16 percent of the total population (Kilborn, 1999a). The number of children under the age of 18 without health insurance in 1998 was greater than 11 million (Pear, 1999b). The uninsured include many working families whose employers do not provide health care coverage and who cannot afford to purchase their own insurance. Often adults in these families earn too much to be eligible for Medicaid coverage for themselves, even though their children may be covered by this federal program. African Americans and Hispanic Americans are disproportionately without health care insurance, with the uninsured including approximately 34 percent of Hispanic Americans and 22 percent of African Americans, as compared to only 12 percent of non-Hispanic whites (Kilborn, 1999b). This problem is particularly acute for Hispanic immigrants because of cultural, bureaucratic, and political barriers such as the following:

- the waiting period to apply for Medicaid is five years for legal immigrants;
- Hispanic immigrants often work for small employers in low-wage jobs with no health benefits;
- health care providers often do not speak Spanish;
- some Hispanic immigrants prefer to use *curanderas* and *curanderos* (female and male indigenous healers, often concerned with spiritually related illnesses) for health care.

In response to these problems, many Hispanic American immigrants seek care from unlicensed practitioners in storefront clinics, where they obtain illegal pharmaceuticals brought in from Mexico (Associated Press, 1999b). Another response is to use emergency rooms of public hospitals.

Members of Congress have given attention to the problems of lack of medical insurance coverage through proposals related to the marketplace. One proposal involves tax breaks that could be used to buy health insurance (Kilborn, 1999a). For example, tax credits might be extended to low-income individuals and families. These benefits still might not be sufficient to help extremely poor families to purchase adequate insurance. Other proposals would provide benefits to self-employed workers through tax deductions for insurance premiums; tax credits to pay for long-term care; and tax credits for people with disabilities who go back to work (Pear, 1999a).

Proposals on behalf of persons with disabilities, such as the Work Incentives Improvement Act brought to Congress in 1999 by President Clinton, seek to assure them that they will retain health care benefits under Medicaid and Medicare if they return to work, including coverage for prescription drugs and home care assistance.
This bill would contain provisions such as the following:

- People who lose eligibility for Social Security disability benefits because they return to work would be allowed to continue their Medicare coverage.
- People with disabilities could buy Medicaid coverage even if they took jobs and earned income that would otherwise disqualify them. States could charge premiums for such coverage, requiring higher premiums from people with higher incomes.
- States could allow disabled workers to buy Medicaid coverage, even if the workers lost eligibility for cash benefits because of improvements in their medical conditions.
- States could provide Medicaid to workers who are not actually disabled, but have physical or mental impairments that are "reasonably expected" to become severe disabilities in the absence of health care. This provision could help people who have been infected with HIV, the virus that causes AIDS, but have not developed symptoms of the disease (Pear, 1999d).

In regard to the lack of health insurance for approximately 11 million children in the U.S., the Clinton administration initiated efforts to enroll these children in programs for which they are eligible, such as Medicaid. The Children's Health Insurance Program in 1997 allowed states to expand their existing Medicaid programs or to set up new programs for children (Havemann, 1999). However, by July of 1999 only 1.3 million children were enrolled in this program, even though under the welfare reform act of 1996 when families leave welfare, children may still qualify for Medicaid. Because parents may not be aware of this eligibility, advertising efforts to reach these families included a national toll-free telephone number that would refer callers to their state health departments for enrollment in health care programs (Pear, 1999b). Other advertising efforts were initiated through Kmart advertising, General Motors, NBC, ABC, Black Entertainment Television, and the Spanish-language network.

Recognizing that the Children's Health Insurance Program had not succeeded as expected, in the early period of the presidential campaign for 2000, Vice President Gore proposed a plan that would expand the current program "to guarantee access to affordable health insurance for all children by 2005" (Pear, 1999e). The Gore proposal included the following features:

- Expand eligibility for the Children's Health Insurance Program to include children in a family of four with an income of up to $41,750
- Let uninsured parents enroll in this program if their children are eligible
- Penalize states that fail to meet federal goals for insuring children
- Provide tax credits to help individuals and small businesses buy health insurance

Managed Care

Managed care is a term given to various types of plans for the financing and delivery of health care. There are usually three major parties involved in managed care plans: the patients or purchasers of care, the providers (physicians, hospitals, other professionals), and the insurers (third parties such as Health Maintenance Organizations and Preferred Provider Organizations). Both private and public health insurers are involved in managed care that seeks to contain or reduce costs for health care. As a result, abuses in health plans have led to attempts to provide "patients' rights" for health care consumers. Another concern raised by these plans is the trend of physicians to cut back on their "charity work" for uninsured patients. For example, a research study reported in the *Journal of the American Medical Association* indicated "that managed care systematically erodes physicians' willingness to treat people without insurance or money," due in part to the fact that an increased proportion of the physician's income comes from managed care fees (Goldstein, 1999). At the same time, charity care by community clinics and public hospitals has become financially problematic because of changes in the policies of state and federal health programs related to managed care for poor people and the elderly.

Managed care has become a significant influence on the health care choices of Medicare beneficiaries, yet the Health Care Financing Administration found that many older adults are "ill-equipped to handle the brave new world of health care choices envisioned by

Congress" (Toner, 1999). In an effort to make these individuals better informed, during the fall of 1999 the federal government mailed out a guide, *Medicare and You 2000*. One of the important features of this guide was inclusion of information about managed care choices through HMOs. For example, many Medicare beneficiaries have the choice between traditional Medicare and at least one HMO, but they may not understand the basic features of these choices, such as Medicare Part A and Part B, prescription drug coverage, choice of doctors, and Medigap insurance. Some beneficiaries need information on choosing another HMO when their provider withdraws from the Medicare program. The federal government has backed up the mailings of the guide with toll-free telephone service, an expanded Internet site, and outreach efforts to local and national groups.

Managed care has become "the predominant method of financing and delivering health care to Medicaid recipients" (Perloff, 1996). Most of the states have some form of managed care for families and children eligible for Medicaid. In some instances, there is a concern that managed care plans for Medicaid recipients may not meet health and mental health needs of urban poor populations, made up of many "high-risk, multi-problem, chronically ill, and more expensive patients" (Perloff, 1996). Of particular concern is the scarcity of health care providers, public hospitals, and clinics in poor, inner-city neighborhoods, the so-called "safety net providers" that operate with limited budgets and inadequate facilities.

Parity in Mental Health Care

The financing of mental health care has traditionally been different from that of physical health care, with considerable limits placed on insurance coverage for mental health services. Employer-sponsored health plans are generally concerned with cost and access to services, leading to limitations for mental health care. The passage of parity legislation in many states and by the Congress in 1996 illustrates how public policies at the state and national levels of government affect the health care systems of local communities. The lack of parity in coverage of physical and mental health services has been due to concerns on the part of insurers and employers about the costs of mental health care, its unpredictability, and the high risk of insuring people with severe, persistent mental illnesses. Mental health parity is defined in different ways in parity legislation, usually in a much more limited sense than "full parity"—that is, "insurance coverage for mental and addictive disorders that is equal to that provided for any physical disease or illness, in terms of service or dollar limits, deductibles, and co-payments" (Hennessy & Stephens, 1997). Narrow definitions of parity may cover only mental health services that are comparable to physical health care, such as "medical treatment," and may minimize psychosocial treatments, rehabilitative assistance, and long-term care services.

The Mental Health Parity Act of 1996 has been described as a first step in ending discrimination against people who need mental health services (Pear, 1998b). This law requires group insurance policies of companies with more than 50 persons to cover any mental illness requiring mental health services, excluding substance abuse or chemical dependency. The services covered and cost-sharing provisions are as follows (Hennessy & Stephens, 1997):

- Plans with aggregate lifetime dollar limits for medical or surgical benefits must not impose different dollar limits on mental health benefits.
- Plans without annual or lifetime dollar limits for medical or surgical benefits may not impose them for mental health benefits.
- Coverage must be provided for any mental health services defined under the terms of the plan.
- Use of cost-control mechanisms other than dollar limits are permitted (such as deductibles, co-payments, day or visit limits) and can differ for mental and physical health benefits.

Mental health advocates have been active in seeking parity legislation in states, so that by 1999, nineteen states had parity laws prohibiting discrimination in insurance coverage. These laws show considerable variability in regard to health insurers, eligibility criteria, services covered, and cost-sharing provisions (Hennessy & Stephens, 1997). At the federal level, in 1999 the Clinton administration established new standards for health benefits for federal employees so that there would be comparable coverage for severe mental illnesses and for physical health services. Concerning this plan, the coordinator of health policy at the White House said, "The president believes that the Federal Employees' Health Benefits Program should serve as a model for the rest of the health industry. Parity for federal health plans will not only provide better access to needed mental health services, but also illustrates that coverage of these services can be done affordably" (Pear, 1999c). This health plan covers 9 million people through 285 private insurance plans. In a 1999 report by the Surgeon General of the United States, parity is recommended in order to eliminate disparities in insurance coverage for mental disorders and other illnesses and to ensure that mental health care becomes part of mainstream health care.

Patients' Rights

Reflecting public concern over the quality of health care provided through managed health care plans, Congress and the legislatures of many states have developed legislation to regulate these plans in order to protect patients' rights. Protections include mechanisms for appeal to independent groups when coverage is denied, as well as rights related to specific services. For example, patients' rights provisions may include coverage of clinical trials for treatment, a wider range of prescription drugs, round-the-clock availability of authorization for requests for care, 30 days' notice of reduction in benefits, provision of extended care for some illnesses, reasonable emergency room payments, direct access to gynecologists for women, and access to specialists for long-term treatment without first going through a primary-care physician (Baker, 1999; Froomkin, 1998). Patients' rights bills were passed by the U.S. Senate and the U.S. House of Representatives in 1999, and negotiators were working out differences in the bills during the early months of 2000. A major issue concerned whether patients should be able to sue their health plans over coverage.

Chapter 9 Review

Formal organizations in the social welfare and health care systems in the community contribute in large measure to the provision of mutual support for local residents. The functions of health and social welfare systems are carried out within public/governmental, business/corporate, and private/voluntary service sectors in local communities. Human service organizations in these sectors include direct service agencies, community organization/social planning/social policy agencies, and self-help/mutual support groups. These organizations can be classified by fields of service, such as public welfare/income maintenance, families and children, criminal and juvenile justice, physical and mental health, education, occupation/workplace, and older adults. Trends in the social welfare and health care systems of a community were discussed, including (1) new roles for religious groups; (2) for-profit social service organizations; (3) provision of emergency services; (4) ethnicity and social services. A general framework for understanding the health care system of a local community was presented, along with a discussion of several emerging issues in health care: health care insurance; managed care; parity in mental health care; and patients' rights.

10

The Community Educational System

The primary educational institutions in local communities are elementary and secondary public, sectarian, and private nonsectarian schools. The educational functions provided by these schools are supplemented in significant ways by families and other social institutions. The educational system in a community may also include preschool programs, community colleges, universities, technical schools, professional schools, and programs for continuing education of adults. Our principal focus in this chapter is on public education at the elementary and secondary levels.

Local schools are major community and neighborhood-based institutions that interact with families and community organizations. Public education at these levels includes not only schools organized according to traditional models, but also special schools, such as magnet, charter, and other alternative schools. In keeping with our systems perspective of local communities, the educational system in a community operates in a context of interdependence with economic, political, and health and social welfare systems. Schools within the local educational system provide linkages between families and the community at large.

The local community K–12 educational system serves important functions for individuals, communities, and American society. The primary goals of education in public schools are academic, social/cultural, and economic (Rock & Hill, 1992). Academic goals include the learning of basic skills (e.g., reading, writing, basic mathematics), preparation for higher education, lifelong learning, and learning for personal fulfillment. Social/cultural goals involve socialization vis-à-vis the norms of the community and society, and the transmission of a shared national culture as well as the subcultures within the community and society. Economic goals focus on preparing students for participation in employment within community and societal economic systems.

Education offered through K–12 public schools involves interrelationships between the local community, state, and federal governments. Although the fact is not always recognized by local citizens, local community public education is primarily a state responsibility. At the same time, the actual operation of public schools is delegated by states to local school districts and to their school boards. The school district is the locus of governance of local schools, placing school districts and school boards within the political system of a community. The major components of the local community educational system that will be examined in this chapter include the roles of states and federal governments, school districts, school boards, schools (administrators, teachers, students), parents, and other members of the community. A number of controversial issues are examined, including desegregation, church-state relationships, the financing of public education, multicultural curricula, school reform, school choice programs, and school vouchers. Finally, we will explore the role of social workers in community educational systems.

THE ROLE OF STATE AND FEDERAL GOVERNMENTS

State legislatures make the basic policy decisions for community schools, delegating other decisions to state boards and departments of education. Usually state boards of education hold legal responsibility over public elementary and secondary schools, with actual school operations assigned to district school boards. Decisions made at the state level involve the generation and allocation of state public funds spent for public education. Other decisions include determination of policies about the instructional programs, mandatory attendance rules, course of study, academic standards, approval of textbooks, standards for facilities, and limits on taxing powers. State agencies carry out functions such as teacher certification, planning, research and evaluation, provision of technical services, allocation of federal funds, and enforcement of federal regulations.

State boards of education recommend curriculum content to school districts, and sometimes dictate such content. An example is the action of the Kansas Board of Education regarding the teaching of science, and the issues related to content on evolution and creationism. One definition of these terms is that "the theory of evolution holds that today's species evolved from more primitive ones; creationism is the belief that a divine power created the universe in six days" (Associated Press, 1999h). The Kansas Board voted in 1999 to delete "virtually any mention of evolution from the state's recommended science curriculum and its standardized tests" (Steinberg, 1999a). Still, it was left up to the school districts to follow these recommendations or not, leaving elected school boards with the option "to tell the state board to go jump in the lake" (Steinberg, 1999a). In Oklahoma, a State Textbook Committee that screens textbooks for public school districts has established a requirement for new biology texts. These books must include a disclaimer that says that evolution is a "controversial theory" so that attention is given to "alternative explanations of the development of life" (Associated Press, 1999h). In response to this action by the state textbook committee, the American Civil Liberties Union of Oklahoma began examining the question of whether or not this disclaimer violated the First Amendment prohibition on the endorsement of religion (Romano, 1999). The presentation of human origin theories to students in the public schools continues to be a controversial issue in the states and within local school districts, yet a national survey conducted in 2000 showed that most Americans support the teaching of both evolution (83 percent) and creationism (79 percent) (Glanz, 2000).

While it is clear that educational policy is the responsibility of states, and educational services are delivered through schools in local community school districts, the federal government is involved in education in a number of important ways. Examples of service and educational programs at the federal level include Head Start, the National School Lunch Program, health care programs, and programs for children with disabilities who have special educational needs. The federal influence on local education comes from presidential initiatives, Congressional legislation, actions of federal courts, and from policies and programs of the U.S. Department of Education and the Department of Health and Human Services. In 1999 the Congress and the Clinton Administration agreed on a budget that increased the role of the federal government in the funding of K–12 education. Federal funds for school districts were targeted for additional teachers, teacher training, and reduction of class sizes in the elementary grades (Cooper,

1999b). Some selected examples of federal legislation and federal programs dealing with education are cited below.

The Elementary and Secondary Education Act of 1965

The titles of this Act provide funds for education of children of low-income families, for library and instructional resources, for educational centers and services, for research programs, and for strengthening state departments of education. Amendments in 1966 created Title VI, which established the Bureau of Education for the Handicapped. Title VII of the Amendments of 1968 included provision of bilingual education.

Education of the Handicapped Act of 1970

This Act replaced Title VI of the Elementary and Secondary Education Act of 1965. It provided for a grants program with guidelines for states to develop resources and train personnel for special education programs.

The Educational Amendments Act of 1972

This Act included Title IX, which prohibited sex discrimination against students and employees in programs receiving federal funds. While the Act applied to all school programs, special attention was given by local schools to classes designed for a single gender group and to athletic programs that failed to provide opportunities for female students. This Act also provided for a federal grant-in-aid program for school districts involved in desegregation plans.

Education for All Handicapped Children Act of 1975

This Act focuses on education for all handicapped children, providing federal assistance for programs that emphasized special education and related services. The Act covers eight categories of disability: deaf, deaf-blind, hard of hearing, mentally retarded, multi-handicapped, orthopedically impaired, other health impairment, and seriously emotionally disturbed.

Title II of the Education Amendments of 1976

This Title deals with vocational education, providing federal funds on a matching basis to state and local governments for programs such as work study, cooperative programs, placement services, and support services for women.

Education of the Handicapped Act Amendments of 1987

These Amendments emphasized preventive intervention services for high-risk children. One Amendment provided funds for programs serving children from birth through two years of age with regard to developmental delays. Closely related to these children's services was the provision of family education through school settings.

Individuals with Disabilities Education Act of 1990/Amendments, 1997

This Act "established the right of all children with disabilities to a free and appropriate public education (FAPE) in the least restrictive environment. Subsequent amendments to the law have extended services to infants, toddlers, and preschoolers, identifying social workers as qualified providers of early intervention services including home visits, psychosocial assessments, counseling, and coordination of community resources" (Hare & Rome, 1999). Amendments to the Act in 1997 allowed schools more latitude in discipline of special education students and changed the membership of the child's Individualized Education Program team to include the classroom teacher and related services personnel (Whitted & Constable, 1999).

Improving America's Schools Act of 1994

This Act amended the Elementary and Secondary Education Act of 1965, with a focus in Title I on standards of performance for low-income, educationally disadvantaged children in programs of compensatory education. Services were extended to teen parents, migratory children, and neglected or delinquent youth in state institutions and community day programs.

Goals 2000: Educate America Act of 1994

This Act includes six goals identified in President Bush's America 2000 educational reform proposal, along with two new goals added by President Clinton (Hare & Rome, 1999). These eight goals are:

1. All children will arrive at school ready to learn.
2. High school graduation rate will be at least 90 percent.
3. Students in grades 4, 8, and 12 will demonstrate competency in subject matter.
4. American students will be first in the world in math and science achievement.

5. Adults will be literate and able to compete in a global economy.
6. Learning environments will be safe, disciplined, and drug-free.
7. Parental participation will be increased.
8. Professional development for educators will be promoted.

The Goals 2000 Act of 1994 was amended in 1996 to include a new focus on technology in schools and to clarify requirements of states receiving money under the Act.

Charter School Expansion Act of 1998

This Act is designed to provide federal funding for the planning and expansion of charter schools. State charter school laws allow groups to set up schools under a special agreement/charter that allows them to be supported by public funds without being under the jurisdiction of local school boards (Associated Press, 1998a).

Education Flexibility Partnership Act of 1999

This Act gave the states and local school boards more flexibility in regard to spending federal education money. This legislation allows states to seek waivers from the U.S. Department of Education related to funding restrictions. Some examples include hiring of more teachers rather than using funds for teacher training, reduction of federal paperwork requirements, use of funds to reduce class sizes, expansion of pre-kindergarten programs, and hiring of tutors (Dao, 1999a).

Head Start

The Head Start program was established in 1965 as one of the federal social programs of President Lyndon Johnson's War on Poverty. The program is implemented in approximately 1,400 community-based nonprofit organizations and school systems. Its purpose continues to be to provide preschool educational experiences, nutrition, and health care, to disadvantaged children. "Services include early education in and out of the home, home visits, parent education, comprehensive health and nutrition services, case management, and peer support for parents" (Hare & Rome, 1999). In 1994 the Head Start Amendments established Early Head Start, a program that provided services for children under three years of age and for pregnant women. The four components of the Early Head Start program are child development, family development, community building, and staff development (Allen-Meares, 2000).

Overview of Federal Legislation

All of the above-mentioned legislation increased the federal government's involvement in state and local educational programs. With this involvement came increased public acceptance of federal responsibility for local community education, accompanied by some controls over local education through rules and accountability requirements. The legislative acts cited here are closely related to the purposes of the Civil Rights Act of 1964, in that penalties can be imposed for noncompliance in areas of vocational education, education for persons with disabilities, and sex discrimination in the schools. This legislation illustrates the fact that an important source of educational policy is the federal government through the use of federal funds. Congress continues to consider ways in which the federal government can assist school districts in building and renovating schools. The major avenue proposed for this assistance is through tax benefits and subsidization of building funds through bonds. An example of involvement of the federal government in local educational systems is a 1997 law that provides aid for renovating schools in empowerment zones (Cooper, 1999f).

During a 1999 conference on education, the nation's governors reviewed the eight goals established under the Goals 2000: Educate America Act of 1994 and found that American schools had failed to reach any of them. The goals had been monitored by a National Education Goals Panel, which recognized that there had been progress toward reaching them, albeit at a slow pace. Still, the Panel contended that Goals 2000 should be credited for driving a decade of setting high standards. Education Secretary Riley took this position, indicating that "the goals helped set the move toward standards-based education. . . serving as a "north star" that lighted the path and challenged us to keep moving forward" (Wilgoren, J., 1999b).

STRUCTURE OF PUBLIC EDUCATION AT THE COMMUNITY LEVEL

School Districts

Local school districts are quasi-corporations that implement state policies through the management of schools in the district. Local school districts have geographic boundaries, often conterminous with the boundaries of municipalities, counties, or townships. School districts carry out the state's obligations to provide public education at the local community level. There seems to be little uniformity of school districts in the United States, with districts ranging in size from small rural communities to some covering large cities. Local school districts have many of the features of governmental agencies, which reflects the fact that they are in large part creatures of the state government. Intermediate school districts are established at a level between local communities and the state. More than half of the states have intermediate units of school administration that provide local districts with services such as planning, supportive services, special education programs, educational media services, curriculum consultation, data processing services, staff development, and vocational-technical programs and services.

School attendance areas are established within the geographic boundaries of local school districts. Normally, residential location determines which school a student is required to attend. In recent years some school boards have introduced policies of "choice," or open enrollment, whereby parents can select a different school within the same district. School board decisions regarding attendance areas have been influenced by the 1954 Supreme Court case of *Brown et al. v. Board of Education of Topeka*, in which the court ruled that segregation based on race in school districts deprived students of equal educational opportunity. Efforts to bring about school desegregation through busing, magnet schools, and schools with special programs have challenged the customary school board approaches to determining attendance areas.

Local Boards of Education

School districts are governed by local community school boards. Board members are usually elected by residents of the district on a nonpartisan basis, although in some localities the school board members are appointed by a mayor, judge, or governor. Although board members are constrained by mandates from the state, members are beholden in large measure to their local constituencies. School boards are responsible for hiring superintendents, administrative staff, and teachers; engaging in collective bargaining with teachers' unions; building and maintaining school buildings; and spending tax dollars from the local community, the state, and the federal government.

School boards have a tradition and reputation of exercising local political control over educational matters, always within the statutes of the state and federal government. Even though school boards are run by elected officials, some 23 states have legislation that allows the state to take over the board and replace its members. Challenges to these laws come from residents who believe such actions by a state are unconstitutional, depriving them of their voting rights. Takeovers of local boards by state government have usually occurred in districts that include inner-city schools, especially under conditions of fiscal or other administrative mismanagement, such as has been found in the communities of Jersey City, New Jersey; Compton, California; Chicago and East St. Louis, Illinois; and Detroit, Michigan.

Teachers and Administrators

The success or failure of individual schools within a community educational system is often attributed to the performance of school personnel. Teachers belong to professional organizations and to unions, and they influence community educational systems through these groups. When teachers are politically active through these organizations, tensions may emerge between teachers and community residents, including parents. Teacher strikes may result in increased benefits for teachers, but often at a cost of decreased community support. Teachers, as public employees, are increasingly subject to public expectations with regard to performance and accountability.

The qualifications and performance of teachers in public schools continue to be of concern to parents and to educational organizations. Poor performance of students on standardized tests is frequently attributed to unqualified teachers and the fact that schools have generally not been able to sanction or remove poor teachers. The most formidable obstacle to improving schools has been identified by some as the "we don't do windows" contract. "This contract gives automatic salary increases and various perks to teachers based on seniority, making it impossible to evaluate the schools' most important employees for their productivity or their effectiveness" (Stern, 1999). Concerns about the quality of teachers were raised in a study of teacher turnover reported by *Education Week* in 2000 (Cooper, 2000). The *Education Week* analysis of federal data showed that about one in five teachers leave the profession within three years of their teaching, with "the best and the brightest most likely to leave, giving reasons for leaving of working conditions, student misbehavior, and low salaries." In regard to low pay, the study found that "even though unionized teachers generally get raises based on seniority. . .teachers in their late forties get paid about $24,000 less than their college-educated age mates." The study also noted that teachers in their twenties earn almost $8,000 a year less than other graduates the same age. "School systems also evade market pressure to raise teacher pay. . .by waiving their own job requirements and hiring unqualified teachers" (Cooper, 2000).

In regard to teacher qualifications, a 1999 report entitled "To Touch the Future" by the American Council on Education indicated that "nationwide, more than half of students in seventh through twelfth grades were recently taught physical science by unqualified teachers" (Wilgoren, 1999a). This report was critical of teacher education programs at colleges and universities, recommending that these institutions give increased attention and resources to their schools of education, and that these schools be audited and accredited by an independent agency. Commenting on teacher shortages and qualifications at the beginning of 2000, Secretary of Education Richard Riley noted that "schools have been forced to put any warm body in front of the classroom"(*New York Times*, 2000). Secretary Riley predicted that over the next decade there will be a shortage of two million teachers, attributed in part to low salaries and difficulties in attracting talented individuals into the profession.

Students

Student rights are usually established by school districts and by individual schools, as well as by the courts. School districts and local schools control student behavior through the use of disciplinary measures, including suspensions and expulsions. Recent studies show racial differences in use of discipline, with black students suspended or expelled at a much higher rate than their white peers. A study of 12 large public school districts throughout the United States attributes these differences to institutionalized racism, a conclusion challenged by some educational experts (Lewin, 2000). Students, parents, and local organizations concerned with rights often become involved in litigation related to the schools. A controversial area of student rights has to do with the extent to which schools have the right to search students. This issue reflects incidents of violence in the schools involving the use of guns and other weapons by students. Numerous court cases have dealt with this matter, some upholding and others overturning searches of students. Rights regarding student records were established by the Buckley Amendment (Family Educational Rights and Privacy Act of 1974), which set the rules for parent and student rights in this area, both for public schools and private schools that receive public funding.

HEALTH AND RELATED SERVICES

School districts often establish immunization requirements for prevention and control of communicable diseases. The courts have supported the rights of school districts to establish health regulations. In general, courts have ruled that persons carrying the AIDS virus may attend school. This is in keeping with the protections of the Rehabilitation Act of 1973 concerning persons with disabilities. The Individuals with Disabilities Education Act of 1990, as amended in 1997, assures students the right to receive (without charge) appropriate public education and related services, such as developmental, corrective, and psychological services, physical and occupational therapy, recreation, medical and counseling services. A significant result of this legislation has been a move by schools to embrace the concept of "full inclusion" of students with disabilities into "mainstream," regular classrooms.

SEX EDUCATION

The topic of sex education in the public schools continues to be controversial. Approximately 40 states require or encourage sex education in the schools. The inclusion of instruction about homosexuality continues to draw community opposition. Some large American cities, such as Los Angeles, New York, and Philadelphia, have taken leadership in developing programs that include instruction on sexual orientation. For example, Project 10 in Los Angeles was developed in 1984 as the first formal instructional program to focus on the needs of gay, lesbian, and bisexual youth (Trimer-Hartley, 1993). Since that time, a number of communities, usually culturally diverse ones, have developed diversity programs that include instruction about homosexuality.

Findings from two surveys on sex education in secondary schools in 1999 reported an increase in programs that focus on abstinence. Information from school principals and superintendents showed that more than one in three school districts used an abstinence-only curriculum that permitted discussion of contraception only in terms of its failures (Wilgoren, 1999c). Most school districts were found to have changed their sex education policies over the past ten years to emphasize abstinence, and were receiving federal funds for abstinence-only programs. Challenging this type of program are advocates who want discussions of contraception and safer sex along with instruction on abstinence, an approach followed by a majority of schools. These two surveys found that fewer than half of the schools offered information on where to obtain methods of birth control, and only one third included discussion of sexual orientation in a sex education curriculum.

SEXUAL HARASSMENT

Sexual harassment is reported to be prevalent among young people at elementary and secondary educational levels. At the secondary school level, sexual harassment in the schools received renewed attention as a result of a 1993 study conducted by the American Association of University Women (AAUW, 1993). This study of public school students in 79 schools in the U.S. found that "four out of five students reported being sexually harassed," with most of the harassment being carried out by peers (Fineran & Bennett, 1999). The study defined a number of types of sexual harassment, e.g., "made sexual comments, jokes, gestures, or looks; spread sexual rumors about you; said you were gay or lesbian; flashed or "mooned" you; touched, grabbed, or pinched you in a sexual way; pulled your clothing off or down; forced you to kiss him or her" (AAUW, 1993).

Student-on-student harassment is viewed in the context of sex discrimination by the courts. In the case of *Davis v. Monroe County Board of Education*, the Supreme Court "ruled that a Georgia school district can be held financially responsible for the sexual harassment of a fifth-grade girl if officials with the authority to help her knew about the harassment but were 'deliberately indifferent' to it" (Associated Press, 1999k). This school harassment ruling reversed a federal appeals court decision that Title IX of the Education Amendments Act of 1972 never applies to student-on-student harassment. In another Supreme Court case, *Gebser v. Lago Vista Independent School District*, the court determined "when school districts can be found liable under federal law for a teacher's sexual harassment of a student" (Greenhouse, 1998b). The case involved sexual harassment by a high school teacher with a ninth-grader, with the student never telling school officials about the affair with the teacher. The court "held that the school district could be liable only if a supervisory employee "actually knew of the abuse, had the power to end the abuse, and failed to do so" (Greenhouse, 1998b). Another area of sexual harassment in the public schools involves harassment of gay and lesbian students. Some schools have initiated efforts to provide support services for gay students, including anti-harassment seminars, policies that protect gay students from discrimination, and the formation of coalitions of gay and straight students.

SCHOOL VIOLENCE

Violence in schools usually refers to attempts of students to do physical harm to other students, such as by fistfights, bullying, and shoving, especially on school grounds and in hallways. A more severe form of violence, involving the carrying and use of guns, has become one of the most problematic issues for students in elementary and secondary education. In recent years, the fear of gun violence has emerged as the outstanding concern of students, teachers, parents, and other community residents.

There has been a dramatic change in the nature of school violence, from disputes between individuals, to the presence of guns in schools, to multiple shootings (Lewin, 1998b). A number of multiple shootings in schools by teenagers, taking place in communities such as West Paducah, Kentucky; Jonesboro, Arkansas; Springfield, Oregon; and Littleton, Colorado, have raised concerns within local communities as well as in Congress. For example, the 1999 shootings at Columbine High School in Littleton, Colorado, left 15 dead (Bruni, 1999). The Columbine shootings led to a national debate over the societal causes of youth violence, as evidenced in Congressional proposals for more stringent restrictions on the sale and possession of guns.

Another school shooting that gained national attention and debate occurred in February 2000 in an elementary school in Mt. Morris Township, Michigan. In this incident, a six-year-old boy shot and killed a six-year-old girl in his first-grade classroom. The boy had taken a gun from a bed in the house where he had lived with an uncle since his mother was evicted from her household. The uncle's house, loaded with guns and drugs, was described as a flophouse and crack house by local officials. Prior to the shooting, Child Protective Services social workers had approached the family to discuss allegations of abuse and other family problems.

Violence prevention programs such as classes on conflict resolution have been conducted in public schools for many years (Astor, 1995; Cooper, 1999c). An example is a program used in 60 primary and secondary schools in New York City, financed by the New York City Board of Education. The program "teaches students techniques to control potentially violent situations through negotiation and reasoning. It includes classroom instruction, a student peer mediation program, teacher training and a series of workshops for parents" (Banner, 1999). An evaluation of elementary school children in this program by the national Center for Children in Poverty at Columbia University "found that students in the program tended to be less hostile, were less likely to resort to aggression and more likely to choose verbal rather than physical strategies to resolve conflicts" (Banner, 1999).

SCHOOL-COMMUNITY RELATIONS

A major issue in American schools involves the extent to which school personnel are integrated into or isolated from the community. One of the objectives stated in the Goals 2000: Educate America Act (1994) is that "Every school will promote partnerships that increase parental involvement and participation in promoting the social, emotional, and academic growth of children" (Pryor, 1996). One approach to reducing isolation and increasing school-community relationships and activities has been through voluntary organizations. The primary example of such organizations is the Parent-Teacher Association (PTA). Parent-Teacher Associations are made up of parents of children attending a specific school, the school's principal, and teacher and student representatives. PTAs vary in their purposes and activities. They are advisory in nature, providing parent input in regard to school programs and school rules and regulations. They raise money for special projects that are not funded by the school system. Sometimes these organizations become involved in community issues, such as school reorganization plans and proposals for increasing taxes for schools.

In addition to PTA activities and other parental involvement, sometimes schools form special ad hoc committees for giving advice on educational matters. This is especially true of programs receiving federal funds, because of the need to comply with governmental regulations. At times citizen advisory groups emerge to promote school reform, to protest school reorganization, or to lobby for or against school board issues. Individual parents and parent groups periodically get involved in school activities, such as the selection of books assigned by teachers for student reading. Objections to specific books are sometimes brought to the attention of school administrators and school boards. The following examples illustrate the kinds of controversies that may emerge when parents or organizations object to mandatory or optional reading assignments in the schools.

Examples of Controversies Over Books

In the first example, a white teacher used a book entitled *Nappy Hair* in her third-grade class in a largely black and Hispanic school in Brooklyn, New York. The author of the book, a black writer and scholar, had written "about an African-American girl coming to terms with her hair," using "nappy hair as a metaphor for the tenacity, resilience and creativity of people of African descent" (Nelson, 1998). Some black parents asserted that *Nappy Hair* was a racially insensitive book. These parents interpreted "nappy hair" as a racial slur and were "offended by the book's colloquialisms and illlustrations, which they construed as negative cartoon characterizations" (Holloway, 1998c). Although school officials backed the teacher and her use of the book as extracurricular reading, she requested and received a transfer out of the school (Holloway, 1998a, 1998b). The acceptability of references to "nappy" hair was supported by an illustrated storybook for young children, *Happy to Be Nappy*, written by Bell Hooks and Chris Raschka (1999).

A second example of parents becoming involved in books available for reading in the public schools involves author J. K. Rowling's popular series of "Harry Potter" books, with titles such as *Harry Potter and the Prisoner of Azkaban, Harry Potter and the Chamber of Secrets*, and *Harry Potter and the Sorcerer's Stone*. Parents, some of whom have been labeled as members of the "religious right," have objected to these books, about a British boy's life at a school for witchcraft, because they believe "the books promote interest in the occult." Parents in several states and communities "have called for their removal from classrooms and school libraries" (Blume, 1999). At the same time, the three volumes appeared in the top three spots of The New York Times Best Sellers List from October 1999 to January 2000, and continued to be used in many public schools. Journalists and writers of children's books were critical of the objections of parents' groups, noting: "Their crusade is pitifully misplaced. Harry Potter is the product of one of God's greatest gifts: creativity" (Malkin, 1999). Judy Blume (the author of several children's books that have been banned by some schools), noted, "The real danger is not in the books, but in laughing off those who would ban them...And now the gate is open so wide that some parents believe they have the right to demand immediate removal of any book for any reason from school or classroom libraries" (Blume, 1999).

A third example of controversies over books involves long-standing complaints against use of Mark Twain's *Adventures of Huckleberry Finn* because of its references to "niggers" (Hentoff, 1999). Most recently, in 1999 the Pennsylvania State Conference of the NAACP asked its state chapters to file grievances with the state's human rights commission in order to have local school boards remove this book from mandatory reading lists. The action of the Pennsylvania organization, supported by the national NAACP, claimed that "tax dollars should not be used to perpetuate a stereotype that has psychologically damaging effects on the self-esteem of African American children" (Hentoff, 1999). In contrast, a former assistant national director of the NAACP called the book "a great anti-slavery classic" and described it as anti-racist. When a 1998 lawsuit in Phoenix, Arizona by an African American parent asked that the book be removed from mandatory lists, a three-judge panel of the Ninth Circuit Court of Appeals rejected the lawsuit, stating that

"Words can hurt, particularly racist epithets, but a necessary component of any education is learning to think critically about offensive ideas. Without that ability, one can do little to respond to them" (Hentoff, 1999). Support for the use of the book in schools has come from Jocelyn Chadwick-Joshua, an African American author of *The Jim Dilemma: Reading Race in Huckleberry Finn*, who instructs teachers about the book.

A somewhat different form of censorship of books in schools is represented in the assignment of the book *Kaffir Boy* by Mark Mathabane. *Kaffir Boy* describes the author's growing up in a South African ghetto during apartheid. The book has been controversial since its publication in 1986, when it was made required reading in a number of high schools nationwide (Mathabane, 1999). The crux of the controversy has been passages about a prostitution scene involving young boys and men in a hostel. In a Flint, Michigan, high school, a committee of administrators, teachers, and staff responded to parental complaints by taping over some sentences and parts of sentences in the book. In response to this type of censorship, the author stated, "assign the whole book, or nothing at all."

RELATIONSHIPS TO THE ECONOMIC SYSTEM

Schools interact with the private economic sector of the community in various ways. Of special note is the development of school-to-work transition programs in which teachers link students in poverty-area schools to workplace training and apprenticeship activities (Newman, 1999). The federal government has supported these efforts through laws such as the School-to-Work Transition Opportunities Act of 1994. Still, these programs depend heavily on local community support and operation. An example of such a program is the National Youth Apprentice Program developed in selected high schools in Chicago that involves McDonald's, the Hyatt hotels, and Walgreen's drugstores. One focus of this program is on making changes in the curriculum to more closely reflect the needs of employers. This program is designed to "make a real, meaningful, ongoing bridge between teachers, the workplace, and the curriculum they develop jointly" (Newman, 1999). While programs like this one receive a small amount of governmental support, they are not government programs. They mainly involve private industry and schools in making school-to-work transitions for young people who plan to move directly into the work force from secondary schools. Summer youth work programs are often a part of these efforts to link students to the work force.

PARENT INVOLVEMENT APPROACHES

Increasingly, elementary school principals and teachers have taken "aggressive new action to get parents more involved in their children's education" (Mathews, 1999a). These activities include holding a Saturday morning "report card pickup party" where parents can stop in for a visit and conference with school staff; setting up voice mailboxes for teachers so that parents can phone in for information on classroom activities and homework; and having teachers stroll through community commercial districts visiting with parents. One of the reasons principals and teachers are making efforts to increase linkages with parents is researchers' discovery that making contacts with parents and keeping them informed about school programs appears to lead to higher "reading scores and reduces the need for remedial work" (Mathews, 1999a). As one expert on family and community partnerships notes, "Family involvement is something that schools must decide they want to do as consistently and meaningfully as they want to do reading and mathematics" (Mathews, 1999a).

Linkages of school personnel to parents are difficult in school districts with students and parents who do not speak English. An example of a program designed to reach out to such parents is found in Montgomery County, a Washington, D.C., area suburban community. School officials have initiated a program that provides translation services by telephone in 140 languages. The program is a way of "improving services and communication with the parents of immigrant and minority students," with one of its goals being the improvement of academic performance of these groups (Perez-Rivas, 1999). The school contracts with a private Language Line service, so that when someone who cannot speak English calls a school office, staff members can make an interpreter available through the service. Teachers, staff, and administrators may use the service whenever they need to contact parents or guardians who do not speak English.

In many communities, parents are able to obtain "report cards" on K–12 schools through the Internet. For example, information available to parents in Washington, D.C., and its surrounding suburbs includes school statistics and achievement test scores. Information provided by school officials is available for individual schools, along with system averages, concerning items such as student-teacher ratio, number of students eligible for free or reduced-price lunches, students with limited English proficiency, special education students, retention rate, student absentee rate, and teachers with a master's degree or higher. Stanford 9 Achievement test levels are available on the Internet for math and reading tests administered in these schools.

DESEGREGATION OF SCHOOLS

In regard to desegregation, "the Equal Protection of the Fourteenth Amendment to the U.S. Constitution requires that public schools not be operated by the state on a racially segregated basis" (Data Research, 1988). Numerous court cases have followed the mandate of the U.S. Supreme Court in *Brown v. Board of Education, 1954*. Two criteria have been employed when investigating alleged violations of the Supreme Court decision: "There must be a current condition of racial segregation...and this condition must have been caused or maintained by intentional state action" (Data Research, 1988). An important distinction has been made between de jure segregation (current and intentional segregation), and de facto segregation (beyond control of the government). Local community boards have not been required by the courts to eliminate de facto segregation, but they may make efforts to do so.

School boards usually have had considerable discretion in choosing solutions to the segregation problem, such as closing schools, reducing staff, and busing. Busing children in order to desegregate schools emerged as an important effort to achieve desegregation of schools following a 1971 Supreme Court decision mandating school busing (Applebome, 1997). However, due to legal, political, and parental opposition to busing, other alternatives have been created in most communities, such as school choice plans, vouchers, or magnet schools. Federal courts continue to be involved in supervision of desegregation plans of local school districts, but the trend has been toward lifting desegregation orders imposed by the courts (Barrett, 1993a). For example, desegregation orders have been lifted in Nashville, Tennessee; Oklahoma City, Oklahoma; Denver, Colorado; Wilmington, Delaware; Prince George's County in Maryland; Grand Rapids, Michigan; and Cleveland, Ohio (Lewin, 1998c). An example of continuing court supervision is provided in the attempt by the Tampa, Florida schools to end desegregation orders. In 1998 a Federal District Court required continuation of federal supervision by ruling that Hillsborough County, which includes the City of Tampa, "had not demonstrated a commitment to complying with the order and had not "desegregated to the maximum extent practicable" (Associated Press, 1998b). In contrast, in 1999 a Federal District Court judge ordered the Charlotte-Mecklenburg school system to end busing and stop assigning students to schools based on race. Busing in this school district, the first in the United States to implement such a program, began in 1969 when a federal district judge ruled that the schools had been intentionally operating a racially segregated system.

One of the most controversial plans to integrate schools has been admission systems that use affirmative action methods. In a case before the United States Court of Appeals for the First Circuit, the court ruled against racial preferences for admissions to Boston Latin School, a prestigious public high school (Lewin, 1998c, 1998d). In another example of desegregation plans dealing with admissions, San Francisco's public schools operated under an admissions system that allowed no more than 45 percent of the enrollment of any neighborhood school nor more than 40 percent of a magnet or alternative school to consist of one of nine racial and ethnic groups. A Chinese American parent brought suit against the schools over this admission policy, which had established separate cutoff levels for various racial and ethnic groups, with the highest qualifying score assigned to Chinese Americans and the lowest score assigned to blacks and Spanish-surnamed applicants (Siskind, 1994). This plan prevented some Asian American and white students from enrolling in the top public schools, such as Lowell High, even though their test scores were high and they lived in the area. In February 1999, the San Francisco school system, the NAACP, and Chinese American parents agreed to a settlement declaring that children would no longer be assigned to a public school based on race or ethnicity (Reuters, 1999). The settlement called for the school district to develop other plans to assure racial, ethnic, and economic diversity in the schools, such as use of socioeconomic status and the redrawing of school boundaries. Innovative alternatives to busing are being tried in some communities. The Palm Beach County school system has proposed that the community's 37 incorporated communities and unincorporated developments engage in marketing efforts to integrate neighborhoods. Such efforts are expected to result in children attending neighborhood schools with a mix of majority/minority students (Celis, 1991).

Reports from the Harvard Graduate School of Education's Civil Rights Project from 1995, 1997, and 1999 have indicated that a process of resegregation in schools has been occurring over the past decade (Applebome, 1997; Bronner, 1999). The authors of the most recent Harvard project study, Gary Orfield and John Yun, attribute this trend of resegregation to "the shift on court decisions freeing school districts from desegregation orders and growing public indifference to the role of education in racial integration" (Bronner, 1999). These authors used data from the U.S. Bureau of the Census and the National Center for Education Statistics for the 1996-97 school year to show an increase in segregation in most states, especially a drop of southern African Americans in majority white schools from 43.5 percent to 34.7 percent. Hispanic Americans were most likely to attend the most segregated schools. Of the general school population, white students were, on the average, likely to attend schools with more than 80 percent white students.

CHURCH-STATE ISSUES

An important aspect of school-community relations involves the activities of individual parents and voluntary associations, such as the American Civil Liberties Union, in regard to litigation related to religion and the public schools. The basis for court decisions on this topic is the Establishment Clause of the First Amendment of the U.S. Constitution ("Congress shall make no law respecting an establishment of religion. . ."), which applies to school districts. A test established in the *Lemon v. Kurtzman* case in 1971 is used by the courts in cases involving religion and the public schools. "The Lemon test provides that (1) a government practice or enactment must have a secular purpose, (2) its principle or primary effect must be one that neither advances nor inhibits religion, and (3) it must not foster an excessive government entanglement with religion" (Data Research, 1988).

Challenges to the activities of local schools often come about due to state statutes or local school district actions related to religious activities in the public schools (Epstein, 1993). For example, controversies have arisen over efforts to allow voluntary prayer in classrooms, resulting in these activities being declared unconstitutional. The U.S. Supreme Court has ruled that clergy invited by school officials cannot deliver graduation prayers. However, the Fifth U.S. Circuit Court of Appeals in New Orleans ruled in favor of allowing student-led prayers, and the U.S. Supreme Court reviewed the case and left the decision standing (Barrett, 1993b). This Court decision has led a number of states to propose legislation that would allow student-led prayers at assemblies, sports events, and graduations (Hayes, 1990b; Hetter, 1993). In 1998, members of the House of Representatives defeated a proposal for a Constitutional amendment that would have allowed organized prayer in public schools (Seelye, 1998). In 1999, an appeals court in Texas ruled that allowing pre-game prayers by students at football games was unconstitutional. The U.S. Supreme Court reviewed the ruling of the appeals court and declared that such prayers were unconstitutional.

Local communities have made various arrangements in their school systems for dealing with the closing of schools for religious holidays. Schools make different arrangements, depending on practicality related to the size and interests of the religious groups in a school district (Perlstein, 1999). For example, some schools close on Jewish High Holy

Days and on the Christian holidays of Good Friday and Easter Monday. Due to the increased diversity in student bodies, new cultural and religious groups have been seeking recognition of their holidays, e.g., Muslims for Islamic holidays, and Chinese, Korean, and Vietnamese for Chinese New Year.

In 1980 the U.S. Supreme Court ruled that posting the Ten Commandments in public schools was unconstitutional. In 1999, display of the Ten Commandments was supported by the House of Representatives, but at present, such display remains unconstitutional (Grunwald, 1999). Some school boards, such as one in Riverside County, California, have overturned votes to display the Ten Commandments because of a fear of lawsuits by the American Civil Liberties Union. Teaching about the Bible is usually permitted "when presented objectively as a part of a secular program of education" in keeping with the Supreme Court's discussion of the 1963 decision on school prayers. In 1999 a group of 20 national organizations published a booklet entitled "The Bible and Public Schools" that guides these schools as to how to teach about the Bible without risking a lawsuit. For example, the booklet's authors suggest teaching about the Bible's influence in history and its value as literature (Brozan, 1999).

In regard to the use of public facilities by religious organizations, the U.S. Supreme Court ruled that excluding church group activities violates free speech rights if the schools allow other groups access to the facilities (*Lamb's Chapel v. Center Moriches School District*). In another case involving instruction, the U.S. Supreme Court ruled that public funds could be used to provide services for a deaf student attending a parochial school (Barrett, 1993c). However, a Supreme Court decision in 1985 ruled out the use of a religious school site for counseling and remedial help by public school teachers and social workers as an "excessive entanglement of church and state." As a result, school systems in New York City have delivered federally financed remedial education and counseling to more than 20,000 students per year enrolled in parochial schools by renting mobile classrooms, vans, and other "neutral sites" (Sengupta, 1996). In 1997, the Supreme Court "overturned one of its own precedents…to declare that the Constitution permits public school systems to send teachers into parochial schools to teach remedial and supplemental classes to needy children" (Greenhouse, 1997). In a related case, the U.S. Supreme Court will consider "whether the Constitution permits public schools to provide computers and other instructional equipment for use in religious school classrooms" (Greenhouse, 1999d). At this time, the Court has allowed federal money to be used only for textbooks in parochial schools.

Vouchers and Religious Schools

Perhaps the most controversial church-state issue is the use of tuition vouchers by students to attend religious-based schools. The Wisconsin Supreme Court ruled in 1998 that the voucher program of the City of Milwaukee did not violate state laws or the First Amendment. The Milwaukee Parental Choice Program provided vouchers for children of families below a certain income level that would allow them to choose to send their children to any K–12 school of their choice, private or public (Bronner, 1999). The program provides vouchers of $5,000 per student, and has a cap of about 15 percent of the total public school enrollment. In November 1998 the U.S. Supreme Court refused to review the Wisconsin Court decision. State Supreme Courts in several states have been hearing cases on the use of voucher programs in religious schools, leading to predictions that the U.S. Supreme Court will eventually hear and rule on the constitutionality of these programs (Cooper, 1999a).

In the fall of 1999, just prior to the opening day of school in Cleveland, a U.S. District Judge issued an injunction that suspended the state's voucher program that pays tuition for children who attend private and religious schools (Associated Press, 1999g). The state-funded voucher program began in 1995, covering up to $2,500 in tuition per child for poor families whose children attend private schools. The Judge then rescinded his injunction for the fall school term, leaving students able to attend schools with vouchers while the courts debated the constitutionality of the program established by the state legislature. In response, the state of Ohio took the issue to the U.S. Supreme Court, with a ruling still pending in regard to the federal judge's injunction (Associated Press, 1999b).

An alternative approach to allocating funds for students' tuition at religious schools is represented in a tax credit plan used in Arizona. The Arizona Private School Tax Credit applies to religious and nonsectarian private schools, giving taxpayers a way of contributing up to $500 a year to a form of charity called a School Tuition Organization. The organizations then make scholarship grants to children attending private schools. When the tax credit was challenged in the U.S. Supreme Court, the Court refused to hear the case brought against the Arizona plan (Greenhouse, 1999e). In another case related to school vouchers, in 1999 the Supreme Court refused to hear "a challenge to a Maine law that subsidizes students who attend private high schools but specifically excludes religious institutions" (Biskupic, 1999). The challenge came from parents of students attending Catholic high schools, as the lower courts had ruled that reimbursement "would violate the constitutional requirement of separation of church and state."

The State of Maine permits students in rural school districts with no public high school to "send their children to the private school of their choice and be partially reimbursed," but religious schools are exempt from the benefit (Biskupic, 1999). In a similar case involving Vermont's tuition reimbursement program for students attending private schools, but not religious institutions, the Supreme Court rejected a challenge to this state policy.

FINANCING OF PUBLIC EDUCATION

Funding for public education generally comes from local community, state, and federal sources. However, in recent years there has been an increase in aid to public schools and their students from wealthy donors, such as filmmaker George Lucas; T. J. Forstmann, a Wall Street financier; Leonard Riggio, chairman of Barnes & Noble; Eli Broad, chairman of Sun America; John Walton of Wal-Mart; John Doerr, technology venture capitalist; Walter H. Annenberg; and Eugene Lang (Steinberg, 1999b). For example, Broad has given money to urban school systems for training superintendents, principals, and staff. Lang "adopted" 54 sixth-graders at a Harlem, New York, school with a commitment to send them to college. Forstmann and Walton co-founded the Children's Scholarship Fund, which distributed $200 million to permit 40,000 inner-city public-school children to attend parochial and private schools. The Annenberg Foundation has joined public and private partners in a number of large cities such as Detroit, Chicago, Houston, and Philadelphia. Funds are matched for the development of "educational models that demand intense teacher training, frequent testing and evaluation, and continuous participation from parents and businesses" (Ortiz, 1999). The Annenberg grants may be coupled with federal Title I funding, which helps disadvantaged children in basic subjects, and with state funding reserved for schools in which students are at risk for dropping out.

On the average, about 40 percent of local school funding is provided by the state, about 40 to 50 percent by local communities, and about ten percent through federal grants distributed under Title I for special educational purposes. States differ in the extent to which they support public education, as do local school districts. Local school districts usually obtain funds by taxing residents, based on general property taxes related to assessed value of property. The amount of a local community millage is established by citizen vote. School reform movements, at the local as well as state levels, have attempted to bring about "equalization" of educational resources for school districts.

School districts approach voters with two major types of funding requests, for millage renewals and increases for their operating budgets, and bond proposals, usually for new schools and school renovations. State legislatures continue to debate school tax issues, especially with regard to property tax reform. The debate centers on ways of raising more money for public schools, such as channeling tax revenues into a statewide fund that is redistributed to school districts, and ways of closing the gap between rich and poor school districts. Proposals sometimes involve raising sales taxes and lowering property taxes for education. Local community school districts share a common problem: how to create public support for educational funding. A special problem confronts districts with low-income neighborhoods where the tax base is low. Serving the educational needs of ethnic minority populations in inner-city areas is particularly problematic because of the lack of adequate local school district funding.

There are a number of issues surrounding the financing of public education at the K–12 levels. Since most local communities pay their part of public education through the use of property taxes, a rather large disparity in funding of education has developed between rural, suburban, and urban schools. A number of states and local communities have developed alternative proposals for funding schools through sales and other taxes, in combination with property taxes. In 1993 the *Congressional Quarterly* reported that "about 25 states are being sued for operating unconstitutional school financing systems and that supreme courts in 11 states have ruled that their systems violate state constitutions" (Rowan, 1993). An example is found in the decision of the Texas Supreme Court, which noted "glaring disparities between rich and poor school districts" and declared the state's system of financing the education of public school children unconstitutional (Green & Marcus, 1989). In yet another example, the New Jersey Supreme Court "struck down the state's system of financing public schools, ruling that the system doesn't provide enough money for schools in poorer, urban districts" (Felsenthal, 1990). The court based its decision on the "state's constitutional guarantee of a 'thorough and efficient' education" (Felsenthal, 1990). The State of New Jersey was ordered to develop a plan for guaranteeing equal funding among school districts.

In New York State, a coalition of advocacy groups called the Campaign for Fiscal Equity brought a suit in 1999 against the state regarding the disparity of funds for city schools vis-à-vis the rest of the state. The suit charges that the state plan for financing schools violates the Federal Civil rights laws "by discriminating against black and Hispanic children, who make up the majority of public school students in New York City" (Hartocollis, 1997). The suit has been supported by a brief on the part of the U.S. Justice Department that the suit is a valid claim under the Civil Rights Act of 1964.

Voucher programs have important implications for the financing of public education, especially in poor urban school districts. Sometimes publicly funded vouchers are used to permit students to attend public schools outside their school districts, with the area of residence losing school funds. At other times, public fund vouchers are permitted for students attending private and/or religious-based schools, as discussed earlier under church-state relations. Private vouchers, funded by non-public groups, allow some students to attend any private school that will admit them. In all of these instances, the school district of the student receiving the voucher loses funding, both local district and state funds.

In the case of private vouchers, school districts lose money indirectly through lower enrollments. One of the arguments against vouchers as funding devices has been that vouchers leave already "poor" schools with even less money for students left behind, particularly in low-income areas of large cities. Some communities and states have responded to the concern over loss of funds by assuring school districts a minimum level of funding. Others have raised property taxes, reduced staff, and delayed building repairs in order to continue to fund the public schools at pre-voucher levels. In Florida, a state law allowed for vouchers to private schools for students in public schools where a defined proportion of students failed standardized tests. The Florida voucher law was the nation's first statewide program allowing students in failing schools to attend private schools. When two schools in Pensacola, Florida, lost students to vouchers because of poor test performance by students, grants from the state and the district were used to hire more teachers, reduce class size, extend the school year, and add tutoring programs (Wilgoren, 2000). After one year, the voucher law was declared unconstitutional by a state judge.

The proponents of tuition vouchers believe that voucher systems encourage competition among schools to attract students, and this competition, when accompanied by public school loss of funds and students, will provide the impetus for public schools to improve their educational system. In keeping with these arguments, voucher programs promote the idea of "school choice," although school choice programs need not be linked to voucher funding plans. Caroline Hoxby, an economics professor at Harvard, has studied the impact of competition on public schools (Cassidy, 1999). Hoxby has taken models of competition by business firms and applied them to the public schools. Based on data from every school district in the country, Hoxby found "that in areas where there was competition, public-school students obtained higher test scores, even though total spending on schools was significantly lower there" (Cassidy, 1999).

At the same time, Hoxby found that the role of families is central to educational achievement. She stated that "One of the strengths of charter schools and voucher schemes is that they can have a contract with parents that says, this is what we expect you to do...the parents don't necessarily need sanctions, but they need encouragement. Because they have made the choice, and they have made the investment, they get more involved." Drawing from her study of vouchers, Hoxby has described what she calls an ideal voucher system: "one in which every public-school student in the country would receive a voucher to cover tuition costs at the school of his or her parents' choice." She argues that such a plan would force public schools to provide a better education, and could be used to promote racial integration as well. "For example, vouchers applied to tuition at racially integrated schools might be assigned a higher value than those used at poorly integrated schools" (Cassidy, 1999).

A major factor in the development of voucher programs has been concern over the limited educational opportunities for youth who reside in inner-city poverty neighborhoods. Congressional debate on Title I legislation in 1999 included "a limited step to broaden the choice of public schools available to disadvantaged students. Under the bill, those enrolled in low-performing schools—currently about 20 percent of Title I supported schools—would be able to transfer to another public school within the same school district" (Cooper, 1999e, 1999f). Another response to the educational problems of inner-city youth has been an experimental voucher program in New York City, funded by private donors and foundations under the banner of School Choice Scholarships Foundation (Hartocollis, 1997). This program began in 1997 by providing vouchers for 1,200 public school students to attend private or religious schools, with expansion of the program the next year by doubling the number of students involved. Students are selected from school districts with the lowest reading scores, with 91 percent of the students either African American or Hispanic American. A national voucher program funded by private donors, the Children's Scholarship Fund, was initiated in 1998 as a mechanism for businesses to invest in education, so that students from low-income families in more than 50 cities could enroll in non-public schools (Steinberg, 1998). In a 1999 survey by the Gallup Organization, Americans expressed a preference for governmental involvement in the improvement of public schools over the alternative of voucher programs for private or church-sponsored schools (Holloway, 1999). However, in regard to vouchers, "A small majority of Americans (51%) continues to favor allowing parents to send their children to any public, private or church-related school if government pays all or part of the tuition" (Holloway, 1999).

SCHOOLS AS COMMUNITIES

Even though non-public schools at the elementary and secondary levels account for only about 10 percent of the total student enrollment at these levels, they play an important role in the educational system of a community. Parents choose non-public schools for their children for a variety of reasons, with a general expectation that the non-public school will provide a "better" or different education. Studies by Coleman et al. (1982) and Coleman and Hoffer (1987) suggested that non-public schools do "better" because of different orientations toward education and different types of communities with which the schools are associated—that is, functional communities and value communities. These researchers identify three parent orientations to schools: "the school as agent of the larger society or the state; the school as agent of the (religious) community; and the school as agent of the individual family." It is recognized that public and private schools may include a mix of all three orientations, but the emphasis differs. The first orientation is associated with the public schools, the second with sectarian schools, and the third with independent private schools. The second and third orientations are similar in that they both emphasize the importance of the role of the family in education. In the sectarian orientation, the family is a part of a community of families, with community based on religion (and/or residence), or on other factors.

An example of private schools as communities is provided by Islamic schools that focus on a school community based on religion, nationality, culture, language, and a standard academic curriculum (Sachs, 1998). Islamic schools in New York City, Long Island, and New Jersey are characteristic of at least 200 Islamic schools nationwide, with school uniforms, classes in Islamic studies and Arabic, strict rules and discipline, and prayer. A focus on "community comes from the definition, for themselves and for others, of what it means to be a Muslim in the United States" (Sachs, 1998).

Public schools vary in the extent to which they are functional communities, i.e., "an environment characterized by caring and supportive interpersonal relationships, opportunities to participate in school activities and decision making, and shared norms, goals, and values" (Battistich & Hom, 1999). In schools where students have a sense of their school as a community, studies show that they "enjoy school more, are more academically motivated, are absent less often, engage in less disruptive behavior, and have higher achievement than students who do not" (Battistich & Hom, 1999). One such study of fifth- and sixth-grade students in six school districts across the United States found that "higher levels of school sense of community were associated with significantly less student drug use and delinquent behavior" (Battistich & Hom, 1999).

In metropolitan areas such as Los Angeles, with school districts where many new schools need to be built, decisions are necessary in relation to the location and design of schools. Some educators have recommended that the new schools become community centers with facilities that can be used by neighborhood residents, with a school building being available for activities 12 to 18 hours a day. An example of such a school design is a New Schools/Better Neighborhoods project created by David Abel in Los Angeles. The idea of this project is to build small, community-centered schools, where there is less need for busing, opportunities for walking/biking to school, and sharing of neighborhood community and school facilities, such as libraries, auditoriums, parks, sports fields, and gymnasiums. This project emphasizes community input from parents, churches, youth groups, and government, with a goal of "schools as centers of communities, and communities as centers of learning" (Peirce, 1999).

HOME SCHOOLING

An alternative to public and private schools is home schooling. Estimates of the number of U.S. students at the elementary and high school levels who are taught by parents in their own homes range from one to one and a half million (Yarnall, 1998). The choice of home schooling is often based on religious, educational, and/or philosophical reasons. "Traditionally, people chose to home-school for four reasons: to strengthen family relationships, to pass on particular beliefs and values, strong academics and guided social interactions" (Sink, 1999). Maintaining children's safety has become an additional reason for home schooling, especially in reaction to school shootings in 1999, with parents "concerned with safety at school, whether it's physical violence or illegal drugs or psychological and emotional safety" (Sink, 1999).

Home schooling is legal in all states, with each state having somewhat different regulations, curriculum requirements, and teacher/parent qualifications. Parents involved in home schooling usually base teaching on core books and learning materials specified by the state, along with other teaching materials available through home schooling organizations. Ordinarily public funds are not granted to home schooling parents, but Alaska is an exception, with the provision of a voucher of $5,400 per student. In a Gallup poll conducted by Phi Delta Kappa, a professional association of educators, "the public showed strong support for providing public school services to children who are schooled at home" (Holloway, 1999). Supported services included special education, home school teacher development and training, and participation in public school extracurricular activities.

The Internet has become an important partner in home schooling for many parents. "The emerging role of the Internet in home schooling has cracked open the door to more collaboration between home schoolers and schools and led to more interest in home-based learning" (Yarnall, 1998). An example of extensive use of the Internet in home schooling is a program in the Galena City School District of Alaska, where "the town is now home to an innovative program that uses the Internet to provide access in the bush and throughout the state to school resources for parents who are educating their children at home" (Chervokas & Watson, 1997). This district has benefited from corporate and government grants that have permitted the purchase of computers for families. Grants have made possible the development of "an online curriculum designed to be of particular relevance to the largely Native American population in and around Galena" (Chervokas & Watson, 1997). This Web-based curriculum has been financed by the U.S. Department of Education, and the Internet makes it easy for students, parents, teachers, and volunteers to communicate with each other, thus fostering "communities of home-schooling families" and "new learning communities."

Some preliminary findings related to the evaluation of home schooling programs show that test scores of home-schooled students were "exceptionally high." A study involving more than 20,000 home-schooled students sponsored by the Home School Legal Defense Association found that "Home-schooled children score well above the national median on standardized tests, often study above their normal grade level and have parents with better incomes and educations than do most American students" (Mathews, 1999b). Still, the study's author cautioned that "the study does not demonstrate that home schooling is superior to public or private schools," as family factors rather than the school setting may be responsible for these results (Mathews, 1999b).

SCHOOL REFORM

School reform is a term used to describe a variety of efforts to improve the public school system. Our discussion of vouchers represents one approach to school reform. In recent years school reform initiatives have been introduced at all levels of government, including proposals made by both Republicans and Democrats in the Congress prior to the elections of 2000.

"Academic standards" has become the label given to a school reform movement focused on standards-based curriculum and educational accountability. As of 1999, all states except Iowa had standardized assessment tests related to specific learning standards for English, math, and science. Test results may be used to "determine whether students will be held back a grade, stopped from graduating or sent to tutoring sessions, Saturday classes or summer school" (Lewin, 1999b). Test scores are used by 36 states to publish annual report cards on individual schools. In some school districts the pay of teachers is related to the test scores of students. A major concern among some parents and teachers with regard to standardized tests is that this approach "may crowd out creative thinking, arts education and character development." There is also a concern among some parent groups that the tests may be unfair to students whose native language is not English, who have learning disabilities, or who are ethnic minority students in poor inner-city schools.

Among the concerns of parents and boards of education about tests to measure "standards" is the possibility that teachers might cheat in order to raise their students' scores. For example, in 1999 allegations were brought against some teachers in New York City for cheating in administering and scoring tests. Questions also have been raised about the nature of the standards, asserting that they "can be ludicrously unrealistic" (Kohn, 1999). For example, one standard in Virginia requires fourth-graders to be able to "evaluate the social, political, and economic life in Virginia from the Reconstruction period to the twentieth century...and its impact on politics and government, the economy, demographics, and public opinion; the impact of segregation...and the economic and social transition from a rural, agricultural society to a more urban, industrialized society" (Kohn, 1999).

Having joined in a movement toward higher academic standards for schools, state policy makers have recently found that many students are failing to reach these standards. For example, in Arizona only one of ten high school sophomores had passed a new state math test. In Virginia, only 7 percent of schools in the state met standards related to testing requirements. In Massachusetts and New York the standards for passing grades are extremely low. In other states, plans to end "automatic promotion" are being reconsidered. There has been a recognition in many states that a lack of finances to provide teacher training programs and extra services for students is related to students' difficulty in reaching standards (Steinberg, 1999c).

Issues over how to prepare all students, including African American, Hispanic, and poor youth, to meet high standards in education have been expressed by the term "achievement gap." These concerns led to the establishment by the College Board of a six-year Equity 2000 pilot program involving more than 500,000 students from 14 districts, in 700 K–12 schools, in six cities. This program "uses the power of high standards for all students, coupled with the support to achieve them, to help whole school districts reach the goal of excellence and equity in education" (Jones, 1998). The goal of the program is "closing the gap in college-going and success rates between minority and non-minority, advantaged and disadvantaged students, through a series of efforts such as eliminating low-level student tracking policies." The Equity 2000 program is built on six components:

1. District-wide policy and practice changes related to mathematics standards;
2. Ongoing professional development for teachers, counselors, and administrators;
3. Establishment of academic "safety nets" such as Saturday and summer programs;
4. Development of initiatives that involve and empower parents and families;
5. Formation of school-community partnerships;
6. Effective use of student enrollment and achievement data for decision-making and monitoring (Jones, 1998).

Another approach to closing the achievement gap between white and minority students has been developed in the schools of Houston and Forth Worth, Texas. In 1999 this program was cited by the Council of Great City Schools as the most successful of 48 urban school districts in closing achievement gaps. In both of the Texas school districts more than 70 percent of the students were either Hispanic or African American. The success of these programs was attributed to teacher training (particularly for math teachers), a new curriculum for reading instruction, and "a methodical but hardly novel marshaling of good principals, well-trained teachers and sound curriculum" (Cooper, 1999d).

SCHOOL CHOICE PROGRAMS

A variety of school choice programs have been established, with a goal of improving education of elementary and high school students, especially students in impoverished inner-city areas. A number of states have passed legislation that permits school districts to develop school choice programs. Under a school choice program involving public schools, parents are not restricted to sending their children to a school in a particular attendance area. Some permit choice within a set of schools, within a school district, or within a broader area of several school districts or an entire state. Most choice programs restrict the selection of a school to those within the public school system, although a few make it possible for students to attend private schools. Since 1990, Milwaukee, Wisconsin has had a choice program that uses public funds for low-income parents to enroll children in private nonsectarian schools. A federal suit by some Milwaukee parents seeks to extend choice to enrollment in sectarian schools (McGroarty, 1993).

Goals of choice programs usually focus on enhancing the education of children in low-income areas by permitting them to leave "poor" schools and attend schools offering higher quality and/or specialized education. One of the arguments in support of school choice is that such programs will promote competition among schools. This competition is expected to force schools with poor-quality education to improve themselves. Opponents of such programs reject this argument and believe that choice plans will leave some inner-city schools with fewer students and a reduced quality of education. Because there are great variations among school choice programs, generalizations cannot be made concerning their success or failure (MacGuire, 1992; Staudt, 1992). A number of programs have been evaluated and judged to improve education. Examples of programs declared to be successful are East Harlem (Fliegel, 1992); Milwaukee Parental Choice Program (includes public funds for tuition at private schools) (Chira, 1991a); programs in Minnesota (choice of any school in the state) (Nathan, 1993); and a magnet school system in Kansas City, Missouri (Farney, 1992).

The theory behind choice programs has been presented by Chubb and Moe (1990) in a book entitled *Politics, Markets, and America's Schools.* These authors propose "a new system of public education that eliminates most political and bureaucratic control over the schools and relies instead on indirect control through markets and parental choice." Such a system is expected to produce more effective schools, since "Schools compete for the support of parents and students, and parents and students are free to choose among schools. The system is built on decentralization, competition and choice." The benefits of a choice program are believed to be twofold: the student gets a better education, and the public schools improve because they must compete for students. These programs are thought to have special benefits for poor and minority children, since the urban, inner-city schools appear to provide inferior education. It is also argued that choice programs will result in public savings, because the operating costs per student in private schools are considerably lower than in the public schools.

Opposition to choice programs has come most forcefully from school boards, teachers' unions, and public school administrators. Among the anti-choice arguments are the following:

- school choice will upset desegregation plans, leaving inner-city schools even more heavily populated by ethnic minority students;
- resources will be drained from inner-city schools;
- there is no mechanism for assuring that schools which lose students will improve;
- some plans allow for state funding of sectarian schools, out of keeping with the establishment clause of the Constitution regarding separation of church and state;
- the private schools would not be accountable to the standards of the states (Putka, 1990; Chira, 1991b).

Despite the fact that the impact of choice programs on students and on the public school system is unknown, the movement has been supported by the federal government, by some state legislatures, and by some local communities.

Charter Schools

The charter school is an example of a school choice program. A principal feature of charter schools is that they operate in local communities under state laws that permit them to be funded by public monies. "Under charter laws, depending on the state, parents, community activists, teachers, or even private companies may set up schools under a special agreement or charter" (Associated Press, 1998a). As of 2000, thirty-four states and the District of Columbia had passed legislation permitting charter schools with public funding. State universities, especially in large urban areas, may operate charter schools. In 2000 there were more than one thousand charter schools in the states that allowed them. An example of the rapid growth of charter schools is the District of Columbia, where approximately 30 charter schools have been developed since 1996 and a congressional mandate allows for 20 new schools to open each year. Charter schools in the District are diverse, with "some schools designed for children with learning disabilities, adjudicated youths and high school dropouts. Others emphasize technology, math and science, language immersion, the arts or vocational training" (Strauss, 1999).

An important feature of charter schools is that they are not under the administrative control of a local school district board, and are accountable directly to the state granting the charter. As a result, proponents claim that these schools offer "an alternative to the bureaucratic and regulated public education system, opening the door for more variation in the delivery of educational services, greater local community input into how schools are run, and, in theory, more competition between schools" (Wells, 1999). Charter schools are designed to be experimental, innovative, and nontraditional in curriculum and/or teaching methods. The creation of charter schools in the states is encouraged by the availability of federal funds through the Charter School Expansion Act of 1998. However, in order to receive federal funds states must meet criteria established by the U.S. Department of Education. Virginia is an example of a state's charter school plan not being in conformity with federal rules (Nakamura, 1998). The U.S. Department of Education turned down Virginia's application in 1998 for federal funds on the grounds that this state's law left the charter schools under the control of local school boards; that its law did not specify how school districts would hold charter schools accountable for student's performance; and that the law did not adequately define "at-risk" students to be targeted by the charter schools (Nakamura, 1998). In contrast, there are a growing number of charter schools in the District of Columbia, which has one of the most liberal school chartering laws in the country, receives federal funds, and operates through two charter-creating boards (*Washington Post*, 1998).

At the time of the passage of the Charter School Expansion Act, President Clinton noted, "As the charter school movement spreads throughout the country, it is important that these schools have clear and measurable educational performance objectives and are held accountable to the same high standards expected of all public schools" (Associated Press, 1998a). The U.S. Department of Education plans to carry out a study of the performance of students at charter schools. In the meantime, the Center for School Change at the University of Minnesota studied charter schools in eight states and found that charter students raised their test scores in relation to concrete, realistic goals related to areas such as reading and math ability (Archibold, 1998). In another study of charter schools, Eric Rofes, a researcher at the University of California, Berkeley, "studied 25 school districts for signs of competition, and found that a quarter of them made big changes to their programs because of charter schools (Kronholz, 1999a; Lewin, 1999a). Charter schools compete with the regular public schools for a variety of reasons. One example is the charter schools in Mesa, Arizona, which have implemented a "back to basics" curriculum, e.g., the use of phonics, teaching of history rather than social studies, drills and memorization in math, use of classic children's books instead of modern novels, a dress code, and insistence on orderly behavior: "even kindergartners sit in desks, in straight rows that face a teacher and chalkboard" (Kronholz, 1999a).

Of the states that have charter school legislation, most require that the charter holders be nonprofit organizations, such as parent, teacher, or civic groups (Kronholz, 1999b). However, many charter schools use education-management companies to assist them in running the schools. Increasingly, for-profit companies have applied for charters to run schools, indicating that school privatization may become the norm for charter schools. One of the reasons for this prediction has been the fact that new housing developments in suburban communities need schools, and developers may become involved in constructing schools to be run by for-profit companies as charter schools. Also, established charter schools may decide to hire management companies to handle the complexities of running a school (Kronholz, 1999b).

MULTICULTURALISM AS CURRICULUM REFORM

Most local community school systems throughout the United States have given some attention to curriculum reform, which includes teaching and learning beyond traditional Western culture, Anglo-American content. The recognition of cultural pluralism in American society by public school educators has led to inclusion of histories of people of color, including content on African American, Asian American, Native American, and Hispanic/Latino American cultures. Changes in curriculum to include content on ethnic minorities, as well as on women and sexual orientation, have been introduced under the label of "multiculturalism." There are a number of approaches to increasing the cultural diversity of a curriculum. For example, plans for assuring that reading lists included books by authors of color were considered by the school board in San Francisco (Lewin, 1998a). Such proposals vary in terms of how many such books by "multicultural authors" would be required and whether specific books would be mandated, e.g., the San Francisco district has in the past required three of ten books read in a year be Chaucer's *Canterbury Tales*, Shakespeare's *Romeo and Juliet*, and Mark Twain's *Huckleberry Finn*.

At the same time, critics have argued that the movement to multicultural curricula in the public schools has led to a de-emphasis on the role of a unifying culture of Americanism (Hymowitz, 1993; Verhovek, 1991). Schlesinger (1992) has articulated this position, claiming that multicultural curricula, especially Afrocentricity, contributes to a "disuniting of America." Proponents of a multicultural curriculum claim that both approaches in education are needed—the unifying components of Americanism as well as recognition of the diversity and ethnicity of population groups within the United States. Glazer (1997), a prominent authority on multiculturalism, has declared that the proponents of multiculturalism in the public schools have won— that "we are all multiculturalists now."

An example of controversy over the elements of a multicultural curriculum is found in Glazer's (1997) work on the debate over multicultural education in New York State in the early 1990s. In response to the "cultural wars," a curriculum committee under the State Commissioner of Education produced two reports: *A Curriculum of Inclusion*, and *One Nation, Many Peoples: A Declaration of Cultural Interdependence*. While these reports revealed the controversies inherent in multiculturalism, they also demonstrated the rapid introduction of cultural materials in the public schools of New York.

Another example of controversy over multiculturalism is provided in the "Children of the Rainbow" curriculum approved by the New York City Board of Education. This curriculum was based on a 1989 resolution by the Board that "Multicultural education values cultural pluralism and rejects the view that schools should seek to melt away cultural diversity; rather, multicultural education accepts cultural diversity as a valuable resource that should be preserved and extended" (Miller, 1993). Critics objected to a number of aspects of the Rainbow curriculum, particularly those dealing with bilingualism, with feminism, with homosexuality, and with "family situations found in New York, including, most controversially, children being raised by gay and lesbian couples" (Hiss, 1993).

Bilingual education continues to be a controversial area in public education. The most common form of bilingual education has been teaching classes in both English and Spanish. Long-time bilingual educational programs in California have recently been discontinued as a result of the passage of Proposition 227 in 1998. Court challenges to the Proposition by civil rights and education groups have failed, with a federal judge refusing to block implementation of the Proposition in the fall of 1998. An alternative for assisting students to learn English is a one-year program of English immersion prior to entry into regular classes (Purdum, 1998). The campaign to stop bilingual education in

California revealed the fact that the Latino community was divided in support and opposition to the Proposition (Terry, 1998). However, most seemed to agree on one issue: "for immigrant children, whether they are from Mexico or Vietnam, the key to unlocking the treasures of America is to learn English as quickly as possible" (Purdum, 1998).

Another example of bilingual education is a program on the Lower East Side of New York City. A small alternative public school, known as Shuang Wen Academy, is a dual-language school that "seeks to teach students the language and culture of their homeland for their own sake" (Toy, 1998). The goal of the school is to have students master both Chinese and English languages, with the core Chinese instruction offered from 3:00 to 5:30 in the afternoon by teachers paid with private funds raised mainly from foundations. This type of program differs from traditional bilingual education that "seeks to educate non-English-speaking children by teaching them in their native language until they are confident enough to learn exclusively English" (Toy, 1998).

SOCIAL WORK IN THE SCHOOLS

Social work services are provided in public schools by professional social workers. The nature of these services has changed over the years, especially in light of federal legislation related to children with special educational needs (Allen-Meares et al., 2000; Constable, McDonald, & Flynn, 1999). Social workers are members of interdisciplinary teams organized to assist children who have special needs. Federal legislation has established obligations of states and school districts with regard to services and full educational opportunities for all children with disabilities. As a result, an inclusive education movement has moved ahead, based on "the philosophy that children with disabilities benefit when they are educated in age-appropriate general classroom settings" with the support of special education (Pryor et al., 1996). School social workers have responded to this movement by implementing a variety of strategies to promote inclusion, including:

- preparing students to celebrate human differences;
- facilitating the transition process for newly included students;
- consulting collaboratively with teachers;
- revising the school curriculum to address social and emotional needs;
- providing services to students in general educational settings;
- expanding inclusive education concepts throughout each school (Pryor et al., 1996).

In addition to helping students who have disabilities, social workers provide services for high-risk children, family education, case management, and service evaluation. Developing an understanding of the educational subsystem of a local community is particularly important for social workers who practice in the schools.

Books on the social services and on school social work usually include discussions of the design and delivery of social work services in the schools (Allen-Meares et al., 2000; Constable et al., 1999; Freeman et al., 1998). Guidelines for practice in schools are provided by the National Association of Social Workers through a publication of the NASW Standards for School Social Work Services (NASW, 1992). These works highlight the need for social workers to recognize the significance of the local community in relation to the functioning of the educational system, especially in regard to the assessment of community needs and resources.

School social workers must develop an understanding of the interdependence of the various subsystems of the community, including the educational system, in the provision of resources for families and children. One element of school reform has been the linking of services provided in the public schools to human services in the local community (Franklin & Streeter, 1995; Franklin & Allen-Meares, 1997). These linkages are most likely to be with programs within the health and social service system of the community. Individual schools, as well as school districts, often take different approaches toward serving students and families through the linking of schools to health and human services. Franklin and Streeter (1995) have identified some of these "school-linked services": e.g., informal relations, coordination, partnerships, collaboration, and integration. A number of factors are related to implementation of these approaches, such as level of commitment, amount of planning and in-service training, leadership patterns, resources, funding, scope of change, and impact.

Linking public schools to community resources is especially needed in low-income, inner-city poverty neighborhoods where education is a principal source of employment skills. One response in some communities has been to "make schools 'hubs' for community development through family resource centers" (Dupper & Poertner, 1997). These centers provide their own direct services as well as linkage to human services agencies in the community in order to support parents and children in achieving goals of education, health, growth, and development. Some of the characteristics of school-linked family resource centers include the following (Adler & Gardner, 1994):

- Families and children can access all services at a center located at a school or other facility in their neighborhood.
- A wide variety of services are available, such as health, mental health, recreation, job development, child development and care, education, and housing.
- Service providers work collaboratively to meet all of the needs of children and their families in a holistic way.
- Services stress community development and family support that prevents problems, rather than being crisis driven.
- Both families and social workers who provide direct services are empowered through their participation in planning to meet the needs of the community.
- There is flexibility in how categorical funding can be used, or ideally, new funding streams are created to support collaborative services on an ongoing basis.
- Professionals who work in community and family services will need training and preparation to develop new skills.
- System-wide changes will be necessary to achieve these goals.

Social workers play significant roles in both the schools and the related social service agencies that are involved in family resource center programs. An important element of the social worker's role is the development of relationships with parents in the community, "empowering them to become active advocates involved in the shaping of parent-driven services" (Dupper & Poertner, 1997). These relationships are based on a model emphasizing empowerment and family strengths, which is especially important in working with poor, ethnic minority, immigrant, and homeless parents.

Services for homeless families and their children in the public schools involve "unique and numerous complexities related to assisting these children and supporting their families" (Wall, 1996). The role of the social worker in serving homeless children and families involves collaborative interventions within the school and in the community. Wall (1996) has noted a number of obstacles that interfere with the development of cooperative relationships between school systems and homeless families, such as residency requirements, restricted access to schools, space limitations in schools, lack of transportation, lack of available academic records, special education requirements, guardianship requirements, as well as stereotyping and prejudice against homeless people. Social workers in the schools are in a position to collaborate with community agencies to provide special services to homeless families and children, as well as to be involved in educational planning within the schools through work with teachers and support staff.

Chapter 10 Review

The educational system of a community carries out major functions for individuals, communities, and American society. The primary goals of education are academic (learning of basic skills), social/cultural (socialization, citizenship development), and economic (providing training for future employment). The principal focus of this chapter was the structure and functioning of a community's public elementary and secondary school systems, in the context of their relationship to state and federal governments. Examples of federal legislation and educational programs were presented, along with a description of the structure of public education at the local community level. Special issues related to teachers, students, school-community relations, student services, parental involvement, desegregation, church-state relations, and school reform were discussed. Issues related to financing of public education and to school choice programs were introduced, especially with regard to tuition vouchers for attendance at private schools. The discussion of issues related to the community educational system highlighted the fact that this system serves to integrate people into the community, providing opportunities for social interaction and social identity. At the same time, the community educational system is an arena for community controversies, illustrated through discussions about academic standards, achievement gaps, multicultural education, the provision of specialized services to students in private schools, and the development of school choice programs, including charter schools. The last section of the chapter focused on the services provided by school social workers in community educational systems.

11

Community Economic System

A community's economic system includes organizations, groups, and individuals engaged in the production, distribution, and consumption of goods and services. The economy of local geographic communities is related horizontally to other local community economic systems, and vertically to state, regional, national, and world economies. Central cities, the surrounding suburban communities, and metropolitan areas are integral parts of an urban economic system. Rural and other non-metropolitan communities usually have economic systems that are less complex than those in metropolitan areas, with an interdependence between urban and rural economies. A local community's economic system has interrelationships with other community subsystems, especially the political system. The term *political economy* refers to the interconnections between economic and political systems. To carry out their functions, other community subsystems, such as education, health, and social welfare, depend on the strength of a community's economic system.

The economic system of a local community includes (1) numerous formal bureaucratic organizations, such as local government departments, industrial companies, commercial businesses, hospitals, and social agencies; (2) offices of professionals in private or group practice (e.g., accountants, lawyers, physicians, social workers, and psychologists); (3) small, less formal businesses, home industries, and service operations; (4) other sources of income from social security entitlements and social welfare benefits. A local community's economic system may also have an underground economy, which includes a variety of legal and illegal monetary transactions by individuals and groups.

An ecological perspective is useful in examining the functioning of a local community's economic system. Human ecologists view the city as a marketplace, with people living off trade and commerce. Hence, they consider the economy to be the most important element of a community, with *community* defined as a physical environment where people live and work. A similar approach is taken by Marxist economists, who focus primarily on how the forces and modes of production and ownership affect social and economic problems and result in a class struggle. The importance of the local economic system is emphasized in early community studies such as the Middletown study by Lynd and Lynd (1929) and the "Yankee City" studies by Warner and Lunt (1941). These investigators looked at how social class structure is both defined and affected by the economic life of the community.

Ecological factors such as a community's size, age, geographical location, natural resources, climate, and other demographic features all have a bearing on a community's (1) production base, (2) labor market, and (3) income levels. The production base involves manufacturing, commercial, and financial functions—that is, economic productivity and accumulation of assets. U.S. Census data can be used to describe the labor market through the creation of an occupational profile of a community and through the analysis of employment and unemployment statistics. Per capita income is also a measure of the viability of a community's economic system. Comparisons of income and occupational levels of specialized populations, such as ethnic minorities and women, are used to examine the social and economic stratification of a community's population and the extent of economic inequalities.

ECONOMIC SYSTEM AS A SET OF WORKPLACES

Formal organizations within a community make up the bulk of employment opportunities for residents, providing the actual locations for most work activities. Workplaces are functional communities in that employees are likely to share a common interest or function. Economic organizations allow individuals to perform work, to derive satisfaction from engaging in a specialized occupational activity, to earn income, to obtain health and welfare benefits, and to establish a financial basis for retirement income and other benefits. "Virtually all our benefits (especially health care but including unemployment insurance, life insurance, child care tax credits, etc.) are provided through the employment system" (Newman, 1999). The community economic system, in providing work for people, serves a significant function for members of the community. As Newman (1999) has observed, "Americans have always been committed to the moral maxim that work defines the person." People gain respect and personal satisfaction through work, with stratification based on the type of job and the level of income it provides. Newman further notes that "given our tradition of equating moral value with employment, it stands to reason that the most profound dividing line in our culture is that separating the working person from the unemployed."

There are clear interdependencies between workplaces and the total community. For example, management and labor in work organizations have specialized needs, many of which must be met from within the community. Workplace organizations require physical facilities, a pool of employees, local services (fire, police protection), water, energy, and education and health services. Most communities need employment opportunities for their residents; property taxes from employed workers; taxes from employers; and an organized means of providing health and welfare benefits for community residents. Interdependencies develop in a community between the economic system and other subsystems, such as education. Many local businesses give financial support to local high schools, colleges, and universities, as a way of insuring a pool of well-qualified employees. Business organizations benefit from community health and welfare agencies, which provide services that support employees in need of professional help.

EQUAL EMPLOYMENT OPPORTUNITIES

Workplaces vary in the extent to which they provide equal opportunities for employment, pay, and advancement. Nationwide, women, people of color, persons with disabilities, gay and lesbian persons, and older adults are most likely to encounter discrimination in the workplace. Programs of affirmative action, pay equity, and promotion seek to minimize and eliminate workplace discrimination. Income comparisons for men and women, based on U.S. Census data, consistently show lower earnings for women compared to men, especially for women of color. Comparisons between white women, Latinas, and African American women show inequalities between whites and minority women with regard to participation in the labor market, wages, and rates of unemployment (Browne, 1999). Given the plight of Latinas and African American women in the labor force, Misra (1999) has made a number of policy recommendations that would help rectify this condition, including improvement of opportunities for educational attainment and job training, desegregation of occupations, creation of comparable worth policies, reduction of residential segregation, improvement in wages and tax policy, increased access to health care, provision of subsidized day-care and family supports, expansion of anti-discrimination policies, and restructuring of work.

In comparisons of women to men, in 1998 the U.S. Labor Department reported that the gender wage gap had narrowed, with women earning 76 cents for every dollar men earned. Challenges to the validity of wage gap studies, such as those produced by Catalyst, focus on how the data are collected and analyzed. Some economists contend that the wage gap disappears when the analysis of wages deals with the question, not of how much women vs. men earn, but how much equally qualified women and men earn. They conclude that "the adjusted wage gap between men and women. . .the difference in wages after accounting for differences in occupation, age, experience, education and time in the work force. . .is far smaller than the average wage gap, which is the difference in wages found by comparing averages of all men's and all women's wages" (Furchtgott-Roth & Stolba, 1998). Based on this system of analysis, the claim is made that gender wage differences do not reflect discrimination in employment. Countering this argument is the fact that gender segregation of employment contributes to wage gaps between men and women.

Accurate analysis of wage gap studies depends on understanding the concepts of pay equity and comparable worth. Pay equity involves a "principle of fairness that different people who do the same work be compensated equally" (NASW, 1996). Comparable worth involves the analysis of job skills and responsibilities as a basis for compensation for work in similar but not identical jobs. An example of legislation based on the concept of comparable worth can be found in a Human Rights Act in Ontario, Canada that requires "equal pay for work of equal value." Under this Act the value of a job is classified by four criteria: comparable education, responsibility, mental demands, and working conditions. Thus, the jobs of nurses can be compared to the work of secretaries, telephone operators, chefs, and janitors. In 1999, federal workers in Canada used this Act to challenge the government's compliance, with an equity settlement by the Canadian government awarded to about 230,000 workers, most of whom were women (Brooke, 1999).

In the U.S., basic employment rights were established in the Civil Rights Act of 1964, which included an Equal Pay Act, monitored through the Equal Employment Opportunity Commission. Monitoring employers for compliance, however, often is not carried out in a timely manner or is neglected altogether. For example, a 1999 report from the General Accounting Office of the U.S. Government found the EEOC deficient in monitoring job discrimination among federal workers (Hsu, 1999). The report stated that "EEOC does not collect and report data. . .in a way that would help answer some fundamental questions about the nature and extent of workplace conflicts," and "The reliability of the data that EEOC collects from agencies and reports is questionable." A dramatic illustration of the untimely resolution of a sex-bias hiring lawsuit is a settlement in March 2000 by the U.S. government of a case initiated in 1977. The suit was brought against the government-run service, Voice of America, by 1,100 women who claimed they had been denied jobs and promotions within the agency. The federal government agreed to pay $508 million to settle the claim, with each woman receiving at least $450,000.

DIVERSITY IN THE WORKPLACE

Issues related to the work force have been examined in surveys of American workers concerning their work and personal lives. One study found that "workers of all ages said they prefer working with people of the same race, sex, gender and education" (Shellenbarger, 1993a). Most employees had not had an experience of working or living with people of other races and ethnic groups. Individuals with such experiences were more likely to express positive feelings toward diversity in the workplace. Most employees agreed that members of other racial and ethnic groups had poorer chances for advancement than non-minority workers, and there was a widespread perception of discrimination against minority workers. Women were much more likely than men to rate their opportunities for career advancement as "poor" or "fair." These findings suggest a need for educational programs and equal opportunity policies in the workplace focused on gender and multicultural diversity.

Many companies now seek to develop a corporate culture that promotes comfortable and productive relationships between women, ethnic minorities, and white males (Arrendondo, 1996). Mechanisms to promote this culture include affirmative action hiring, programs for advancement of women and minorities, and special "multicultural" training programs. Small companies have begun to provide "diversity" workshops as a way of easing tensions between workers and making them aware of the values and lifestyles of people from other cultures. Such companies see diversity training as a survival technique, because workplace confrontations tend to disrupt the work environment and inhibit productivity.

Companies such as Xerox, Avon Products, and Motorola have initiated programs to move ethnic minorities and women into management jobs, motivated in part by the fact that growth in the work force beyond the year 2000 will require increased involvement of ethnic minorities and women. Still, in a Catalyst survey in 1999, minority women "view their company's diversity programs as largely ineffective" (Abelson, 1999a). More than half of the women in the survey, including Asian Americans, African Americans, and Hispanic Americans, "thought that the diversity programs failed to address subtle racism or sexism in the workplace, compared with a third that agreed that diversity programs at their company created a supportive environment." Only one quarter of the women found career development to be an important aspect of diversity programs (Abelson, 1999a). One of the major reasons given by these women for not being able to advance in a company was the "lack of a mentor or the chance to network informally with colleagues" through activities such as playing a game of golf.

Multicultural workshops focus on fostering participants' understanding and appreciation of differences of people from various cultures as well as differences and similarities of men and women (Daly, 1998). Such workshops are not without controversy, as diversity training programs sometimes backfire, that is, they are designed to promote harmony but reinforce race and gender divisions. This sometimes happens when workshops use negative and positive stereotypes that offend participants, when blame is given to one group in relation to another, or when a "winners-losers" situation arises because a program is tied to affirmative action goals.

The employment of low-wage workers in the hotel and restaurant industry provides an example of the challenges of workplace diversity. In these organizations, the workplace may "resemble a modern-day Tower of Babel, presenting multiple opportunities for miscommunication and misunderstanding, as people seek to work together across steep barriers of language, culture, gender and economic class, and racial, educational and religious differences" (Grimsley, 1999). The challenges for managers and supervisors are especially evident in working with new immigrants, as expressed by a general manager at a Hilton hotel: "If you don't have empathy and aren't able to communicate in diversity, or are uncomfortable around a multicultural work force. . . you'll be a miserable failure as a manager" (Grimsley, 1999).

SEXUAL ORIENTATION AND WORKPLACE DISCRIMINATION

Discrimination based on sexual orientation occurs for gay men, lesbians, and bisexual persons in the workplace. Federal laws regarding discrimination in employment, such as Title VII of the 1964 Civil Rights Act, the Civil Rights Act of 1991, and the Americans with Disabilities Act of 1990, do not prohibit discrimination based on sexual orientation. However, civil rights protection in employment for gay persons is provided in some cities, counties, and states. For example, the State of California passed legislation in 1999 that prohibits job and housing discrimination on the basis of sexual orientation. The State Fair Employment and Housing Department has authority over such cases (Associated Press, 1999a). In 39 states men and women can be fired solely because of their sexual orientation, with no reference to job performance. In 1999 members of the U.S. Congress, with the support of President Clinton, proposed an Employment Non-Discrimination Act that would have extended basic employment discrimination protections to gay and lesbian persons. Such legislation had not been passed as of 2000. At the same time, President Clinton issued an executive order that made permanent a federal policy against discrimination based on sexual orientation in the civilian federal workplace.

In regard to employee benefits, an appeals court in the state of Oregon ruled in 1998 that "the State Constitution gave homosexual government employees the right to health and life insurance benefits for their domestic partners" (Lewin, 1998e). In 1999 the Vermont Supreme Court ruled that gay and lesbian couples are entitled to the same benefits and protections as heterosexual couples. An exception to the position of federal laws in relation to sex discrimination occurred in a 1998 ruling of the U.S. Supreme Court in the case of *Oncale v. Sundowner Offshore Services*. In this case, the Supreme Court ruled that Title VII of the Civil Rights Act of 1964 protects employees from being sexually harassed in the workplace by people of the same sex (Greenhouse, 1998a).

Communities vary in the extent to which workplaces provide equal opportunities for gay people with respect to employment, pay, benefits, and advancement. In many workplaces, gay employees must make decisions about "coming out" (disclosing their sexual orientation) or "remaining in the closet," since such decisions often affect their professional lives. Many times the closet has been viewed as the realistic option because "The penalties for coming out were too severe and the protections too few" (Woods, 1993). Gay employees are likely to be at risk of discrimination in hiring practices and job retention if they disclose their sexual orientation to employers. In 1993, Congress enacted a policy that "allows homosexuals to serve in the armed forces as long as they keep their sexual orientation private" (Myers, 2000). This policy, which has been described as "don't ask, don't tell," was upheld by a federal appeals court in 1998, while still holding that the military may ban all homosexual activity (Finder, 1998). Hillary Rodham Clinton, a candidate in New York's Senate race in 2000, called the policy "a failure," declaring that "Gays and lesbians already serve with distinction in our nation's armed forces and should not face discrimination" (Nagourney, 1999). A Pentagon report in March 2000 on a survey conducted within the armed services found anti-gay bias common in the military service, especially in the form of offensive speech and gestures, but including graffiti, vandalism, threats, unfair discipline, discrimination in training or career opportunities, and even physical assaults. In response to the report, Defense Secretary William Cohen initiated a program to combat such harassment based on the Defense Department's Homosexual Conduct Policy. Cohen stated that "The report showed that military leaders must do more to make it clear that harassment based on sexual orientation violates military values" (Myers, 2000).

There are companies, professions, industries, and communities that have acquired a positive reputation for providing employment, advancement, and benefits for gay employees. The city of San Francisco has led the nation in establishing legislation "to prohibit the city government from contracting with companies that do not make the same benefits available to employees' domestic partners that they do to the married spouses of their workers" (Golden, 1996). Many companies have developed "domestic partner" policies that provide benefits for gay persons and for straight unmarried partners, but studies show that a very low percentage of gay employees sign up for these benefits. The low level of requests for benefits is mainly attributed to a fear that disclosure will interfere with one's career advancement (Jefferson, 1994). Members of the gay community have been active in pressing large U.S. companies to adopt domestic partner benefits that cover gay persons. A primary concern believed to be a factor in the provision of benefits has been the perception that health-related costs would be higher for gay persons; however, health insurance companies such as Blue Shield have not found this to be the case.

Dilemmas related to disclosure and the visibility of gay individuals in the workplace are illustrated by case studies, such as a case described in the *Harvard Business Review*, "Is This the Right Time to Come Out?" (Williamson, 1993), and a case discussed in the *New Yorker*, "Coming Out at Chrysler" (Stewart, 1997). In the HBR case, "The corporate culture is traditional. The star employee is gay and wants to bring his partner to a company/client function." The employee discloses this information to his superior, leading to the question, "How should the manager respond?" Seven experts examined the issues of discrimination involved in this case. One of the first issues arises because the company does not have a nondiscrimination policy that includes sexual orientation. As one of the experts noted, "A growing number of companies. . .including AT&T, Levi Strauss & Co., and Digital. . .currently have nondiscrimination policies that include sexual orientation." This expert advises that out of fairness and a sense of ethics, the manager should encourage the employee to bring his partner to the company/client functions, even though some clients at the event are likely to be homophobic and thus there may be some negative economic consequences for the company.

The case described in the *New Yorker* deals with a gay employee of Chrysler Corporation who had established "a string of sterling job-performance evaluations" over a three-year period as an electrician. Due to unpleasant experiences he encountered from other employees when they came to believe he was gay, the employee became active in trying to gain employee protection for gay employees at Chrysler. Due to this activism, he lost support of his union and began to be harassed by his co-workers. He continued trying, without success, to bring pressure on the company and the union to adopt nondiscrimination policies regarding sexual orientation. This case illustrates the types of negative experiences a gay person may encounter after "coming out" at the workplace and engaging in efforts to change company and union policies and practices.

CAREER TRACKS

The concept of career tracks is related to ideas of equal employment opportunities and barriers to promotion and advancement. This concept has mainly been applied to the lack of representation of women in management circles of large corporations. For example, a 1999 study by Catalyst found that women held approximately 12 percent of the corporate officer positions in America's largest companies, and only 3 percent of top executive positions at Fortune 500 companies (Jacobs, 1999; Smart, 1999). Only 11 percent of all female corporate officers were women of color. This survey showed that women hold 11 percent of the board seats in the top 500 companies, and only 8.5 percent of the seats in the 501 to 1000 largest companies. Not until 1999 did a woman, Carleton Fiorina, cross the "gender barrier" to become the CEO at

Hewlett-Packard, one of the 30 companies whose performance determines the Dow Jones Industrial Average. A 1999 study by the Center for Women in Government showed that less than 30 percent of appointees by governors to state government leadership positions were women, and only 22 percent of state legislators were women. The lack of career tracks for women has been especially apparent in low-wage positions, such as "dead end" employment positions available for women trained in government welfare programs (Associated Press, 1999 l).

For a number of years the U.S. Labor Department has recognized that job bias and sex discrimination in promotions continues to exist in subtle ways in most large U.S. corporations. During President Bush's administration, Labor Secretary Elizabeth Dole announced special efforts to "shatter the glass ceiling" by examining promotion practices in companies with government contracts and by threatening to cancel such contracts if companies did not cooperate (Kilborn, 1990). Despite efforts such as these, a 1993 survey of executive women found that these individuals made major gains in pay and status, but executive women's average compensation still lagged behind that of men by more than one-third (Shellenbarger, 1993a). More than 90 percent of the female executives in this study reported that a "glass ceiling" was still intact and that "being a woman" was their greatest single career obstacle. Similar findings were found in 1996 and 1999 by Catalyst, a research organization that focuses on women professionals. At the top of the list of barriers to advancement was "male stereotyping and preconceptions of women," with the second reason being "Exclusion from informal networks of communication" (Dobrzynski, 1996). In a 1999 Catalyst study, many women of color reported that there were few cracks in the "concrete ceiling"—the social barriers preventing them from reaching the top of Corporate America (Abelson, 1999a).

Based on their ongoing research on gender discrimination, Meyerson and Fletcher (2000) have concluded that "It took a revolution to get women where they are in business today. But now, to push hard-won gains wider and deeper, a different approach is necessary. It is a strategy based on small wins—incremental changes that have the power to transform organizations positively for both men and women. . . . changes aimed at biases so entrenched in the system that they're not even noticed until they're gone." This approach to breaking through the "glass ceiling" is based on these professors' belief that "It's not the ceiling that's holding women back; it's the whole structure of the organizations in which we work: the foundation, the beams, the walls, the very air. The barriers to advancement are not just above women, they are all around them."

New opportunities for women in business leadership positions have been opening up in the "dot.com" world of Internet commerce. Women are entering top management positions in venture capital Internet firms, where there is a "leveling of the playing field" and a welcoming of women due to an "unquenchable need for talent" (Kaufman, 2000).

While some women who believe they are being denied a promotion because of sex discrimination "stay and fight" through a complaint or litigation, a Catalyst study in 1999 indicated that many choose to leave their companies and seek positions elsewhere. In this study of women in Wall Street organizations, it was found that "For many, the glass ceiling is easier to go around than to break through" (Abelson, 1999b). In interviews with women managers who left their companies, Catalyst was told by almost three-quarters of these women that their departure for other employment was "greatly influenced by their belief that there was a lack of opportunity for advancement." Another reason for leaving was a reluctance to bring a lawsuit, as sometimes it was unclear that there was discrimination, and at other times a lawsuit was perceived as simply making "the workplace even less friendly" (Abelson, 1999b).

A controversial response to the problems for women in climbing the corporate ladder was voiced over a decade ago by Felice Schwartz (1989), who proposed a plan whereby corporations could overcome the fact that "the cost of employing women in management is greater than the cost of employing men." For women to succeed in management, she suggested, businesses need to "recognize that women are not all alike"—that "Like men, they are individuals with differing talents, priorities, and motivations." Based on these assumptions, she proposed that companies address their own needs and those of women by establishing two career tracks: a career-primary track and a career-and-family track. The latter track was quickly dubbed "the mommy track" by the mass media.

Schwartz contended that introducing optional career tracks would promote flexibility in a woman's work life, facilitate the management of maternity and work, reduce stresses, and benefit both women and companies. She suggested that building flexibility, along with family supports, into careers would be desirable for both women and men. This approach has not been without its critics, as demonstrated in numerous letters to the editor of the *Harvard Business Review* following publication of Schwartz's proposal. Debates about career tracks have served to highlight the problems women face in the workplace in terms of work assignments, pay, and career advancement. Schwartz (1992) continued to support the idea that "Treating women as a business imperative is the equivalent of a unique R and D product for which there is a huge demand." In keeping with this approach to women in the workplace, Schwartz developed a quiz for business leaders (*Wall Street Journal*, 1993). A 20-item questionnaire was used to rate companies on their treatment of female employees. "The quiz includes such questions as: Do you trust a woman to be the chief liaison with one of your top 10 clients/customers? Do you support talented women who choose to limit their career paths to spend more time with their families? Do female and male managers in your company routinely have lunch together?" Some companies have used the findings of the questionnaire to develop sensitivity training and recruitment plans.

Issues surrounding women in the workplace versus stay-at-home mothers are controversial, as exemplified in the women's movement and in the popular media. Usually the arguments center around three positions: support for women in the workplace, in the home, or combining career and home. There continues to be some evidence that "stay-at-home moms are fashionable again in many communities" (Swasy, 1993). These women believe that they provide better care for their children than do "working" women, and that they have adequate opportunities for work satisfaction through activities and leadership in community voluntary associations. Women with careers in the workplace often have opposite views, leaving both types of women with pressures to be "maternally correct" (Swasy, 1993). One response to the pros and cons related to work at home or work outside the home has been a call for "ridding our language of the absurd term 'working mother.' All mothers work: inside the home, outside the home, or both" (Kim, 1993).

AMERICANS WITH DISABILITIES ACT

Discrimination in hiring is one of the major problems addressed by the Americans with Disabilities Act of 1990. In this Act, Congress recognized that more than 43 million Americans have one or more physical or mental disabilities, and that these individuals encounter discrimination economically, socially, vocationally, and educationally. The Act applies to all businesses with 15 or more employees, and it includes provisions that seek to eliminate discrimination in employment, as well as to provide supports and accommodations that will assist disabled persons in performing their jobs (Moss et al., 1999).

The American with Disabilities Act includes the following provisions: (1) it prohibits an employer from inquiring into a job applicant's disability with questions concerning topics such as medical history, prior workers' compensation/health insurance claims, work absen-

teeism due to illness, and past treatment for alcoholism or mental illness; (2) it requires employers to make "reasonable accommodations"
for disabled workers by acquiring or modifying work equipment, providing qualified readers or interpreters, adjusting work schedules, and
making existing facilities, such as restrooms, telephones, and drinking fountains accessible; (3) it defines a disabled person as one who
has a physical or mental impairment that limits one or more life activities, has a record of such an impairment, and is regarded as having
such an impairment; and (4) it defines a qualified disabled worker as
one who can perform the "essential functions" of a job, with or without
reasonable accommodation (Equal Employment Opportunity Commission, 1980; Quintanilla, 1993). Although many states have had laws
with regard to discrimination toward the physically disabled, this Act
covers job rights of persons with physical and mental disabilities. The
Equal Employment Opportunity Commission, the Access Board, and
the U.S. Department of Justice have initiated a program to make
known to the public the rights of persons with disabilities. Booklets
printed in nine languages (Spanish and eight Asian languages) have
been distributed through ten federal disability assistance centers to
meet the needs of persons whose primary language is not English.

A number of U.S. Supreme Court cases have brought about clarification of the legal meaning of disability under the Americans with
Disabilities Act of 1990. In 1998 the Court ruled that people infected
with HIV, the virus that causes AIDS, are protected from discrimination
under the Act even if they suffer no symptoms of AIDS. In another
case the Supreme Court in 1999 ruled that the Act does not protect
people with poor eyesight or other conditions that can be corrected
with medication or devices such as eyeglasses or contact lenses (Associated Press, 1999c). In a suit over a disabled person's right to accommodation, a judge ruled in favor of a professional golfer's request for
a change in a PGA Tour event's rules that required walking and prohibited riding in a golf cart. The player asked for the cart accommodation based on a physical disability involving his leg. This request
"ignited a debate over a disabled person's right to accommodation
versus a private sports organization's ability to set rules of competition" (Chambers, 1998).

The U.S. Equal Employment Opportunity Commission (EEOC)
shares responsibility with state and local Fair Employment Practices
Agencies (FEPAs) for enforcement of the employment discrimination
charges of the ADA (Moss et al., 1999). Individuals may file charges
of discrimination with either the EEOC or the FEPA or may "dual-file"
with both agencies. In a study by Moss et al. (1999) of the outcomes of
employment discharges under the ADA from 1992 to 1998 (a total of

175,226), 15.7 percent resulted in a benefit to the charging parties. Monetary benefits were the most common outcomes among the possible benefits, with only 7 percent resulting in a new hire or reinstatement. While a relatively low percentage of persons filing charges actually received benefits, the researchers concluded that the ADA is still effective. They indicated that the ADA influences employment decisions in many ways not included in their study. Thus, their data did not show compliance with the Act without enforcement, that is, voluntary non-discriminatory behavior. Also, in many other instances, employers arrived at settlements without charges being made. They also suggest that the low level of successful charges may be influenced by the narrow interpretation of the ADA by the lower courts.

During the latter part of President Clinton's tenure, he "directed federal agencies to step up their efforts to recruit and hire people with disabilities, stating that government should serve as a model for private-sector employers" (Barr, 1999). The president's directive focused on all levels of federal employment, "from entry-level jobs to senior executive ranks." Clinton also asked federal agencies to "reach out" to disabled students in the employment process. The employment plan, called "Accessing Opportunity," urged agencies "to ensure that 'reasonable accommodations'—such as flexible work schedules, modified work sites and special equipment—are provided for applicants and employees with disabilities" (Barr, 1999). In conjunction with this plan, President Clinton signed the Work Incentives Improvement Act, which allows disabled people to keep their government health benefits when they go to work; this legislation received support from both the House and the Senate (Harris, 1999). Under the new law, Medicaid and Medicare were expanded so that people with disabilities could return to work without losing their health insurance benefits (Pear, 1999a, 1999e). This law also included provisions for employment and training of people with disabilities, and for applying Medicaid coverage to workers who are not actually disabled but have impairments "that are 'reasonably expected' to become severe disabilities in the absence of treatment" such as HIV, Parkinson's disease, multiple sclerosis, and other chronic conditions (Pear, 1999a).

ERGONOMICS AND THE WORKPLACE

Responding to the fact that more than 27 million workers annually sustain injuries related to overexertion or repetitive motion, the Occupational Safety and Health Administration (OSHA) proposed a standard to help prevent such injuries (Skrzycki, 1999). OSHA estimated that the rule would prevent 300,000 musculoskeletal disorders a year. The proposal applies to manufacturers and companies with workers involved in manual handling and activities that may cause musculoskeletal disorders, such as work at computers, assembly line production jobs, and heavy lifting. The proposal calls for ergonomics programs that identify problems related to fitting jobs to the physical characteristics of workers, and that respond to workers who report ergonomic injuries. Workplaces would be expected to adjust work conditions in order to avoid injuries, in keeping with principles of ergonomics that involve fitting a job to a worker. Changes in work conditions would be expected to prevent numerous injuries, such as injuries to muscles, tendons, ligaments, and the spine, including carpal tunnel syndrome, back pain, and tendinitis. OSHA's proposal was published in the Federal Register in 1999. The proposal had the support of labor unions, but over the previous eight years it had been strongly resisted by business organizations and some members of Congress. Business organizations have opposed the standard based on a claim that it is too broad and vaguely written to allow for compliance, that compliance would be inordinately expensive, and that there is no scientific evidence to show that ergonomic problems cause injuries. Studies by the National Science Foundation are in progress, but officials at OSHA determined that the need for improvements in the 1.9 million workplaces involved was urgent. As one official stated, "We are compelled to act. Employees are getting hurt. Workers are being sent home. People are suffering" (Crenshaw, 1999).

SEXUAL HARASSMENT IN THE WORKPLACE

Sexual harassment is a form of discrimination in the workplace, and it is illegal. Most sexual harassment cases brought into the legal system involve lawsuits by women against men, but harassment by women toward men, and by same-sex individuals may also be litigated under Title VII of the Civil Rights Act of 1964. Thus, in *Oncale v. Sundowner Offshore Services, Inc. et al.*, the U.S. Supreme Court "agreed that same-sex harassment violates civil rights protections just as opposite-sex harassment does" (MacKinnon, 1998). Increasingly, sexual harassment cases have moved from the lower courts to the U.S. Supreme Court, with the rulings of the courts helping to define the meaning of sexual harassment. Sexual harassment is covered by sex discrimination laws, including Titles VII and IX of the Civil Rights Act of 1964, and it is also covered by criminal, tort, and state employment laws. Title VII states that it is illegal to "fail or refuse to hire or to discharge any individual" or to discriminate in the "compensation, terms, conditions or privileges of employment" on the basis of an employee's or prospective employee's race, color, religion, sex, or national origin (Levy & Paludi, 1997). Based on this title, the Equal Employment Opportunity Commission (1980) established the following guidelines on sexual harassment that serve as the basic definition of this form of discrimination:

> Unwelcome sexual advances, requests for sexual favors, and other verbal or physical conduct of a sexual nature constitute sexual harassment when:
>
> - submission to the conduct is made either explicitly or implicitly a term or condition of an individual's employment;
> - submission to or rejection of such conduct by an individual is used as the basis for employment decisions affecting such individual; or
> - such conduct has the purpose or effect of unreasonably interfering with an individual's work performance or creating an intimidating, hostile, or offensive working environment.

This description by the EEOC includes two types of sexual harassment: quid pro quo and hostile work environment. Quid pro quo cases involve behavior in situations where "the employee is claiming that a supervisor or someone with authority to confer workplace benefits is offering those benefits in exchange for sexual favors or is threatening to take away economic benefits if the employee does not accept the 'offer'" (Levy & Paludi, 1997). Such an offer must be unwelcome to the employee. The existence of a hostile work environment is a complex form of harassment that a person contends affects his or her work performance and denies equal employment opportunities. In the case of *Meritor Savings Bank v. Vinson,* the Supreme Court ruled in 1986 that the Bank had created a hostile work environment in violation of Title VII. Since the time of this case, the courts have continued to be called upon to establish the boundary between appropriate and hostile work environments.

In the 1991 case of *Harris v. Forklift Systems,* the Supreme Court "reaffirmed the definition of what constitutes a sexually hostile workplace environment set out in *Meritor Savings Bank v. Vinson*" (Levy & Paludi, 1997). In the Harris case, the plaintiff worked at an equipment rental company for a man whose behavior was said to involve quid pro quo and hostile environment components. A major issue in this case revolved around the question of whether or not this behavior needed to have caused tangible psychological harm. The Court ruled that Ms. Harris could sue, even when the alleged offense "does not seriously affect employees' psychological well-being" (Mansnerus, 1998).

The quid pro quo and hostile work environment concepts have been taken into consideration in high-profile cases such as the complaint by Anita Hill against Clarence Thomas in the hearings before the Senate Judiciary Committee (Toobin, 1998). "At the hearings, both Thomas's supporters and his opponents agreed that if Hill was telling the truth about what had occurred during her tenure as Thomas's assistant, the nominee was unquestionably guilty of sexual harassment" (Toobin, 1998). The sponsors of the nomination of Thomas to the Supreme Court attacked Hill's version of the facts, not the meaning of sexual harassment, and succeeded in getting the nomination approved. In the complaint by Paula Jones against President Clinton in 1994, Jones invoked both the quid pro quo and hostile work environment definitions of sexual harassment. A Federal District judge dismissed the case due to the finding that the suit "could not prevail under any legal standard because she had offered no evidence that Mr. Clinton had threatened her with job-related consequences" (Greenhouse, 1998b).

One of the areas of sexual harassment that needed clarification because of mixed lower court rulings involved the rights and responsibilities of companies and their employees (Greenhouse, 1998b). The U.S. Supreme Court's rulings in two cases in 1998 helped to clarify the law on sexual harassment. In *Faragher v. City of Boca Raton*, a lifeguard brought suit against the City of Boca Raton for failing to protect her from harassment by her supervisors. In *Burlington Industries Inc. v. Ellerth*, the employee asserted that her supervisor engaged in sexual harassment and forced her discharge. These two cases led the Court to establish the following rules for deciding when an employer is liable in a sexual harassment case:

- Employers are responsible for harassment engaged in by their supervisory employees.
- If the harassment results in "a tangible employment action, such as discharge, demotion or undesirable reassignment," the employer's liability is absolute.
- If there has been no tangible action, an employer can defend itself if it can prove two things: first, that it has taken "reasonable care to prevent and correct promptly any sexual harassing behavior," such as by adopting an effective policy with a complaint procedure, and second, that the employee "unreasonably failed to take advantage of any preventive or corrective opportunities" provided (Greenhouse, 1998b).

Based on these guidelines, the Court ruled that in the Burlington case, the plaintiff, Ellerth, "should have a chance at trial to prove her case and that, at the same time, the company should have the chance to assert a defense" (Greenhouse, 1998b). In the Boca Raton case, the Court awarded judgment to Faragher, the lifeguard, holding that "an employer is vicariously liable for actionable discrimination caused by a supervisor, but subject to an affirmative defense looking to the reasonableness of the employer's conduct as well as that of a plaintiff victim."

The work environment, as emphasized in the idea of a "hostile" environment, is intertwined with the concept of sexual harassment as sex discrimination. MacKinnon (1979), in *Sexual Harassment of Working Women*, has argued that "sexual harassment, because it is a problem primarily for women, is a form of discrimination and as such a violation of federal law" (Patai, 1998). Patai (1998), in *Heterophobia: Sexual Harassment and the Future of Feminism*, has been critical of MacKinnon's arguments and the feminist literature, as well as the ways in which sexual harassment as sex discrimination has been handled in the courts. Patai contends that "Hostile-environment actions are now based upon the subjective experience of 'unwanted' or 'offensive' conduct (including speech), as perceived by the accuser and tested by the 'reasonable women' standard." She takes the position that "this development transfers the burden of proof from the accuser to the accused, in violation of American due process." In her critique, Patai (1998) reviews how the sexual harassment doctrine has been applied in higher education, contending that a "Sexual Harassment Industry" made up of staff and administrators has led to a "policing of the faculty."

FAMILY SUPPORT PROGRAMS

The changing work force in American communities has resulted in increased attention to family-friendly, family-responsive company policies and programs (Lambert, 1993, 1998). The issue of balancing family and work roles continues to be a challenge to employees, especially women with children who work in paid employment outside the home. As of 2000, approximately 65 percent of new entrants into the work force were women. Family support programs developed at the initiative of private companies and governmental agencies have been responsive to some of the changes in the work force. Corporate support for families may include the establishment of child care centers, employee assistance programs, flex-time, job sharing, family leave, and eldercare services.

Although there are ample examples of family support programs in major corporations, most small organizations do not offer such employee benefits. Of the programs that exist, most are found in large corporations that employ professionals. Thus, people employed in smaller companies, secondary labor markets, and low wage jobs do not have the benefits of family support programs. For example, the majority of low-paid workers, women, single parents, and members of ethnic and racial minority groups tend to be employed in organizations without family support programs (Lambert, 1993). With the advent of welfare reform, increased attention has been given to the child care needs of poor families participating in "workfare" (welfare-to-work) programs. In addition, working poor families tend to have limited or nonexistent health insurance for adults and children. In her critique of workplace supports, Lambert (1993) has highlighted the fact that "many so-called family-responsive policies function as work supports to help ensure that workers continue to give priority to work over family." At the same time, Lambert (1993) has noted that employers "can help workers effectively balance their work and family responsibilities. . .at the company policy level, the supervisor level, the work group level, and the job task level."

An important source of family supports has come from federal and state legislation, including "laws and regulations concerning child labor, minimum wage, safety in the workplace, payment for overtime hours, the freedom of workers to organize, and discrimination on the basis of race or gender" (Lambert, 1993). A major federal initiative is the Family and Medical Leave Act of 1993. This Act was implemented in August 1993, for workers employed in companies with 50 or more employees. The law allows workers up to 12 weeks of unpaid leave annually to care for seriously ill or new members of their immediate family (self, children, parents, or a spouse). An important part of the Act is the requirement, under most conditions, of a guarantee of the same or comparable job with equivalent pay, benefits and working conditions, as well as continuation of health benefits during leave. The leave itself, however, is unpaid and this prevents its full use by many working-class families. In 1999, the Clinton administration supported the extension of benefits under the Family and Medical Leave Act by liberalizing the accrued sick leave options for federal workers.

Employer supports for child care and elder care have a significant impact on the ability of families to balance work and family roles, but additional benefits are provided by some companies. For example, in a company studied by Lambert (1998), three types of supports were provided: for dependents, for community, and for self. Supports for dependent children included scholarships, summer camp, onsite child care center, tutoring, and sick-child care; for dependent elderly or ill family members, support included emergency care for an adult, and eldercare referral service. Supports for the community included neighborhood improvement funds and matching-gifts programs. Supports for self included tuition reimbursement, an on-site fitness center, and wellness massage.

PROBLEMS IN COMMUNITY ECONOMIC SYSTEMS

American communities vary considerably in how well their local economic systems operate. It is important to recognize that the local system is highly interdependent with other economic systems, particularly in relation to urban areas, and state, national, and world economies. An effective local community economic system produces a low level of unemployment; an adequate "division of labor" with opportunities for various occupations in the work force; non-discrimination in hiring, promotion, and benefits; a presence of affirmative action programs directed toward employment of special populations; adequate funding for community protection (fire, police, safety); an adequate tax base for public services and recreational programs; opportunities to earn adequate income above the poverty level; and provision of funding of health and welfare services for people without sufficient fiscal resources.

Evaluating a local economic system is a complex task. Community studies and the deliberations of governmental bodies alert us to the extent to which economic forces have a positive or negative effect on the lives of community residents. The community acts through its economic and political organizations in the generation of money and services and the allocation of resources to community residents. The larger the community, the more difficult it is to ascertain the major features of its economic system and the causes of its problems. Special attention in recent years has been devoted to the problems of central cities in large metropolitan areas, and the relationship of the economic conditions of these cities to the economic well-being of suburban communities. Central cities, after losing jobs and population over several decades, recovered somewhat during the economic boom of the 1990s. Nevertheless, about one fourth of large cities in the U.S. lost jobs during this period and had problems maintaining their populations and creating jobs for their residents (*Investors Business Daily*, 1999).

The economic conditions of central cities often have been characterized as an "urban crisis." Observers attribute this crisis to factors such as declines in central city commercial-industrial growth, reductions in population, suburbanization of industry and households, competition between regions of the country for jobs and workers, and high public investment in downtown developments (especially convention centers and sports arenas). Any listing of these complex economic forces suggests the creation of a "fiscal plight" for the central cities, especially the inner-city areas of most large, older U.S. communities. Reasons for the economic difficulties of central cities include the fact that these cities provide daily services for a large number of people, many of whom live outside the city. The cities' fiscal ability to provide these services has been reduced by tax base declines related to "white flight" of middle-class residents to the suburbs, and increased labor costs for city utilities and services. At the same time, suburban municipalities are not without their economic problems, particularly with regard to the delivery of public services. As federal funds to these communities have decreased, many local governments have sought relief through consolidations into larger governmental units. Some suburban communities now look to consolidation with central cities for such services as transportation, water supply, waste disposal, recreation, parks, and public health services. While these local governments retain their political identity, the increased cooperation between them and central city governments signals an emerging form of economic relationships between the units of metropolitan communities (Rusk, 1993).

Among the various efforts by economic and political leaders to revitalize central city communities, three stand out. First, there are efforts to build housing that will attract middle- and upper-middle-income people (new and restored housing, and gentrification areas). Second, there are efforts to develop the inner city as a high-class "playground" offering culture, dining, recreation, entertainment, and casinos to attract tourists and conventions. These efforts require a collaboration of local political leaders with economic leaders, and the provision of incentives such as loan guarantees and tax abatements, designed to lure new business, new housing, and new investments into the central downtown districts. Third, large central cities attempt to obtain special funds from state governments and departments of the federal government, such as assistance to enterprise and empowerment zones designated by the U.S. Department of Housing and Urban Development, and projects from the U.S. Department of Health and Human Services.

Central city mayors and other political leaders continue to seek state and federal aid for their communities. They argue that people from the entire metropolitan area use the facilities, roads, and cultural and entertainment amenities of the city, and that this usage requires unusually high expenditures for police and fire protection, parks, hospitals, and roads. Most people who use the central city's facilities and services contribute very little to the funds needed to maintain them. Often guided by political party interests, state governments have responded in various ways to the special needs of central cities. The federal government has assumed some of the fiscal burdens of the city through revenue sharing and a variety of programs under the Department of Housing and Urban Development, including funding for street repairs, transportation, and water supply. Fiscal assistance from extra-community sources has been advocated on the premise that older urban cities have lost large numbers of people and jobs to the suburbs; have large areas with low tax bases, or no tax base (highways, urban renewal areas); have a large concentration of the poor; and have decaying physical facilities. Federal involvement in problems of central city economic systems is most apparent in the development of enterprise and empowerment zones.

ENTERPRISE ZONES/EMPOWERMENT ZONES

Federal, state, and local governments are interested in creating new job opportunities and enhancing economic strength at the local community level. One way of seeking to accomplish these goals has been to designate inner-city areas as enterprise zones. Economic activities within the zone are expected to respond to the special problems of people in the area, such as high unemployment, high crime, and welfare dependency. Once an area has been declared an enterprise zone, special incentives for businesses are provided to assist in economic development, such as tax relief for new hires, business expansion, and relaxation of regulations. The principle of the enterprise zone is that stimulation of business will generate employment opportunities for residents in the zone.

States have been the principal initiators of enterprise zone programs. Florida established the first enterprise zone legislation in 1981. As of 2000, most states and the District of Columbia had established some variation of enterprise zones. Based on studies by the U.S. Department of Housing and Urban Development, state enterprise zone programs in local communities have been successful in stimulating capital investment and new jobs. Small businesses, through public-private cooperation, have been the main actors in improving the economy in enterprise zones.

Federal government involvement in local community development increased with the passage of the Community Development Act of 1987, which included authorization for HUD to create 100 federal enterprise zones within which usual regulatory controls for businesses would be modified. An "enhanced enterprise zone" was proposed in 1993 by Henry Cisneros, Secretary of the Department of Housing and Urban Development. The proposal included funding from a mix of federal sources: HUD for housing needs, Education for schools, Health and Human Services for clinics and family counseling, Labor for job training, Justice for public safety programs, Transportation for infrastructure needs, the Environmental Protection Agency for cleaning up the environment, and the Treasury for tax abatements. These funding sources focused on a local design and on services "delivered on a scale calculated to lift the neighborhood and its people into the mainstream," emphasizing neighborhood initiatives "to nurture people's sense of responsibility and self-respect" (*Washington Post*, 1993).

Some of the ideas proposed by HUD Secretary Cisneros for enterprise zones were incorporated into President Clinton's budget legislation passed by the Congress in August 1993. Under this legislation, "empowerment zones" were created in Atlanta, Baltimore, Chicago, Detroit, New York City, and Philadelphia-Camden, NJ, with a supplemental zone in Los Angeles and three zones in rural areas. These zones received tax incentives for hiring of area residents, authority to issue tax-exempt bonds to finance businesses, deductions for business property, and social service grants. An additional 95 "enterprise communities" were designated, 65 urban and 30 rural, and provided with special bond rules as well as federal grants. The number of enterprise areas was limited to assure that they would receive sufficient support to be evaluated for effectiveness in reaching the program's goals (McGinley, 1993).

The federal empowerment zone program is similar to the enterprise zone program in that it emphasizes job development and other benefits to residents in neighborhood and community areas, such as physical investment and social service programs. Tax incentives and public/private collaboration of city, state, and federal sources are directed toward establishing businesses, creating jobs, and providing job training (Newman, 1999). Federal funds have been made available to cities with empowerment zones over a ten-year period. A major problem for all the empowerment zone cities has been the cumbersome approval process for projects, with the mix of politics and bureaucracy leading to "millions of dollars going unused" (Waldman, 1999). For example, since the New York City Zone receives money from the federal, state, and city governments, some observers and officials believe that "The pool of money has been frozen largely because each proposal requires the approval of officials in three levels of government" (Waldman, 1999). Another explanation for unused funds in one area of New York City has been that "In Harlem, the picture is complicated by complex and sometimes volatile politics— the layers of Congress and City council members, the different generations and classes, and the competing ethnic and immigrant groups all vying for a piece of the pie" (Waldman, 1999).

Another example of the lack of use of federal funds is the City of Detroit, where critics say red tape ties up millions in aid (Dixon, 1999). A large part of the unspent money was allocated to housing and community development projects, but U.S. Housing and Urban Development Department officials have accused local agencies of mismanagement and withheld funds from some projects. Residents blame city, HUD, and local community groups for delays in removal of abandoned homes and commercial buildings, in handling lead poisoning problems related to children, in responding to housing needs of the homeless, and in rehabilitating public housing projects and private homes.

In addition to addressing the economic needs of residents in large urban areas, in 1999 the Clinton administration provided community development grants to rural areas such as Appalachia. Within Appalachia, which includes portions of 13 states, unemployment and poverty rates are at least one and one half times the national average (Babington, 1999b). Economic developments in these communities have included "highway construction and job-creation initiatives to help residents overcome the economic and psychological isolation caused by poverty and the rugged terrain" (Janofsky, 1998). In 1999 President Clinton sought to encourage economic development in rural areas through "a mix of public and private investment to spur economic activity in some of the nation's forgotten communities." The president's program included community development grants to areas such as the Mississippi Delta region (Associated Press, 1999d).

THE ROLE OF BANKS IN THE REVITALIZATION OF NEIGHBORHOODS

Banks are a significant part of the economic system of a community. The lending patterns of banks affect the purchase and/or rehabilitation of homes, as well as the initiation or expansion of small businesses. A 1977 Community Reinvestment Act emphasizes that banks have "a continuing and affirmative obligation to help meet the credit needs of the communities where they operate." Still, evidence from numerous studies indicates that banks fail to meet this federal requirement in urban, inner-city neighborhoods (Bacon, 1993; Karr, 1993; *Detroit News,* 1999; Kilborn, 1999c). For example, a 1999 study by Acorn found that "African-Americans were twice as likely as whites, and Hispanic-Americans one-and-a-half times as likely, to be denied a conventional, 30-year home loan last year" (Kilborn, 1999c). A second study, commissioned by HUD, "showed that discrimination was the reason for the disparity" and that "African American and Hispanic American homeownership rates are still less than two-thirds the homeownership rate of whites" (Kilborn, 1999b). A third study conducted by the National Community Reinvestment Coalition "found that Americans believe discrimination is still pervasive in lending, despite bank-industry claims to the contrary," with banks favoring white men for loan approval (Pugh, 1999).

In 1999, when proposed federal legislation was perceived by a number of civil rights organizations to undermine the Community Investment Act, the organizations sponsored the following *New York Times* advertisement in support of the Act.

> America is built on its communities. And the Community Reinvestment Act (CRA) has been helping those communities prosper for more than 20 years. It has stimulated billions of dollars in local investment, enhancing the quality of life in thousands of towns and cities across the country.
>
> We need Congress to help ensure that banks continue to invest locally, so that the neighborhoods they serve can continue to prosper. . . Working together under the CRA, banks, civic leaders, and citizens can continue to make our communities stronger. And when our communities are strengthened, so are we (*New York Times*, 1999a).

Three important developments in programs for investment in poor communities have emerged in recent years. The first is a model of commercial and community development banks initiated within urban communities. The second is a new initiative on the part of the federal government to support economic development of inner cities through the creation of community development banks. The third is the creation of banks owned and operated by African Americans, such as Indecorp Inc. and Seaway National Corp. in Chicago. One of the issues related to these minority-run banks has been their limited capacity to help inner-city residents because of their small size, under-capitalization, and limited and conservative loan practices (Wilke, 1995).

The South Shore Bank of Chicago is the exemplar of a community bank involved in lending for purchase or rehabilitation of residential housing and for funding of small businesses (Grzywinski, 1991). When new managers took over this bank in 1973, the bank was failing and planning to leave the neighborhood. The new managers created a "development" bank that helped stop the decline of the neighborhood by making commercial and housing loans within the area. The bank was able to take residents' savings and invest the money in the local neighborhood, thus stopping the flow of money out of the community, and improving residential housing, supporting small businesses, developing and managing business and residential property, and developing rental and cooperative housing.

When the South Shore Bank began its activities, this neighborhood of approximately 80,000 people had changed from a white, middle-class neighborhood to a mostly African American community of middle-class, working-class, and poor residents. Single-family and multifamily housing was deteriorating, small businesses were closing or moving, and the South Shore area faced "abandonment." The South Shore Bank became a major actor in rebuilding the community, with the other major force being residents who became active through "Ma and Pa rehabbing" of residential buildings, improvements of small businesses, and the creation of activist voluntary associations (Grzywinski, 1991). At the same time, the South Shore bank's role in the community has not been without controversy. For example, in 1995 the bank offered to buy Indecorp Inc. and encountered community opposition because the sale was perceived as moving money and economic power away from the African American community (Wilke, 1995).

The South Shore Bank is an example of a bank initiating changes in banking practices that led to the involvement of community residents. Other examples of resident involvement include coalitions of community residents and organizations pressuring banks to make inner-city loans (Bleakley, 1992), and starting new banks (Bacon, 1993; Bleakley, 1992). In the first instance, community residents, African American churches, and community groups in Syracuse, New York worked together to bring about changes in lending practices of the major bank in the city. Deliberations between community groups and the bank led to a "banking community reinvestment agreement" that involved extending home loans to borrowers from poor inner-city neighborhoods and facilitating loan approval for small businesses (Bleakley, 1992). In the second instance, community activists in Grand Rapids, Michigan engaged in efforts to open a start-up bank designed to help minority entrepreneurs in an inner-city neighborhood to obtain business loans. These efforts met with opposition from the mainstream banking community but gained the support of community groups, including a financial investment by a local order of Dominican nuns (Bacon, 1993).

Under the administration of President Clinton, federal initiatives have been introduced with regard to lending in poor communities (Bacon, 1993). These initiatives include encouraging and facilitating commercial banks to increase their loans to residents in poor communities, as well as to help fund new community development banks. The Clinton administration has proposed the creation of a Community Banking and Credit Fund that would provide federal money for community development to financial institutions such as banks, credit unions, and loan funds. The new Fund would operate under new reinvestment rules designed to cut bureaucratic red tape. The major goal of the Fund would be to create a network of 100 community development banks, which would be required to mix federal dollars with local community funds and to move their operations toward independence from federal funding. The proposed bank in Grand Rapids, Michigan discussed above illustrates one of the ways in which the Fund could be used to stimulate community banking—that is, to assist community residents in establishing banks that would focus on community development by issuing loans for minority businesses and for rehabilitation of housing in older, poor neighborhoods (Martin, 1993). The U.S. Department of Agriculture has established programs with guaranteed loans for co-op associations in rural areas as a way of encouraging rural investment to help increase employment opportunities. The Hermitage Tomato Cooperative Association in Arkansas is an example of this type of loan, which enabled tomato farmers to produce and sell their tomatoes to Burger King (Babington, 1999a, 1999b).

In response to concerns that banks often turn down home loan applications from Native Americans, in 1999 the Housing and Urban Development took action to increase this group's access to HUD assistance programs. Under this program, newly formed tribal nonprofit groups would be able to apply for federal money from a range of sources, such as Rural Economic Development funds, housing programs for low-income and disabled seniors, housing programs for homeless persons, a Youthbuild program for training in home-building skills, housing grants for people with HIV and AIDS, sweat-equity homeownership programs, and Ginnie Mae mortgage programs. In announcing these initiatives for Native Americans, Secretary of HUD Cuomo said these housing assistance programs would "bring new opportunities to families on reservations by empowering them to build stronger economies, new homes, and better lives" (Claiborne, 1999c). Some Native American groups and tribal leaders expressed doubt that such programs would have much impact on reservation poverty, pointing instead to "HUD's inaction in addressing Indian concerns over environmental assessments required for reservation housing construction."

WELFARE AS A PART OF THE ECONOMIC SYSTEM

A number of social programs provide income and other benefits to local community residents. These programs are usually considered to be part of the health and social welfare subsystem of a community. At the same time, they constitute an important component of the local economic system. These programs provide economic benefits for families, and for individuals who are retired, unemployed, and/or disabled. Most programs are financed through federal and state governments, and these programs have been described in Chapter 2. Some programs, such as Social Security and Unemployment Insurance, are based on social insurance, a system under which employed individuals contribute a portion of their income in order to receive future benefits. The Social Security system also provides for in-kind benefits in health care through the Medicare and Medicaid programs. Of particular import on the community economic system are benefits to older adults from the Social Security programs. For example, a 1999 study by the Center for Budget and Policy Priorities found that Social Security benefits keep a sizable number of elderly men and women out of poverty (Associated Press, 1999a).

The care of children is the major focus of the Temporary Assistance for Needy Families program. The care of older adults, blind persons, and disabled individuals who have not been covered by the Social Security system is the focus of the Supplemental Security Income (SSI) program, which includes income and health care benefits (Medicaid). General Assistance programs are provided by state and local funds for individuals not covered by federal or state programs. These public assistance programs are "means tested" and provide income and in-kind benefits (food stamps and food) based on need. The number of individuals and families in a community who are receiving public assistance has an impact on other local subsystems, such as the social welfare, education, religion, and political systems. For example, eligibility for additional benefits for schoolchildren, such as health and nutrition programs, is established by their status within the public welfare system. The social welfare and religious community subsystems provide a variety of services for people living below the federal poverty line. Under workfare programs, employable individuals on welfare are required to receive training for work or to obtain jobs as a condition of receiving public assistance. Such programs are highly dependent on the development of occupational opportunities in communities, highlighting the close interconnections between social welfare and economic subsystems.

THE ECONOMY OF THE GHETTO

Wilson (1998) has observed that as of the late 1990s "most adults in many inner-city ghetto neighborhoods were not working in a typical week" and many were "on welfare," especially Temporary Assistance for Needy Families (Wilson, 1998). In his book, *When Work Disappears*,

Wilson (1996) provides evidence of high levels of joblessness in ghetto poor neighborhoods, that is, lack of regular employment in the formal economy. Of some financial help to the residents of large, urban, inner-city neighborhoods is the presence of an "underground economy." Much of this economy involves odd jobs: "Women cut hair and take care of children in their homes. Men repair houses and fix cars. They rarely pay income tax, and often work covertly while collecting food stamps and welfare" (Templin, 1995).

In their classic studies of the ghetto economy, Fusfeld (1973) and Fusfeld and Bates (1984) provide insight into the economic problems of an urban ghetto. Their analysis highlights the role the welfare economy plays in the ghetto and the relationship of the ghetto economy (the work and wages of residents) to the larger economic system of the community. The findings of these studies were similar in some respects to those by Wilson (1996) in showing that the welfare system helps perpetuate the poverty of ghetto residents, as it isolates them from the labor market of the larger community. Welfare payments and informal income sources support the internal flow of spending. These sources keep the ghetto economy somewhat isolated from the larger society, except that there is an outflow to the larger economy that is detrimental to the ghetto because it prevents asset accumulation by residents.

The ghetto is a residual economic subsystem. Social and economic barriers such as high unemployment, relatively low income, and low occupational and residential mobility prevent movement out of the ghetto. Wilson (1987, 1996) and Wacquant and Wilson (1989) argue that "the dramatic rise in inner-city joblessness and economic exclusion is a product of the continuous industrial restructuring of American capitalism" (Wilson, 1989). Studies by these authors have demonstrated that the ghetto poor, living in high-poverty areas (where more than 40 percent of the residents have incomes below the poverty line), lack the kinds of resources, job opportunities, economic and social capital available to residents of non-ghetto, low-poverty areas.

Even in times of national "economic boom" such as the 1990s, many residents in ghetto poor areas such as Watts and its surrounding communities in South Central Los Angeles do not benefit from the economic system of the larger community (Sanchez, 1999a). In these areas, one third of the families live in poverty, and unemployment is nearly twice the national average. These conditions have been attributed to problems of public transportation for getting to work, to lack of businesses and manufacturing in the area, personal problems of residents, such as lack of technical skills, "bouts with crime, drug abuse or reluctance to prepare better for changes in the job market," and fears and neglect by employers. "And the few jobs that community organizers manage to find for residents often seem to be of little more than low-paying scraps—temporary construction or carpentry work, night security posts, or entry positions in food service" (Sanchez, 1999a). One hope for employment opportunities for residents in Watts and nearby ghetto areas, with a high proportion of urban poor African American and Latino residents, is to attract new businesses through funds provided from the federal empowerment zone program.

THE WORKING POOR AND MINIMUM WAGES

In many inner-city and rural communities a high proportion of households live in poverty, even if at least one person in the household is working. This group, which is often referred to as the "working poor," includes "millions of poor workers occupying the lowest rungs of the occupational ladder. . . .The working poor are perpetually at risk for becoming the poor of the other kind; they are one paycheck away from what is left of welfare, one sick child away from getting fired, one missed rent payment short of eviction" (Newman, 1999). A federal report issued in March 2000 by HUD Secretary Andrew Cuomo highlighted the difficulties faced by working poor families in finding affordable housing—that is, housing that costs less than a third of a family's income. The study found that 5.4 million working poor families were paying more than half of their incomes for housing.

A "living wage" movement in many communities has resulted in ordinances that establish minimum wages for organizations doing business with the city or county government. Approximately 40 cities and counties in 17 states have enacted living wage laws that require hourly minimum wages that are higher than the federal minimum wage level. For example, minimum hourly wages range from $6.50 to $8.75 in the cities of Baltimore, Milwaukee, Tucson, Jersey City, Los Angeles, New Haven, Boston, Duluth, Durham (NC), and Chicago (Uchitelle, 1999a). A community organization, Build, supported the passage of the living wage ordinance in Baltimore, and more recently, organized residents in poor neighborhoods to go to the polls. In Los Angeles, a Living Wage Coalition made up of community groups, churches, and unions organized residents to gain support for the passage of an ordinance related to wages for employees of restaurants and other businesses in a subsidized tourist zone. In many communities, the wage movement seeks to improve the wages of janitors, cleaning people, restaurant workers, health care personnel, security guards, school bus drivers, and parking attendants. Community groups join together in social action activities that involve local politics in order to support wage ordinances.

Newman's (1999) study of working poor adults in Latino and African American neighborhoods of Harlem provides insights into the problems of community economic systems for people in low-wage and minimum-wage jobs. In the United States, the working poor actually constitute a larger group of poor people than those on welfare. The working poor "cannot afford decent housing, health care, or child care" and often "lack access to government supports that cushion those out of the labor force: subsidized housing, medical care, and food stamps" (Newman, 1999). The working poor are disproportionately African American and Hispanic American, and welfare reform has placed new pressures on women who leave TANF and enter the work force. Still, Newman (1999) found that work means more than money for the working poor, as "what they have that their non-working counterparts lack is both the dignity of being employed and the opportunity to participate in social activities that increasingly define their adult lives."

Many working poor families live in rural areas, where "minimum wage jobs give many Americans only a miserable life" (Horwitz, 1993). For example, in some communities in rural Vermont, working poor families are mostly white, mostly high-school educated, and are unable to pay bills on time, such as car and utility payments, but they do not qualify for public assistance. Ongoing financial struggles lead some to quit jobs in order to get benefits. Social and economic changes in rural areas in the 1990s, such as the economic restructuring of business and industry related to a global economy, have weakened the infrastructure of many small towns. During this period there was a loss of "living wage" jobs that would keep families above the poverty level, migration of young people to larger cities, and reduced federal funding for public and social services. These changes have diminished the developmental potential of rural communities and have contributed to the persistence of rural poverty. More recently, federal budgets have expanded funding for rural economic development in "distressed communities." At the same time, some rural communities have been able to create jobs by attracting manufacturers with municipal bonds, low taxes, and the promise of reliable workers. Some small towns in Minnesota have become boom towns, supported by new service businesses and factories, as well as by successful farming families (Quintanilla & Rose, 1996).

COMMUNITY CONTEXT FOR WELFARE, GHETTO, AND WORKING POOR

Issues involving community, neighborhood, poverty, and work are interconnected for inner-city residents. As Coulton (1996) has observed, "A growing body of research has identified the community and neighborhood as a factor in the reproduction of social and economic disadvantage." Our discussions of some of the economic issues related to people on public welfare, the working poor, and the underclass, have highlighted the need to understand how neighborhood conditions influence residents' capacity to obtain work. Coulton (1996) identifies the following connections between communities and work:

- Socialization within communities may be an important mechanism for fostering the ability to hold a job. Socialization for work can come from successful role models, from community efforts in schools, youth programs, family centers.
- Communities can transmit expectations and definitions of success that foster work.
- Crime and disorder interfere with residents' abilities to work and discourage business development, a condition that requires both formal and informal social controls over behaviors.
- The quality and effectiveness of schools, training programs, and post-secondary educational institutions available to community residents have a powerful effect on employment, a condition that involves institutions that build human capital.
- Social networks and supports in the community influence employment possibilities.
- Informal networks are by far the most important sources of information about jobs, and employers rely on these networks to find employees, especially those in the lower-skill categories.
- Poor people rely on public transportation to a greater degree than other workers.
- The possibility of working, especially for new or marginal labor force participants, is affected by the demand for workers, a condition that requires strategies such as those in enterprise and empowerment zones.

As noted in Chapter 1, a number of communities have organizations that sponsor IDA programs that encourage savings and asset development for people in low-income households (Sherraden et al., 2000).

EFFECTS OF ECONOMIC CONDITIONS ON THE MIDDLE CLASS

There is a strong belief among people who identify themselves as "middle class" that taxes, inflation, and other economic forces make it difficult to maintain a satisfactory lifestyle. As a result, many middle-class households include two adults in the work force, but still feel it is difficult to "make ends meet." For these families, national and local community economic forces are viewed as barriers to upward mobility. Increasingly problematic is the experience of downward mobility for some members of the middle class. This experience is captured by Newman (1988), who states, "Hundreds of thousands of middle-class families plunge down America's social ladder every year. They lose their jobs, their income drops drastically, and they find themselves suddenly powerless and in economic hardship, often for the first time. In the face of this downward mobility, people feel unable to direct their lives."

A variety of economic conditions, at the international, national, and/or local community level, such as economic restructuring and downsizing by corporations, bring about job loss for people accustomed to well-paid blue-collar and white-collar work. Most of these individuals find other jobs and do not skid into poverty. Still, they may find it difficult to maintain their customary middle-class status and lifestyle. "They must therefore contend not only with financial hardship but with the psychological, social, and practical consequences of 'falling from grace,' of losing their 'proper place' in the world" (Newman, 1988, 1993). The nature of downward mobility through economic dislocation varies. Sometimes it involves collective losses when companies carry out mass layoffs or dismissals, or when strikes fail and employees cannot return to work. At other times the loss involves only the individual or selected individuals. In other instances downward mobility is caused by divorce, after which some women are forced to enter the work force in positions that do not support the previous family lifestyle.

The experience of downward mobility in the middle classes is illustrated by Newman (1988) in her discussion of the fate of four different groups: former managers and executives, fired air traffic controllers, blue-collar workers in a plant shutdown, and divorced mothers. The experiences of these groups provide convincing evidence that their fate depends in part on the economic system of the local community. Some communities provide alternatives for work, educational and training opportunities, supportive health and social services for families and children, and community economic development programs, all of which may cushion downward mobility or assist in movement back up the occupational ladder and restoration of one's class identity and self-esteem. In short, employment is a central component in the local community economic system, and the competence of a community is measured in part by its ability to prevent downward mobility at all social class levels and to create employment opportunities at all occupational levels.

IMMIGRATION AND THE ECONOMY

Federal immigration policies and patterns of immigration into the United States continue to be of great interest to local community residents, especially with regard to the effects of immigration on national and local economies (Smith & Edmonston, 1998). Native-born citizens, as well as governmental officials and business/corporate organizations, pay close attention to immigration policies because of concerns about the costs and benefits of immigration. As Borjas (1999) has observed, "the American people care about who the immigrants are"— Americans want to know whether the immigrants will need social welfare services and whether they will compete with natives in the labor market. These concerns are related to the number of immigrants admitted to the United States, and the skills they possess when entering the country. At times U.S. immigration policy has been based on the idea that the nation's economy would benefit most through the entry of highly skilled workers (Finch, 1990). Borjas (1999) demonstrates that changes in immigration policies in 1965 show a "relative decline in the skills and economic performance of immigrants since that time" (Borjas, 1999). Especially during the 1980s and 1990s, the "immigrant flow" of about one million persons a year (including about 730,000 legal immigrants, 200,000 illegal aliens, and 100,000 refugees) has been disproportionately composed of less-skilled workers, due in large part "to a single factor, the changing national origin mix of the immigrant population" (Borjas, 1999).

Recently a major concern of U.S. native-born citizens has involved the impact of low-skilled immigrant workers on employment opportunities and wages. Studies in the 1980s on this topic indicated that competition from unskilled immigrants did not adversely affect the income of persons born in the U.S. and that immigration made substantial contributions to the U.S. economy (Reischauer, 1989; Simon, 1990, 1993). Contrasting findings about the effects of immigration are presented by Borjas (1999) in *Heaven's Door: Immigration Policy and the*

American Economy. Borjas concludes that the effect of immigration on the U.S. economy is offset by the costs of providing services to immigrants. He suggests that immigration generates enormous wealth for employers and highly skilled workers at the expense of unskilled and disadvantaged natives. According to this analysis, immigration is thought to have negative effects on the economic opportunities of the least-skilled native-born Americans—high school dropouts, particularly those who belong to minority groups.

In some areas of the United States. most notably California, residents have expressed concern about the effects of illegal immigrants on local economies. Anti-immigrant sentiments about illegal aliens are strong in communities such as Los Angeles, where citizens believe that "What is really happening is that employers of this labor are taking advantage of the local taxpayers, who are covering the difference in public benefits" (Ferguson, 1992). Or, as Freeman (1991) stated, "To live here is to know that Los Angeles is becoming a vast sea of the undocumented and the illegal. Many of them work hard; some even spend their money here. Many try to send it out of the country, mostly to Mexico and Latin America." A major problem for illegal immigrants has been their lack of protection from dismissal or discrimination based on their race, sex, age, or religion. In response to this situation, particularly exploitation by employers, the Equal Employment Opportunity Commission extended broad anti-discrimination rights to illegal immigrants in 1999. These immigrants were already protected by minimum-wage and occupational safety laws (Greenhouse, 1999f).

It is difficult to determine the number of illegal immigrants who enter the U.S. annually or their impact on local economies. Most of these immigrants are farm workers and domestic workers. A large number of the domestic workers settle in New York City, New Jersey, Los Angeles, Chicago, Miami, Houston, and Washington, D.C. As an immigration lawyer noted about Washington, D.C., "They're working in the homes of our lawyers, our journalists, and our government officials" (Kilborn, 1993). The Immigration and Naturalization Service has been unable to control such immigration into the nation's communities, despite a 1986 Act designed to curtail illegal immigration and 1999 Senate appropriations to hire new agents for the U.S. Border Patrol. Borjas' (1999) study of immigration policy includes proposals for "stiffer penalties on those who employ illegal aliens" and financial penalties on illegal persons themselves (Skerry, 1999). These proposals are controversial in political circles, due in part to resistance by employer groups.

It is clear that some immigrant groups, particularly Asians, have been successful in achieving the benefits of the local community economy

(Kasarda, 1989, 1992). Dominican immigrants in New York City have displayed a capacity for entering into the economic life of the city and the surrounding areas, often accumulating funds to send to relatives in their homeland (Rimer, 1991). Many Central and South American immigrants have become suburbanites, establishing employment and residence in the New York City suburbs (Berger, 1993). Kasarda (1989) draws from studies on ethnic entrepreneurism to compare Asian immigrants and some Hispanic groups to African American native residents. Important elements that appear to foster the economic success of Hispanic immigrants include the fact that self-employment is supported by ethnic solidarity, kinship networks, household structures, use of family labor, thriftiness, long hours of work, reinvestment of profits, and purchasing by members of the ethnic community.

An example of the entrepreneurial success of Asian immigrants can be found in Flushing, New York, a community in Queens that has attracted Asians into residential neighborhoods and into the business and professional community (Wysocki, 1991). There has been a dramatic increase in Asian-owned businesses, such as restaurants, beauty salons, banks and trading companies, led by Chinese and Korean immigrants but including Asians from many countries. A decade ago, nearly 100,000 Chinese and Korean immigrants had moved into Flushing neighborhoods since the late 1970s, but not without conflicts with long-time residents of the area. Cultural and racial frictions have emerged, particularly between white and African American residents and Asian immigrants. In the community of Flushing, there is evidence that some members of the Asian immigrant families have been engaged in social and economic mobility, moving to suburbs and "toward the middle-class mainstream of suburban and corporate America" (Wysocki, 1991).

During the 1990s, communities in the Washington, D.C., area became a major destination for immigrants (Bredemeier, 1999). This is especially apparent in Asian-oriented shopping centers. "As the inner suburbs of Washington attract increasingly diverse pockets of ethnic cultures, some of its older strip shopping centers have been transformed into veritable international bazaars of goods, services, and restaurants" (Bredemeier, 1999). The suburbanization of immigrants in this area has influenced the growth of start-up stores and restaurants, and "some ethnic groups have come to be identified with certain trades, such as Koreans with dry cleaning, Indians with doughnut shops, Vietnamese with cosmetology, and Latinos with construction and landscaping" (Bredemeier, 1999).

A somewhat different story of successful immigration patterns has emerged in Miami, where immigration over the past several decades has made Miami distinctly Cuban (Navarro, 1999). As of 1999, many of the political leaders in the area are either Cuban-born or of Cuban descent, including the mayors of the city and county, nearly half of the county's delegation in the legislature, and two of its six members of Congress. Due in part to shifting patterns of immigration over the years, one journalist has observed that "Cuban Miami has become less cohesive, encompassing a people who differ in social class, race, generation and politics, who increasingly come from different worlds" (Navarro, 1999). The U.S. government gives special treatment to Cuban immigrants, granting 20,000 visas by lot each year. Thus, Miami's Cuban population encompasses both American-born generations and newcomers, making it the largest Latin American group in the community, accounting for about 60 percent of the Hispanic population. New arrivals may face a difficult transition both socially and economically, especially if they lack education and work-related skills.

Traditionally, many new immigrants have become migrant workers, especially in states where farm products are grown. An emerging economic opportunity for immigrants is the ownership of small farms, such as Asian vegetable growers and Latino apple raisers. Opportunities for farming often occur as Anglo farmers find that their children do not want to be in the farming business, and as the market for organic and ethnic specialty crops increases. Although a majority of the new farmers are Mexican American, many other nations are represented in this economy. A report of the 1997 Census of Agriculture indicated that there were more than 27,000 Hispanic-run farms, an increase of 32 percent over the previous five years. The number of Hispanic farm owners in about one-third of the states had doubled during this period (Kilman & Millman, 1999).

Chapter 11 Review

The economic systems of local urban and rural communities are inextricably linked to the economies of metropolitan areas, states, the nation, and the world. A community's economic system provides sustenance functions of production, consumption, and distribution of goods and services. Important ecological and demographic features in the system are the community's production base, labor market, and income opportunity structures. The community economic system includes a set of workplaces that are interdependent with the other community subsystems and with the total community. Special issues within these workplace organizations include equal employment and advancement opportunities, diversity in the workplace, sexual orientation and workplace discrimination, career tracks, family support programs, effects of the Americans with Disabilities Act, ergonomics and work-related injuries, and sexual harassment.

Problems in the local economic system are most glaring in the inner-city areas of large urban municipalities and in rural areas of poor states. Economic policies and programs to revitalize these areas include enterprise zone and empowerment zone programs, and community development programs, including community banks. Social welfare programs, such as social insurance and public assistance, are viewed as a part of the local economic system, as they provide income for residents. Groups with special needs and demands on the local community economic and social welfare systems include working-class poor, ghetto poor, underclass, and homeless people. Members of ethnic minorities fall disproportionately into the lower segments of the social class structure, due in large part to barriers to full participation in the work force. Of these groups, Native Americans are the most economically disadvantaged and the most likely to live in poverty.

Members of the middle class depend heavily on the local economic system to maintain their lifestyles and status. Within this group are individuals and families who experience downward mobility, a condition that has negative effects on self-esteem and family lifestyles. As a consequence, it is clear that while the community economic system affects people at all social class levels, problems in the system have more devastating effects on selected groups in the community, such as ethnic minorities, women, the downwardly mobile, the working poor, and the unemployed. Changing federal policies regarding immigration are related to concerns about national and local community economies and the effects of new immigrants on these systems. There are mixed findings concerning the impact of legal and illegal immigration on employment opportunities and income of native-born Americans, and on the economic costs versus benefits of immigration. Illustrative examples of successful immigration patterns and new immigrant groups were provided.

12

Community Political System

The political system of a community consists of formal organizations of local government, people involved in informal political processes and activities, and community leaders and organizations within the various community subsystems. As the size of the community increases, the political system becomes more complex, and thus political processes in small communities differ considerably from those in mid-sized and large municipal communities. The local community political system carries out several significant functions:

- Local governments provide services, such as public health, social services, parks and recreation, protection of person and property, street maintenance, water utilities, planning and building, waste collection, and recycling. Most communities provide these kinds of services to some degree, but services vary in their range and quality.
- Local governments are responsible for developing community policies concerning public expenditures for service programs. This "communal decision-making" function applies to matters

such as human services, land use, economic development, and tax and budget issues.

- The local political system plays a major role in the creation of community decision-making and advisory groups. Decision making is assigned to groups such as a local community zoning board, a property tax review board, a local planning commission, and a mental health board.
- Local governments, along with other social units in the community, function as instruments of social control, using regulations and coercive power to maintain social order.
- The political system, through its governmental units, engages in conflict management. Examples of conflicts include zoning disputes, business-commercial and neighborhood group conflicts, and controversies between individuals and interest groups over privileges, rights, and resources.

Social work professionals practicing within the health and social welfare system are influenced by, and exert their own influence on, the community political system. Reisch (1997) refers to this interaction as "the political context of social work," recognizing "the intrinsically political nature of the work" that social workers do. The organizations and activities within the political system offer a range of arenas for the involvement of social workers in advocacy and political action, both as individuals and as members of organized community groups. As Reisch (1997) emphasizes, a political framework calls for social workers to engage in "partisanship" and use of power on behalf of clients and their communities, to link an "an agency's empowerment strategy to the demands of the political environment," to educate clients and constituents about their rights and available resources, and to "facilitate intra-agency and intra-community cooperation" in order to bring about "intra-organizational change in social service agencies."

THE STRUCTURE OF A COMMUNITY POLITICAL SYSTEM

Municipal Government

The primary structure of the political system of a local community is the municipal government, its various administrative and service units, and the official positions within these units. These positions usually include key elected officials, political appointees, and civil service employees. Some of these individuals are policy makers, but many are "administrative actors, that is, non-elected city officials" (Keller, 1992).

These officials are involved in the administration of programs, such as parks and recreation, fire and police departments, public works, legal services, library services, zoos, museums, and school districts. As a result, governance in a municipality "requires coordination of the diverse organizations" within it. Community office holders and leaders "must create and sustain complex systems of people and organizations with efficient and effective policies implemented under an appropriate and 'constitutional' arrangement of public authority" (Keller, 1992).

The specific structure of local government varies from one community to another, depending on the size of the community. Most municipalities are governed by either (1) a mayor and city council; (2) a manager and a city council; (3) a council, mayor, and city manager; or (4) a mayor, council, and/or manager, with commissions or planning boards. Depending on the amount of jurisdiction and influence over decision making, local governments may have strong mayors and weak councils; strong councils and weak mayors, or various other combinations of power relationships. Township and village governments are common in many local communities, representing residents of areas not within a municipality. These local governments provide some of the services offered within municipalities, such as police and fire protection, planning and building services, roads and public works. These community areas are mainly residential, with many services provided by municipal and county governments.

County Government

Municipalities are under the jurisdiction of county governments, created by state legislatures to provide specialized services through the offices of county administrator, county assessor (property tax assessment), county treasurer, county clerk (records and elections), public defender, prosecuting attorney, county sheriff's office, county courts, county jail facilities, county hospitals, roads, parks, fire and police protection, and environmental health agency (Rusk, 1993). In particular, county governments provide a range of services to unincorporated areas. County governments, especially in large urban areas, usually dominate the local community political system, due to their large tax base and to their service and zoning responsibilities. These governments have a board of commissioners—an elected, policy-making body that adopts ordinances, oversees county operations and facilities, approves budgets of county service departments, and makes appointments to county boards, committees, and commissions. County governments are agents of the state and have overlapping jurisdiction with the governments of cities and townships located within the county. In the area of human services, county governments usually act on behalf of the state in funding local health and public welfare services.

Metropolitan Government

This type of government consolidates several local governments under a single metropolitan government. Examples of this form of government include Jacksonville, Indianapolis, and Nashville. Metropolitan government has been proposed as the ideal type of governance for consolidating central cities with suburban communities, especially as a way of solving the fiscal and social problems of large central cities. Metropolitan governments have the potential for overcoming the fiscal imbalances of cities and suburbs, of reducing the racial and economic segregation of these communities, and of promoting area-wide economic development (Rusk, 1993). Most municipalities resist consolidation, however, and therefore the number of metropolitan governments in the U.S. is very small.

Many problems of communication and cooperation between central cities and suburban communities remain unresolved. Varying types of metropolitan government offer limited solutions to urban social problems. One option is to empower county government and eliminate municipal governments within a county. A second option is to create a consolidated government, merging a central city with a single county, as has been done by Indianapolis–Marion County, Nashville–Davidson County, and Jacksonville–Duval County. A third option involves combining counties into regional governments. New York City is the classic example of this type of government, wherein five boroughs make up New York City (Rusk, 1993).

In recent years there has been a movement by some local communities "to retain or create smaller governments, by seceding from existing city governments, by incorporating new, smaller jurisdictions carved out of larger ones or by resisting annexation by larger governments" (Husock, 1998). For example, four new municipalities have been created within Dade County, Florida. Some suburbs around Tucson, Arizona have avoided annexation by the central city by incorporating as independent cities. A major reason "localism" has become popular is that "Voters' common sense tells them that the closer they are to government, the more it will respond to their demands" (Husock, 1998). Some advocates of small government go so far as to suggest breaking up cities "into an array of independent, neighborhood-based governments that would set their own property tax rates, elect their own officials, and give city residents the same control and sense of community that their suburban counterparts take for granted" (Husock, 1998). Los Angeles is an example of a city that has acted to avoid secession of local areas by adopting a new city charter. In 1999 this city created a charter that increased the power of the mayor, created neighborhood advisory councils, and instituted five neighborhood boards with power related to zoning decisions. The creation of advisory councils is guided by a Department of Neighborhood Empowerment and the City Council (Purdum, 1999).

CITIZEN PARTICIPATION IN LOCAL GOVERNMENT

The local government is under the control of local citizens through their participation in the voting process. Key figures in the system are elected by the "body politic." Citizens also participate in the political system by contacting public officials, seeking to influence them individually or through special interest groups. Some citizens serve leadership roles in political parties and interest groups and engage in activities designed to influence community decision-making. The role of political parties varies in different communities, but political offices provide a major avenue for the emergence of community leaders through the election process.

Representation and influence in the political system varies for different population groups in a community. In past years people of color and poor people have had low levels of participation in the political process. However, since the passage of the Voting Rights Act of 1965, some ethnic minority groups have been able to increase their involvement and representation in local governments. Thernstrom and Thernstrom (1997) contend that this is especially true of African Americans, "because their numbers are growing and because they have become politically mobilized" through increases in voter registration, voting rates, and the election of officials in the political system. In many communities, Hispanic/Latino Americans have struggled to gain political power, as illustrated by the emergence of new Hispanic groups seeking to play a part in the political "game" of the community. Leaders in the Arab American community have sought political empowerment by encouraging members to form a "voting bloc" and to become candidates for political office. These goals were emphasized in a conference in Detroit, Michigan, with the theme "Campaign 2000: Empowering Arab Americans," that included one of their members, Senator Spencer Abraham, and other national and state political figures. Voter turnout efforts have been the most common strategy for minority groups seeking to increase their participation in the political system. Some groups, such as a number of Native American tribes, have become more active in their lobbying efforts regarding "Indian issues" and in their financial contributions to state political parties.

Given the diverse ethnic identities within the Asian American population, there seems to be no pattern of affiliation with a single political party. However, controversy over the nomination by President Clinton of Bill Lann Lee to become Assistant Attorney General for Civil Rights stimulated an increased interest and involvement of Asian Americans in the political process. In response to objections by some members of Congress to the appointment of Mr. Lee, the executive director of the national Asian Pacific American Legal Consortium, a civil rights group in Washington, stated that to have Asian Americans in high levels in the government required "more involvement in the grass-roots political work of the community" (Purdum, 1997). At the same time, in states such as California that include large groups of Asian Americans, there continues to be an increase in voter registration and voting by Asian groups.

In a statement called an "important civic challenge," the National Conference of Catholic Bishops announced to American Catholics that "In the Catholic tradition, responsible citizenship is a virtue; participation in the political process is a moral obligation" (Niebuhr, 1999). The statement, "Faithful Citizenship: Civic Responsibility for a New Millennium" explicitly disavowed the idea of trying to create "a religious voting bloc" or a party position. The Catholic bishops emphasized the practical implications of the church's teachings on issues such as abortion, physician-assisted suicide, environmental protection, workers' rights, the death penalty, loans to poor nations, aid to poor children, and programs to provide families with affordable housing. Thus, civic responsibility and political participation have been encouraged by the leaders of the Catholic Church, a religious group with a socially and ethnically diverse membership that encompasses nearly a quarter of the U.S. population.

CREATION OF POLITICAL DISTRICTS

A long-standing controversy with regard to citizen participation in the political system involves the creation of voting districts. New districts are constructed at ten-year intervals when population shifts occur. For example, the 1990 census data demonstrated shifts of population from central cities to suburban communities, which in turn resulted in redistricting related to representation in state legislatures and the U.S. House of Representatives. Migration to the suburbs has led to new political maps and a shift in political power to people who live in these areas. A controversial way in which redistricting occurs is "gerryman-dering," which involves establishing boundaries for voting districts in such a way that white or non-white groups "vastly outnumber" the other group, assuring the majority residential group of representation in local, state, or federal government. In 1996, the U.S. Supreme Court decided in *Shaw v. Reno* that a gerrymandered 12th Congressional District in North Carolina was unconstitutional. The Court rejected the stereotype that "members of the same racial group, regardless of their age, education, economic status or the community in which they live think alike, share the same political interests, and will prefer the same candidates at the polls" (McCaughey, 1993). The district, which had been created to assure representation of African Americans, was about 160 miles long and included parts of 12 counties.

Even in the light of the Supreme Court's decision in *Shaw v. Reno*, the "place of race in distributing electoral power" has continued to be an issue in the courts (Kennedy, 1993). As noted by Kennedy (1993), an important question remains unanswered: "What is required to create political institutions that address the needs and aspirations of all Americans, not simply whites, who have long enjoyed racial privilege, but people of color who have long suffered racial exclusion from policy-making forums?" After the North Carolina legislature redrew the 12th Congressional District in 1997, a three-judge court ruled that it was unlawfully drawn because it was too race-conscious. The U.S. Supreme Court, in 1999, reversed this decision and sent the case back to the three-judge federal court. The Supreme Court decision appeared to make it "harder for federal judges to strike down election districts as products of unlawful racial gerrymandering" (Carelli, 1999).

In an effort to change the boundaries of three congressional districts in Florida that had been drawn to increase minority representation in 1992, a new plan was devised in 1999 in response to a lawsuit claiming that the boundaries were unconstitutional. After the districts were redrawn in 1992, two black Democrats and a Hispanic Republican were elected to represent voters in the three districts. The plan developed in 1999 would have reduced the percentage of minority voters in each of the districts. Since the plan did not receive the support of the governor of Florida, the state attorney general's office indicated it would proceed to fight the lawsuit.

COMMUNITY POWER PERSPECTIVES

The community political system is not limited to the formal structure of local government. Elected representatives in local governments make numerous decisions that affect the residents of a community. Rather than making these decisions in isolation, however, elected officials are subjected to pressures from individuals outside the formal governmental political system. Many other decisions that affect community residents are made within the various subsystems of the community and do not require the formal approval of local government. Such decisions may also be made by individuals or organizations that wield "community power" but are outside the formal institutions of the community. In short, local government is a part of the community power structure. It may be a major part, or its role may be overshadowed by individuals and organizations outside the local government. Thus, in order to discover the power structure of a community, one must be able to identify the leaders in the local government and the political system as a whole.

In examining the power structure of a community, it is helpful to consider the conceptual differences between "power" and "influence." Power involves the potential ability to reach selected goals within a social system, with an emphasis on "potential." In contrast, "influence" is the exercise of power that brings about change in a social system. A power structure is a patterned distribution of power in a social system. A decision-making structure is a patterned distribution of influence, based on decisions on specific issues. Individual leaders make up a power/influence structure within a community. Leaders can be identified at all community levels: in the larger metropolitan community and in local districts; in community subsystems, such as health and welfare, religion, and in education; and in voluntary groups, such as the League of Women Voters, Kiwanis clubs, welfare rights organizations, and civil rights organizations. When community leaders are found to participate with each other frequently in decision making, in social activities, and through membership on boards, they can be viewed as a group, often labeled a "power elite."

Identifying Community Leaders

Community leaders can be identified according to position, reputation, or policy decisions. A positional approach directs attention to leaders in government, business, health and social welfare, education, and religious subsystems of a community. These leaders occupy important offices as elected public officials, business executives, executives of voluntary associations, and leaders of religious groups. Hunter's (1953) classic study of community power in Atlanta is an example of a reputational approach, which basically involves asking informants to name and rank the leaders in their community. With a decisional approach, individuals who are involved in major policy decisions are identified as leaders.

Once leaders have been identified, the next step is to determine whether they constitute a structure of community power. Although some "ideal types" of structures have emerged in the social science literature on community power, many variations of these types exist in American communities. One such variation is an "elitist" or "monolithic" power structure made up of economic and/or political elites. Leaders at lower levels carry out the policies supported and/or developed by a power elite. In contrast, in a pluralistic structure, power is distributed among various leaders of organized groups within the community, with decision making depending on the nature of the issues.

In seeking to identify leaders and power structures, four salient characteristics of leadership should be considered: legitimacy, visibility, scope of influence, and cohesiveness (Bonjean & Olson, 1966). The leadership structure is legitimate when a high proportion of leaders occupy political or associational offices. It is visible when there is public recognition of a high proportion of leaders. The leadership structure can be described in terms of the scope of influence of individual leaders and the kinds and numbers of issues and decisions with which they are involved. Finally, a most interesting aspect of community power structures is the extent to which individual leaders form a cohesive group in relation to their community, business, and social activities. Community power may reside with leaders of community-wide voluntary organizations, such as local community Ministerial Alliances, the League of Women Voters, the Chamber of Commerce, Parent-Teacher Associations, and coalitions of neighborhood organizations. Other important sources of leadership are grassroots organizations: local neighborhood groups organized as block clubs, affiliates of churches, or boards of neighborhood community service agencies. Leaders within these organizations, especially ministers, priests, and rabbis, carry local power and often are involved in the broader community power structure.

Community Leaders: Local and Cosmopolitan

Merton's (1949) classic discussion of community leadership continues to be an interesting and useful conceptual approach to understanding community power and influence. Merton labeled community leaders as local or cosmopolitan. Both types of leaders were viewed as being actively involved in community affairs, but their orientations to community differ considerably. These basic orientations toward community, the one parochial and the other ecumenical, can be distinguished as follows. First, the structure of social relations of these leaders differ, with the local leader strongly identified and attached to the local community, while the cosmopolitan leader does not feel "rooted" in the community. A local leader is interested in knowing as many people as possible, whereas a cosmopolitan is more selective in choosing to get to know the "right" kind of people. The local leader belongs to voluntary associations in order to make contacts and extend personal relationships, while the cosmopolitan leader joins organizations whose activities call on his or her knowledge and skills. The local leader is an "old-timer" in the community who has influence based on a network of personal relationships, while the cosmopolitan leader is likely to be a relative newcomer who comes into the community with prestige from business or professional associations.

Merton's ideas about community leaders are relevant to the social work professional's efforts to gain public support and resources for a social agency. In particular, this distinction in leadership qualities has applicability to the creation and maintenance of agency board membership. An "ideal" community board of directors would include a mix of local and cosmopolitan leaders. Local leaders can be expected to have social contacts that will bring public support to the agency, while cosmopolitan leaders can provide expertise and links to the resources of the wider community, to state and federal government, and to organizations at these levels in the private sector.

COMMUNITY POWER FROM AN ORGANIZATIONAL PERSPECTIVE

Examination of the power and decision-making structures of the total community helps determine the extent to which the various subsystems are a dominant force in the community. This perspective assumes that organizations, rather than individuals, hold the key resources that form the bases of power. As Piven and Cloward (1997) observe, "Institutions reflect power, and they enhance power. Patterned rules and practices are constructed by those who have power, with the aim of stabilizing power over time." Arrangements between organizations provide a strong organizational claim for community power and influence. The community as a social system, made up of formal organizations within various community subsystems, constitutes the institutional context of community leadership. The ideas generated by Perrucci and Pilisuk (1970) in this regard continue to be applicable to the identification of institutional power. These social scientists argued that "power is contained within institutional systems and it is differentially available to individuals and groups according to their place in the larger social subsystems of which they are a part." Under this formulation, resources for decision making reside in either several persons or in organizational and inter-organizational networks. In some communities there are community decision-making organizations, such as the United Way, business associations, community development agencies, welfare councils, and health departments, that constitute a center of power. These organizations play special roles in the community through their involvement in the planning, coordination, and delivery of services.

The idea that "organization is power" was advanced by Saul Alinsky as a guide for community organizers in low-income neighborhood communities. The Alinsky approach to community change was to build "organizations of tenants, organizations of welfare recipients; organizations in neighborhoods, and to unite them citywide, then statewide, and ultimately in national federations" (Cloward & Piven, 1999). However, Cloward and Piven (1999) have questioned this approach, especially in regard to electoral influence. They argue that "evidence shows that this theory of power from below does not work in practice," because poor people lack conventional political resources and do not develop mass membership, and grassroots organizations are characterized by high membership turnover and a lack of permanence. Cloward and Piven also suggest that grassroots organizations, despite not empowering lower-class communities, are important for nurturing subcultures of poor people and keeping the ideal of justice alive.

EXAMPLES OF COMMUNITY EMPOWERMENT

Historically, communities of color and members of the gay community have been left out of local communities' political systems. Wilson's (1999) examination of race and class politics in *The Bridge Over the Racial Divide* indicates the need for a multiracial political coalition to gain political power and reduce social inequality. Involvement of people from these groups in local governmental positions has increased, as noted earlier in this chapter in regard to citizen participation. Examples of political organizations that are effective in mobilizing minorities in city politics include neighborhood associations, citywide issue organizations, crime watch groups, and social service/self-help organizations (Portney & Berry, 1997). In a study of five American cities that have strong neighborhood association systems (Birmingham, Dayton, Portland, St. Paul, and San Antonio), Portney and Berry (1997) found that these organizations serve to build a sense of community and to provide opportunities for face-to-face interaction.

Of these types of organizations, neighborhood associations were found to be the most successful "for mobilizing African Americans and bringing them into the political process." Poor black neighbors and black neighborhoods in general demonstrated "relatively high levels of political participation in neighborhood associations."

Still, under-representation of people of color in the local political system continues to be a major barrier to community competence. Concern over the disenfranchisement of these groups in local community political structures has stimulated the development of an "empowerment" perspective within the profession of social work, with an emphasis on empowering people of color (Solomon, 1976; Gutierrez, Parsons, & Cox, 1997; Gutierrez, 1997; Gutierrez & Lewis, 1999). Empowerment is defined by Gutierrez (1990) as "the process of increasing personal, interpersonal, or political power so that individuals can take action to improve their life situations." A major feature of empowerment in relation to political power is the "capacity to work with others to control aspects of public life and access to the mechanisms of public decision making" (Gutierrez et al., 1997). In this regard, social workers work with clients "in the political aspects of their problems. This includes social action or other collective efforts to impact environmental forces that contribute to individual problems" (Gutierrez et al., 1997). In order to illustrate issues related to community power and empowerment, we will examine these power perspectives in relation to the African American community and the gay community.

Community Power and the African American Community

Empowerment is gained by individuals who belong to communities of color through citizen participation in the electoral process, usually through voting and membership in advocacy organizations. The most visible signs of power in a local community's political system are the positions occupied by elected officials and political appointees. In the case of African Americans, "exclusion from mainstream social and political processes" before the Voting Rights Act of 1965 and the Civil Rights Movement has been replaced by the rise of a new "political class" (Kilson, 1998). This group is most prominently represented by the election of African American mayors and other officials and a dramatic increase in the number of appointed and civil service officials, especially in cities with high proportions of African American citizens.

The rise of a black political class has been conceptualized by Kilson (1998) in terms of three stages of political development: a Protest Stage, an Electoral Empowerment Stage, and a Power Consolidation Stage. Protest politics were practiced during the Protest Stage and supported by leaders in organizations such as the National Urban League, the NAACP, professional societies, and religious organizations. The Electoral Empowerment Stage has seen the election not only of mayors and other city officials but also county and state officials and members of Congress. At the national level, African Americans in Congress are organized through membership in the Congressional Black Caucus, with an increase in membership from the South since 1992 due in part to racially gerrymandered districts. At present, Kilson (1998) observes that African Americans have been able to achieve only a low level of Power Consolidation, especially in achieving goals for the working class and poor members of the black community. One of the obstacles to consolidation has been a lack of support from white politicians, voters, and interest groups. Another obstacle has been the existence of two major streams of leadership in the African American community: the mainline leadership groups and organizations, and the black nationalist ethnocentric groups, such as the Nation of Islam.

Given the attention directed to these two categories of African American leadership, some observers have asked, "Who speaks for Black America?" The mass media often convey the idea that national leaders are the principal, if not sole, representatives of leadership in the African American community. These leaders receive the most attention in the media, especially as organizers of protest rallies, and can be characterized as "cosmopolitan" leaders. Another view has been advanced by Pearson (1995), who points out that the leaders of local black churches and other grassroots organizations make up an important segment of the leadership in black America. These "local" leaders are active in neighborhoods and cities, working in schools, churches, small business enterprises, housing agencies, and social welfare organizations.

The importance of both cosmopolitan and local leaders of the African American community has been emphasized by Vernon Jordan, Jr. (1995) in his identification of the new black leadership classes that have emerged since the 1960s. Jordan enumerates the following categories of leaders:

- Black elected officials, many of whose constituents are of other races
- Managers of predominantly white institutions, ranging from school superintendents and police chiefs to foundation heads, college presidents, and cabinet officers
- Indigenous community leaders whose organizations represent welfare families, public housing tenants and other groups, and whose backgrounds are similar to those of their constituents

- Black entrepreneurs who produce goods and services for markets that extend beyond the black community
- Blacks in corporate America, as exemplified by the Executive Leadership Council

Jordan (1995) indicates that what is common to all of these leadership groups is the fact that "They can bring resources, skills, and knowledge of the world beyond the confines of dysfunctional communities." Jordan goes on to say that these leadership groups "all share the experience of negotiating the deep and sometimes treacherous waters of majority institutions" and are most likely to succeed in creating "The Beloved Community" advocated by Martin Luther King, Jr., by working "within the context of an open, pluralistic, integrated society."

Community Power and New Immigrants

The emergence of political leaders and political power among new immigrant populations is exemplified in New York City by the rise of "a new breed of immigrant politicians from Asia, the West Indies, and Latin America (Dao, 1999b). A number of avenues to power are being followed, such as the rebuilding of dying political clubs, development of civic associations and coalitions, and running for local offices, such as school boards and city councils. This participation in the local political system resembles in many ways the patterns of Italian and Eastern European Jews in the early 1900s, especially through the Democratic Party. However, the ethnic diversity of the new immigrants appears to have hindered the political involvement and success of these groups. As Dao (1999b) has noted, "Today's immigrants come from more countries and speak more languages than the last wave of European immigrants" and are more difficult to unite into political movements, especially since many do not register to vote. Still, many immigrants are becoming active in politics, agreeing on one thing: that it is "time to have a voice, perhaps many, in American politics" (Dao, 1999b). As one Venezuelan immigrant leader in a political organization has stated, "We have to show them we belong" (Dao, 1999b). Examples of newly gained political power include the Dominicans in Washington Heights, Puerto Ricans in the Bronx, West Indians in Flatbush and Crown Heights, and Hispanics in Queens. As a leader of a political club in Queens stated, "Politics is the same everywhere in the world. Nobody wants to give up their power. But times are changing" (Dao, 1999b).

Community Power and the Gay Community

In response to the question, "Why do gay people need political power?" Vaid (1995) has stated, "We need political power to protect and defend ourselves as we work to eradicate homophobia." At the national level, in the late 1980s a political action committee, the Human Rights Campaign Fund, was active in raising funds from gay and lesbian people in local communities as a "politics of access" strategy for gaining political power. Since that time, some gay leaders have advocated for voter registration and a gay-supportive voting bloc as a more effective way of gaining legislative change on behalf of the gay community at state and local levels. Vaid has recommended moving away from the PAC strategy that involves gaining support from the "rich and privileged" and national groups, and putting more emphasis on the development of state and local political organizations.

In the meantime, Vaid observes that gay organizations tend to be small, and "Our difficulty in supporting gay leadership disempowers us." Consistent with the social work empowerment approach, Vaid sees gay social services and AIDS organizations as promising "outposts" that "can strengthen gay and lesbian political power because they are the bridges between the cultural sphere (where gay and lesbian people live, make a family, raise children, and create a life) and the political realm (where the gay movement fights discrimination)." These service organizations, including community centers, clinics, hotlines, support groups, and cultural groups, involve a large number of participants, and can be utilized as grassroots communities to expand gay and lesbian political clout. However, "The biggest obstacle such groups face is the persistence of political apathy and despair among gay, lesbian, and bisexual people" (Vaid, 1995). Vaid calls for a local civil citizenship "with each of us being registered and politically aware": a citizenship "made real by our action—both in how we live our lives (our praxis) and in how we come together to solve the problems facing both our local gay community and the broader community in which we live." An example of this approach is the $300,000 contribution to fight Proposition 22 in California (legislation banning same-sex marriages) provided by Kathy Levinson, President and Chief Operations Officer of E-Trade Group, Inc., and her partner, Jennifer Levinson (Bank, 2000).

A number of county and city governments have voted to include sexual orientation within their anti-discrimination laws. Gay rights activists at the local community level have promoted gay rights legislation, facing considerable opposition from conservative religious leaders and groups such as the Christian Coalition. As of 1998, 11 states, 27 counties, and 136 cities had passed anti-discrimination laws protecting gay people, and only a few of these laws (ten) had been repealed (Navarro, 1998). An example of local government controversies over gay rights laws took place in Miami-Dade County. A gay rights law passed in 1977 was repealed that year, and it took until 1998 for this County to pass a new law banning discrimination based on sexual orientation, with the campaign for the ordinance led by a local group under the banner of SAVE Dade, "Safeguarding American Values for Everyone." The group gained support from political and civic leaders who used the argument "that intolerance is bad for an economy that depends on tourism and new investment" (Navarro, 1998).

During the 1990s, gay and lesbian activists in local communities worked for the election of openly gay people to public offices. Openly gay public officials have been elected through the support of gay and non-gay citizens (Button, Wald, & Frienzo, 1999). In a study of a sample of 126 cities and counties, Button and colleagues found "the nature and pattern of electoral activities of lesbians and gay men were similar to those of other disadvantaged minorities." Gay candidates for public office have several disadvantages, including hostility and antipathy of non-gay individuals, as well as a "lack of the dense organizational networks that promote the development, transmission, and politicization of social 'identity.'"

Gay political empowerment in local communities is most likely to be found in urban areas that are large and diverse. Due to the small size of the gay community, "gay voters must often depend on the support of gay-friendly or tolerant heterosexual allies to win elections" (Button et al., 1999). At the same time, fundamentalist religious organizations often mobilize to oppose gays' efforts to gain political power. Success for gays in election to public office is more likely when there is a political opportunity structure that is open, especially in a state that has nondiscrimination legislation regarding gay and lesbian people. In short, Button et al. (1999) found that the chances of success for openly gay and lesbian candidates are best in "large, diverse communities with sizable gay populations and electoral structures that are hospitable to minority candidates."

CRIMINAL AND JUVENILE JUSTICE SYSTEM

An important component of the local political system is the criminal and juvenile justice system. Our extensive discussion of community issues and problems related to the justice system will illustrate how the political system operates in an area crucial to the provision of social control, safety, and service functions in local communities. We will look at community problems that involve the justice system (including discrimination, hate crimes, and family, youth, and workplace violence) as well as community responses to these problems.

Community governments have a primary role in providing protection and social control for community residents through the criminal justice system, including law enforcement, the judicial (court) system, and the correctional system. Law enforcement is a responsibility of local community police departments, as well as agencies at the county, state, and federal levels of government. At the local community level, the principal functions of the police department are to help control crime through crime prevention and apprehension of criminal offenders; to provide aid to people in crisis; to serve justice through arrests and prosecution; and to deliver non-emergency services, such as controlling traffic and providing assistance when cars break down (Eck & Rosenbaum, 1994). The second component of the justice system is the judicial system, which includes adult and juvenile courts. The third component of the justice system includes correctional institutions and programs, such as incarceration in jails, community service, work release, halfway houses, probation and parole, and diversion programs. The major responsibility for criminal and juvenile justice resides with city and county governments, and hence, belongs to the community political system. At the same time, the federal government and the Congress engage in activities and produce legislation related to criminal justice both at the state and local levels of government. Governmental responses to the social problems of crime, delinquency, and violence continue to create controversy in local communities, particularly in regard to special populations at risk for discrimination.

Discrimination

Over-representation of racial/ethnic minority groups and poor people in the criminal and juvenile justice system has been a fact for some time in the United States. The differences in how members of these groups and other residents are treated by law enforcement officials, such as the police, by the courts, especially in sentencing, and in terms of correctional alternatives, are often the result of discrimination (Cole, 1999). There is considerable evidence that members of racial/ethnic minority groups and poor people are treated negatively and more harshly than other community members in each of the components of the justice system (Walker, Spohn, & Delone, 1996). A poll conducted for the American Bar Association in 1999 sought to ascertain the public's understanding and perceptions of the American justice system. The survey found that nearly half (47 percent) of the public viewed the legal system, including the courts and law enforcement authorities, as being unfair to poor people and ethnic and racial minority groups (Greenhouse, 1999a). In Los Angeles, charges involving police corruption included more than 20 lawsuits and 15 claims of abuses in the police department's Rampart Division. The alleged misdeeds ranged from use of excessive force to planting evidence such as guns and drugs. City attorneys estimated that the scandal could result in more than 100 lawsuits, costing the city as much as $125 million (Leung, 2000).

The actions of police in handling suspected criminals represent one of the most controversial issues concerning the justice system in many American cities. This involves the use of "aggressive preventive patrol" activities, e.g., frequent stops and frisks, the treatment of individual suspects with excessive force, and police responses to street violence and civil disturbance (Walker et al., 1996). In discussing this issue, First Lady Hillary Rodham Clinton referred to a "trust divide" in characterizing "the suspicion and hostility that have created such a devastating gap between the law-abiding residents of some big-city neighborhoods and the police officers who are supposed to protect and serve them" (Herbert, 2000). Fatal shootings of unarmed persons of color in New York City have been viewed by critics of the mayor as symptomatic of police brutality and problems in the city's approach to policing. The principal issue regarding the use of force involves the extent to which police policies and behaviors assure protection of self (local police, state troopers) versus protection of the rights of crime suspects.

Racial profiling, the police practice of using race or ethnicity as the basis for stopping and questioning and/or searching motorists, is common in many American communities (Segal, 1999). In a settlement directed toward ending racial profiling and discrimination in New Jersey, the U.S. Department of Justice appointed in 1999 an outside agency to monitor the New Jersey Police Department, keeping records of arrests and traffic stops by race, with the goal of revamping the state's Department of Internal Affairs system. In 1999 President Clinton spoke out against racial profiling, stating that "Racial profiling is in fact the opposite of good police work where actions are based on hard facts, not stereotypes...It is wrong, it is destructive, and it must stop" (Holmes, 1999). President Clinton ordered the collection of demographic data by federal law-enforcement agencies that would aid in assessing when and where racial profiling occurs, so that efforts could be made to eliminate it. At its 1999 annual convention, the governing board of the American Bar Association opposed racial profiling, and called for "state and local municipalities to collect data about police traffic stops" to assist in ending discriminatory practices (Segal, 1999).

Hate Crimes

Hate crimes are criminal activities that come under the jurisdiction of municipal, state, and/or federal governments. These crimes are defined in the Hate Crime Statistics Act as crimes that "manifest prejudice based on race, religion, sexual orientation, or ethnicity." This Act requires the Justice Department to collect data on hate crimes from law enforcement agencies throughout the United States and to report findings annually. Information gained from these reports is useful for law enforcement agencies and for local communities, since geographic distribution and other patterns of hate crimes can be ascertained and used to develop programs for prevention. Another federal act, the Violent Crime Control and Law Enforcement Act of 1994, expanded coverage of the Hate Crime Statistics Act to include crimes based on disability, and provided a sentencing enhancement on hate crimes. This Act further defined a hate crime as a "crime in which the defendant intentionally selects a victim, or in the case of a property crime, the property that is the object of the crime, because of the actual or perceived race, color, religion, national origin, ethnicity, gender, disability, or sexual orientation of any person." An Act specifically related to violent crime against women is the Violence Against Women Act of 1994, with this Act providing authority for domestic violence and rape crisis centers and for education and training programs for law enforcement and prosecutors.

Church arson is an example of hate crimes directed toward the property of religious organizations. Although the majority of attacks against houses of worship have been on churches of African Americans, attacks have also been made against other religious groups, such as the mosques of Arab Americans, the synagogues and cemeteries of Jews, and churches attended by white congregations. In response to these crimes, Congress enacted legislation that broadened federal criminal jurisdiction and facilitated criminal prosecutions for attacks against houses of worship, increased penalties for these crimes, established loan programs for rebuilding houses of worship after such attacks, and increased personnel assigned to "investigate, prevent, and respond" to incidents of crime involving places of religious worship.

A major limitation for federal prosecution under these hate crime acts is that the crime must be motivated by bias and the assailant must have intended to prevent the victim from exercising a federally protected right, e.g., voting, attending school, travelling on interstate highways, and so on. Congressional leaders continue to make proposals for expanding the federal jurisdiction over hate crimes. At the same time, a number of states and local governmental units have passed hate crime laws that govern criminal activity in local communities. Nineteen states do not have hate crime laws that prohibit anti-gay crimes based on bias related to sexual orientation, yet each year gay people are murdered in apparent hate crimes, and in 1997 through 1998 a coalition that monitors anti-gay violence and harassment documented 2,445 episodes in 14 American cities (Gillis & Gaines, 1998). The killing in 1998 of Matthew Shepard, a gay college student in Wyoming, resulted in candlelight vigils and marches in communities throughout the United States to protest anti-gay violence.

East Peoria, Illinois, is an example of how a mostly white community of approximately 23,000 people reacted to a hate crime that took place near their community. A local community leader contacted the Southern Poverty Law Center, a nonprofit civil rights organization, and was advised to "speak out immediately and form a broad-based coalition on race issues" (Thomas, 1999). As a result, the mayor appointed a new Human Relations Commission "to oppose hate, preach tolerance and celebrate diversity." Similar groups have been formed in other communities, such as Boise, Idaho, and Boyertown, Pennsylvania—communities with reputations of having white supremacist groups. The experiences of communities such as these have been described in a booklet entitled *Ten Ways to Fight Hate* distributed by the Southern Poverty Law Center.

Family, Youth, and Workplace Violence

Family violence, especially spouse abuse, has emerged as a significant problem in communities. An important issue concerns the extent to which reported victimization is addressed appropriately by law enforcement officials. One response to the problem of spouse abuse has been the creation of "safe houses" in the community for women and children who are in need of protection from family violence. Another response has been court-ordered treatment programs for males who have abused family members. Increasingly, violence occurs in the workplace. This violence ranges from homicides at work sites to injuries, beatings, shootings, and rapes. One response to this type of violence has been providing training for supervisors and managers, and developing employee assistance programs that respond to the stresses of family and of the workplace.

Youth violence and other criminal behavior have become extremely problematic in many American communities. Schools have become a focal point for teen violence. In 1999, at Columbine High School in Littleton, Colorado, two students, armed with guns and explosives, killed 13 people and wounded 23 in a six-hour siege, and then killed themselves. Within a month after the Columbine incident, a student at a high school in Georgia shot six classmates. Other school shootings in 1999 occurred in the states of Oregon, Arkansas, Kentucky, Tennessee, Pennsylvania, and Mississippi. This gun violence led to deliberations in Congress, and in the states and local communities, about gun control legislation. Since 1994 there has been a Gun-Free School Act that requires school districts to expel any student who brings a weapon to school. Studies in 1999 by the Centers for Disease Control showed "that fewer young people are carrying guns or taking them into schools," "the overall rate of school violence is down," and expulsions for carrying guns onto school property dropped by one third between 1997-1998 and the previous school year (*New York Times*, 1999b).

Teen gangs are prevalent in all major U.S. cities, and tend to operate in some neighborhoods and not in others. Social scientists have given considerable attention to trying to explain delinquent behavior. For example, Figueira-McDonough (1991) has hypothesized certain relationships between the structure of communities and delinquency rates. She suggests that communities with strong primary and secondary networks, that is, kin, friends, and informal groups, as well as community organizations, are likely to have low delinquency rates, while "disorganized" communities that lack these networks are likely to have the highest rates.

COMMUNITY GOVERNMENT RESPONSES TO CRIME

Fighting Drugs

One of the most problematic areas of crime in local communities is the sale of illegal drugs on streets and in drug houses. Drug dealing and crack houses generate a "fear of crime" on the part of many residents, especially older adults. One response to the problem has been for neighborhood block clubs to organize against the houses and report drug "traffic" to the police. Sometimes barricades and one-way streets are set up in order to discourage suburban drug buyers from entering a neighborhood to buy drugs (Rosen, 1997). Drug crackdowns by the police often result in the arrest of drug sellers, but also may leave law-abiding residents believing that law enforcement is not fair, especially in its treatment of members of minority groups in the inner city.

One type of response to this issue has been proposed by Meares and her colleagues at the University of Chicago Law School. They suggest that the police engage in reverse-sting operations, posing as drug dealers and arresting the buyers, who tend to be from suburban communities. It is believed that this approach would not only scare away suburban buyers, but "create an appearance of fairness that works to undercut the mistrust of police in black neighborhoods" and would lead to social norms that foster "cooperation with the police among people of color" (Rosen, 1997). Another response to neighborhood drug problems has been the organizing of prayer vigils, cosponsored by local ministers and the police. These vigils assert "a faith in their community's norms of good behavior" and seek to embarrass and chasten suburban buyers and local dealers by gathering to pray for them. Events such as vigils are examples of establishing social norms based on "partnerships between local governments and the traditional sources of moral values: local community groups, schools, and churches. And they may involve activities that bear little resemblance to traditional law enforcement" (Rosen, 1997).

Community Policing

Community policing is an "elastic notion" that includes a wide range of police activities and programs that are based on four principles: policing that is "(1) decentralized, (2) problem oriented, (3) responsive to citizens with respect to tactics employed and priorities set, and (4) committed to joint solutions to neighborhood crime and order problems" (Manning, 1998; Skogan & Harnett, 1997). An important feature of community policing is the effort "to reorganize policing to reduce social distance between citizens and the police"(Manning, 1998). Advocates of community policing support "the idea that organized citizens can control crime and improve neighborhood conditions, and therefore police should mobilize neighborhood groups" (Eck & Rosenbaum, 1994). Eck and Rosenbaum (1994) have identified several means by which citizens can assist in crime control and improve the quality of community life: watch and report suspicious behavior to police; patrol neighborhood areas; take personal safety precautions; engage in political action and lobby governmental agencies for public resources.

Community policing, in which police officers are assigned to specific neighborhood areas, is an effort to make the police "a part of the community, not apart from the community" (Lardner, 1993; Rosenbaum, 1994). Community policing programs are often identified in terms of foot patrols, ombudsman police officers, drug enforcement units, home visits, innovative management structures, police substations, community response teams, and intensive enforcement tactics. A number of successes of these programs, showing positive effects on neighborhood residents, have been reported in research evaluation studies of community policing in Baltimore, Oakland, Birmingham, Madison, Houston, and Newark (Skogan, 1994).

Community policing approaches are not problem-free. A concern arises if the police who are selected are not sympathetic to the needs, values, and interests of the neighborhood residents (*New Yorker*, 1993). There is a belief on the part of some observers that recruitment of qualified and interested personnel, as well as what is learned on the job, is essential to make a community policing program work. In some instances, in order to establish a partnership between police and citizens, neighborhood groups must be organized and supported. Evaluations of community policing programs indicate that this is a challenge when police departments do not have personnel skilled in community organizing and development and when neighborhood residents lack education and interest in citizen participation. Moreover, programs may not be successful if police departments are unable to develop interagency relationships within the public and private sectors of the community (Sadd & Grinc, 1994).

"Weed and Seed" is a form of community policing initiated by the federal government. "The basic idea of Weed and Seed is to involve the federal government with state and local governments in 'weeding out' crime from targeted neighborhoods and then in 'seeding' those communities with programs designed to aid economic and social development." As a part of these programs, police "help residents identify and resolve common problems," "move against violent street gang members," and participate in "safe haven" arrangements so that residents can safely use local neighborhood schools at night (Eastland, 1992). A program called COMPASS in Hartford, Connecticut is an example of a "weed and seed" approach to improving neighborhoods hit by crime and drugs (Tien & Rich, 1994). The Hartford program began with a drug market analysis, followed by a "variety of community policing and other antidrug tactics to weed out the underlying drug problem in the target area. Once the area is weeded, the stabilization phase attempts to seed the target area with businesses and activities that can replace the weeded out drug businesses and activities—this phase requires a strong partnership between the community, the city, and the police" (Tien & Rich, 1994).

Many local community political systems, through their police departments, political leaders, citizens, social agencies, and the media, have used community policing to assist in solving problems within the criminal justice system. Trojanowicz (1994) has suggested that "Community policing can be the catalyst for stimulating the partnership between the government and its citizens." He goes on to suggest that effective community policing depends on participation of several groups:

- Citizens need to get involved in efforts ranging from providing information for crime prevention to volunteering for neighborhood projects.
- Social agencies need to become partners to help deal with the conditions that lead to crime and to address the needs of victims and perpetrators.
- Political leaders need to support long-term policies to prevent and control crime.
- The media needs to educate community residents about the complexity of social problems and the importance of becoming involved in the problem-solving process.

SECURITY IN SCHOOLS

Given the rash of gun violence incidents in elementary and high schools during 1998 and 1999, especially in the aftermath of the shootings at Columbine High School in Littleton, Colorado, public schools have responded with programs for increased security. Measures for safety include assignment of security guards and police officers to schools; preparation of school staff through simulated crisis situations; conflict mediation programs; telephone hot lines for reporting trouble; cameras and metal detectors; development of crisis response manuals; placement of mental health professionals in schools; and installation of video-linked intercom entry systems (Wilgoren, D., 1999a). Measures such as these have been regarded by some observers, such as the director of the Center for the Prevention of School Violence in Raleigh, N.D., as dramatic steps that are required because "The public expects when they drop their children off in the morning that they will be safe" (Wilgoren, D., 1999a). Still, some school districts are concerned about whether some of the security measures could make the school less inviting and violate students' rights.

GUN CONTROL

Local governments come under the jurisdiction of state and federal laws on the possession of guns. An example at the federal level is the Brady Bill, which requires a waiting period for the purchase of guns. The bill also has strong punishment provisions related to certain crimes, such as the killing of federal law enforcement officers. At the federal level the Bureau of Alcohol, Tobacco and Firearms regulates the sale of guns. States have varying laws governing firearm ownership and possession. For example, the State of Michigan distinguishes between rifles/shotguns and handguns. For rifles/shotguns no permit is required for purchase, and registration or licensing of purchasers is not required. Handguns, on the other hand, require a permit/license to purchase and a record of sales.

One example of local government attempts to control the sale of guns is the District of Columbia's Operation Gun Tip, a gun buy-back program. This program is a guns-for-cash exchange designed to get illegal weapons off the streets, with a goal of purchasing handguns, assault weapons, or other illegal firearms in the city's seven police districts. This program is based on the idea that "fewer guns mean fewer police shootings, gun accidents, and gun violence" (*Washington Post,* 1999). Another approach to local government efforts at gun control is the use of lawsuits against gun retailers, gun makers, and wholesale gun dealers. For example, in Chicago, "police officers posed as local gang members and went shopping for firearms" in suburban gun stores. The targeted stores were ones that had sold "the largest number of guns recovered from city crime scenes or seized by police from people carrying them illegally" (Meier, 1999). In their lawsuits, Chicago and some twenty other cities have sued the gun industry for its marketing practices, "seeking to make the manufacturers responsible for gun control, charging that they and the distributors and dealers do too little to keep guns out of the hands of criminals" (Meier, 1999). In another example, Detroit and Wayne County conducted an undercover operation against ten stores and gun-show dealers, and then sued the dealers, manufacturers, and distributors. "One of the aims of the cities' lawsuits is to establish a line of responsibility for guns used in crimes from dealers up through distributors to gun makers" (Meier, 1999).

NATIVE AMERICANS AND VIOLENT CRIME

The U.S. Justice Department has responded to the high levels of violent crime among Native Americans by awarding grants to their communities in more than 25 states. These grants are a response to an analysis of crime statistics by the Justice Department that showed Native Americans were "victims of violent crime more than twice as often as any other major group and are more likely than others to be attacked by people of other races" (Associated Press, 1999f). The analysis showed that "in nearly three-quarters of the cases their assailants are not Indian" (Claiborne, 1999a). These programs focus on Native American communities and were developed by the Justice and Interior Departments of the U.S. Government, in consultation with Native American tribes. The grants were for "tribal communities to hire more police officers or to train or better equip existing ones; new regional jails and detention facilities; technical assistance to devise new justice systems, such as inter-tribal courts to share limited resources; programs for at-risk youths to combat gang violence and drug and domestic abuse" (Associated Press, 1999f).

Chapter 12 Review

The key functions of the political system of a local community were identified, recognizing that this system plays a major role in making community policies and delivering community services. The primary structure of a local community political system is made up of governmental units at municipal, county, and metropolitan levels. Citizen participation in local government was discussed in terms of voting and the controversies that have emerged in the creation of political districts, especially in regard to representation of people of color. Community power perspectives were presented to highlight the major dimensions of community leadership and issues involving empowerment. These power perspectives suggest frameworks for conducting a "power analysis" in local communities as a basis for the enhancement of personal, interpersonal, and political power. These frameworks assist in the identification of community leaders, influential community organizations, inter-organizational networks, and dominant community power subsystems. The concept of empowerment was introduced as a perspective of particular relevance for groups within communities who lack fair and equitable representation in the community's political system. Examples were provided of the community empowerment of African Americans, new immigrants, and the gay community. Finally, in order to illustrate how some social problems have challenged the political systems of local communities, we provided an extensive discussion of problems and operations of the criminal justice system as it functions within the community political system. Problems discussed include discrimination, hate crimes, and family/youth/workplace violence. A number of responses of the political system to crime were discussed, including fighting drugs, community policing, security in schools, gun control, and federal programs in Native American communities.

13

Community Conflict

Conflicts and controversies are common in American communities. Examples of community controversies include legal action by residents against a local government to remove adult entertainment businesses (Holly, 1993; Lam, 1993); city government versus organizers of a youth rally in Harlem (Barstow, 1999b, 1999c); cleanup of graffiti and public art in Los Angeles (Sanchez, 1999b); disagreements of neighbors and city officials over the building of sidewalks (Morley, 1999); a clash between residents and city officials over an ordinance that prohibits putting old furniture on porches and in yards (Halbfinger, 1998); the establishment of group homes and treatment centers (George, 1992; Petrila, 1995). These examples suggest a number of dimensions of community conflict. First, controversies arise when groups seek to change the equilibrium of the community. When individuals, ad hoc groups, voluntary associations, or racial/ethnic groups seek to change the community system, these changes may be resisted by formal organizations within the community, such as local governments, schools, hospitals, and businesses. Controversies also occur when formal community organizations seek to bring about changes in communities, such as social agencies seeking to establish group homes or shelters for homeless people. Community controversies, then, may arise through efforts of residents, informal groups, or formal organizations to bring about change or to protest some decision or action within the community.

A second dimension of community conflict involves its scope—that is, how widespread is the conflict, how many people are involved, and how many people does the conflict affect? School strikes may involve large numbers of families in a school district, and hence be viewed as community-wide in scope. On the other hand, a dispute over the location of a small nighttime shelter for homeless people might affect only immediate neighbors or businesses and be viewed as narrow in scope. Some labor-management strikes, such as a public bus drivers' strike, usually have an impact on the total community and hence are broad in scope. A strike by nurses in a single hospital of a large city may begin with a narrow scope, but become community-wide if professional associations and nurses from other hospitals join in the controversy.

A third dimension of community conflict involves whether it is conventional or rancorous. Conventional conflicts are handled within established political and organizational rules and procedures, usually created by local governments and settled by decision-making bodies such as city councils or courts. Arbitration, mediation, and negotiation are processes through which many conventional controversies are settled. Rancorous conflicts are those wherein acceptable and legitimate norms for settling differences are not followed and a high level of hostility and/or violence occurs during the controversy. For example, such conflicts may involve physical attacks made on individuals in picket lines, the burning of buildings, and disruption of open meetings. This form of conflict is sometimes labeled "disruptive protest" or "disruptive dissensus," which has been defined by Cloward and Piven (1999) as "mass action that is (1) unlawful or marginally lawful, (2) institutionally disruptive, (3) electorally divisive, and (4) sometimes spurred and guided by cadre organizations."

THE PROCESS OF COMMUNITY CONFLICT

The dimensions of conflict initiation, scope, and convention/rancor provide a context for examining the actual processes of community controversies. Within this context, Coleman's (1957, 1983) classic discussions of the dynamics of community conflict contribute to our understanding of problem solving in local communities. Coleman maintained that "the most striking fact about the development and growth of community controversies is the similarity they exhibit despite diverse underlying sources and different kinds of precipitating incidents. Once the controversies have begun, they resemble each other remarkably."(Coleman's framework helps us understand the changes that occur in regard to the issues of a controversy, as well as changes in the structure of organizations and associations in the community.)Community controversies appear to proceed according to the following stages:

1. Initial single issue emerges.
2. Equilibrium of community relations is disrupted.
3. Disruption allows previously suppressed issues against opponent to appear.
4. More and more of opponent's beliefs enter into the disagreement.
5. The opponent appears totally bad.
6. Charges are directed against opponent as a person.
7. Dispute becomes independent of initial disagreement.

During community conflicts, elements of the social organization of the community often change in the following ways: (1) polarization of social relations, (2) formation of partisan organizations, (3) emergence of new leaders, (4) mobilization of ongoing community organizations and (5) increase in word-of-mouth communication (Coleman, 1957).

POSITIVE FUNCTIONS OF COMMUNITY CONFLICT

Community controversies are a form of social conflict. The functions of social conflict can be applied to social groups and social relations within a community. Rather than viewing social conflict as a totally negative phenomenon, it is useful to consider some of its positive functions, which can be applied to transactions among social groups in a community:

- Conflict serves to establish and maintain the identity and boundary lines of societies and groups.
- Conflict provides an opportunity for group members to "vent hostility" and "express dissent" and thereby maintain relationships between groups.
- While there may be hostility and tensions in conflict relationships between groups, this is not necessarily so.
- Conflicts arise in many instances between groups that are interdependent, such as union-management or school-family, and resolutions of conflicts serve to stabilize group relationships as long as the conflicts do not threaten basic consensus.

- Conflict with another group increases the cohesion of a group.
- Conflict allows a group to assess the power and influence of another group, and thus serves as a balancing mechanism to maintain the overall system.
- Conflicts provide a unifying function by bringing together people and groups into coalitions and temporary associations.

These propositions emphasize the positive functions of social conflicts (Coser, 1956). They may not hold for all incidents involving community conflicts, but they give us a framework for assessing and understanding specific conflicts.

COMMUNITY CONFLICTS AND THE COMMUNITY SYSTEM

Social system and ecological system perspectives on communities both employ the concept of conflict. From the ecological point of view, conflict is a process that governs the allocation of resources and leads to the establishment of dominant and subdominant social units within community and society. Conflict is considered to be a natural phenomenon that is to be accepted, not eliminated. In contrast, a social system perspective views conflict as a disruption of the equilibrium of the system, one that should be controlled or prevented. System maintenance requires the minimization of social conflict. Conflictual activities are considered to be essentially negative because they disturb the social order. For example, social conflict in the form of controversies between social classes, ethnic, cultural, or religious groups is seen as disturbing the stability of a community. Patterns of community conflict are illustrated in the cases presented here. These represent various types of controversies that occur in local communities, involving issues such as ethnic minority relations; community-based homes, shelters, and treatment centers; and urban redevelopment. The reader can find cases such as these in the daily press and in televised news programs.

COMMUNITY-BASED TREATMENT CENTERS

The movement of patients and residents of public institutions into the community has engendered community controversies in many American communities. Conflicts of this kind are expressed in terms of community opposition to facilities, homes, or other housing arrangements that vary from the usual dwellings and households in residential neighborhoods. Group homes and treatment centers often house unrelated individuals who have been deinstitutionalized. Opposition at the neighborhood level is often associated with fears of declining property values, concern for safety of residents, or negative consequences of abnormal behavior of the new residents. This type of opposition has been labeled a "Not In My Back Yard" reaction (Gilbert, 1993).

When community conflicts arise over proposals to establish community-based residential care centers, they often result in preventing these centers from being developed in local neighborhoods. If a center is established in spite of local opposition, it may be difficult for the center to function in the aftermath of conflict conditions. This is especially true if one of the purposes of locating individuals in the center is the reintegration of patients into the local community, a goal difficult to achieve if opposition to the center has been strong. Gilbert (1993) has suggested that some of the negative reaction to the establishment of group homes, shelters, and treatment centers comes from deficiencies on the part of the social agencies. She suggests that social service agencies need to plan more carefully, reach out to neighborhood residents and organizations, and understand more fully the impact of the agency facility on the neighborhood. In this way, social workers would not only serve their clients, but also meet the needs of the neighborhood and community.

Davidson's (1981, 1982) work on community-based treatment centers provides some useful insights into local community conflict and resistance to the location of treatment centers in local neighborhoods. Davidson suggests that resistance to these centers will be low in neighborhoods in which "deviant" behavior is tolerated, in neighborhoods with residents who do not regard the neighborhood as sufficiently valuable to defend it against intrusions, and in neighborhoods that lack the resources necessary for effective political mobilization. Such "transitional" neighborhoods are likely to be located in inner cities, not in suburban communities where resistance is high and residents have resources to become politically organized.

Davidson's analysis suggests that some neighborhoods seem to have the capacity, through formal and informal resources, to mount "effective campaigns to influence local officials with respect to neighborhood issues." Community opposition through such campaigns is regarded as a significant barrier to the survival and effective functioning of community-based treatment centers. Even under the best of circumstances, these centers operate in a potentially turbulent environment, especially if the clients' behavior is of concern to the local neighborhood residents.

An interesting example of a controversy that can be examined within Davidson's framework concerns the establishment of a group home in an affluent neighborhood in Grand Rapids, Michigan (George, 1992). When a program run by the Sisters of the Good Shepherd to help women escape prostitution needed a new "home" for up to ten women and their children, the Dominican Sisters offered a former rectory on their 34-acre campus that had been used to house aspiring nuns. Community opposition was voiced by some residents of a 750-home neighborhood that surrounded the Dominican Sisters' campus. Residents opposed to the program contended that "the women will attract pimps and drug pushers and threaten safety," and that the group home would "jeopardize property values," and "pave the way for more institutions in the neighborhood." The social worker involved with the program indicated that "many of the residents' fears stem from inaccurate perceptions of prostitutes as over-sexed women who choose their life-style and make a lot of money." At the same time, some residents did not oppose the location of the program in their neighborhood. However, one person who signed the petition against the home said, "I want the women to be able to get out of prostitution and break the cycle, but I don't want it in my neighborhood" (George, 1992).

In this example, the controversy occurred when a formal organization sought to establish a social service program in a residential neighborhood. The controversy was moderately narrow in scope, affecting a rather large upscale neighborhood, and conventional methods of resolving the conflict were employed, such as petitions to the local government and the use of zoning laws. Elements of social organization of the neighborhood were already in place, including the existence of a neighborhood association whose leaders who could represent the neighborhood to the local government.

Residents opposed to housing for people with disabilities often invoke city zoning ordinances that cover housing in single-family residential areas. Organizations seeking to place clients in group homes in these areas have challenged housing use restrictions by invoking the Fair Housing Amendments Act of 1988. This act prohibits discrimination in housing based on race or on mental or physical disability. In a 1995 case related to the Fair Housing Act, an organization named Oxford House established a new group home in Edmonds, Washington for ten to twelve adults recovering from alcoholism and drug addiction. The home was established in an area zoned for single-family residences, with "family" defined as "an individual or two or more persons related by genetics, adoption, or marriage, or a group of five or fewer persons who are not related by genetics, adoption, or marriage" (Petrila, 1995). The Supreme Court ruled that the city ordinance that set limits on the number of unrelated people that could be defined as "family" could be challenged under the Fair Housing Amendments. In

City of Edmonds v. Oxford House, "the Supreme Court held that use restrictions imposed on residences for people with disabilities but not
on families or other groups of unrelated people have a discriminatory
effect and therefore are covered under the Fair Housing Act" (Psychiatric Services, 1995).

URBAN REDEVELOPMENT

The relocation of people to new residential and business sites in urban
redevelopment projects provides another example of community conflict. A classic case in point is the Poletown Project in Detroit, where the
city of Detroit, the General Motors company, and other involved parties cooperated to redevelop 465 acres for a new Cadillac auto plant. A
319-acre portion of the site in the city of Detroit "included 1,176 residential, commercial, and industrial structures, as well as major community institutions. The demolition of these and the displacement of
the people owning and using them were at the heart of the Poletown
controversy" (Warner et al., 1982).

A total of approximately 3,800 persons in the Poletown community
were displaced. The city of Detroit promised to provide relocation assistance and financial compensation to those displaced for the "larger
community's welfare"—that is, to enhance the industrial employment
and revenue base for the city of Detroit. The city of Hamtramck was the
location of another part of the 465-acre project. Two major community institutions, the Catholic Archdiocese of Detroit and St. Joseph's Hospital, did not oppose the project. However, while some residents
welcomed the opportunity to move, a number opposed the plan for redevelopment. Prominent among the resisters were older Polish residents, especially those attached to Catholic churches in the area. Many of
these residents had already been involved in revitalization efforts for
the neighborhood and were joined in their opposition to the project by
young political activists and outside groups, such as Ralph Nader's people, and inside area leadership from the parish pastor. After much talk,
protest, and an unsuccessful court challenge, demolition proceeded, and
the General Motors Cadillac factory was built (Auerbach, 1985).

Another example of controversy over urban redevelopment involved plans for large-scale construction projects in downtown Los
Angeles, including a sports arena and a cathedral (Terry, 1997). These
projects were viewed as hemming in Skid Row and not meeting the
needs of the poor. This downtown neighborhood had been designated
a "sleeping zone" by the City, which supported the development of
social services and shelters in the area. One intention was to keep the

homeless in a confined area, Skid Row, a neighborhood of some 12,000 people, most of whom lived in single-room-occupancy hotels, missions, shelters, and on the streets. Competing with this development were plans to bring in recreational facilities, shops, and theaters in order to attract tourists. As one homeless advocate noted, "Our priorities are messed up—we are willing to sell out entire communities in the name of economic development, and forget the poor" (Terry, 1997).

KEEPING OUT THE HOMELESS

The question of where to house homeless people has created controversy in a number of American communities. One such example is Santa Monica, California, where the community of 87,000 people became "fiercely at war with itself over the swelling homeless population of between 1,500 and 2,000 that dominates some city parks and sidewalks, harasses pedestrians for money and commits crimes ranging from public urination to murder" (Lubman, 1992). While the community provides for a number of services for homeless people, such as shelter and food, the principal controversy involves the use by homeless persons of public places, especially parks, parking structures, beaches, and playgrounds. The principal groups seeking restrictions on the homeless have included an anti-crime Citizens' Protection Alliance of local citizens and a Santa Monicans for Renters' Rights group. These groups have sought to influence the city council in passing ordinances that would place restrictions on the use of public places by the homeless.

The City of Miami, Florida, provides another example of controversy over the behavior of homeless persons in local communities. A federal judge ordered the City of Miami to "create 'safe zones' where the homeless can eat, sleep, bathe and cook without fear of arrest" (Rohter, 1992). A number of groups, such as public officials, lawyers, and advocates for the homeless, have been in conflict over the conditions under which the homeless can be arrested. Many cities have ordinances controlling vagrancy, begging, and park curfews that have been used against the homeless. The safe zones to be created in Miami are essentially "arrest-free" zones where an estimated 6,000 homeless persons "can eat and sleep and exist in a healthy, safe environment" (Rohter, 1992).

CONTROVERSIES OVER ADULT ENTERTAINMENT

Residents of some neighborhoods in large cities are involved in constant battles against the presence of certain types of adult entertainment. These controversies occur when a concentration of businesses such as topless bars, massage parlors, and adult bookstores develops near a residential neighborhood (Holly, 1993; Lam, 1993). Residents organize to influence the local government to revoke business licenses, limit the issue of new licenses, and prosecute violations of local laws related to adult entertainment. The most usual complaint is that these establishments bring with them prostitution and crime. Residents usually seek to intervene by bringing lawsuits against the establishments or in seeking to change city zoning ordinances. These controversies tend to be narrow in scope, and the patterns for resolution are usually conventional. Successful opposition to adult entertainment establishments usually occurs only when the neighborhood is highly organized through involvement of residents as leaders and members of neighborhood associations, church groups, and school groups.

CONFLICT OVER ART AND GRAFFITI

A controversy in Los Angeles occurred between the City and County governments and the Hispanic community. This controversy arose when maintenance crews attempted to cover up graffiti and at the same time destroyed outdoor murals created as street art by members of the Hispanic community. As the city covered up graffiti that "gangs constantly use to threaten and taunt one another," it also destroyed some public art, including murals viewed as "bright expressions of joy or pain that like nothing else reveal the soul of this complicated city" (Sanchez, 1999b). For example, a seminal work of public art, "The Wall that Cracked Open" described as "a haunting two-story portrait of how violence was tearing up Hispanic families in the barrios of East Los Angeles," was ruined by a city maintenance crew. In this controversy of limited scope, a governmental unit took actions that were resisted by members of the Hispanic community who sought to save its public art.

CONFLICTS OVER MARCHES/RALLIES

Controversies arise when local city governments refuse to allow a particular group to hold marches or rallies within the city. These conflicts usually pit the organizers against community leaders and local government officials. An example of such a controversy arose when a Million Youth March in Harlem was proposed in 1999 by Khallid Abdul Muhammad, leader of the New Black Panther Party in New York City. Prominent black politicians condemned both the march and its organizers, citing as reasons the "racially charged speeches and violent clashes with the police at last year's rally" (Barstow, 1999b). A 1998 rally was allowed through a federal appeals court decision. In 1999, Mayor Giuliani's office refused to grant a march permit, blaming the media for giving too much attention to the organizers, and saying, "They don't have political support, they don't have social support, they don't have support in the community." Muhammad and his organization warned that there would be "a state of emergency in Harlem" if the Police Department attempted to block the event. "He said the organization was committed to focusing attention on high unemployment, high drop-out rates and a 'raging asthma epidemic' among black youth." In a decision by Judge Chin of the United States District Court in Manhattan, city officials were told they "had no right to use the content of Muhammad's inflammatory speeches as a basis for denying him a rally permit." The judge "ordered city officials and the organizers to promptly meet to discuss the specifics of the rally, and to 'agree on measures to avoid the confrontation that occurred last year'" (Barstow, 1999c). This is an example of a community controversy that threatened to become rancorous in its protest activities.

CONTROVERSIES OVER BARRICADES

Crime is a major social problem in American communities, especially in urban areas and in inner-city neighborhoods. Efforts to combat crime through local neighborhood organizations, such as block clubs, neighborhood associations, and Neighborhood Watch Programs, rarely generate any controversy. However, controversies have developed when neighborhoods organize to prevent crime by prevailing upon a city to construct street barriers dividing one neighborhood community from another. The barriers may take the form of gates into a neighborhood or as other types of physical barriers that keep traffic away from the neighborhood. Examples of the "Do Fence Me In" approach to crime prevention can be found in many large cities, such as Los Angeles, Chicago, Miami, Detroit, and in some suburban communities such as Oak Park, Illinois, and Shaker Heights, Ohio (Etzioni, 1992; Holly, 1993; Wilkerson, 1993).

An example of a controversy between neighbors over the erection of street barriers occurred in neighborhoods of Detroit and Grosse Pointe Park, Michigan (Holly, 1993; Mathews, 1993). Residents of the Grosse Pointe Park neighborhood petitioned the city council to construct barriers at selected streets that adjoin the dividing line between the two communities. In a nearby area, street barriers were erected to prevent traffic from moving on these three streets from one major artery to another, both leading into the inner city and downtown area of Detroit. The controversy was characterized as racial, since the community erecting the barriers was almost entirely white and affluent, and the neighboring community was mostly African American and working class. Residents of the Detroit neighborhood perceived the barriers as "offensive" and as symbolic of negative attitudes toward African Americans. In this controversy, the Grosse Pointe Park community gained the support of the local government and succeeded in having the barriers constructed.

In another example of a controversy over street barricades, Mayor Richard Daley proposed that some streets in Chicago be blocked off in order to restrict the movement of criminals in these communities. This plan was viewed as an effort to "cul de sac" the entire city of Chicago (Wilkerson, 1993). Opposition to the plan came from "poor black wards" of the city, whose residents saw the effort as "dangerous," "oppressive," and a way to further segregate the races. In this case the plan was not implemented because of the controversy as well as financing problems related to construction of the barricades.

COMMUNITY ASSOCIATIONS AND RESIDENTS

Many suburban community residential areas are governed by rules of homeowners' associations. These associations are usually made up of a board of directors that acts on complaints concerning noncompliance with the rules. Many times these associations are created by the real estate industry, and have strict standards and rules that are the basis of emotional disputes between homeowners and the associations (Pacelle, 1994). Although many residents like rules, the rules become less popular when they interfere with residents' sense of freedom and right of ownership. Issues creating conflict between residents and homeowners' associations include pet bans, architectural restrictions (e.g., bans on window air conditioners, truck parking, and curbside auto repairs, and regulations involving on-street parking and location of basketball hoops), and limits on outside sheds, backyard fences, and home additions. Much to the distress of many residents who go to court, the courts usually side with the associations, most which are governed by volunteer boards of directors that act on complaints and requests for noncompliance with the rules.

LOCAL GOVERNMENTS AND RELIGION-BASED COMMUNITIES

Sometimes the rules and regulations of local community governments clash with the interests and culture of religious groups. Controversies arise in regard to the law and the behavior of the members of the religious community. An example of such tensions and conflicts is found in the Monsey area of New York, the home of members of Hasidic and ultra-Orthodox Jews. Disputes over a number of years have centered around zoning laws, in terms of numbers of people in households, construction of multiple-family housing, enforcement of traffic safety regulations, location of synagogues in homes, and school safety regulations for yeshivas (Berger, 1997).

LOCAL GOVERNMENTS AND IMMIGRANTS

A housing law proposal in Brookhaven, New York, a small town on Long Island, became the basis for a "highly charged conflict." The local government sought to limit the number of people who could legally occupy rental property, requiring a certain amount of space per occupant, with no more than four people sharing a bedroom. The proposal also stipulated that rental property could be inspected by town officials. The local government initiated the proposal as a way of assuring the safety of new immigrants in crowded housing, improving their living conditions, and protecting "renters from landlords who crowd them into unsafe houses" (Cooper, 1999g). The new immigrants were mainly day laborers from central Mexico who, along with other immigrants, were coming to Brookhaven where work was plentiful in areas such as construction and gardening and where housing was scarce. Immigrants and their advocacy groups opposed the housing proposal as discriminatory, calling it "just another attempt to drive out immigrants."

Behind the issue over the new housing law was a tension between the new immigrants and local "old-timer" residents. Homeowners accused the newcomers of "everything from littering to selling drugs to molesting women to driving down property values." They objected to the equinas, or street corners, where laborers lined up to get jobs, as snarling traffic, creating hazards, and making the residents feel unsafe. The immigrant laborers complained "of beatings, harassment, and constant taunts," while the landlords claimed that the proposed law was aimed at them. Both sides used conventional methods of supporting and opposing the new housing proposal, e.g., public hearings by the Brookhaven town council and a candlelight vigil outside the town hall. New organizations emerged in support of the proposal, such as a civic group called the Sachem Quality of Life Organization, and the Workplace Project, a nonprofit immigrant rights group created to fight the proposed law.

Chapter 13 Review

In this chapter we identified the various dimensions of community conflicts, the elements involved in most controversies at the community level, and some of the functions such controversies serve for the groups involved. What is apparent in community controversies is the fact that conflicting groups believe they make legitimate claims. In some cases the efforts of small community groups serve to modify the actions of formal organizations, but it is difficult for them to succeed in "defeating" the larger institutional forces. Examples of a range of controversies in local communities were presented, including community-based treatment centers, urban development, housing for the homeless, adult entertainment, art and graffiti, marches and rallies, barricades, community associations, religious groups, and housing of new immigrants. Controversies are likely to arise when group homes for mentally ill persons, people from the criminal justice system, and children and youth with developmental disabilities move into local community neighborhoods (Fellin, 1993). Efforts to achieve goals of social integration for these individuals have been met with barriers such as protective zoning ordinances, neighborhood group opposition, and social rejection by neighbors. Although informal resistance to community care of individuals who cannot care for themselves continues through a "Not In My Back Yard" attitude on the part of neighbors, the courts have often ruled in favor of community residential care organizations.

14

Social Integration in Communities

The concept of social integration guides our assessment of residents' attachment and involvement in the social institutions of a community. This concept also helps us see how the parts of the various community subsystems operate in relation to each other—that is, how these systems fit together in the community as a social system. Social integration has a number of dimensions that can be defined, observed, and measured. Landecker's (1951) classic discussion of social integration distinguishes four subtypes: "cultural, or consistency among the standards of a culture; normative, or conformity of conduct in the group to cultural standards; communicative, or exchange of meanings throughout the group; and functional, or interdependence in the group through exchange of services."

Internal consistency of values, norms, and standards of the community is a sign of cultural integration. An important dimension of cultural integration within a multicultural society is the degree to which the cultural aspects of social groups within the community correspond to each other and to those of mainstream society. Normative integration focuses on the extent to which the behaviors of residents conform to the cultural standards of the community. Various subsystems within a community establish standards, especially the political, educational, and religious community systems, with normative integration representing the conformity of members of a community to these standards. Communicative integration is attained in a community when residents share common meanings through social participation across various cultural groups. An example of functional integration is the "division of labor" in a community and the degree to which different occupational and social groups contribute to the wellbeing of the community. Special issues surround the extent to which sub-groups, such as ethnic minority groups, social class groups, gay groups, persons with disabilities, and older adults, are socially, economically, and politically integrated into a community.

The major focus of this chapter is on the sources of social integration of residents in a local community. The concept of social network is used to examine the individual's social integration into a community. Next, we will look at the ways in which communities of interest foster social integration on the part of their members. Religion as the basis for a community of identification is examined in terms of its integrative functions. Less obvious sources of integration include recreational activities, sports spectatorship, and patronizing specific eating and drinking establishments. Finally, attention is directed to groups of individuals who have difficulty integrating or reintegrating into local communities of place and of interest.

SOCIAL NETWORKS

A major source of social integration is an individual's social network. This network includes one's significant others, often drawn from family, kinship, friendship, neighborhood, voluntary association, and work-related groups. Rather than thinking of these discrete groups as separate sources of community integration, social network analysis identifies a configuration of social relationships that encompasses a mixture of individuals from these groups. Social networks differ with regard to a number of dimensions, such as size, frequency of contacts, strength of ties, and similarities and differences in gender, age, religion, race, ethnicity, ability, or social orientation. Sometimes the relationships in social networks are supportive, warm, and helpful, or they may be hostile, cold, and disapproving. The nature of one's social network is closely related to the provision of social, emotional, physical, economic, and informational support. One's social network not only provides access to resources, but also serves to link individuals with local community institutions and social groups.

Since social networks are likely to include a mixture of individuals, such as family members, friends, relatives, neighbors, and co-workers, it is natural that some ties will be stronger than others. Granovetter (1973) has highlighted the fact that both strong and weak network ties can be functional for individuals. In fact, weak ties often serve to hold people in urban communities together, providing links that help individuals find employment, associate with others in the workplace, gain occupational and social mobility, and connect to the resources of the larger community.

VOLUNTARY ASSOCIATIONS AND SOCIAL INTEGRATION

Voluntary associations serve as an important source of social integration for members of geographic communities. These voluntary groups are communities of interest and identification. They provide avenues for integration and attachment to the local community, while at the same time providing identification with communities that may have no geographical bounds. Terms such as "we-feeling," community sentiment, common bonds, values, psychological identification, and cultural ties are associated with these voluntary group communities. Most American communities include the following voluntary associations:

- religious, faith-based groups;
- occupational groups, such as unions and professional organizations;
- social groups, such as dance clubs, card clubs, and sports clubs;
- advocacy groups, such as NAACP;
- political groups, such as political party organizations and community advisory groups;
- self-help groups, such as AA, Recovery, and the Alliance for the Mentally Ill;
- service groups, such as hospital auxiliaries;
- client groups, such as tenants' organizations;
- neighborhood groups, such as homeowners' associations and Neighborhood Watch groups.

In most cases, membership in these voluntary groups provides opportunities for social, educational, and professional activities that serve to integrate members into the local community. At the same time, members of local community groups often identify with organizational units at state, national, and/or international levels. In some instances, membership in voluntary groups may substitute for local ties, thus reducing community integration by inhibiting individuals from participating in activities at the local community level.

Social participation is one of the primary functions of many of these social groups. For example, religious denominations provide opportunities for social participation through worship as well as service-oriented activities. A parent-teacher association or volunteer group within a social agency may act in a support or service capacity, linking its volunteers to the local community. Civic associations link members to the larger community through participation of their members in the political process. Groups with political orientations connect citizens to local, state, and national political structures. Citizens may use these civic groups to engage in local community conflicts, especially in opposing actions of local groups and/or local government that infringe upon their interests. They also use such memberships to promote actions that will further their private interests. These political and parapolitical groups are instrumental in raising the consciousness of members regarding issues of concern, placing local issues on the political agenda of a community, producing new leaders, and creating or maintaining political identities.

Racial, ethnic, and/or religious groups are examples of communities of identification that integrate persons into local communities of place. Often membership in one or more of these groups coincides with the place of residence, as in some Italian, Polish, Irish, Jewish, Catholic, African American, Hispanic, and Asian American neighborhood communities in large urban areas. As noted in our previous discussion of ethnic minority neighborhoods, a member of a specific group may change residence and still retain psychological identification with former neighborhood groups. Most often in these types of communities, individuals develop a sense of belonging to the local community as well as to a much broader, even worldwide group. Again, attachment to the local geographic community is often determined by involvement in local activities emerging from membership in these non-place communities.

RELIGION AND COMMUNITY INTEGRATION

For many Americans, religious affiliation provides a community of identification that integrates people with their communities of place. Although many religious groups have churches, synagogues, mosques, or other places of worship in local community areas, their members generally identify with their religion on a basis that goes beyond geographic bounds. This is most vividly highlighted by the response to religious appeals for funds for national and international needs and projects. Religious groups serve to link their membership to the local geographic community through participation in religious services, social and educational activities, and volunteer services. Membership in churches and other religious organizations serves as a mechanism for integration into the local community of place, but such membership may also lead to community conflict and controversy. Inasmuch as those who belong to religious organizations often identify with a specific set of norms and values, they may find these values to be at odds with those of other members of the local geographic community. Controversial issues related to the values of religious groups include sex education, prayer in public schools, abortion, sale and use of liquor, and enforcement of laws on pornography.

Religious organizations function as instruments of socialization, education, social control, and mutual support. As a result, religion offers a number of avenues, formal and informal, for individuals and families to develop attachments and social interactions with other people in the local community. Some of the major formal ways religious organizations facilitate community integration include religious-oriented schools, social agencies, and volunteer groups. For example, schools establish a basis for the development of child and adult ties to religious and school communities, and as such, serve to integrate families into the local community. Members of religious organizations often participate in volunteer services under the direction of sectarian social welfare and health care organizations. In addition, some religious organizations create their own volunteer groups with goals of assisting members of the community. Finally, informal relationships may be developed between members of religious organizations, leading to mutual aid and social supports among families connected to a religious congregation.

One of the ways in which religious groups serve an integrative function is through youth and young adult groups. Programs for these individuals, while oriented toward the development of religious values, also include social activities such as dances, dinners, picnics, and ski trips. In New York City, Bible reading and other types of discussion groups have attracted young adults, so that they "have become popular singles scenes," or the "new church social—defined broadly as any gathering outside conventional rites of worship, often on weekdays" (Yazigi, 1998). Religious leaders of some of these young adult groups, such as Hineni, sponsored by a Jewish congregation, see them as functioning to foster marriages between people of the same faith. In general, religious leaders attribute the new popularity of these social groups "to a seeking of spirituality and a longing for community" (Yazigi, 1998).

MASS SOCIETY, RESIDENCE, AND SOCIAL INTEGRATION

As noted in Chapter 1, local American communities operate within a larger context, sometimes labeled a national "mass society." There is little agreement as to the influence of a national society on local communities and their residents. Some social scientists describe the relationship as coexistence, stressing the importance of both the national society and the local community. Others suggest that the local community has diminished in influence and as a source of social integration. The issues focus on the nature of a "mass society" that has emerged from the social processes of urbanization, bureaucratization, and industrialization. Among the features of "mass society" are an emphasis on secondary over primary group relations (a movement from *gemeinschaft* to *gesellschaft* relationships), the development of mass media, large-scale bureaucratic institutions, high levels of residential mobility, and an increase in size and density of urban populations. The claim is made that these societal features have negative effects on residents, increasing their sense of isolation, alienation, and anomie. Under this formulation, social residence is said to be a relatively unimportant source of social integration. With this perspective, the social significance of the local geographic community is considered to be minimal, at least in terms of local social bonds, community sentiments, social participation, and social control.

A contrasting model of the relationship between mass society and local communities has emerged from studies of American communities. This model, which may be characterized as the "community of limited liability" (Janowitz, 1978), is based on the proposition that participation in local institutions and local attachments persist within the larger society, although they are more limited than in previous traditional forms of community. The concept of a "community of limited liability" suggests that personal community involvement is partial and voluntary in relation to primary group friendship, kinship, and neighboring bonds. The same is true of participation in voluntary associations, formal organizations, and informal and formal social activities in the local community. These latter kinds of relationships appear to reinforce primary contacts, rather than replace them.

In short, the qualities associated with a good community, such as citizen involvement, participation, commitment, and local attachment, appear to be possible in communities within a "mass society." This does not mean that there are many communities that resemble the traditional autonomous community of yesteryear described by Keillor (1985) in *Lake Wobegon Days*, but it does mean that citizens of contemporary mass society can have local sentiments and attachments that integrate them into the local community. However, the degree of social integration appears to vary among social classes, ethnic and racial groups, and occupational groups. A number of barriers, such as residential segregation, inhibit the social integration of ethnic minorities into many neighborhoods and municipal communities. Ties to these communities are also affected by factors such as residential mobility, length of residence, and stage in the life cycle. Some observers suggest that continued urbanization and decentralization of populations make integration into local communities increasingly problematic.

The importance of residence as a source of social integration is illustrated in a study of Chicago neighborhoods by Sampson et al. (1997). In this study, social cohesion among neighbors was found to be an important factor in creating informal social controls that reduced violent crime in neighborhoods. Solidarity and trust among neighbors, and a willingness to intervene for the common good, are related to the tasks of supervising children and maintaining public order. A "collective efficacy" of residents in these neighborhoods emerges in the presence of social cohesion, especially when "residential tenure and homeownership promote collective efforts to maintain social control." In these neighborhoods, "One central goal is the desire of community residents to live in safe and orderly environments that are free of predatory crime, especially interpersonal violence."

OBVIOUS AND LESS OBVIOUS SOURCES OF INTEGRATION

Traditionally, religious, educational, and economic institutions have been the major forces for cohesion and integration of citizens into their communities. These institutions, especially through their related voluntary associations, continue to serve integrative functions for a large portion of the population of a community. However, less obvious forces outside the customary social institutions also serve important integrative functions. There are a number of such examples, such as local newspapers, disc jockeys, radio personalities and talk shows, Meals-on-Wheels programs for the elderly, suburban neighborhood swimming pools, recreational activities of YMCA/YWCA centers, neighborhood ethnic restaurants, country clubs, golf courses, youth recreational programs, libraries, community colleges, shopping malls, food markets, and street corners.

Bars, coffeehouses, bookstores, and local neighborhood restaurants serve integrative functions for their patrons by promoting a sense of community. Television shows often use these locations as a setting for social interactions among the principal characters. For instance, the show *Friends* uses a coffee shop; *Ally McBeal* uses a nightclub as a gathering place for lawyers after the work day; *Seinfeld* used a restaurant as a gathering place; and reruns of *Cheers* show most social interaction taking place in a neighborhood tavern. As in television shows, in real life it is not uncommon for the same people to show up regularly at the same location to drink, eat, and socialize. It is clear that patrons develop loyalties to particular locations, and that their social contacts are a significant form of social integration with a group and with a local neighborhood community.

An example of a location that provides opportunities for social ties to the local community is the bookstore/café, which provides a place for people to read books and newspapers, have discussions, make social contacts, drink coffee, and eat snacks or lunch (Richman, 1999). Such establishments in Washington, D.C., include the following:

- The Barnes & Noble Café in Georgetown, described as being "like a college library, but one that allows snacking." "The café is a restful forest-green place. . ..It's such a gracious café that people bring not only their books and newspapers, but sometimes their own lunches, and nobody challenges them."
- Borders Books, Music & Café, in downtown Washington, featuring "small round tables for two, stretching along one side of the store's first floor," with coffee, sweets, cookies and biscotti, sandwiches and soup: "Given the noisy cash register, some talkative patrons and the clatter of plates and cups, this café couldn't be mistaken for a library."
- Footnotes, offering sandwiches, bagels, soup made in-house, desserts, espresso drinks and teas, and a wine list: "The café draws an artistic-looking group, at least outside the business-lunch crush. In one corner, everyone is under 25 and wearing black. On a sofa, a romantic twosome are reading a children's book aloud to each other."
- Kramerbooks & Afterwords Café, with a complete restaurant at the rear of the bookstore, pages-long menu, and full bar. "If you want quiet and a bookish environment, come for breakfast or in mid-afternoon; late in the evening there's live music."
- Politics & Prose Coffeehouse, a basement café with "the best qualities of a surrogate home and an extended family." "The plush Victorian sofas and slightly baroque dining chairs are occupied

by parents and children, students with yellow highlighters, newspaper readers and occasional budding artists with pads and colored pens." "Like the bookstore surrounding it, Politics & Prose's café is homey and tasteful, its coffee served in handmade pottery mugs and its walls decorated with a lush array of calendars."

More often than not, drinking and eating establishments develop personalities of their own, due to the atmosphere of the place, the patrons, and the personnel. These establishments take on identifications, based on their clientele, as gathering places for people from certain social classes, racial or ethnic groups, "singles," people of gay or lesbian orientation, sports figures, or neighborhood residents.

Music clubs have traditionally provided patrons with opportunities to listen to music, dance, and dine. An example is the Conga Room in Los Angeles, "sometimes called the House of Blues for Latin entertainment" (Anderton, 1998). This club's "combination of top-notch salsa bands and sizzling interior design has brought sophisticated Hispanic style to an ethnically mixed audience." The club draws an upscale crowd including "white residents from the Westside, and Hispanic, Asian, and black patrons from the city's eastern and southern neighborhoods. The club may well mirror a future Los Angeles—ethnically mixed but predominantly, and confidently, Hispanic."

Bars located near baseball or football stadiums in large cities serve a varied clientele. During non-game days and noontime periods, sports bars tend to draw patrons from tourists and the surrounding neighborhood areas. On game days, some members of the usual crowd come in, but the size of the crowd is swelled by outsiders, many of whom identify themselves with the bar. An example is the Lindell A.C., which claims to be America's first sports bar, founded more than 50 years ago in Detroit near Tiger Stadium. This bar has the traditional sports celebrity photos, cheap beer, cheap food, and a true sports atmosphere. Umberto's, near the old Kingdome in Seattle, is an example of a popular stadium restaurant/bar and hangout for sports fans. Other neighborhood bars appeal to patrons who share the same ethnic or racial identification. They tend to be located in working-class neighborhoods or in ghetto areas. These bars and restaurants offer opportunities for socializing, and assist newcomers in becoming part of a neighborhood group community.

Cheap bars or "dives" are usually found in deteriorated sections of large urban areas, in ghetto neighborhoods, on "mean streets" and skid rows. They generally offer a place to hang out for unemployed men and women, persons with alcohol and drug problems, homeless people, and prostitutes and pimps. They often provide a location for illegal activities, such as drug sales and gambling.

From large cities to college towns, singles bars seem to be every-where—in residential neighborhoods, in downtown areas, in suburban business areas, in restaurants, and in motels or hotels. The clientele range from college-age young adults to young urban professionals, to middle-aged men and women who are single, married, or divorced. For some, especially college students, "the bar" near campus is a place to hang out, listen to music, and socialize.

Communities vary as to how easy or difficult it is for gay and lesbian persons to integrate into the social activities of the local area. In some communities, gay bars are among the few places at which gay males and lesbians can congregate comfortably. Gay bars, lounges, and clubs are most often found in communities with large populations of gay and lesbian people, and these establishments serve to link their patrons to each other and to the local community. In recent years there has been a "new generation of gay bars" in New York City, where changes in décor "mirror a broader change in attitude among patrons of gay bars: a self-confidence about being out of the closet, a rising economic prosperity and less fear of harassment by non-homosexuals" (Colman, 1998). The "new bars" have exchanged "dark and dingy interior designs for cleaner, airier, more creative spaces" where "many gay men appear to be embracing some of the values and freedoms of mainstream society, from which they have often been excluded."

Drinking and eating establishments in American communities serve integrative functions for their patrons because people feel comfortable in these places and form primary group relationships with the staff and other patrons. For some local residents, these places can have negative consequences, if they lead to alcoholism or other illness. For some, these places provide the primary source of social contact and identification with the community. The theme song for the TV series *Cheers* expresses one meaning of these experiences: the sense of community that comes from going to a place "where everybody knows your name" (Portnoy & Angelo, 1982).

And then there are hotel bars, with the bars in New York hotels serving as places where "you can relax over a well-mixed drink, be treated like a king or simply be as anonymous as the bars themselves" (Hesser, 1999). Thus, they can serve as refuges from social contact or provide connections to friends and/or the bartender. As Hesser (1999) notes, "Spending time in one, in fact, can be as much of an escape as a walk in Central Park—a brush with seclusion and quiet, a moment to step out of your citified soul and collect your thoughts." The character of hotel bars varies, as does the clientele, which "can vary from delicate women sipping on rum to portly businessmen lighting up cigars. Some may be hiding, hovering over a Scotch; others may be waiting nervously for a date to arrive. Travelers drift in and out. Regulars cling to their corners. Women feel comfortable walking in alone" (Hesser, 1999).

BUSINESS AND ENTERTAINMENT NEIGHBORHOODS

Neighborhoods that include a combination of the types of establishments identified above may provide a major source of social integration for residents of local communities. The Fort Greene neighborhood in Brooklyn is a good example of how neighborhoods serve an integrative function. This neighborhood has a long history of providing housing to African American residents as well as serving as a cultural center. As of 1999 the neighborhood had become revitalized with "a burst of cultural energy," breaking away from its past when "crack and other drug dealers made it a dangerous place." The neighborhood still has "deep pockets of poverty," but increasingly "changes in the neighborhood have drawn young, black professionals from the film, music and art worlds and from Wall Street. Real estate values have risen, as once-decrepit brownstones have been restored" (Pierre-Pierre, 1999).

In the Fort Greene neighborhood there has been an infusion of upscale businesses, such as art and fashion boutiques, new restaurants and cafes. New performance spaces attract people to recite or listen to poetry readings, tell stories, have jam sessions, or attend fashion shows, films, or theatrical productions. There are new events in the Brooklyn Academy of Music and the Paul Robeson Theater, art galleries, and hair salons. Many of the businesses have distinctively African themes, such as the hair salons and boutiques, all of which "foster a greater sense of community pride." This pride is conveyed among some residents and merchants by use of a new name for the area, Bogolan, "an abbreviation of bogolanfini, which means 'mud cloth' in the bambara language that is widely spoken in Mali" (Pierre-Pierre, 1999).

The San Francisco neighborhood of North Beach is another example of a residential/business area that seemed to be disappearing in the 1980s but has since been revived (Reichl, 1998). "Storefronts stood empty, one by one the restaurants started to close, and even the cafes seemed sad. The people who loved North Beach began to anticipate its demise. And then, something remarkable happened: North Beach reinvented itself through food." With new and old restaurants, shops and bakeries, coffee roasters and pottery shops, North Beach regained its personality and its character: "North Beach feels raucous, alive, vibrant. It feels loved." For example, in Enrico's, "one of the area's most venerable institutions, there is almost no time of the day or night when the joint doesn't jump. . . .The food is more likable than fabulous, but the room has a raw energy that is fueled by live jazz and a sense of history. Looking around, you expect Jack Kerouac to show up any moment."

Then there is the Black Cat, where "The food honors Chinatown with dishes like brightly colored chow mein with roast duck, chanterelles and Chinese chives and soothing salmon jook" as well as Italian food such as fragile ravioli filled with red snapper and wild greens, and an awesome capponada; the Rose Pistola, "a chic, modern homage to the Ligurian people who first populated North Beach"; and the L'Ostria del Forno, "a tiny little place that has recaptured the old spirit of the neighborhood," with just eight tables, cash only accepted, and "all the cooking is done in the pizza oven." As Reichl (1998) observed after a visit in 1998, "Looking around the sweet little restaurant, you could easily persuade yourself that nothing had changed in North Beach. When the ghosts gather to play boccie in front of the church across the street, I am sure they are smiling." And so this "gentle old Italian neighborhood that ambles up the hill from San Francisco Bay, in the shade of Telegraph Hill" has once again become a source of social bonds and attachments for people in the community.

SPORTS TEAMS AND COMMUNITY ATTACHMENT

Organized sports provide mechanisms for citizens to identify with their home communities, their neighborhood schools, their local colleges, and their cities and metropolitan areas. Communities become known for the successes and failures of their sports teams, and residents take pride in winning teams. Sports fans follow their teams by newspaper, radio, television, and attendance at games. The sports pages make up a major section of any community newspaper. A winning team increases the sense of belonging and pride in the community, but a losing team may still engender loyal fans and identification with the underdog team. Both spectator and participant sports serve to link individuals to their local community. Participation in sports, especially team sports, and other recreational activities builds ties to local communities. Summer baseball and softball teams for all ages, bowling leagues, bingo halls, pool rooms, informal sports in parks, lake areas, and cross-country ski areas all play integrative roles for community residents. The playing of games "acts as a social glue"—a source of social integration—for many people. Examples include bingo, bridge, and other card games. The game of mah-jongg is particularly popular in the New York City metropolitan area, in Chinese and Jewish neighborhoods, community centers, restaurant kitchens, and private homes.

People of all ages find "camaraderie in the music of mah-jongg tiles" (Brawarsky, 2000). The tile pieces with designs that represent different numbers are used to complete a hand, with each player accumulating set combinations of tiles. There are many versions of mah-jongg, which has its origins in China during the fifth or sixth century B.C. Variations include Chinese classical, Hong Kong old style, Shanghai new style, American, Western, and Filipino. The game is usually played in foursomes and is also played on the Internet (Brawarsky, 2000).

REINTEGRATION INTO COMMUNITIES

A special dimension of social integration is the movement back into the community of persons who have been institutionalized. Major treatment goals for these persons includes reintegration into their former communities. Reintegration has a variety of meanings, depending on the needs of the clientele, who may be mental patients, drug abusers, retarded adults, homeless persons, or participants in work-release programs of correctional facilities. Children and adolescents, including neglected children, developmentally disabled children, juvenile delinquents, and children in foster care, also may require reintegration into the community. Reintegration usually means becoming involved in everyday experiences within the community, developing acceptable behaviors, participating in social networks, and using local resources.

Our conception of multiple communities, both geographical and identificational, can be applied to the community reintegration of special populations, such as mentally ill persons (Fellin, 1993). From this perspective, patients returning from institutional care to community-based care have a range of communities from which they can derive the benefits of group membership, such as social interaction, collective identity, shared interests and social resources. Within this context, a personal community serves as a context for the development of treatment and social service goals. Thus, a personal community may include people in informal and formal helping networks, such as families, kinship and friend groups, self-help groups, daytime drop-in centers, clubhouse programs, church groups, recreational groups, and mental health and social welfare organizations.

Most communities have social service programs that assist individuals in community reintegration. These programs include different types of community-based treatment centers. Treatment programs range from halfway houses and group homes to apartment-style arrangements, all involving "least restrictive environments" compared to institutionalization. The major problem these programs encounter is community opposition to their location in residential areas. This opposition is less pronounced in programs for children than for adults, and less pronounced for the aged than for the mentally ill or criminal offenders.

Community-based treatment centers for adults are usually found in low-resistance neighborhoods located within "transitional" and deteriorating neighborhood areas in a central city. The major limitation of such locations is the existence of crime and other social problems, which restricts free movement within the community. Opportunities to join positive social networks are often limited in these areas. Residents in neighborhoods that are free of these limitations usually resist the establishment of community-based treatment centers, and negative attitudes of residents are likely to limit reintegration (Davidson, 1982).

Another obstacle to reintegration may be the failure of social practitioners to recognize the most relevant part of the community for the client. For example, an ethnic minority person may be living at some distance from individuals of his or her own cultural group, thereby limiting opportunities for reintegration and social interaction. In such cases the client is returned to the community, but is not within a relevant local community area such as an ethnic neighborhood. Another example is elderly persons who live in nursing homes in the community but are isolated by rules and restrictions from social interactions with neighbors, family, and friends.

SOCIAL INTEGRATION AND THE UNEMPLOYED

For most people, participation in the workplace serves as an important integrative link to the local community. As Miller (1997) has observed, "One does not have to be a Freudian, a Marxist, a political conservative, or a union leader to believe that work is a major anchor of people's lives." Work serves as a personal and social anchor, whether it be work in a household, as a volunteer, or in paid employment. People in some social groups are more likely than others to lack this avenue to social integration due to unemployment, such as homeless people, persons with physical and mental disabilities, able persons who lack employment skills and training, and female heads of households receiving benefits from public welfare programs. According to a report of the President's Committee on Employment of People with Disabilities, among people between the ages of 18 and 64, persons with disabilities have a much lower labor force participation rate (52 percent) than those without disabilities (83 percent). This finding indicates the limited opportunities for social integration through work for about one half of persons with disabilities, and opportunities are especially limited for Native Americans and African Americans who are disabled persons (Novoselick, 1999).

There have been a number of federal, state, and local responses to the problems created by unemployment, including the welfare reform legislation enacted in 1996, the Americans with Disabilities Act of 1990, and federal legislation related to homeless people, such as the McKinney Act. Still, even with very low unemployment rates in the 1990s, African American youth in inner cities had high unemployment rates, due in part to discrimination and to a lack of the social capital necessary to obtain jobs. As Wilson (1996) notes in *When Work Disappears*, there is a high level of joblessness in inner-city poverty ghettos, due in large part to the restructuring of the economy, with unemployment highly associated with a decline in social organization in poor neighborhoods.

The Watts area and surrounding neighborhoods in South Central Los Angeles illustrates how, even in times of economic growth, many African Americans and Hispanic Americans are left out of the marketplace (Sanchez, 1999a). While some of the residents of this area may remain unemployed because of characteristics of the job seekers, such as "bouts with crime, drug abuse or reluctance to prepare better for changes in the job market," other residents are victims of substantial fear and neglect (Sanchez, 1999a). Often transportation is a major problem, due to lack of cars and to undependable public bus systems, leading employers to reject workers from these areas. As a result, many are employed only in temporary, low-paid positions in the food service industry or in construction work. One response to these problems has been programs within the federal empowerment zone plans, especially those that provide training programs and tax breaks for businesses to hire local residents. In the Watts area, community organizations such as the Watts Labor Community Action Committee offer social service and employment training to assist residents with job placement. However, the large number of businesses destroyed in the 1992 rioting after the Rodney King trial caused a loss of some 6,000 jobs, and it has been difficult for the area to attract new businesses. As a result, many residents eager to work are left spending much time standing in line for jobs, without much success, leaving them without work connections or social integration with the Los Angeles community.

SOCIAL INTEGRATION AMONG THE HOMELESS

One of the major social characteristics associated with homeless persons is their lack of social integration and attachment to the local community (Fellin, 1996). Homeless persons lack social ties that come from living in a home in a residential neighborhood, and most lack employment as a source of integration. A national study of homeless persons conducted by the Census Bureau found that, while 44 percent had worked at least part-time in the previous month, 42 percent said what they most needed was help in finding a job (Bernstein, 1999). There is an image in the media of homeless people as lacking in normative integration, in that their lifestyles are inconsistent with the standards and expectations of mainstream society. Communicative and functional integration are viewed as minimal among the homeless, in that these persons are characterized as disaffiliated, uprooted, socially isolated, and lacking in social networks and social supports. The Census Bureau study found that approximately 39 percent of homeless persons suffered from mental illness, and about two thirds from chronic or infectious diseases, considered to be strong barriers to social integration into the community. For many homeless persons there is "both a lack of adequate and permanent shelter and the absence of community and social ties" (ADAMHA, 1980).

Sociological and anthropological studies present a picture of three major levels of social integration among homeless persons. The majority of homeless persons are disaffiliated from family, relatives, friends, and the community, with a weak system of social supports. This condition is especially prevalent among the homeless mentally ill. A second level of integration is found among some homeless people, especially women, who have limited social integration through social contacts and supports from their social networks in the community. A third level of social integration is derived from membership of some homeless persons in subcultures of homeless persons. These subcultures include skid row culture, street culture, and shelter culture. These cultures emerge when homeless people "adapt to the rigors of survival outside by joining together in loose-knit communities" (Wolch, 1995). In these communities homeless people "establish and maintain their social ties and access to various sources of formal assistance such as soup kitchens, shelters, or thrift shops" and "resources of the urban environment, like parks, libraries, shopping malls, but also restaurants, grocery stores, and transit facilities."

An exemplar of skid row culture is found in the Bowery in New York City. Integration into this culture was described by Giamo (1989), who found homeless Bowery men belonging to an ordered community, with an identity, structure, and affiliative network of supports. He indicated that as Bowery men find food, shelter, and alcohol, they become "enculturated into their subculture. . .integrated within their community and have daily attachments to bars, restaurants, flops, liquor stores, social agencies, missions, used clothing stores, and bottlegang groups." Many homeless people live in public places, while others are sheltered on a temporary basis and spend most of the daylight hours on the streets and in drop-in centers. These individuals handle day-to-day living in ways that can be described as "street culture," that is, "a loose sense of cohesiveness and an irregular but often effective communication network" (Sosin, Colson, and Grossman, 1988). Homeless people within such networks usually have a strong resistance to institutional living arrangements and to health and welfare services. Whether they have regular contacts with other street people, pedestrians, and merchants, or are "loners" and shy away from social relationships, over time they develop a minimal level of social integration through their street culture.

With the increased use of homeless shelters into the 1990s, a form of social integration has emerged that has been described as "shelterization" (Grunberg & Eagle, 1990; Gounis & Susser, 1990). Some shelter residents begin to "attach and adapt" to shelter life in order to survive, with an increase in dependency on the providers. While these homeless persons may come into a shelter with a high degree of disaffiliation, they soon affiliate with shelter residents, incorporate the lifestyle of the shelter, and become more isolated from the outside world. Residents become involved in efforts to improve life within the shelter, rather than using the shelter as a bridge to permanent housing.

Social welfare agencies and other community groups concerned with housing the homeless encounter strong resistance within the community to the establishment of emergency shelters, transitional housing, and permanent, low-cost, affordable housing. Resistance is particularly strong when homeless persons have been involved with the mental health system or the criminal justice system. As a consequence, integration and reintegration of homeless persons into the local community is a complex task, one that requires cooperation of organizations within the various subsystems of a community. Multidimensional networking, along with models of intensive case management, represent examples of innovative approaches to overcoming the lack of community integration for homeless people (Hutchinson et al., 1986; Leshner, 1992).

SOCIAL INTEGRATION OF NEW IMMIGRANTS

The arrival of predominantly nonwhite immigrants to the United States in recent years has raised questions as to whether these new residents are willing or able to assimilate into the primary social institutions of American society and its communities (Smith & Edmonston, 1997). Historically, "Over time, many immigrants, and especially their children, have become integrated into the mainstream of American society." In considering the nature of social integration of new immigrants, it is important to recognize that the mainstream society is not monocultural, but multicultural. As a result, it can be expected that for many new immigrants, acculturation rather than assimilation may be the major sign of social integration.

In the first phase of immigration, newcomers are likely to live in ethnic residential neighborhoods and participate in ethnic economies for employment. However, as changes in social class, social mobility and residential mobility occur, immigrants are likely to become integrated into the mainstream American society. As stated in a report by the National Research Council on the New Americans, "With the notable exception of Mexican immigrants, the geographic concentration of most immigrant groups is not great, especially compared with geographic segregation among black Americans. The available evidence also indicates that geographic segregation weakens as later generations succeed the immigrant generation" (Smith & Edmonston, 1997). Increasing rates of intermarriage suggest that immigrants are becoming integrated into American society, leading to ethnic identity becoming voluntary rather than automatic. (Illustrative examples of ways in which social integration occurs for new immigrants have been provided in Chapter 8 in the discussion of the emergence of ethnic/cultural neighborhoods and in Chapter 11 in relation to new immigrants and the economy.)

Chapter 14 Review

Social integration of local communities and their residents is a sign of a competent community. The focus of this chapter was on the major sources of integration of residents in a local community. Social integration is facilitated by social networks and involvement of individuals with family members, kin, friends, neighbors, co-workers, and social groups. Members of social networks come from a variety of local communities, such as neighborhoods, community areas, and municipalities, as well as from communities of interest. Voluntary associations, serving as communities of interest and identification, contribute to the social integration of individuals into geographic communities. An important voluntary association is the religious organization, through which social integration is generated by means of religious services, volunteer activities in social welfare, and educational programs.

It is clear that social integration usually comes from involvement and ties to "multiple communities" of place and interest, and that for many residents the importance of some of these communities has diminished due to the emergence of a "mass society." Thus, for many people the neighborhood no longer plays as strong an integrative role as it did in the past. At the same time, other community organizations continue to serve as avenues for social integration, such as school systems, ethnic minority organizations, and religious groups. Less obvious sources of social integration have been identified, including drinking and eating establishments, sports participation and spectatorship, and business and entertainment neighborhoods and enclaves.

The integration and reintegration of special populations in American communities is of particular concern to human service professionals. Persons with mental and physical disabilities, ex-offenders, unemployed persons, and the homeless stand out among these populations, especially when there are negative attitudes toward these individuals on the part of neighborhood and local community residents. Human service professionals in health and social welfare service agencies, as well as in housing and income maintenance programs, have developed community-based programs and services for these special client groups.

15

Communities and
Social Work Practice

This final chapter highlights some important topics that are helpful in explaining how communities function in American society. We encourage the social worker to continue to think about how knowledge of communities can assist in carrying out the purposes of social work. This knowledge is particularly relevant to two specific purposes of social work: (1) "The promotion, restoration, maintenance, and enhancement of the social functioning of individuals, families, groups, organizations, and communities by helping them to accomplish tasks, prevent and alleviate distress, and use resources"; (2) "The pursuit of policies, services, resources, and programs through organizational or administrative advocacy and social or political action, to empower groups at risk and to promote social and economic justice" (Council on Social Work Education, 1992).

For the student in social work education, this summary will assist in exploring how the information presented in this text may be integrated into other parts of the professional foundation curriculum, including social work values and ethics, diversity, social and economic justice, populations at risk, human behavior and the social environment, social welfare policy and services, social work practice, research, and field practicum (CSWE, 1992). The primary focus of the book is on knowledge that will contribute to an understanding of human behavior and the social environment, especially knowledge about communities as an important part of the range of social systems in which individuals live (families, groups, organizations, institutions, and communities). The reader should reflect upon how the knowledge presented about communities gives attention to "the impact of social and economic forces on individuals and social systems" and "the ways in which systems promote or deter people in maintaining or achieving optimal health and well being" (CSWE, 1992).

In regard to social work values and ethics, the reader should identify knowledge that will help promote the principles that "Social workers are committed to assisting client systems to obtain needed resources," and "Social workers demonstrate respect for and acceptance of the unique characteristics of diverse populations." The reader should be alert to principles involving communities of interest and identification, especially with regard to service with diverse populations, such as groups distinguished by race, ethnicity, culture, class, gender, sexual orientation, religion, physical or mental ability, age, and national origin. The reader should give attention to discussions in the text that deal with the impact of discrimination, economic deprivation, and oppression on these groups as populations-at-risk, and the role of communities in the pursuit of individual and collective social and economic justice (CSWE, 1992).

THE SOCIETAL CONTEXT OF COMMUNITIES

Local communities of place and of identification/interest exist within, and have interactions and interdependencies with, national and global social systems. There is general recognition that globalization affects vulnerable populations within American society and its local communities, especially those populations affected by social welfare and health policies and benefits. Consequently, social workers need to give special consideration to the economic profiles of local communities, exploring how the national and international communities affect the nature of work, employment opportunities, and economic and social justice for residents in local municipalities and metropolitan areas.

Our discussion of American society emphasizes the fact that local communities operate within larger social systems, i.e., a national society and a worldwide global system. The American national society provides a most influential context for the functioning of the various subsystems of local communities examined in the text, including health and social welfare, education, economic, and political systems, since similar systems exist at the societal level. The nature of American society as a national culture—that is, what it is and what it should be—continues to be an issue. Communitarians assert that a national community exists with shared values in terms of identity, history, and culture. This conception of American society as a community of communities poses the question of how the unity of the national community can be maintained in the presence of diversity and pluralism of population groups within the nation and its local communities.

One view of the United States is that it is a multicultural society, with a number of equal subcultures based on characteristics such as race, ethnicity, religion, and national origin. Another perspective recognizes the pluralistic nature of the nation as well as the influence of a dominant, mainstream American culture. This second perspective asserts that American citizens have multiple identities and belong to multiple communities within a national community, holding layered loyalties to these communities. A central issue of this perspective concerns the need for acceptance and equal opportunity for people of color and other cultural groups in order for them to participate in the political and economic institutions of mainstream American culture. The social worker will find identification and discussion of issues about multiculturalism in relation to social work practice in De Anda (1997), *Controversial Issues in Multiculturalism*; Ewalt et al. (1996), *Multicultural Issues in Social Work*; and Fellin (2000), "Revisiting Multiculturalism in Social Work."

The concept of a civil society has direct relevance for communities of place and identification/interest because such a society involves the roles of citizenship in civil engagement and voluntarism at the local community level. Our discussion of a civil society emphasizes the fact that the civic condition of local communities is a measure of the health of a civil society. Thus, a National Commission on Civic Renewal (1998) emphasized the responsibilities of citizens in overcoming the civic ills of American society, expressing the belief that "democratic citizenship must be nurtured in institutions such as families, neighborhoods, schools, faith communities, local governments, and political movements." Social workers can extend their knowledge about American democracy and the elements of a civil society by reading *Civil Engagements in American Democracy*, edited by Skocpol and Fiorina (2000). This book examines patterns of civic engagement in the United States in terms of the influence of social groups, government, and electoral politics on the society. Attention is given to the impact of advocacy groups and socioeconomic inequalities on democratic processes, voluntary associations, and civic participation.

Closely related to the idea of a civil society is the question of how social order and social control are maintained within a national society,
and how the mechanisms for achieving social order affect local communities. A principal issue in this regard concerns the extent to which
the national and local communities can balance rights and autonomy
with the need to avoid anarchy and to maintain social order. Within
this context, social and economic justice are identified as goals of American society. Attention is given to how social movements are able to
respond to discrimination and oppression of specific groups in their efforts to promote justice. An important issue in regard to these groups,
such as people of color, is how American society relies on law and law
enforcement for maintaining social order, through the courts, legislation, and the criminal justice system. This issue is examined in Chapter
12 in our discussion of the U.S. criminal and juvenile justice system
within the society and local communities.

Illustrations of American society as a social system are provided
from ecological and social systems perspectives. The influence of the
social structures of American society on local communities is examined in Chapter 1 by reference to the functioning of the federal government and the relationships between federal, state, and local
governments. A salient issue in this regard is the extent to which laws
and courts at the federal level have powers and jurisdiction over state
and local community governments. Issues related to the activities of
the U.S. Bureau of the Census focus on the demographics of American society and its communities, and how the collection of census data
can overcome problems of undercount and the definitional problems
related to racial and ethnic self-identification.

AMERICAN SOCIETY AS A WELFARE STATE

A feature of American society that is most closely connected to the
profession of social work is the combination of health and social welfare policies, programs, and services of the nation that make up a welfare state. The goal of this welfare state is to create a condition of social
welfare that "exists when families, communities and societies experience a high degree of social well-being" (Midgley, 1995). Social workers play important roles in the American welfare state, roles specified
in the profession's Code of Ethics (NASW, 1997) in relation to promoting "social, economic, political, and cultural values and institutions
that are compatible with the realization of social justice." A continuing
issue in a welfare state is the extent to which the provision of social
assistance and health care is carried out by the private, corporate, or

public sectors of the society. These relationships are in large part influenced by the political and economic systems of the nation, systems that are influenced in turn by the ideologies of the American people along a continuum of conservatism to liberalism. A key question noted in our discussion of the welfare state is, "What is an appropriate role for the national government, vis à vis state and local governments, in social welfare?" especially in regard to financing and delivery of social and health programs. The Personal Responsibility and Work Opportunity Reconciliation Act of 1996 provides a focal point for discussion of this question. The Medicare and Medicaid programs of the Social Security Act, and the various forms of managed health care, illustrate the role of the federal government in the health care system of the welfare state.

Of special interest to social workers is the issue of what the American welfare state will be, or should be like in the future. Trends and proposals regarding the future of the welfare state are explored in terms of an "enabling welfare state," a "reluctant welfare state," "welfare reform," and "welfare capitalism." These forms of a welfare state are described briefly in the text, but should be explored more fully by the reader through the excellent books on the topic cited in Chapter 2. As we have noted, it is difficult to predict the future of the federal welfare state and to determine its impact on states, counties, districts, and municipalities of the United States. However, it is clear that the future of the American welfare state is intertwined in the political economy of the nation, one that relies heavily on the values of the American people that support health and social welfare policies and programs, as well as the rights and responsibilities of citizens and the roles of private/voluntary and corporate sectors of the society.

DEFINING COMMUNITIES AND COMMUNITY COMPETENCE

Communities have traditionally been viewed as locality-based, geographic entities that provide residents with sustenance, social interaction, and collective identity. A definitional issue related to social work practice concerns the need for expansion of the meaning of the concept of community. Thus, we introduce the idea of multiple communities, including not only the several geographic areas clients may belong to (neighborhoods, community areas, municipalities, and metropolitan areas), but "non-place" communities of identification and interest as well. This discussion leads to the concept of a personal community, which includes all of the interactions and identifications a person has with individuals, informal groups, and formal organizations through membership in multiple communities.

The concept of a personal community serves as a context for the development of clinical treatment and social service goals in the interpersonal practice of social work. From this perspective, to be effective the social worker must ascertain the nature of the client's membership in multiple communities. For the practice of social work at community and/or administrative levels, recognition of these multiple communities provides a comprehensive focus for community organizing, community planning, and social policy development. Thus, reformulations of the concept of community are related to both micro and macro social work practice, since practice at both levels seeks to mobilize informal and formal resources on behalf of individuals, families, and other groups in need of service. Consulting a special issue of *Social Work* (1997, vol. 42, issue 5) on "Revitalization of Impoverished Communities" will provide the social worker with an understanding of a range of comprehensive community-building strategies that relate to our discussion of multiple communities.

The extent to which communities function well for the benefit of their membership is captured by the concept of community competence. Community organizers, planners, and policy makers involve themselves in identifying the problems, needs, and interests of communities, in working to foster competence, and in creating conditions that lead to a positive social environment. One of these conditions that has particular relevance for populations at risk is empowerment, defined as the capacity to use existing resources and to create opportunities for self and group fulfillment. An empowerment perspective related to communities will assist social workers in meeting their professional responsibilities to society. For example, the social work profession's Code of Ethics calls upon social workers to assist in reducing the barriers to community competence, to improve social conditions, and to promote social justice, especially for special population groups that historically have been subjected to oppression and discrimination. Social work practice issues regarding empowerment and special population groups can be explored in more depth by reading Gutierrez and Lewis (1999), *Empowering Women of Color*; Gutierrez et al. (1997), *Empowerment in Social Work Practice*; and Icard et al. (1999), "Empowering Lesbian and Bisexual Women of Color."

Chapter 4 gives special attention to communities distinguished by social class, people of color, white ethnic groups, religious groups, gay groups, groups of persons with disabilities, and women's groups. Social work practice can be informed by an understanding of the barriers to community competence that come from the values, attitudes, and practices of citizens and institutions toward these identificational communities. Culturally competent social work practice requires that professionals recognize the barriers and limitations imposed upon at-risk populations by the community, its organizations, and its social institutions. These barriers are often expressed by using the terms *racism, sexism, homophobia, ableism, anti-Semitism, classism,* and *ageism.*

SYSTEMS PERSPECTIVES FOR UNDERSTANDING COMMUNITIES

Ecological Perspective

A principal issue related to understanding communities centers around the lack of fully developed theoretical perspectives of community structure and function. Although the nature of communities does not allow for a perfect match to ecological and social systems theories, these perspectives provide a useful set of concepts to guide social work practice. Of special relevance to social workers is the focus of the ecological perspective on the spatial organization of the community—that is, the characteristics, distribution, and interdependence of the population and services in a locality-based community. This perspective can be used to explore the demographic development and social stratification of communities, with special attention to social class, race and ethnicity, migration and immigration.

The demographic changes that have occurred within inner-city neighborhoods of major metropolitan areas have special significance for social work practice. Residents in these areas are viewed as needing a wide range of health and social welfare services, many of which are provided through social programs staffed by social workers. Articles by Wilson (1989) on "The Underclass: Issues, Perspectives, and Public Policy" and Coulton, Pandey, and Chow (1990), "Concentration of Poverty and the Changing Ecology of Low-income, Urban Neighborhoods" can serve as a foundation for considering the practice roles of social workers in relation to residents of urban inner-city communities. It is recommended that the social worker focus on the needs of the residents in these communities who are dislocated from mainstream society and trapped in an underclass ghetto environment, consider ways in which social workers can intervene to enhance the empowerment of these inner-city residents, and examine practice models that include attention to culturally sensitive interventions with ethnic minorities in these neighborhood communities.

The ecological perspective of communities guides the social worker in considering various dimensions of neighborhoods in American society, especially those identified with specific social classes and ethnic, racial, and cultural groups. Neighborhood communities may enhance or detract from community and interpersonal competence. The reader is encouraged to consider possible roles for social workers in relation to neighborhood associations and residents in changing the social conditions of the neighborhood, particularly drug trafficking, school problems, lack of safety, and the lack of social services. Journal articles by Queralt and Witte (1998a, 1998b, 1999) provide an understanding of social mapping and geographic information systems. These articles include illustrations of how maps can be developed with regard to social work practice in areas with high levels of child poverty, and how the maps can be used to assess public assistance and child care center capacities in a given area. Queralt and Witte demonstrate that "by mapping the location of problems of concern in specific localities, one can develop a service strategy that is sensitive to the needs of the community."

Social Systems Perspective

The social systems perspective contributes to our understanding of the competence of a community by focusing on the extent to which the various subsystems of a community meet the functional needs of residents. This view of a locality-based community is particularly salient to social work practice, as one of the major community subsystems is social welfare and health care. However, social workers may also play significant roles in the political, economic, and educational subsystems of a community. A major issue of social work practice involves how well the social welfare and health care systems operate in a given geographic community, and to what extent their interdependencies with other subsystems result in a competent community. The ideas proposed by Norton Long (1958) in "Community as an ecology of games" can help us examine how social workers might use this framework to examine professional leadership roles in local community subsystems. This perspective can be used to examine the health and welfare "game" in relation to other "games" being played in a local community, considering how this approach gives direction to strategies for community change.

DEMOGRAPHIC DEVELOPMENT OF COMMUNITIES

The population size, density, and diversity of local metropolitan, municipal, and neighborhood communities change over time. Achieving an understanding of these demographic features of communities is enhanced by use of data from the U.S. Bureau of the Census. Of special interest to social workers is the composition of communities in terms of diversity, measured by demographic factors such as social class, race, ethnicity, religion, family composition, age, and gender. Census data not only provide a description of these factors in communities, but allow for the study of the development of communities over time. These data can be used to study community changes such as movements of population groups, patterns of migration, immigration, and population growth dynamics, patterns of residential segregation and integration, patterns of social stratification, land use, and the impact of technological forces on communities. An important issue with regard to the Census is the problem of undercount of children, renters, racial and ethnic minorities, and new immigrants. Special efforts were made by the Census Bureau to overcome the undercount problem for the 2000 census. When there is an undercount of ethnic minorities and new immigrants, the communities in which these groups live are disadvantaged in terms of distribution of federal and state funding, eligibility for health and social welfare programs, and the determination of political boundaries.

Our discussion of demographic changes in communities considers the impact of urban sprawl and the emergence of "edge cities" at the fringe of central city and suburban areas on residents of these areas and on the employment opportunities of people in central cities, especially people of color and female-headed households. The growth of these "edge cities" and of small towns and rural communities raises the issue of how residents can create and maintain social integration into their communities, while at the same time benefiting from interchanges with other communities and the broader society. Some of the problems of a lack of various forms of capital in these communities are also found in inner-city poverty neighborhoods. Acquiring an understanding of the potential for economic and social development in these increasingly segregated neighborhoods is of particular relevance for social work practice in high-poverty areas. This topic can be explored further by reading Midgley and Livermore (1998), "Social Capital and Local Economic Development," and Fellin (1998), "Development of Capital in Poor, Inner-City Neighborhoods."

STRATIFICATION BY SOCIAL CLASS

Individuals, households, and communities can be distinguished by characteristics of occupation, income, education, and lifestyles that are commonly referred to in terms of socioeconomic status (SES) or social class. Membership in a social class is related to access to and control over resources involving one's life chances, lifestyle, and quality of life. Hence, social workers need to understand the social class system in local communities, as well as the impact of social class on individuals and social groups. Several aspects of social class, especially in terms of inequalities, are of particular concern to social workers, such as downward occupational and social mobility, movement from a working class into an underclass, restrictions on mobility from an underclass into a working class, and the location of people of color in the class structure.

Our discussion of the location of members of ethnic minority groups in the American class structure highlights the fact that each specific group constitutes a non-dominant class location in relation to prestige, power, and privilege by comparison to the white majority population.

NEIGHBORHOOD COMMUNITIES

The significance of neighborhood communities for the psychosocial development of individuals and families depends in part on the characteristics of these communities. Renewed emphasis in social work practice on the neighborhood as a geographic area and a primary group for residents is related to recognition of the potential of these communities as a source of connections for residents, including social, functional, cultural, and circumstantial connections. For an in-depth examination of these connections, the reader should consult Chaskin (1997), "Perspectives on Neighborhood and Community." Neighborhood community social interactions and connections can provide a basis for creating primary group relationships, for organizational formation and participation, for acquiring resources for daily living, and for developing a collective identity and sense of community. Social workers can play active roles in neighborhoods that fail to provide residents with these opportunities and resources, especially through community building that involves practice strategies of social planning, community social and economic development, community organizing, social action, and empowerment practice. Increasingly, neighborhood communities provide the location for community-based services for people with special needs, such as people with mental and physical disabilities, ex-offenders, older adults, and people living in poverty.

Our presentation of neighborhood types in Chapter 7 is intended to provide the social worker with a conceptual framework for assessing the strengths and weaknesses of neighborhood communities for individuals, families, and social groups. For example, Figueira-McDonough's (1995) neighborhood types reported in "Community Organization and the Underclass" can be used to guide the social worker in assessing the extent to which informal and organizational resources for youth exist in underclass poverty neighborhoods. Figueira-McDonough's neighborhood types and research findings suggest practice strategies that involve collaboration between organizers in a number of underclass neighborhoods. These strategies focus on finding and developing resources, e.g., seeking to develop human and social capital among residents through community development.

SOCIAL CLASS AND ETHNIC/CULTURAL COMMUNITIES

Traditional bases for describing neighborhood communities are social class, ethnicity, culture, and religion. Changes of the proportion of residents in a neighborhood community classified by one or more of these characteristics are often viewed as involving processes of white flight, segregation, integration, and/or succession.

Neighborhoods usually display both the characteristics of communities of place and of identification/interest, so that for the residents, the neighborhood is a spatial as well as a sociopsychological community. Illustrative case examples of social class and ethnic/cultural neighborhoods are provided in Chapter 8 as a basis for examining the creation and maintenance of residential integration and segregation. Attention is also given to the residential patterns of a widely diverse population of new immigrants, including examples of the suburbanization of new immigrants into ethnic enclaves. The changing residential patterns of members of the gay community are cited to illustrate the enclave model of gay neighborhoods and the suburbanization of gay people. Abrahamson (1996) describes this model in *Urban Enclaves: Identity and Place in America.*

COMMUNITY SOCIAL WELFARE AND HEALTH CARE SYSTEMS

Mutual support is provided within a community by formal human service organizations and by a variety of other social support systems, such as family, kin, neighbors, friends, and voluntary associations. Mutual support functions are shared by public and private formal organizations and by informal helping systems. An important question concerning these shared functions involves who takes responsibility for the care of people who cannot care for themselves. The public sectors of social welfare and health care have been delegated some responsibilities through local, state, and federal government legislation, policies and practices, but the private/voluntary sector is increasingly involved in the delivery of health and social services.

Social workers who practice at community, administrative, and policy levels can apply their knowledge of communities to the generation of a wide range of resources, from volunteers to fiscal resources. In our examination of the various fields of social welfare services, we noted that the delivery of services is influenced by the functioning of social workers in both direct service and planning agencies. A basic understanding of community subsystems is necessary for social workers to successfully engage in inter-organizational relations, through activities within communities, as well as through the extra-community political and economic environment. Social workers can enhance the competent functioning of the social welfare and health care systems by advocating for community supports, qualified personnel, and development of institutional responses to the needs of local residents. As social workers participate in these systems, they are in a position to advocate for special populations at risk, such as people of color, families and children in poverty, homeless people, and mentally or physically disabled people. Readings relevant to social work practice with these population groups include Mackelprang and Salsgiver (1996), "People with Disabilities and Social Work"; Segal et al. (1993), "Empowerment in Self-Help Agency Practice"; and Rivera and Erlich (1998), *Community Organizing in a Diverse Society.*

COMMUNITY EDUCATIONAL SYSTEM

One of the principal indicators of a competent community is the functioning of the local educational system. Using Long's (1958) view of the community as an ecology of games, there are a number of ways in which residents and professionals can "keep score" concerning how well the community educational system is functioning. Important indicators include test scores, dropout rates, graduation rates, student per capita funding, and quality of teachers. An important issue with regard to community educational systems concerns the discrepancies between communities in terms of funding and student performance, especially in relation to the quality of education provided in inner-city schools within poverty neighborhoods compared to schools in suburban communities. The financing of public education and the quality of education in central city schools are directly related to support for voucher programs. Issues related to vouchers are discussed in Chapter 10, especially in regard to educational opportunities for youth in inner-city poverty neighborhoods, and to the controversial church-state issue of use of vouchers by students to attend religious-based schools.

School reform refers to a variety of efforts to improve the public school system. Such efforts include voucher programs, standards-based curriculum, educational accountability, and programs to overcome achievement gaps between white students and students of color and between advantaged and disadvantaged students. School choice programs, including charter schools, are one of the most popular and most controversial approaches to school reform. The rapid growth of charter schools has been supported by federal funds, state legislation, and many local community school districts. The emergence of charter schools and taxpayer-financed voucher programs highlights the fact that public education is being redefined under school reforms. Public education is being expanded to include "any school that is open to the public, receives public dollars, and is accountable to public authorities for results" (Olson, 2000).

As noted in Chapter 10, social work services provided in public schools by professional social workers have been influenced by federal legislation related to children with special educational needs. As a result of this legislation, social workers have been involved in school efforts to provide full educational opportunities for children with disabilities through an "inclusion" movement. The social worker can learn about the shifting roles of social workers in response to the call for inclusive education by reading the work of Pryor et al. (1996), "Redesigning Social Work in Inclusive Schools." At the same time, school social workers serve all students, particularly in regard to high-risk children, family education, case management, and service evaluation. In order to carry out these activities, school social workers need to understand the educational subsystem of the local community and its interdependence with other community subsystems, especially economic and political systems. For example, one of the elements of school reform has been to promote linkages of services provided in the public schools to human services and other resources in the local community. Social work practice approaches for such linkages are discussed in the work of Franklin and Streeter (1995), "School Reform: Linking Public Schools with Human Services," and of Dupper and Poertner (1997), "Public Schools and the Revitalization of Impoverished Communities: School-Linked, Family Resource Centers."

THE COMMUNITY ECONOMIC SYSTEM

The practice of social work is connected to the economic system in a variety of ways. As we discussed in Chapter 9, social welfare and health care programs are a part of the economic system, providing income and other benefits to eligible community residents. These programs provide economic benefits for families and children, and for people who are retired, unemployed, and/or disabled. Social workers play important roles in the delivery of these welfare and health care services. Increasingly, social workers are employed in workplaces, are involved in employee assistance programs, and have practice roles related to emerging programs under the Americans with Disabilities Act of 1990. Social workers in direct service agencies work with clients who have problems related to the economic system, such as discriminatory hiring practices, unemployment, need for job training, sexual harassment, and entitlements related to disabilities. A basic understanding of the community economic system is especially necessary for social workers who are active in community organizing, service planning, and resource development in economically disadvantaged neighborhood communities. Social workers may be involved in the development of economic policies and programs, as well as delivery of services, in community development enterprise and empowerment zone areas. Social work practice applications at the community level are illustrated in Page-Adams and Sherraden (1997), "Asset Building as a Community Revitalization Strategy."

THE COMMUNITY POLITICAL SYSTEM

In most communities the representation of social workers in political positions, such as elected officials, city or county council members, is minimal. However, social workers develop contacts with elected officials in order to influence the political system in providing resources for meeting social welfare and health care needs. Social workers in elected and appointed positions within the political structure, as well as social welfare agency executives, are in strategic positions for seeking support of social welfare programs from other community leaders. A discussion of the role of social workers in the political system appears in Reisch (1997), "The Political Context of Social Work." Our discussion of the community political system in Chapter 12 alerts the social worker to important sources of support for social welfare programs, including political and economic system leaders, as well as leaders in grassroots organizations and voluntary associations, particularly neighborhood, ethnic, and religious organizations.

Our view of community power from an organizational perspective is relevant to the practice of social work at community and organizational levels. Although individual social welfare organizations may have limited community influence, membership of such agencies in community decision-making organizations such as United Way, agency coalitions, and national organization affiliations, increases the opportunities for gaining support within the political system. Influence on the part of clients of the social welfare system is gained through empowerment, a process that can be facilitated by social workers, especially in their work with populations at risk. An understanding of power perspectives is necessary for carrying out a "power analysis" in local communities as a basis for enhancing personal, interpersonal, and political power of residents. Examples are provided in Chapter 12 of community empowerment of African Americans, new immigrants, and members of the gay community. Finally, Chapter 12 includes an extensive discussion of the criminal justice system as it functions within the community political system. Problems related to this system and community responses to these problems are examined, especially in relation to discrimination, hate crimes, and family/youth/workplace violence.

COMMUNITY CONFLICT AND COMMUNITY INTEGRATION

Several examples of community conflict discussed in Chapter 13 are relevant to the practice of social work, such as controversies over community-based treatment centers, urban redevelopment, homeless shelters, and group homes for mentally and physically disabled persons. The implications of these controversies for social work practice are discussed in terms of the social integration needs of consumers of social welfare, health, and mental health services. On this point, the reader is directed to the article, "Reformulation of the Context of Community-Based Care" (Fellin, 1993), which focuses on planning for community-based care for mentally ill persons. This discussion explores various levels of social integration and their relationship to social work intervention at the community level. Efforts on the part of residents and human service professionals to achieve goals of social integration for these individuals, as well as persons from the criminal justice system, children and youth with developmental disabilities, and homeless people, have been met with barriers such as protective zoning ordinances, neighborhood opposition, and social rejection by neighbors.

Chapter 14 emphasizes that the social integration of local communities and their residents is a sign of a competent community. Thus, we consider major sources of integration into geographic and identificational communities, such as social networks, voluntary associations, and faith-based groups. The reader will find a useful discussion of "Multicultural Community Organizing: A Strategy for Change" (Gutierrez, 1997) as a social work practice approach that builds on strengths, and deals with conflicts, in ethnically, culturally, and racially diverse communities. Such practice recognizes that social integration comes from ties to multiple communities of place and interest. An important role for social workers is engagement in professional activities that strengthen the integration and solidarity of community groups, social welfare programs, and voluntary associations, so that they become significant sources of well-being through the generation of resources and community attachment.

References

AAUW (American Association of University Women). (1993). Hostile hallways: The AAUW survey on sexual harassment in American schools. Washington, DC: Harris/Scholastic Research.

Abelson, R. (1999a, July 14). Study finds diversity programs ineffective at getting women minorities to the top. New York Times.

Abelson, R. (1999b, August 3). If Wall Street is a dead end, do women stay and fight or go quietly? New York Times.

Abrahamson, M. (1996). Urban enclaves: Identity and place in America. New York: St. Martin's.

Abrams, E. (1997). Faith or fear: How Jews can survive in a Christian America. New York: Free Press.

ADAMHA (Alcohol, Drug Abuse, and Mental Health Administration). (1980). Problems of the homeless. Rockville, MD: ADAMHA.

Adler, L., & Gardner, S. (Eds.). (1994). The politics of linking schools and social services. Washington, DC: Falmer.

Alba, R. D., Logan, J. R., & Stults, B. J. (1999, June). Immigrant groups in the suburbs: A reexamination of suburbanization and spatial assimilation. American Sociological Review, 64.

Allen-Meares, P., Washington, R. O., & Welsh, B. L. (1996). Social work services in the schools (2nd ed). Boston: Allyn & Bacon.

Allen-Meares, P., Washington, R. O., & Welsh, B. L. (2000). Social work services in the schools (3rd ed.). Boston: Allyn & Bacon.

Andersen, K. (1999, September 6). Pleasantville: Can Disney reinvent the 'burbs? New Yorker.

Anderson, R. E., Carter, I., & Lowe, G. R. (1999). Human behavior in the social environment (5th ed.). New York: Aldine de Gruyter.

Anderton, F. (1998, August 9). The Conga room: Where Nuevo Los Angeles is converging. New York Times.

Andrews, A. C., & Fonseca, J. W. (1995). The atlas of American society. New York: New York University.

Applebome, P. (1997, April 8). Schools see re-emergence of "separate but equal." New York Times.

Archibold, R. C. (1998, March 16). Charter schools said to raise pupils' performance on tests. *New York Times*.

Arrendondo, P. (1996). *Successful diversity management initiatives*. Thousand Oaks, CA: Sage.

Associated Press. (1998a, October 23). Clinton signs charter school act. *New York Times*.

Associated Press. (1998b, October 29). Tampa schools fail to end desegregation order. *New York Times*.

Associated Press. (1998c, November 17). HUD to study housing discrimination. *New York Times*.

Associated Press. (1999a, April 9). Social Security found to save third of elderly from poverty. *New York Times*.

Associated Press. (1999b, June 19). Immigrants seek secret medical care. *New York Times*.

Associated Press. (1999c, June 22). Court limits reach of disabilities law.

Associated Press. (1999d, July 16). Clinton announces development grants.

Associated Press. (1999e, October 4). California moves to extend gay rights with new laws. *New York Times*.

Associated Press. (1999f, October 13). Indians get $89M to fight crime. *New York Times*.

Associated Press. (1999g, October 21). Ohio appeals voucher ruling. *New York Times*.

Associated Press. (1999h, November 11). Oklahoma textbooks to carry evolution disclaimer.

Associated Press. (1999i, December 2). WTO protest issues.

Associated Press. (1999j, December 3). States cutting welfare rolls awarded. *New York Times*.

Associated Press. (1999k, May 24). Schools may be sued for student-on-student harassment. *New York Times*.

Associated Press. (1999l, December 9). Women gaining state leadership posts. *New York Times*.

Astor, R. (1995). School violence: A blueprint for elementary school interventions. *Social Work in Education, 17*.

Auerbach, J. (1985). The Poletown dilemma. *Harvard Business Review, 63*(3).

Babington, C. (1999a, July 6). Clinton urges corporate investment to fight pockets of poverty. *Washington Post*.

Babington, C. (1999b, November 5). Clinton encourages rural investment. *Washington Post*.

Bacon, K. H. (1993, January 19). Inner-city capitalists push to start a bank for their community. *Wall Street Journal*.

Bailey, E. (1997, October 12). Welfare reform gives rise to commuting dilemma. *Los Angeles Times*.

Baker, D. P. (1999, February 27). Patients' Bill of Rights approved in Virginia. *Washington Post*.

Bank, D. (2000, March 3). A big donation for gay rights puts executive in the spotlight. *Wall Street Journal*.

Banner, R. (1999, September 15). Study finds programs in schools can curb violence among young. *New York Times*.

Barbarin, O., Tyler, F., & Gatz, M. (Eds.). (1981). *Institutional racism and community competence*. College Park. MD: University of Maryland.

Barker, R. L. (1992). *Social work in private practice* (2nd ed). Washington, DC: NASW Press.

Barker, R. L. (1995a). *The social work dictionary* (3rd ed.). Washington, DC: U.S. Government Printing Office.

Barker, R. L. (1995b). Private practice. In the *Encyclopedia of Social Work* (19th ed). Washington, DC: NASW.

Barr, S. (1999, October 17). Agencies told to recruit disabled. *Washington Post*.

Barrett, P. M. (1993a, April 1). Justices ease rules on school desegregation. *Wall Street Journal*.

Barrett, P. M. (1993b, June 8). School policy on religion is struck down. *Wall Street Journal*.

Barrett, P. M. (1993c, June 21). Court's ruling on help for deaf student cheers backers of parochial-school aid. *Wall Street Journal*.

Barringer, F. (1991, June 12). Immigration brings new diversity to Asian population in the U.S. *New York Times*.

Barron, J. (1990, October). The social whirl. *Detroit Monthly*.

Barstow, D. (1999a, June 1). Annual new-money plague descends upon celebrity-mad Hamptons. *New York Times*.

Barstow, D. (1999b, August 26). Harlem politicians turn against a planned rally for black youth. *New York Times*.

Barstow, D. (1999c, September 1). Rebuking Giuliani, U.S. judge orders permit for rally. *New York Times*.

Battistich, V., & Hom, A. (1999). The relationship between students' sense of their school as a community and their involvement in problem behaviors. *American Journal of Public Health, 87*(12).

Beaulieu, L. J., & Mulkey, D. (Eds.). (1992). *Investing in people: The human capital needs of rural America*. Boulder, CO: Westview Press.

Belluck, P. (1998, September 6). Razing the slums to rescue the residents. *New York Times*.

Berendt, J. (1999). *The Celebration chronicles*. New York: Ballantine.

Berger, J. (1993, July 28). For many Hispanic immigrants, a search for opportunities skirts the cities. *New York Times*.

Berger, J. (1997, January 12). Growing pains for a rural Hasidic enclave. *New York Times*.

Berger, J. (1998, February 25). "Ragtime" to rich mosaic in diverse New Rochelle. *New York Times*.

Bernstein, N. (1999, November 8). Homeless are impoverished and ill, survey finds. *New York Times*.

Betancourt, H. L., & Lopez, S. R. (1993). The study of culture, ethnicity, and race in American psychology. *American Psychologist, 48*(6).

Biskupic, J. (1998, December 1). Little to count on after census hearing. *Washington Post*.

Biskupic, J. (1999, October 12). Court refuses to hear vouchers case. *Washington Post*.

Blau, J. (1989, March). Theories of the welfare state. *Social Service Review*.

Bleakley, R. R. (1992, September 22). How groups pressured one bank to promise more inner-city loans. *Wall Street Journal*.

Blume, J. (1999, October 22). Is Harry Potter evil? *New York Times*.

Bonjean, C., & Olson, D. (1966). Community leadership. In R. Warren (Ed.), *New perspectives on the American community*. Chicago: Rand McNally.

Borgatta, E. F., & Borgatta, M. L. (1992). *Encyclopedia of sociology*. New York: Macmillan.

Boris, E. (1999). The nonprofit sector in the 1990s. In C. T. Clotfelter & T. Ehrlich (Eds.), *Philanthropy and the nonprofit sector in a changing America*. Bloomington, IN: Indiana University Press.

Borjas, G. J. (1999). *Heaven's Door: Immigration policy and the American economy.* Princeton, NJ: Princeton University Press.

Bragg, R. (1999, October 21). Fearful of isolation in retirement, gay generation is seeking havens. *New York Times.*

Brandwein, R. A. (1995). Change for social justice. In D. A. Gil & E. A. Gil (Eds.), *Toward social and economic justice.* Cambridge, MA: Schenkman.

Branigin, W. (1999, March 9). "Chilling effects" seen from welfare reform. *Washington Post.*

Brawarsky, S. (2000, March 17). Finding camaraderie in the music of mahjongg tiles. *New York Times.*

Bredemeier, K. (1999, May 26). Serving up a medley of cultures. *Washington Post.*

Brilliant, E. L. (1997). Nonprofit organizations, social policy, and public welfare. In M. Reisch & E. Gambrill (Eds.), *Social work in the 21st century.* Thousand Oaks, CA: Pine Forge.

Bronner, E. (1999, June 13). Study finds resegregation in U.S. Schools. *New York Times.*

Brooke, J. (1999, November 19). Equity case in Canada seen as redress for women. *New York Times.*

Brown, M. K. (1999). *Race, money, and the welfare state.* Ithaca, NY: Cornell University Press.

Brown, D. (1999, October 8). Officials urge broader flu, pneumonia immunization. *Washington Post.*

Browne, I. (Ed.). (1999). *Latinas and African American women at work: Race, gender, and economic inequality.* New York: Russell Sage Foundation.

Brozan, N. (1999, November 12). Groups offer way to teach bible in class. *New York Times.*

Bruni, F. (1999, July 15). Littleton students listen to gun debate, wondering if they have been heard. *New York Times.*

Button, J. W., Wald, K. D., & Frienzo, B. A. (1999). The election of openly gay public officials in American communities. *Urban Affairs Review, 35*(2).

Carelli, R. (1999, May 17). High court limits federal judges on redistricting. Associated Press.

Carlton-LaNey, I. B., Edwards, R. L., & Reid, P. N. (Eds.). (1999). *Preserving and strengthening small towns and rural communities.* Washington, DC: NASW Press.

Cassidy, J. (1995, October 16). Who killed the middle class? *New Yorker.*

Cassidy, J. (1999, October 18). Schools are her business. *New Yorker,* p. 25.

Castle, E. N. (1993). Rural diversity: An American asset. *Annals AAPSS,* p. 529.

Celis, W. (1991, September 4). District finds way to end segregation and restore neighborhood. *New York Times.*

Chafets, Z. (1990). *Devil's night and other true tales of Detroit.* New York: Random House.

Chambers, M. (1998, February 12). Judge rules Martin can use golf cart. *New York Times.*

Chaskin, R. J. (1997). Perspectives on neighborhood and community: A review of the literature. *Social Service Review, 71*(4).

Chelf, C. P. (1992). *Controversial issues in social welfare policy.* Newbury Park: Sage.

Cheng, L., & Yang, P. Q. (1996). Asians: The "model minority" deconstructed. In R. Waldinger & M. Bozorgmehr (Eds.), *Ethnic Los Angeles.* New York: Russell Sage.

Chervokas, J., & Watson, T. (1997, September 5). Internet is nurturing home schooling. *New York Times*.

Chira, S. (1991a, June 12). The rules of the marketplace are applied to the classroom. *New York Times*.

Chira, S. (1991b, September 5). Schools open soon (with luck) to more trouble than usual. *New York Times*.

Choldin, H. M. (1985). *Cities and suburbs.* New York: McGraw-Hill.

Chubb, J. E., & Moe, T. M. (1990). *Politics, markets, and America's schools.* Washington, DC: The Brookings Institution.

Claiborne, W. (1999a, February 15). Violence hits American Indians hard. *Washington Post*.

Claiborne, W. (1999b, March 29). Indian health chief crusades for his people. *Washington Post*.

Claiborne, W. (1999c, March 30). HUD seeks to expand housing aid to Indians. *Washington Post*.

Clotfelter, C. T., & Ehrlich, T. (Eds.). (1999). *Philanthropy and the nonprofit sector in a changing America.* Bloomington, IN: Indiana University Press.

Cloward, R. A., & Piven, F. F. (1999). Disruptive dissensus: People and power in the industrial age. In J. Rothman (Ed.), *Reflections on community organization.* Itasca, IL: Peacock.

Cnaan, R. A. (1997). Recognizing the role of religious congregations and denominations in social service provision. In M. Reisch & E. Gambrill (Eds.), *Social work in the 21st century.* Thousand Oaks, CA: Pine Forge.

Cnaan, R. A. (1998). *Bowling alone but serving together: The congregational norm of community involvement.* Mimeo. Grand Rapids, MI: Calvin College.

Cohn, D'Vera. (1999, July 28). Urban problems, suburban sprawl linked. *Washington Post*.

Cohn, L. M. (1999, April 18). Women business owners assemble. *Detroit Free Press*.

Cole, D. (1999). *No equal justice: Race and class in the American criminal justice system.* New York: New Press.

Coleman, J. (1957). *Community conflict.* New York: Free Press.

Coleman, J. (1983). The dynamics of community conflict. In R. Warren & L. Lyons (Eds.), *New perspectives on the American community.* Homewoood, IL: Dorsey.

Coleman, J. D., Hoffer, T., & Kilgore, S. (1982). *High school achievement.* New York: Basic Books.

Coleman, J. S. (1988). Social capital in the creation of human capital. *American Journal of Sociology, 94.*

Coleman, J. S., & Hoffer, T. (1987). *Public and private high schools.* New York: Basic Books.

Collins, C. (1999. March 21). Some communities span cradle to gray. *New York Times*.

Colman, D. (1998, February 1). New York's gay bars go bourgeoise. *New York Times*.

Constable, R., McDonald, S., & Flynn, J. P. (1999). *School social work.* Chicago: Lyceum.

Cooper, K. J. (1999a, June 2). Vouchers' use for religious schools barred. *Washington Post*.

Cooper, K. J. (1999b, August 17). Higher ed: Department of Education. *Washington Post*.

Cooper, K. J. (1999c, September 16). Education chief: Smaller schools may curb violence. *Washington Post*.

Cooper, K. J. (1999d, October 14). Some schools closing the achievement gap. *Washington Post.*

Cooper, K. J. (1999e, October 22). House rejects school voucher plan, boosts main aid program. *Washington Post.*

Cooper, K. J. (1999f, November 12). Analysis: Federal role in education again expands. *Washington Post.*

Cooper, K. J. (1999g, November 28). Laborers wanted on Long Island, but not at close quarters. *New York Times.*

Cooper, K. J. (2000, Jan. 13). "Best and brightest" leave teaching early, study says. *Washington Post.*

Coser, L. (1956). *The functions of social conflict.* Glencoe, IL: Free Press.

Cottrell, L.S., Jr. (1983). The competent community. In R. Warren & L. Lyon (Eds.), New perspectives on the American community. Homewood, IL: Dorsey.

Coulton, C. J. (1996). Poverty, work, and community: A research agenda for an era of diminishing federal responsibility. *Social Work, 41*(5).

Coulton, C. J., Pandey, S., & Chow, J. (1990). Concentration of poverty and the changing ecology of low income, urban neighborhoods. *Social Work, 26*(4).

Council on Social Work Education. (1992). *Curriculum policy statement.* Alexandria, VA: CSWE.

Crenshaw, A. B. (1999, November 23). Business attacks OSHA rule proposal. *Washington Post.*

Daly, A. (Ed.). (1998). *Workplace diversity issues and perspectives.* Washington, DC: NASW.

Dao, J. (1999a, April 22). Congress passes flexible school-money bill. *New York Times.*

Dao, J. (1999b, December 28). Immigrant diversity slows traditional political climb. *New York Times.*

Data Research. (1988). *Desktop encyclopedia of American school law.* Rosemount, NH: Data Research, Inc.

D'Augelli, A. R., & Garnets, L. D. (1995). Lesbian, gay, and bisexual communities. In A. R. D'Augelli & C. J. Patterson (Eds.), *Lesbian, gay, and bisexual identities over the life-span.* New York: Oxford.

Davidson, J. (1981). Location of community-based treatment centers. *Social Service Review, 55*(2).

Davidson, J. (1982). Balancing required resources and neighborhood opposition in community-based treatment center neighborhoods. *Social Service Review, 56*(1).

Davidson, J. (1986). The urban sociology of community-based treatment: Ignored issues and future concerns. In H. R. Johnson & J. E. Tropman (Eds.), *Social work policy and practice: A knowledge-driven approach.* Ann Arbor, MI: University of Michigan.

De Anda, D. (Ed.). (1997). *Controversial issues in multiculturalism.* Boston: Allyn & Bacon.

Dedman, B. (1999, February 13). Segregation persists despite Fair Housing Act, Chicago study finds. *New York Times.*

De Rothschild, G. (1985). *The whims of fortune.* New York: Random House.

Dershowitz, A. M. (1997). *The vanishing American Jew.* Boston: Little Brown.

Detroit News Special Report. (1999, February 7). The race gap in lending. *Detroit News.*

Devine, J. A., & Wright, J. D. (1993). *The greatest of evils: Urban poverty and the American underclass.* New York: Aldine De Gruyter.

Devore, W., & Schlesinger, E. G. (1996). *Ethnic-sensitive social work practice* (4th ed.). Boston: Allyn & Bacon.

Dixon, J. (1999, March 24). Funds sit unused as residents seek help. *Detroit Free Press*.

Dobelstein, A. W. (1999). *Moral authority, ideology, and the future of American social welfare*. Boulder, CO: Westview Press.

Dobrzynski, J. H. (1996, February 28). Gaps and barriers, and women's careers. *New York Times*.

Dodenhoff, D. (1998). Is welfare really about social control? *Social Service Review, 72*(3).

Dozier, M. (1993, April 23). Fund to boost Oakland integration. *Detroit Free Press*.

Drake, St. C., & Cayton, H. (1945). *Black metropolis: A study of Negro life in a northern city*. New York: Harcourt, Brace, Jovanovich.

Dryze, J. (1996). Political inclusion and the dynamics of Democratization. *American Political Science Review, 90*(1).

Duany, A., Plater-Zyberk, E., & Speck, J. (2000). Suburban nation: The rise of sprawl and the decline of the American dream. New York: North Point.

Duffy, M. (1998, June 29). For gays, a place to call home. *Detroit Free Press*.

Dupper, D. R., & Poertner, J. (1997). Public schools and the revitalization of impoverished communities: School-linked family resource centers. *Social Work, 42*(5).

Eastland, T. (1992, May 14). Weed and seed: Root out crime, nurture poor. *Wall Street Journal*.

Eck, J. E., & Rosenbaum, D. P. (1994). The new police order: Effectiveness, equity, and efficiency in community policing. In D. P. Rosenbaum (Ed.), *The challenge of community policing*. Thousand Oaks, CA: Sage

Edwards, B., & Foley, M. W. (Eds.). (1997). Social capital, civil society, and contemporary democracy. *American Behavioral Scientist, 40*(5).

Edwards, E. D., & Egbert-Edwards, M. (1998). Community development with American Indians and Alaska Natives. In F. G. Rivera & J. L. Erlich (Eds.), Community organizing in a diverse society (3rd ed.). Boston: Allyn & Bacon.

Elazar, D. J. (1995). *Community and polity: The organizational dynamics of American Jewry*. Philadelphia: The Jewish Publication Society.

Elshtain, J. B. (1996, December). Democracy at century's end. *Social Service Review*.

Epstein, A. (1993, June 8). High court allows church groups to hold meetings in public schools. *Detroit Free Press*.

Equal Employment Opportunity Commission. (1980, April 11). Guidelines on discrimination because of sex. Title VII, Sec. 703. *Federal Register, 45*.

Escobar, G. (1999, November 29). Immigration transforms a community. *Washington Post*.

Esping-Andersen, G. (Ed.). (1996). *Welfare states in transition: National adaptations*. Thousand Oaks, CA: Sage.

Etzioni, A. (1992, December 1). Do fence me in. *Wall Street Journal*.

Etzioni, A. (1996a). *The new golden rule*. New York: Basic Books

Etzioni, A. (1996b). The responsive community: A communitarian perspective. *American Sociological Review, 61*(2).

Ewalt, P., Freeman, E. M., Kirk, S. A., & Poole, D. L. (Eds.). (1996). *Multicultural issues in social work*. Washington, DC: NASW Press.

Ewalt, P., Freeman, E. M., & Poole, D. L. (Eds.). (1998). *Community building: Renewal, well-being, and shared responsibility*. Washington, DC: NASW.

Farley, R., & Frey, W. H. (1994). Changes in the segregation of whites from blacks during the 1980s: Small steps toward a more integrated society. *American Sociological Review, 59*(2).

Farney, E. (1992, January 7). Can big money fix urban school systems? A test is under way. *Wall Street Journal.*

Fay, B. (1996). *Contemporary philosophy of social sciences.* Cambridge, UK: Blackwell.

Fein, E. B. (1998, March 18). New York to aid Chinese and Korean-speaking mental patients. *New York Times.*

Fellin, P. (1993). Reformulation of the context of community-based care. *Journal of Sociology and Social Welfare, 20*(2).

Fellin, P. (1996). The culture of homelessness. In P. Manoleas (Ed.), *The cross-cultural practice of clinical case management in mental health.* New York: Haworth Press.

Fellin, P. (1998). Development of capital in poor, inner-city neighborhoods. *Journal of Community Practice, 5*(3).

Fellin, P. (2000). Revisiting multiculturalism in social work. *Journal of Social Work Education* (in press).

Fellin, P., & Litwak, E. (1968). The neighborhood in urban American society. *Social Work, 13,* p. 3.

Felsenthal, E. (1990, October 25). New Jersey's public school financing is struck down by state's highest court. *Wall Street Journal.*

Ferguson, T. W. (1992, December 29). California feels anti-immigrant tremors. *Wall Street Journal.*

Fichen, J. M. (1998). Rural poverty and rural social work. In L. H. Ginsberg (Ed.), *Social work in rural communities* (3rd ed.). Alexandria, VA: CSWE.

Figueira-McDonough, J. (1991). Community structure and delinquency: A typology. *Social Service Review, 65,* p. 1.

Figueira-McDonough, J. (1995, March). Community organization and the underclass: Exploring new practice directions. *Social Service Review.*

Finch, W. A. (1990). The immigration reform and control act of 1986: A preliminary assessment. *Social Service Review, 64,* p. 2.

Finder, A. (1998, September 24). Court backs the Pentagon on gay rights. *New York Times.*

Fineran, S., & Bennett, L. (1999). Peer sexual harassment and the social worker's response. In R. Constable, S. McDonald, & J. P. Flynn (Eds.), *School social work.* Chicago: Lyceum.

Firestone, D. (1999, March 25). Georgia setting up tough anti-sprawl agency. *New York Times.*

Fisher, H. (1999). *The first sex.* New York: Random House.

Fisher, R., & Karger, H. J. (1997). *Social work and community in a private world.* New York: Longman.

Fletcher, M. A. (2000, March 4). Asian Americans coping with success. *Washington Post.*

Fliegel, S. (1992, October 29). Public school choice works...Look at East Harlem. *Wall Street Journal.*

Flynn, J. (1994). Social justice in social agencies. In R. Edwards (Ed.), *Encyclopedia of social work* (19th ed.). Washington, DC: NASW.

Franklin, C., & Streeter, C. L. (1995). School reform: Linking public schools with human services. *Social Work, 40*(6).

Franklin, C. G., & Allen-Meares, P. (1997). School social workers are a critical part of the link. *Social Work in Education, 19.*

Frantz, D., & Collins, C. (1999). *Celebration, U.S.A.* New York: Holt.
Freeman, D. (1991, September 9). A different wave of immigrants. *Wall Street Journal.*
Freeman, E. M., Franklin, C. G., Fong, R., Shaffer, G. L., Timberlake, E. M. (Eds.). (1998). *School social work practice.* Washington, DC: NASW Press.
Frey, W. H. (1993, August 23). *Newhouse study.* Newhouse News Service.
Frey, W. H., & First, C. L. (1997). *Investigating change in American society.* Belmont, CA: Wadsworth.
Frey, W. H., & Liaw, K.-L. (1998). The impact of recent immigration on population redistribution within the United States. In J. P. Smith & B. Edmonston (Eds.), *The immigration debate.* Washington, DC: National Academy Press.
Froomkin, D. (1998, October 16). Backlash builds over managed care. *Washington Post.*
Furchtgott-Roth, D., & Stolba, C. (1998, September 20). American women aren't really so cheap. *Wall Street Journal.*
Fusfeld, D. R. (1973). *The basic economics of the urban racial crisis.* New York: Holt, Rinehart and Winston.
Fusfeld, D., & Bates, T. (1984). *The political economy of the urban ghetto.* Carbondale, IL: Southern Illinois University Press.
Galster, G. (1992). The case for racial integration. In G. C. Galster & E. W. Hill (Eds.), *The metropolis in black and white.* New Brunswick, NJ: Rutgers.
Galster, G., & Glazer, L. (1998). *Connecting the urban poor to work: A framework and strategy for action.* Ann Arbor, MI: Michigan Future.
Galster, G., & Glazer, L. (1999, April 15). Combat handicaps of urban poor with training, economic opportunity. *Detroit Free Press.*
Galston, M. A. (1999). Does the Internet strengthen community? *Philosophy and Public Policy, 19*(4).
Gans, H. J. (1996). Symbolic ethnicity. In W. Sollors (Ed.), *Theories of ethnicity: A classical reader.* New York: New York University Press.
Garreau, J. (1991). *Edge city.* New York: Doubleday.
Garvin, C. D., & Tropman, J. E. (1998). *Social work in contemporary society.* Englewood Cliffs, NJ: Prentice Hall.
George, M. (1992, December 3). *House divides Grand Rapids neighborhood.* Detroit Free Press.
Germain, C. B., & Bloom, M. (1999). *Human behavior in the social environment* (2nd ed.). New York: Columbia University.
Germain, C. B., & Gitterman, A. (1995). Ecological perspective. In *Encyclopedia of Social Work.* Washington, DC: NASW.
Giago, T. (2000, January 3). Indians aren't eager to join a club that long excluded them. *St. Paul Pioneer Press.*
Giamatti, A. (1998). *Take time for paradise: Americans and their games.* New York: Simon and Schuster.
Giamo, E. (1989). *On the Bowery: Confronting homelessness in American society.* Iowa City: University of Iowa Press.
Giese, J. (1990, September 27). A communal type of life with dinner for all and day care, too. *New York Times.*
Gil, D. G. (1994). Confronting social injustice and oppression. In F. G. Reamer (Ed.), *The foundations of social work knowledge.* New York: Columbia.
Gil, D. G. (1998). *Confronting justice and oppression.* New York: Columbia.
Gil, D. G., & Gil, E. A. (1995). *Toward social and economic justice.* Cambridge, MA: Schenkman.

Gilbert, D. (1993). Not in my backyard. *Social Work, 38*(1).

Gilbert, N. (1983). *Capitalism and the welfare state.* New Haven: Yale.

Gilbert, N. (1998, July/August). Remodeling social welfare. *Society.*

Gilbert, N., & Gilbert, B. (1989). *The enabling state: Modern welfare capitalism in America.* New York: Oxford.

Gillis, J., & Gaines, P. (1998, October 18). He looked like a sweet kid. Brutal slaying focuses the nation on violence against gays. *Washington Post.*

Ginsberg, L. (1994). *Understanding social problems, policies, and programs.* Columbia, SC: University of South Carolina Press.

Ginsberg, L. H. (1998). *Social work in rural communities* (3rd ed). Alexandria, VA: CSWE.

Gladwell, M. (1997, March 17). The coolhunt. *New Yorker.*

Glanz, J. (2000, March 11). Survey finds support is strong for teaching two origin theories. *New York Times.*

Glazer, N. (1993). Is assimilation dead? *Annals AAPSS,* p. 530.

Glazer, N. (1997). *We are all multiculturalists now.* Cambridge, MA: Harvard University Press.

Goldberg, C. (1999, January 3). Rural town takes on obstacles to an Internet connection. *New York Times.*

Goldberger, P. (2000, May 24). It takes a village. *New Yorker.*

Golden, T. (1996, November 5). San Francisco near domestic-partner rule. *New York Times.*

Goldstein, A. (1999, April 5). Physicians cutting back charity work. *Washington Post.*

Gonzalez, D. (1992, September 1). Dominican immigration alters Hispanic New York. *New York Times.*

Gopnik, A. (1999, May 24). Culture vultures. *New Yorker.*

Gounis, K., & Susser, E. (1990). Shelterization and its implications for mental health services. In N. Cohen (Ed.), *Psychiatry takes to the streets.* New York: Guilford Press.

Graham, L. O. (1999). *Our kind of people: Inside America's Black upper class.* New York: HarperCollins.

Granovetter, M. (1973). The strength of weak ties. *American Journal of Sociology, 78*(5).

Green, D. P., Strolovitch, D. Z., & Wong, J. S. (1998). Defended neighborhoods, integration, and racially motivated crime. *American Journal of Sociology, 104,* p. 2.

Green, J. W. (1999). Cultural awareness in the human services (3rd ed.). Boston: Allyn & Bacon.

Green, W. E., & Marcus, A. D. (1989, October 3). Texas school funding is unconstitutional. *Wall Street Journal.*

Greenhouse, L. (1997, June 24). Court eases curb on aid to schools with church ties. *New York Times.*

Greenhouse, L. (1998a, March 5). Law prohibits same-sex harassment in the workplace, justices rule. *New York Times.*

Greenhouse, L. (1998b, June 27). Court spells out rules for finding sex harassment. *New York Times.*

Greenhouse, L. (1999a, February 24). 47% in poll view legal system as unfair to poor and minorities. *New York Times.*

Greenhouse, L. (1999b, March 4). In ruling, schools must pay for needs of disabled pupils. *New York Times.*

Greenhouse, L. (1999c, April 19). Pivotal rulings ahead: Supreme Court to begin review of Americans with Disabilities Act. *New York Times.*

Greenhouse, L. (1999d, June 15). Justices agree to consider case on public aid to religious schools. *New York Times*.

Greenhouse, L. (1999e, October 5). Justices again avoid church school aid issue. *New York Times*.

Greenhouse, S. (1999f, October 28). U.S. to expand labor rights to cover illegal immigrants. *New York Times*.

Grimsley, K. D. (1999, March 20). Workplace diversity creates challenges. *Washington Post*.

Gronbjerg, K. A. (1977). *Mass society and the extension of welfare: 1960–1970*. Chicago: University of Chicago Press.

Grunberg, J. & Eagle, P. F. (1990). Shelterization: How the homeless adapt to shelter living. *Hospital and Community Psychiatry, 41*(5).

Grunwald, M. (1999, June 18). Culture wars erupt in debate on hill. *Washington Post*.

Grzywinski, R. (1991, May-June). The new old-fashioned banking. *Harvard Business Review*.

Gutierrez, L. (1990). Working with women of color: An empowerment perspective. *Social Work, 35*(2).

Gutierrez, L., Ortega, R. M., & Suarez, Z. E. (1990). Self-help and the Latino community. In T. Powell (Ed.), *Working with self-help*. Silver Spring, MD: NASW Press.

Gutierrez, L., Parsons, R., & Cox, E. D. (Eds.). (1997). *Empowerment in social work practice: A sourcebook*. Pacific Grove, CA: Brooks/Cole.

Gutierrez, L. M. (1997). Multicultural community organizing. In M. Reisch & E. L. Gambrill (Eds.), *Social work in the 21st century*. Thousand Oaks, CA: Pine Forge Press.

Gutierrez, L. M., & Lewis, E. A. (1994). Community organizing with women of color: A feminist approach. *Journal of Community Practice, 1*(2).

Gutierrez, L. M., & Lewis, E. A. (1999). *Empowering women of color*. New York: Columbia University Press.

Guzzetta, C. (1995). White ethnic groups. *Encyclopedia of social work* (19th ed.). Washington, DC: NASW.

Halbfinger, D. M. (1998, May 18). In Washington Heights, drug war survivors reclaim their stoops. *New York Times*.

Hanley, R. (1999, November 15). Reality catches up to a New Jersey town founded as a utopia. *New York Times*.

Hansan, J. E., & Morris, R. (Eds.). (1997). *The national government and social welfare: What should be the federal role?* Westport, CT: Auburn House.

Hansan, J. E., & Morris, R. (Eds.). (1999). *Welfare reform, 1996–2000*. Westport, CT: Auburn House.

Hare, I., & Rome, S. H. (1999). The changing social, political and economic context of school social work. In R. Constable, S. McDonald, & J. P. Flynn (Eds.), *School social work* (4th ed.). Chicago: Lyceum.

Harper, K. V., & Lantz, J. (1996). *Cross-cultural practice*. Chicago: Lyceum.

Harris, D. R. (1999, June). Property values drop when blacks move in, because. . . . *American Sociological Review, 64*.

Harris, J. F. (1999, October 20). House passes job benefits for disabled. *Washington Post*.

Harrison, B. G. (1999, December 31). Relics of an Italian village called New York. *New York Times*.

Harrison, R. J., & Weinberg, D. H. (1992, April). *Racial and ethnic segregation in 1990*. Washington, DC: U.S. Bureau of the Census.

Hartocollis, A. (1997, November 26). NYC school voucher experiment will be extended and expanded. *New York Times.*

Hasenfeld, Y. (1983). *Human service organizations.* Englewood Cliffs, NJ: Prentice Hall.

Hasenfeld, Y., & Gidron, B. (1993). Self-help groups and human service organizations: An interorganizational perspective. *Social Service Review, 67*(2).

Havemann, J. (1999, April 13). Child health program gets off to slow start. *Washington Post.*

Hawley, A. (1950). *Human ecology: A theory of community structure.* New York: Roland Press.

Hawley, A. (1986). *Urban ecology.* Chicago: University of Chicago Press.

Hayes, A. S. (1990a, October 4). Is town's housing plan the key to integration or a form of racism? *Wall Street Journal.*

Hayes, A. S. (1990b, May 24). Judge clears way for students to conduct graduation prayer. *Wall Street Journal.*

Health and Human Services. (1999). *HHS: What we do.* www.hhs.gov/.

Hennessy, K. D., & Stephens, S. (1997). Mental health parity: Clarifying our objectives. *Psychiatric Services, 48*(2).

Hentoff, N. (1999, November 27). Expelling "Huck Finn." *Washington Post.*

Herbert, B. (2000, March 9). A delicate balance. *New York Times.*

Herek, G. M. (1989). Hate crimes against lesbians and gay men. *American Psychologist, 44*(6).

Hernandez, J. (1985). Improving the data: A research strategy for new immigrants. In L. Maldonado & J. Moore (Eds.), *Urban ethnicity in the United States. Urban Affairs Annual Reviews, 29.*

Hesser, A. (1999, February 24). A grand oasis: New York's hotel bars. *New York Times.*

Hetter, K. (1993, August 18). States move to allow prayer in schools. *Wall Street Journal.*

Hirsch, J. S. (1991, May 9). Planned communities promise a new calm with the new home. *Wall Street Journal.*

Hirsch, J. S. (1992, February 27). Columbia, Maryland, at 24, sees integration goal sliding from its grasp. *Wall Street Journal.*

Hiss, J. (1993, April 12). The end of the rainbow. *New Yorker.*

Hollinger, D. A. (1995). *Postethnic America: Beyond multiculturalism.* New York: Basic Books.

Holloway, L. (1998a, November 25). School officials support teacher on book that parents call racially insensitive. *New York Times.*

Holloway, L. (1998b, December 1). Threatened over book, teacher leaves school. *New York Times.*

Holloway, L. (1998c, December 10). Brooklyn parent who stepped forward still dislikes "nappy hair." *New York Times.*

Holloway, L. (1999, August 25). Government tops voucher in new survey. *New York Times.*

Holly, D. (1993, March 28). Neighborhood battles adult entertainment. *Detroit Free Press.*

Holmes, S. A. (1998, August 25). Court bars "sampling" method in next census. *New York Times.*

Holmes, S. A. (1999, June 10). Clinton orders investigation on possible racial profiling. *New York Times.*

Hooks, B., & Raschka, C. (1999). *Happy to be nappy.* New York: Jump at the Sun.

Hoover, R. (1999, April 4). Urban sprawl under fire. *Detroit News & Free Press.*

Hooyman, N., and Gonyea, J. (1995). *Feminist perspectives on family care*. New York: Sage.

Horton, L. E. (1985). Equality, cooperation, and the American tradition: Reflections of directions for movements for social justice. In D. G. Gil & E. A. Gil (Eds.), *Toward social and economic justice*. Cambridge, MA: Schenkman.

Horwitz, T. (1993, November 12). Minimum-wage jobs give many Americans only a miserable life. *Wall Street Journal*.

Hsu, S. S. (1999, July 5). GAO: EEOC fails to track workers' complaints. *Washington Post*.

Hunter, F. (1953). *Community power structure*. Chapel Hill: University of North Carolina Press.

Husock, H. (1998, January 12). Breaking up cities more promising than merger with 'burbs. *Detroit News*.

Hutchinson, W. J., Searight, P., & Stretch, J. J. (1986). Multidimensional networking: A response to the needs of homeless families. *Social Work, 31*(6).

Hymowitz, K. S. (1993, March 25). Multiculturalism is anti-culture. *New York Times*.

Icard, L., Jones, T., & Wahab, S. (1999). Empowering Lesbian and bisexual women of color: Overcoming three forms of oppression. In L. M. Gutierrez & E. A. Lewis (Eds.), *Empowering women of color*. New York: Columbia University Press.

Iglehart, A. P., & Becerra, R. M. (1995). *Social services and the ethnic community*. Boston: Allyn & Bacon.

Ignatiev, N. (1995). *How the Irish became white*. New York: Routledge.

Investors Business Daily. (1999, December 29). How cities grow.

Ivillage. (1999, March 27). World Wide Web.

Jackman, M., and Jackman, R. (1983). *Class awareness in the United States*. Berkeley: University of California Press.

Jacobs, K. (1999, November 12). Women have scaled corporate ladder, but climb continues to be a slow one. *New York Times*.

Janofsky, M. (1998, February 9). Pessimism retains grip on region of poverty. *New York Times*.

Janofsky, M. (1999, January 12). Gore offers plan to control suburban sprawl. *New York Times*.

Janowitz, M. (1978). *The last half-century: Societal change and politics in America*. Chicago: University of Chicago Press.

Jansson, B. S. (1997). *The reluctant welfare state* (3rd ed.). Pacific Grove, CA: Brooks/Cole.

Jefferson, D. J. (1994, March 18). Gay employees win benefits for partners at more corporations. *Wall Street Journal*.

Jeffrey, N. A. (1993, March 19). Gays find suburbs along Woodward to be home. *Detroit Free Press*.

Jenkins, S. (1981). *The ethnic dilemma in social services*. New York: Free Press.

Jensen, G. V., Cayner, J. J., & Hall, J. A. (1998). Social services in the health care field. In H. W. Johnson (Ed.), *The social services* (5th ed.). Itasca, IL: Peacock.

Johnson, D. (1997, August 27). Chicago hails district as symbol of gay life. *New York Times*.

Johnson, D. (1999, October 20). A suburbiascape grows in inner-city Chicago. *New York Times*.

Johnson, H. W. (1998). The social services (5th ed.). Itasca, IL: Peacock.

Jones, L. (1990, September 29). Balancing act. *Detroit Free Press*.

Jones, V. C. (1998). Improving black student performance on a large scale: The lessons of Equity 2000. In *The state of black America*. Washington, DC: National Urban League.

Jordan, V. E., Jr. (1995, October 27). Look outward, Black America. *The Wall Street Journal*.

Karger, H. J., & Stoesz, D. (1998). *American social welfare policy* (3rd ed.). New York: Longman.

Karr, A. R. (1993, August 13). Consumer group finds marketing bias in mortgage lending in 16 large cities. *Wall Street Journal*.

Kasarda, J. D. (1989). Urban industrial transition and the underclass. *Annals AAPSS*, p. 501.

Kasarda, J. D. (1992, May 28). Why Asians can prosper where Blacks fail. *Wall Street Journal*.

Kaufman, L. (2000, March 9). The dot.com world opens new opportunities for women to lead. *New York Times*.

Keillor, G. (1985). *Lake Wobegon days*. New York: Viking Penguin.

Keller, L. F. (1992). Leadership and race in the administrative city: Building and maintaining direction for justice in complex urban networks. In G. C. Glaster & E. W. Hill (Eds.), *The metropolis in black and white*. New Brunswick, NJ: Rutgers.

Kemp, S. P. (1995). Practice with communities. In C. H. Meyer & M. A. Mattaini (Eds.), *The foundations of social work practice*. Washington, DC: NASW Press.

Kennedy, R. (1993, July 21). Still a pigmentocracy. *New York Times*.

Kerchis, C. Z., & Young, I. M. (1995). Social movements and the politics of difference. In D. A. Harris (Ed.), *Multiculturalism from the margins*. Westport, CT: Bergin and Garvey.

Kilborn, P. T. (1990, July 30). Labor department wants to take on job bias in the executive suite. *New York Times*.

Kilborn, P. T. (1993, February 11). Law failed to stem illegal immigration, panel says. *New York Times*.

Kilborn, P. T. (1999a, March 12). Help for the uninsured may rest in tax code. *New York Times*.

Kilborn, P. T. (1999b, April 9). Third of Hispanic Americans do without health coverage. *New York Times*.

Kilborn, P. T. (1999c, September 16). Bias lingers for minorities buying homes. *New York Times*.

Killian, M. S., & Beaulieu, L. J. (1992). Current status of human capital in the rural U.S. In L. J. Beaulieu & D. Mulkey (Eds.), *Investing in people: The human capital needs of rural America*. Boulder, CO: Westview Press.

Kilman, S., & Millman, J. (1999, August 12). Immigrants find hope in a life of farming as others sour on it. *Wall Street Journal*.

Kilson, M. L. (1998). The state of African-American politics. In L. A. Daniels (Ed.), *The state of Black America 1998*. Washington, DC: The National Urban League.

Kim, C. H. (1993, August 13). We're too busy to fight a "mommy war." *Wall Street Journal*.

Klibanoff, J. (1984, October 8). Chicago suburb actively seeks racial diversity. *Detroit Free Press*.

Klinghoffer, D. (1999, October 24). The conversion of Loralei Lee. *New York Times Book Review*.

Kohn, A. (1999, December 9). Tests that cheat students. *New York Times*.

Kotkin, J. (2000, February 27). A revival of older suburbs as ethnic business takes hold. *New York Times*.

Kramer, R. M. (1994, March). Voluntary agencies and the contract culture: Dream or nightmare? *Social Service Review.*

Kronholz, J. (1999a, February 12). Charter schools begin to prod public schools toward competition. *Wall Street Journal.*

Kronholz, J. (1999b, August 13). Tesseract and others march briskly ahead in school privatization. *Wall Street Journal.*

Krupat, E. (1985). *People in cities.* Cambridge, UK: Cambridge University Press.

Kugel, J. F. (1999, August 17). The electronic block party. *New York Times.*

Kurtz, L. F. (1997). *Self-help and support groups.* Thousand Oaks, CA: Sage.

Lam, T. (1993, February 10). Residents, topless bar owners reach pact. *Detroit Free Press.*

Lambert, S. J. (1993, June). Workplace policies as social policy. *Social Service Review.*

Lambert, S. J. (1998). Workers' use of supportive workplace policies. In A. Daly (Ed.), *Workplace diversity issues and perspectives.* Washington, DC: NASW.

Landecker, W. S. (1951). Types of integration and their measurement. *American Journal of Sociology, 56*(4).

Lardner, J. (1993, July 5). A new kind of cop. *Wall Street Journal.*

Lee, A. (1999, February 21). Black like us. *New York Times.*

Leonard, P. (1997). *Postmodern welfare.* Thousand Oaks, CA: Sage.

Leshner, A. I. (1992). *Outcasts on main street.* Washington, DC: U.S. Government Printing Office.

Leung, S. (2000, March 3). L.A. considers how to pay claims due to police corruption. *Wall Street Journal.*

Levine, H., & Harmon, L. (1992). *The death of an American Jewish community.* New York: Free Press.

Levine, R. (1990, July 30). Young immigrant wave lifts New York economy. *New York Times.*

Levy, A. C., & Paludi, M. A. (1997). *Workplace sexual harassment.* Englewood Cliffs, NJ: Prentice Hall.

Lewin, T. (1998a, March 11). Multicultural book list considered in San Francisco. *New York Times.*

Lewin, T. (1998b, May 22). Experts see shift in the nature of school violence. *New York Times.*

Lewin, T. (1998c, November 20). Court ruling blocks affirmative action at a public school. *New York Times.*

Lewin, T. (1998d, November 29). Affirmative-action dilemma spreads in public schools. *New York Times.*

Lewin, T. (1998e, December 10). Oregon's gay workers given benefits for domestic partners. *New York Times.*

Lewin, T. (1999a, June 13). Arizona district profits from charter schools. *New York Times.*

Lewin, T. (1999b, September 6). Schools apply tougher stance with standards. *New York Times.*

Lewin, T. (2000, March 11). Study finds racial bias in public schools. *New York Times.*

Lewis, R. G. (1995). American Indians. In *Encyclopedia of social work* (19th ed.). Washington, DC: NASW Press.

Lie, G. (1999). Empowerment: Asian-American Women's Perspectives. In L. M. Gutierrez & E. A. Lewis (Eds.), *Empowering women of color.* New York: Columbia University Press.

Lind, M. (1998, August 16). The beige and the black. *New York Times.*

Lipsky, M., & Smith, S. R. (1989). When social problems are treated as emergencies. *Social Service Review, 63,* p. 1.

Liska, A. E. (1992). Social control. In E. F. Borgatta & M. L. Borgatta (Eds.), *Encyclopedia of sociology.* New York: Macmillan.

Litwak, E. (1985). *Helping the elderly.* New York: Guilford Press.

Locke, D. C. (1992). *Increasing multicultural understanding.* Newbury Park: Sage.

Logan, A. (1993, April 26). Cry the beloved community. *New Yorker.*

Long, N. E. (1958). The local community as an ecology of games. *American Journal of Sociology, 64,* p. 3.

Longres, J. (1995). *Human behavior in the social environment* (2nd ed.). Itasca, IL: Peacock.

Lubman, S. (1992, November 9). Santa Monica grows hostile to the homeless who consider it home. *Wall Street Journal.*

Lugones, M., & Price, J. (1995). Dominant culture. In D. A. Harris (Ed.), *Multiculturalism from the margins.* Westport, CT: Bergin & Garvey.

Lynd, R. S., & Lynd, H. M. (1929). *Middletown: A study in contemporary American culture.* New York: Harcourt Brace.

MacFarquhar, N. (1997, October 1). The changing face of Riverdale. *New York Times.*

MacGuire, J. (1992, November 25). The Carnegie assault on school choice. *Wall Street Journal.*

Mackelprang, R., & Salsgiver, R. (1996). People with disabilities and social work: Historical and contemporary issues. *Social Work, 41*(1).

Mackelprang, R., & Salsgiver, R. (1999). *Disability: A diversity model approach in human service practice.* Pacific Grove, CA: Brooks/Cole.

MacKinnon, C. (1979). *The sexual harassment of working women.* New Haven, CT: Yale University Press.

MacKinnon, C. A. (1998, Fall/Winter). Harassment: A serious and neglected social problem. *Law Quadrangle Notes.*

Maguire, D. J. (1991). An overview and definition of GIS. In D. J. Maguire, M. F. Goodchilde, & D. W. Rhind (Eds.), *Geographical information systems.* New York: Wiley.

Malkin, M. (1999, November 23). Don't banish Harry Potter books; admire their gift. *Detroit News.*

Mann, J. H. (1998). Aging and social work. In H. W. Johnson (Ed.), *The social services* (5th ed.). Itasca, IL: Peacock.

Manning, P. K. (1998). Book review: Community Policing, Chicago Style. *American Journal of Sociology, 104*(1).

Mansnerus, L. (1998, April 5). Perceptions and facts in sexual harassment. *New York Times.*

Marshall, G. (Ed.). (1994). *The concise Oxford dictionary of sociology.* New York: Oxford.

Martin, P. (1993, July 6). Turn ailing thrifts into community banks. *Wall Street Journal.*

Martinez-Brawley, E. (1990). *Perspectives on the small community.* Silver Spring, MD: NASW Press.

Martinez-Brawley, E. (2000). *Close to home: Human services and the small community.* Silver Spring, MD: NASW Press.

Massey, D. S., & Denton, N. A. (1993). *American apartheid: Segregation and the making of the underclass.* Cambridge, MA: Harvard University Press.

Mathabane, M. (1999, November 28). If you assign my book, don't — it. *Washington Post.*

Mathews, L. (1993, April 13). Grosse Pointe Park closes street to Detroit. *Detroit Free Press.*

Mathews, J. (1999a, September 6). Schools forging new links with parents. *Washington Post.*

Mathews, J. (1999b, March 24). A home run for home schooling. *Washington Post.*

McAdam, D., McCarthy, J. D., & Zald, M. (1996). *Comparative perspectives on social movements.* Cambridge, UK: Cambridge University Press.

McCaughey, E. (1993, June 30). Court deals a blow to racial gerrymandering. *Wall Street Journal.*

McGinley, L. (1993, August 9). Some advocates of enterprise-zone concept find little to cheer in Democrats' legislation. *Wall Street Journal.*

McGroarty, D. (1993, October 1). A prayer for a better education. *Wall Street Journal.*

McKenzie, R. D. (1926). The scope of human ecology. *American Journal of Sociology, 32.*

McKnight, J., & Kretzmann, J. P. (1993). *Building communities from the inside out.* Evanston, IL: Northwestern University Press.

Meier, B. (1999, July 22). Local governments attack gun industry with civil lawsuits. *New York Times.*

Mendelsohn, D. (1995, March). The world is a ghetto. *Out.*

Merida, K., & Vobejda, B. (1996, December 15). Promoting a return to "civil society." *Washington Post.*

Merton, R. K. (1949). Types of influentials: The local and the cosmopolitan. In P. Lazarsfeld and F. Stanton (Eds.), *Communications research.* New York: Harper & Row.

Meyerson, D. E., & Fletcher, J. K. (2000, January/February). A modest manifesto for shattering the class ceiling. *Harvard Business Review.*

Midgley, J. (1995). *Social development: The developmental perspective in social welfare.* Thousand Oaks, CA: Sage.

Midgley, J. (1997). *Social welfare in a global context.* Thousand Oaks, CA: Sage.

Midgley, J. (1999). Growth, redistribution. and welfare: Toward social investment. *Social Service Review, 73*(1).

Midgley, J., & Livermore, M. (1998). Social capital and local economic development. *Journal of Community Practice, 5,* pp. 1–2.

Miley, K. K., O'Melia, M., & DuBois, B. L. (1998). *Generalist social work practice.* Boston: Allyn & Bacon.

Miller, J. J. (1993, February 10). The rest of the rainbow curriculum. *Wall Street Journal.*

Miller, S. M. (1997). Employment challenges. In J. E. Hansan & R. Morris (Eds.), *The national government and social welfare.* Westport, CT: Auburn House.

Mishra, R. (2000). *Globalization and the welfare state.* Northhampton, MA: Edward Elgar Publishing.

Misra, J. (1999). Latinas and African American women in the labor market: Implications for policy. In I. Browne (Ed.), *Latinas and African American women at work.* New York: Russell Sage Foundation.

Montana, C. (1986, October 1). Latino schism: Hispanic communities in U.S. are divided by influx of Mexicans. *Wall Street Journal.*

Moreno, S. (1999, March 2). A bit of Mexico flourishes in Manassas. *Washington Post.*

Morley, J. (1999, April 19). Suburban battle lines drawn over sidewalks. *Washington Post.*

Morris, C. R. (1997). *American Catholics.* New York: Random House.

Moss, K., Ullman, M., Starrett, B. E., Burris, S., & Johnsen, M. C. (1999). Outcomes of employment discrimination charges filed under the Americans with Disabilities Act. *Psychiatric Services, 50*(8).

Mowbray, C. T., Chamberlain, P., Jennings, M., & Reed, C. (1988). Consumer-run mental health services: Results from five demonstration projects. *Community Mental Health Journal, 24*, p. 2.

Mullaly, R. (1997). *Structural social work* (2nd ed.). Toronto: McClelland & Stewart.

Myers, S. L. (2000, March 25). Survey of troops finds anti-gay bias common in service. *New York Times.*

Myles, J. (1996). When markets fail: Social welfare in Canada and the United States. In G. Esping-Andersen (Ed.), *Welfare states in transition.* Thousand Oaks, CA: Sage.

Nagourney, A. (1999, December 9). Hillary Clinton faults policy of "don't ask." *New York Times.*

Nakamura, D. (1998, October 30). Virginia denied U.S. funds for charter schools. *Washington Post.*

Nathan, J. (1993, April 22). School choice works in Minnesota. *Wall Street Journal.*

Nathan, R. P. (1991, May 22). Where the minority middle class lives. *Wall Street Journal.*

National Association of Social Workers. (1982). *Standards for social work in health care settings.* Silver Spring, MD: NASW.

National Association of Social Workers. (1992). *NASW standards for school social work services.* Washington, DC: NASW.

National Association of Social Workers. (1996). *NASW speaks: Gender, ethnic, and race-based workplace discrimination.* Washington, DC: National Association of Social Workers.

National Association of Social Workers (1997). *Code of Ethics.* Washington, DC: NASW Press.

National Commission on Civic Renewal. (1998). *Plenary sessions transcripts.* College Park, MD: University of Maryland.

Navarro, M. (1998, December 2). Miami restores gay rights law. *New York Times.*

Navarro, M. (1999, February 11). Miami's generations of exiles side by side, yet worlds apart. *New York Times.*

Neighbors, H. W., Elliot, K. A., & Gant, L. M. (1990). Self-help and black Americans: a strategy for empowerment. In T. Powell (Ed.), *Working with self-help.* Silver Spring, MD: NASW Press.

Nelson, J. (1998, November 28). Stumbling upon a race secret. *New York Times.*

Nes, J. A., & Iadicola, P. (1989). Toward a definition of feminist social work: A comparison of liberal, radical, and socialist models. *Social Work, 34*(1).

New York Times. (1998, November 15). Status.

New York Times. (1999a). Community Investment Act (advertisement).

New York Times. (1999b, August 11). U.S. schools report fewer gun expulsions.

New York Times. (2000, January 11). Coping with teacher shortages.

New Yorker. (1993, July 5). The wobbly blue line.

Newman, K. S. (1988). *Falling from grace.* New York: Free Press.

Newman, K. S. (1993). *Declining fortunes: The withering of the American dream.* New York: Basic Books.

Newman, K. S. (1999). *No shame in my game: The working poor in the inner city.* New York: Knopf and Russell Sage.

Niebuhr, G. (1999, October 20). U.S. bishops urging Catholics to be politically involved. *New York Times.*

Norlin, J. M., & Chess, W. A. (1997). *Human behavior and the social environment: Social systems theory.* Boston: Allyn & Bacon.

Novoselick, P. (1999, October 7). Disabilities prevalent among minority groups. *Ann Arbor News.*

O'Looney, J. (1996). *Redesigning the work of human services.* Westport, CT: Quorum.

Olson, L. (2000, April 26). Redefining public schools. *Washington Post.*

Ortiz, M. G. (1999, October 13). Schools to get millions to experiment. *Detroit Free Press.*

Pacelle, M. (1994, September 21). Not in your backyard, say community panels in suburban enclaves. *Wall Street Journal.*

Page-Adams, D., & Sherraden, M. (1997). Asset building as a community revitalization strategy. *Social Work, 42*(5).

Park, R., Burgess, E. W., and McKenzie, R. D. (Eds.). (1925). *The city.* Chicago: University of Chicago Press.

Parsons, T. (1951). *The social system.* Glencoe, IL: Free Press.

Patai, D. (1998). *Heterophobia: Sexual harassment and the future of feminism.* New York: Rowman & Littlefield.

Pear, R. (1998a, December 30). Most states meet work requirement of welfare law. *Washington Post.*

Pear, R. (1998b, December 26). Insurance plans skirt requirement on mental health. *New York Times.*

Pear, R. (1999a, January 13). Proposal aims at returning disabled workers to jobs. *New York Times.*

Pear, R. (1999b, February 23). President set to establish a toll-free number to enroll children in health insurance plans. *New York Times.*

Pear, R. (1999c, May 25). Federal workers promised gains in mental-health coverage. *New York Times.*

Pear, R. (1999d, June 17). Senate approves health care for disabled. *New York Times.*

Pear, R. (1999e, November 19). Bill expands health benefits for disabled people who work. *New York Times.*

Pearson, H. (1995, August 29). Who speaks for Black America? *Wall Street Journal.*

Peirce, N. (1999, November 10). Designing schools for the modern age. *Detroit Free Press.*

Pepper, J. (1990, August 19). Common ground: Cleveland suburbs work to achieve a racial balance. *Detroit News.*

Perez-Rivas, M. (1999, November 17). Montgomery schools to offer translation service. *Washington Post.*

Perloff, J. D. (1996). Medicaid managed care and urban poor people. *Journal of Health and Social Work, 21*(3).

Perlstein, L. (1999, September 18). Holy days complicate school year. *Washington Post.*

Perrucci, R., & Pilisuk, M. (1970). The interorganizational bases of community power. *American Sociological Review, 35,* p. 6.

Persons, G. A. (1992). Racial politics and black power in the cities. In G. C. Galster & E. W. Hill (Eds.), *The metropolis in black and white.* New Brunswick, NJ: Rutgers.

Petersen, A. (1999, January 6). Some places to go when you want to feel right at home. *Wall Street Journal.*

Peterson, W. C. (1999). *The Social Security primer.* Armonk, NY: M. E. Sharpe.

Petrila, J. (1995). The Supreme Court's ruling in Edmonds vs. Oxford House. *Psychiatric Services, 46*(10).

Phinney, J. S. (1996). When we talk about American ethnic groups, what do we mean? *American Psychologist, 51*(9).

Pierre-Pierre, G. (1999, August 20). New roots for black culture in Fort Greene. *New York Times.*

Piven, F. F., & Cloward, R. (1971). *Regulating the poor.* New York: Vintage.

Piven, F. F. & Cloward, R. (1997). *The breaking of the American social compast.* New York: The New Press.

Pollan, M. (1997, December 14). Town-building is no Mickey Mouse operation. *New York Times Magazine.*

Poplin, D. (1979). *Communities: A survey of theories and methods of research* (2nd ed.). New York: Macmillan.

Portney, K. E., & Berry, J. M. (1997). Mobilizing minority communities. *American Behavioral Scientist, 40(5).*

Portnoy, G., & Angelo, J. H. (1982). *Cheers.* Addax Music Co., Inc.

Powell, T. J. (1987). *Self-help organizations and professional practices.* Silver Spring, MD: NASW.

Powell, T. J. (Ed.) (1990). *Working with self-help.* Silver Spring, MD: NASW.

Prigoff, A. (2000). *Economics for social workers: Social outcomes of economic globalization with strategies for community action.* Belmont, CA: Wadsworth.

Pryor, C. (1996). Techniques for assessing family-school connections. *Social Work in Education, 18.*

Pryor, C. B., Kent, C., & McGunn, C. (1996). Redesigning social work in inclusive schools. *Social Work, 41(6).*

Psychiatric Services. (1995). Supreme Court rules against use of zoning laws to exclude group homes from residential areas. *Psychiatric Services, 46(7).*

Pugh, T. (1999, December 17). Many call lenders biased. *Detroit Free Press.*

Purdum, T. S. (1997, November 14). Asian Americans set to flex political muscle made large. *New York Times.*

Purdum, T. S. (1998, July 16). Judge refuses to block measure ending bilingual education in California. *New York Times.*

Purdum, T. S. (1999, June 10). Los Angeles reinvents itself, adopting new city charter. *New York Times.*

Putka, G. (1990, March 26). Wisconsin to allow some students to use education vouchers at private schools. *Wall Street Journal.*

Putnam, R. D. (1995). Bowling alone: America's declining social capital. *Journal of Democracy, 6(1).*

Quadagno, J. (1994). *The color of welfare.* New York: Oxford University Press.

Queralt, M. (1996). *The social environment and human behavior: A diversity perspective.* Boston: Allyn & Bacon.

Queralt, M., & Witte, A. D. (1998a). A map for you? Geographic information systems in the social services. *Social Work, 43(5).*

Queralt, M., & Witte, A. D. (1998b). Influences on neighborhood supply of child care in Massachusetts. *Social Service Review, 72(1).*

Queralt, M., & Witte, A. D. (1999). Estimating the unmet need for services: A middling approach. *Social Service Review, 73(4).*

Quillian, L. (1999). Migration patterns and the growth of high-poverty neighborhoods, 1970–1990. *American Journal of Sociology, 105(1).*

Quintanilla, C. (1993, September 17). Disabilities Act helps. *Wall Street Journal.*

Quintanilla, C., & Rose, R. L. (1996, September 16). Some tiny towns find a way to create jobs: Attract manufacturers. *Wall Street Journal.*

Rawls, J. (1971). *A theory of justice.* Cambridge, MA: Harvard University Press.

Reichl, R. (1998, October 7). A taste of San Francisco: Culinary lights—North Beach shines again. *New York Times.*

Reisch, M. (1997). The political context of social work. In M. Reisch & E. Gambrill (Eds.), *Social work in the 21st century*. Thousand Oaks, CA: Pine Forge Press.

Reisch, M. (1999). Economic globalization and the future of the welfare state. Ann Arbor, MI: University of Michigan.

Reischauer, R. D. (1989). Immigration and the underclass. *Annals AAPSS*, p. 501.

Reuters News Service. (1999, February 18). San Francisco schools abolish racial quotas. *Washington Post*.

Rich, P. (1999). American voluntarism, social capital, and political culture. *Annals AAPSS*, p. 565.

Richman, P. C. (1999, January 10). By the books. *Washington Post*.

Rimer, S. (1991, September 16). New immigrant group displays its enterprise. *New York Times*.

Rivera, F., & Erlich, J. L. (1995). An option assessment framework for organizing in emerging minority communities. In J. E. Tropman et al. (Eds.), *Tactics and techniques of community practice*. Itasca, IL: Peacock.

Rivera, F., & Erlich, J. L. (Eds.). (1998). *Community organizing in a diverse society* (3rd ed.). Boston: Allyn & Bacon.

Rock, H. M., & Hill, E. W. (1992). Policy prescriptions for inner-city public schooling. In G. C. Galster & E. W. Hill (Eds.), *The metropolis in black and white*. New Brunswick, NJ: Rutgers.

Rohter, L. (1992, November 18). Judge orders safe zones for homeless. *New York Times*.

Romano, L. (1999, December 1). Oklahoma's divisive disclaimer on evolution. *Washington Post*.

Rooney, G. D. (1998). Occupational social work. In H. W. Johnson (Ed.), *The social services* (5th ed.). Itasca, IL: Peacock.

Rose, H. (1976). *Black suburbanization*. Cambridge, MA: Ballinger.

Rosen, J. (1997, October 20–27). The social police. *New Yorker*.

Rosenbaum, D. P. (Ed.). (1994). *The challenge of community policing*. Thousand Oaks, CA: Sage.

Rowan, C. (1993, April 25). Parity must be the goal in funding schools. *North America Syndicate*.

Rozhon, T. (1998, April 16). Dreams, and now hope, among the ruins in Harlem. *New York Times*.

Rucht, D. (1996). The impact of national contexts on social movement structures: A cross-movement and cross-national comparison. In D. McAdam, J. D. McCarthy, & M. N. Zald (Eds.), *Comparative perspectives on social movements*. Cambridge, UK: Cambridge University Press.

Rusk, D. (1993). *Cities without suburbs*. Baltimore: Johns Hopkins University Press.

Ryan, W. P. (1999, January/February). The new landscape for nonprofits. *Harvard Business Review*.

Rybczynski, W. (1996, July 22). Tomorrowland. *New Yorker*.

Sachs, S. (1998, November 10). Muslim schools in U.S. a voice for identity. *New York Times*.

Sachs, S. (1999a, March 19). Reaching out early to those most likely to be missed. *New York Times*.

Sachs, S. (1999b, November 8). As New York immigration thrives, diversity widens. *New York Times*.

Sacks, K. B. (1997). How did Jews become white folks? In R. Delgado & J. Stenfancic (Eds.), *Critical white studies*. Philadelphia: Temple.

Sadd, S., & Grinc, R. (1994). Innovative neighborhood-oriented policing: An evaluation of community policing programs in eight cities. In D. P. Rosenbaum (Ed.), *The challenge of community policing*. Thousand Oaks, CA: Sage.

Salamon, L. M. (1993). The marketization of welfare: Changing nonprofit and for-profit roles in the American welfare state. *Social Service Review, 67*(1).

Salant, K. (1999, June 26). A new town's growing pains. *Washington Post.*

Saleebey, D. (Ed.). (1997). *The strengths perspective in social work practice* (2nd ed.). New York: Longman.

Saltman, J. (1991). Maintaining racially diverse neighborhoods. *Urban Affairs Quarterly, 26*, p. 3.

Sampson, R. J., Raudenbush, S. W., & Earls, F. (1997, August 15). Neighborhoods and violent crime: A multilevel study of collective efficacy. *Science, 277.*

Sanchez, R. (1999a, August 31). Economic boom is a distant rumble in South Central L.A. *New York Times.*

Sanchez, R. (1999b, August 19). L.A.'s artless cleanup causes controversy. *Washington Post.*

Sands, R. G., & Nuccio, K. (1992). Postmodern feminist theory and social work. *Social Work, 37*(6).

Schlesinger, A. M. (1997). *The disuniting of America: Reflections on a multicultural society*. New York: Norton.

Schmidtz, D., & Goodin, R. E. (1998). *Social welfare and individual responsibility*. Cambridge, UK: Cambridge University Press.

Schneider, A. (1998, June 5). Colleges urged to promote "civil society" by stressing the values of liberal education. *The Chronicle of Higher Education.*

Schram, S. F., & Turbett, J. P. (1983, December). The welfare explosion: mass society versus social control. *Social Service Review.*

Schriver, J. M. (1998). *Human behavior and the social environment* (2nd ed.). Boston: Allyn & Bacon.

Schwartz, F. N. (1989, January/February). Management women and the new facts of life. *Harvard Business Review.*

Schwartz, F. N. (1992, March/April). Women as a business imperative. *Harvard Business Review.*

Seelye, K. Q. (1998, May 5). House rejects organized prayer in public schools. *New York Times.*

Segal, D. (1999, August 11). ABA opposes racial profiling. *Washington Post.*

Segal, E. A., and Brzuzy, S. (1998). *Social welfare policy, programs, and practice.* Itasca, IL: Peacock.

Segal, S., Silverman, C., & Temkin, T. (1993). Empowerment in self-help agency practice. *Social Work, 38*, p. 6.

Segal, S., Silverman, C., & Temkin, T. (1995). Measuring empowerment in client-run self-help agencies. *Community Mental Health Journal, 31*, p. 3.

Sengupta, S. (1996, October 3). Public help for parochial students, at a distance. *New York Times.*

Sengupta, S. (1999, June 9). Dumbo's transformation brings mixed feelings. *New York Times.*

Sexton, J. (1997, March 10). In a pocket of Brooklyn sewn by welfare, an unraveling. *New York Times.*

Shatz, E. O. (1995). Human services toward social and economic justice. In D. A. Gil & E. A. Gil (Eds.), *Toward social and economic justice*. Cambridge, MA: Schenkman.

Shellenbarger, S. (1993a, June 30). Executive women make major gains in pay and status. *Wall Street Journal.*

Shellenbarger, S. (1993b, August 18). Longer commutes force parents to make tough choices on where to leave the kids. *Wall Street Journal.*

Shepard, P. (2000, March 19). Feds commit $2 trillion for minorities. *Detroit News.*

Sherraden, M. (1991). *Assets and the poor.* Armonk, NY: Sharpe.

Sherraden, M., Johnson, L., Clancy, M., Beverly, S., Schreiner, M., Zhan, M., & Curley, J. (2000). *Saving patterns in IDA programs.* St. Louis: Washington University.

Simon, J. L. (1990, January 26). Bring on the wretched refuse. *Wall Street Journal.*

Simon, J. L. (1993, August 4). The nativists are wrong. *Wall Street Journal.*

Sink, M. (1999, August 11). Shootings intensify interest in home schooling. *New York Times.*

Siskind, L. J. (1994, July 13). San Francisco's separate and unequal public schools. *Wall Street Journal.*

Skerry, P. (1999, November 14). Immigration book offers thorough research, fairness. *Washington Post.*

Skocpol, T., & Fiorina, M. P. (Eds.). (2000). *Civil engagement in American democracy.* Washington, DC: Brookings.

Skogan, W. G. (1994). The impact of community policing on neighborhood residents. In D. P. Rosenbaum (Ed.), *The challenge of community policing.* Thousand Oaks, CA: Sage.

Skogan, W. G., & Harnett, S. M. (1997). *Community policing, Chicago style.* New York: Oxford University Press.

Skrzycki, C. (1999, November 22). OSHA offers standard to fight injuries in workplace. *Washington Post.*

Smart, T. (1999, July 20). A new presence in the corporate elite. *Washington Post.*

Smith, J. P., & Edmonston, B. (Eds.). (1997). *The new Americans.* Washington, DC: National Academy Press.

Smith, J. P., & Edmonston, B. (Eds.). (1998). *The immigration debate.* Washington, DC: National Academy Press.

Snipp, C. (1996). Understanding race and ethnicity in rural America. *Rural Sociology, 61.*

Social Work. (1997). Revitalization of impoverished communities. *Social Work, 42(5).*

Solomon, B. (1976). *Black empowerment: Social work in oppressed communities.* New York: Columbia University Press.

Sontag, D. (1998, January 7). In Brooklyn, a new "old world" community flourishes. *New York Times.*

Sosin, M. R., Colson, P., & Grossman, S. (1988). *Homelessness in Chicago.* Chicago: Chicago Community Trust.

South, S. J., & Crowder, K. D. (1998, February). Leaving the 'hood: Residential mobility between black, white, and integrated neighborhoods. *American Sociological Review, 63.*

Specht, H., & Courtney, M. (1994). *Unfaithful angels.* New York: Free Press.

Staudt, H. (1992, October 26). School choice programs do not lead to improved education, report finds. *Wall Street Journal.*

Steinberg, J. (1998, June 10). Voucher program for inner-city children. *New York Times.*

Steinberg, J. (1999a, August 25). School districts in Kansas split on evolution ruling. *New York Times.*

Steinberg, J. (1999b, September 23). Nation's wealthy, seeing a void, take steps to aid public schools. *New York Times.*

Steinberg, J. (1999c, December 3). Academic standards eased as a fear of failure spreads. *New York Times*.

Steinhauer, J. (1998, May 3). The shoe as social signifier. *New York Times*.

Steinhauer, J. (1999, December 31). Needed New Year's Eve? It's a job status symbol. *New York Times*.

Stern, G. (1995, December 20). An affluent suburb is racially diverse...but is it integrated? *Wall Street Journal*.

Stern, S. (1999, December 19). What Rudy Crew didn't do. *New York Times*.

Stewart, J. B. (1997, February 21). Coming out at Chrysler. *New Yorker*.

Stoesz, D., & Saunders, D. (1999). Welfare capitalism: A new approach to poverty policy? *Social Service Review, 73*(3).

Strauss, V. (1999, September 11). Chartering a course. *Washington Post*.

Strinati, D. (1995). *An introduction to theories of popular culture*. NewYork: Routledge.

Suttles, G. (1968). *The social order of the slum*. Chicago: University of Chicago Press.

Swasy, A. (1993, July 23). Stay-at-home moms are fashionable again in many communities. *Wall Street Journal*.

Taeuber, K. E., & Taeuber, A. F. (1965). *Negroes in cities: Residential segregation and neighborhood change*. Chicago, IL: Aldine.

Taylor, R. (1979). Black ethnicity and the persistence of ethnogenesis. *American Journal of Sociology, 84*, p. 6.

Templin, N. (1995, April 4). For inner-city Detroit, the hidden economy is crucial part of life. *Wall Street Journal*.

Tenbruck, F. H. (1989). The cultural foundations of society. In H. Haferkamp (Ed.), *Social structure and culture*. New York: Aldine de Gruyter.

Terry, D. (1997, October 19). Redevelopment plans may hem in skid row. *New York Times*.

Terry, D. (1998, June 5). Latino community remains divided over future of bilingual education. *New York Times*.

Thernstrom, S., & Thernstrom, A. (1997). *America in black and white: Race in modern America*. New York: Simon & Schuster.

Thomas, D. (1991, July 11). Young, rich and on a roll. *Washington Post*.

Thomas, J. (1999, September 21). In East Peoria, an intolerance for hate. *New York Times*.

Thompson, J. (1999, October 24). Does Michigan need more laws to stop suburban sprawl? *Detroit News*.

Tien, J. M., & Rich, T. F. (1994). The Hartform COMPASS program: Experiences with a weed-and-seed-related program. In D. P. Rosenbaum (Ed.), *The challenge of community policing*. Thousand Oaks, CA: Sage.

Tifft, S. E., & Jones, A. S. (1999). *The trust: The private and powerful family behind The New York Times*. New York: Little, Brown.

Tilove, J. (1995, October 27). Stereotypes hem in a neighborhood. *Detroit Free Press*.

Titmuss, R. M. (1974). *Social policy: An introduction*. London: Allen & Unwin.

Tobin, G. A. (Ed.). (1987). Divided neighborhoods: Changing patterns of racial segregation. *Urban Affairs Annual Reviews, 32*.

de Tocqueville, A. (Ed.). (1988). J. P. Mayer (Trans.), George Lawrence. *Democracy in America*. New York: Harper.

Toner, R. (1999, September 27). Extensive effort seeks to clarify Medicare maze. *New York Times*.

Toobin, J. (1998, February 9). The trouble with sex: Why the law of sexual harassment has never worked. *New Yorker*.

Toy, V. S. (1998, October 14). Bilingual for its own sake, an alternative school bucks the tide. *New York Times.*

Trimer-Hartley, M. (1993, April 23). Chapter's just begun on accepting gays in school. *Detroit Free Press.*

Trojanowicz, R. C. (1994). The future of community policing. In D. P. Rosenbaum (Ed.), *The challenge of community policing.* Thousand Oaks, CA: Sage.

Tropman, J. E. (1989). *American values and social welfare: Cultural contradictions in the welfare state.* Englewood Cliffs, NJ: Prentice Hall.

Tropman, J. E. (1995). *The Catholic ethic in American society.* San Francisco: Jossey Bass.

Tropman, J. E. (1998). *Does America hate the poor?* Westport, CT: Praeger.

Uchitelle, L. (1999a, November 19). Minimum wages, city by city. *New York Times.*

Uchitelle, L. (1999b, October 1). Rising incomes lift 1.1 million out of poverty. *New York Times.*

U.S. Bureau of the Census. (1998). *Statistical Abstract of the United States, 1998.*

Vaid, U. (1995). *Virtual equality: The mainstreaming of gay and lesbian liberation.* New York: Anchor/Doubleday.

Verhovek, S. H. (1991, June 20). A New York panel urges emphasizing minority cultures. *New York Times.*

Verhovek, S. H. (1999, June 9). Fighting sprawl, a county gets Intel to limit jobs. *New York Times.*

Wacquant, L., & Wilson, W. J. (1989). The cost of racial and class exclusion in the inner city. *Annals AAPSS*, p. 501.

Wakefield, J. C. (1996). Does social work need the eco-systems perspective? *Social Service Review, 70*(1) Part I; *Social Service Review, 70*(2) Part II.

Waldman, A. (1999, April 24). Thin support and red tape mire development zone in New York City. *New York Times.*

Walker, S., Spohn, C., Delone, M. (1996). *The color of justice: Race, ethnicity, and crime in America.* Belmont, CA: Wadsworth.

Wall, J. C. (1996). Delivery of educational and social services to homeless children and their families. *Social Work in Education, 18.*

Wall Street Journal. (1993, February 22). Putting to the text views toward women.

Warner, K., et al. (1982). Detroit's renaissance includes factories. *Urban Land.*

Warner, W. (1949). *Social class in America.* New York: Harper Books.

Warner, W. L., & Lunt, P. (1941). *The social life of a modern community.* New Haven, CT: Yale University.

Warren, D. (1975). *Black neighborhoods.* Ann Arbor, MI: University of Michigan Press.

Warren, R. (1963). *The community in America.* Chicago: Rand McNally.

Warren, R. (1980). The good community revisited. *Social Development Issues, 4*(3).

Warren, R., & Warren, D. I. (1977). *The neighborhood organizer's handbook.* South Bend, IN: University of Notre Dame Press.

Wartzman, R. (1993, September 24). New bus lines link the inner-city poor with jobs in suburbia. *Wall Street Journal.*

Washington Post. (1993, April 12). Cisneros, Bradley have what it takes to fix our aching cities.

Washington Post. (1998, August 18). Editorial: The public schools succession.

Washington Post. (1999, August 24). The House vs. D.C. on guns.

Weeks, L. (1999, September 7). Can a planned community approach the utopian ideal? In Celebration, Fla., it's a question that hits close to home. *Washington Post.*

Weil, M. O. (1996). Community building: Building community practice. *Social Work, 41*(5).

Wells, A. S. (1999). Charter schools as postmodern paradox. *Harvard Educational Review, 69*(2).

Wenocur, S., & Soifer, S. (1997). Prospects for community organization. In M. Reisch & E. Gambrill (Eds.), *Social work in the 21st century*. Thousand Oaks, CA: Pine Forge Press .

Whitfield, S. J. (1999). *In search of American Jewish culture*. Hanover, NH: Brandeis University Press.

Whitted, B. R., & Constable, R. (1999). Educational mandates for children with disabilities: School policies, case law, and the school social worker. In R. Constable, S. McDonald, & J. P. Flynn (Eds.), *School social work*. Chicago: Lyceum.

Whyte, W. H. (1988). *Rediscovering the center city*. New York: Doubleday.

Wilensky, H. (1975). *The welfare state and equality*. Berkeley, CA: University of California Press.

Wilensky, H., & Lebeaux, C. (1958). *Industrial society and social welfare*. (New York: Free Press.

Wilgoren, D. (1999a, August 25). Schools start the year with improved security. *Washington Post*.

Wilgoren, D. (1999b, November 15). Sharp eyes make safe place. *Washington Post*.

Wilgoren, J. (1999a, October 25). Harsh critique of teachers urges attention to training. *New York Times*.

Wilgoren, J. (1999b, December 3). Credit given to failed education goals. *New York Times*.

Wilgoren, J. (1999c, December 15). Abstinence is focus of U.S. sex education. *New York Times*.

Wilgoren, J. (2000, March 14). Two Florida schools become test ground for vouchers. *New York Times*.

Wilke, J. R. (1995, November 13). Plan to sell black bank to a white one stirs protests in Chicago. *Wall Street Journal*.

Wilkerson, I. (1993, January 22). Chicago plans barriers to hinder street crime. *New York Times*.

Wilkinson, K. P. (1992). Social forces shaping the future of rural areas. In L. J. Beaulieu & D. Mulkey (Eds.), *Investing in people: The human capital needs of rural America*. Boulder, CO: Westview Press.

Williams, M. (1999, March 7). Is there a black upper class? *New York Times*.

Williamson, Alistair D. (1993, July-August). Is this the right time to come out? *Harvard Business Review*.

Wilson, W. J. (1978). *The declining significance of race*. Chicago: University of Chicago Press.

Wilson, W. J. (1987). *The truly disadvantaged*. Chicago: University of Chicago Press.

Wilson, W. J. (1989). *The underclass: Issues, perspectives, and public policy*. Annals AAPSS, p. 501.

Wilson, W. J. (1994). The new urban poverty and the problem of race. *Michigan Quarterly Review, 33*(2).

Wilson, W. J. (1996). *When work disappears: The world of the new urban poor*. New York: Knopf.

Wilson, W. J. (1998). Jobless ghettos: The impact of the disappearance of work in segregated neighborhoods. In L. A. Daniels (Ed.), *The state of black America*. Washington, DC: National Urban League.

Wilson, W. J. (1999). *The bridge over the racial divide*. Berkeley, CA: University of California Press.

Wolch, J. R. (1995). Inside/outside: The dialectics of homelessness. In G. J. Demko & M. C. Jackson (Eds.), *Populations at risk in America*. Boulder, CO: Westview Press.

Woods, J. D. (1993). *The corporate closet*. New York: Free Press.

Woolbright, L. A., & Hartmann, D. J. (1987). The new segregation: Asians and Hispanics. *Urban Affairs Annual Reviews, 32*.

Wray, M., & Newitz, A. (1997). *White trash: Race and class in America*. New York: Routledge.

Wrong, D. H. (1994). *The problem of order: What unites and divides society*. New York: Free Press.

Wysocki, B. (1991, January 15). Influx of Asians brings prosperity to Flushing, a place for newcomers. *Wall Street Journal*.

Yardley, J. (1998, September 23). Brooklyn's Russian residents find a "suburb" in a neighborhood next door. *New York Times*.

Yarnall, L. (1998, October 28). On-line courses have given a new impetus to the home-schooling movement. *New York Times*.

Yazigi, M. P. (1998, November 2). Church socials, the new singles bars? *New York Times*.

Yazigi, M. P. (2000, January 6). Fine linens are making their mark as status symbol. *New York Times*.

Young, I. M. (1995). Five faces of oppression. In D. A. Harris (Ed.), *Multiculturalism from the margins*. Westport, CT: Bergin and Garvey.

Index

Acculturation, 8, 94
African Americans: 8, 11, 21, 57, 60,
  94, 107, 110
  and community organizing, 195
  and community power, 294, 295
  and employment, 247, 275, 336
  and neighborhoods, 145, 146,
  154, 157, 167
  and schools, 223, 228, 235
  and social class, 121, 122, 123,
  152
Americans with Disabilities Act, 75,
  76, 256
Asian Americans: 60
  neighborhoods, 155, 169, 171
  and political system, 288
  and social class, 121, 122
Assets development, 40
Assimilation, 8, 9, 94

Banking:
  community, 271
  and neighborhood development,
  268
Biculturalism, 8, 94
Bilingual education, 240

Capital:
  human, 16, 40, 104, 105
  forms of, 108
  social, 16
Capitalism: 2
  welfare, 32, 45

Career tracks: 253
  and the mommy track, 255
Catholicism: 9, 64
  and civic responsibility, 288
Census:
  of American population, 25
Charter schools, 210
Charter School Expansion Act of
  1998, 210
Church-state relations: 224
  and schools, 225
Children's health insurance, 200
Citizen participation: 287
  in local government, 287
Community:
  of color, 60
  competence, 70, 71, 346
  defined, 1, 49
  as an ecological system, 77
  as an ecology of games, 86
  gay, 65
  geographic, 1, 49
  global, 2
  good, 71, 87
  of identification, 1, 50, 56
  of interest, 1, 50, 56
  locational, 51, 52
  national, 6
  personal, 49, 345, 346
  planned, 52
  religious, 63, 64
  retirement, 56
  rural, 91